中国残疾人事业统计年鉴

China Statistical Yearbook on the Work for Persons with Disabilities

2018

（总第17期 No.17）

中国残疾人联合会 编

Compiled By China Disabled Persons' Federation

图书在版编目（CIP）数据

中国残疾人事业统计年鉴. 2018 / 中国残疾人联合会编. -- 北京 : 中国统计出版社, 2018.7
ISBN 978-7-5037-8563-4

Ⅰ. ①中… Ⅱ. ①中… Ⅲ. ①残疾人－社会福利事业－统计资料－中国－2018－年鉴 Ⅳ. ①D669.69-66

中国版本图书馆 CIP 数据核字(2018)第 171254 号

中国残疾人事业统计年鉴－2018
China Statistical Yearbook on the Work for Persons with Disabilities

作　　者/中国残疾人联合会
责任编辑/许立舫
封面设计/王　鹏
出版发行/中国统计出版社
通信地址/北京市丰台区西三环南路甲 6 号　邮政编码/100073
电　　话/邮购（010）63376909　书店（010）68783171
网　　址/http://www.zgtjcbs.com
印　　刷/河北鑫兆源印刷有限公司
经　　销/新华书店
开　　本/880×1230mm　1/16
印　　张/14.75　彩页 0.5
字　　数/460 千字
版　　别/2018 年 8 月第 1 版
版　　次/2018 年 8 月第 1 次印刷
定　　价/180.00 元

如有印装差错，由本社发行部调换。

《中国残疾人事业统计年鉴-2018》
编委会和编辑工作人员

编者说明

《中国残疾人事业统计年鉴-2018》系统收录了全国和各省、自治区、直辖市2017年残疾人工作各方面的统计数据，是一部全面反映中国残疾人事业发展的资料性年刊。

本书内容由六部分组成：第一部分为主要指标数据图；第二部分为2017年中国残疾人事业发展统计公报；第三部分为综合统计资料，是历年统计情况的综合反映；第四部分为2017年度分省统计资料，记录2017年各省任务指标执行情况和全国汇总情况；第五部分为分省统计报告，包括全国31个省（自治区、直辖市）、新疆生产建设兵团和黑龙江垦区的残疾人事业统计公报；第六部分为附录，介绍中国残疾人事业统计有关的政策法规文件。

本年鉴涉及的全国性统计数据均不包括香港、澳门特别行政区和台湾省数据。

本年鉴是根据各地残联报送的统计年报和部分专项业务项目统计结果编制而成。表格中“空格”表示该项统计指标数据不足本表最小单位数、数据不详或无该项数据。

2018年7月

目　录

Contents

第一部分　主要数据图

Part Ⅰ　Charts

第二部分　统计公报
Part Ⅱ　Communiqué

第三部分　综合统计资料
Part Ⅲ　Comprehensive Statistical Data

第四部分　分省统计资料
Part Ⅳ　Statistical Data of Provinces

一、康复
Rehabilitation

二、教育
Education

九、体育

Sports

十、维权

Rights Protection

十一、组织建设

Disabled Person's Organizations

十二、残疾人服务设施建设

Service Facilities for Persons with Disabilities

十三、信息化建设

Informatization

第五部分　分省统计报告

Part V　Statistical Report of Provinces

第六部分　附　　录

Part Ⅵ　Appendix

1

主要数据图

Charts

图-1 2017年各类残疾人接受康复服务情况

Chart 1 Rehabilitation Services Received by Various Persons with Disabilities in 2017

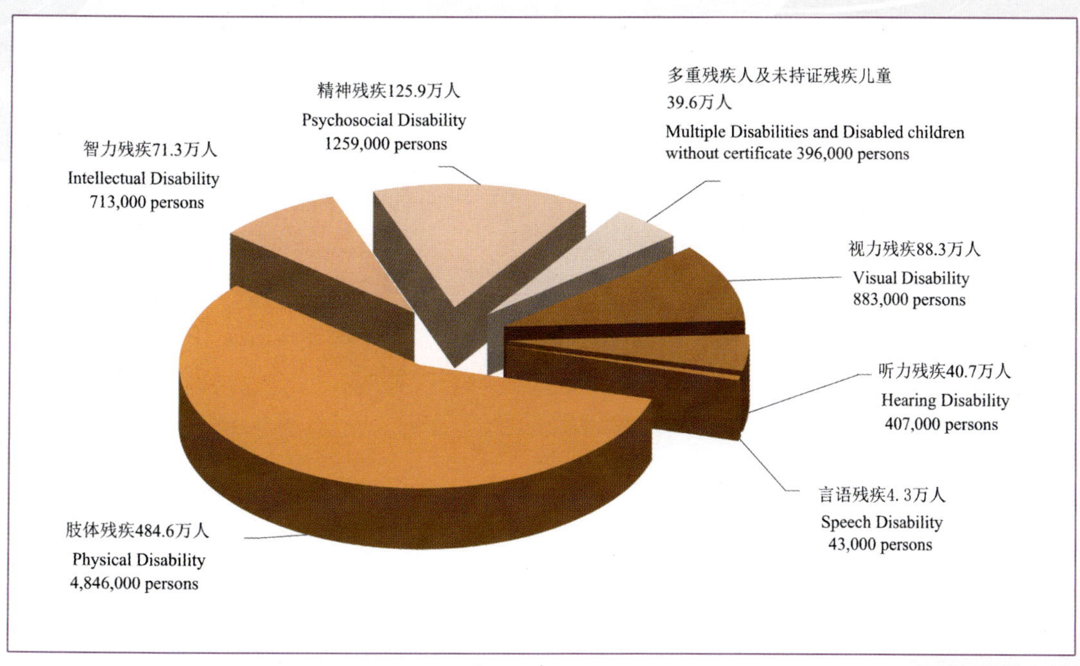

图-2 2013-2017年高等院校录取残疾考生情况

Chart 2 Admission of Disabled Students by Higher Educational Institution during 2013-2017

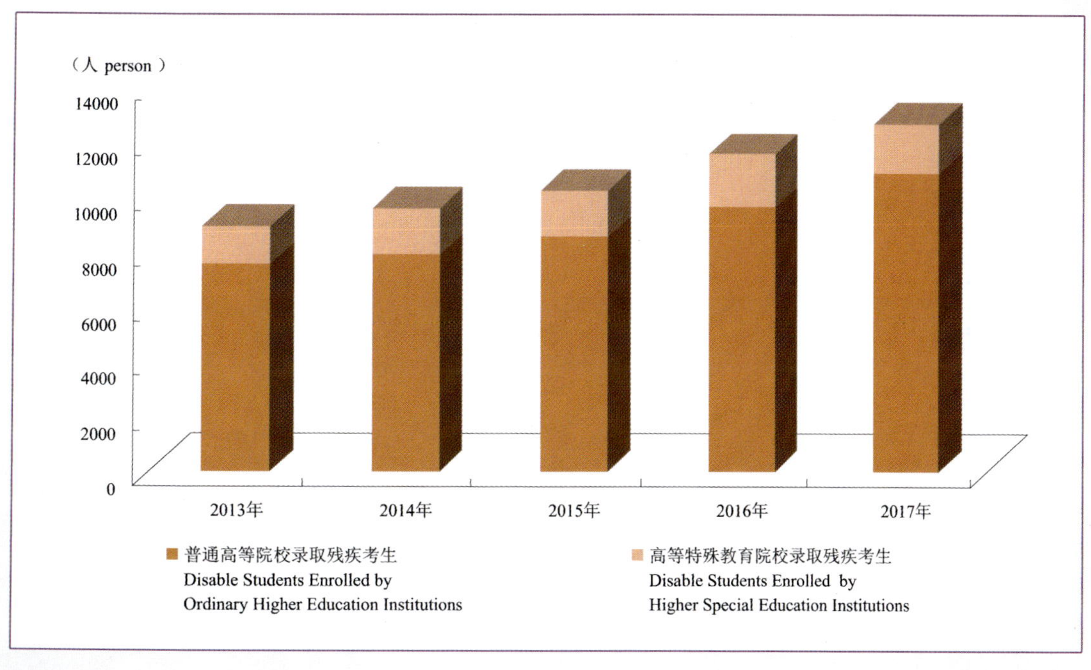

图–3 2017年城乡持证残疾人就业形式

Chart 3 Employment of Persons with Disabilities holding certificates in Urban and Rural Areas in 2017

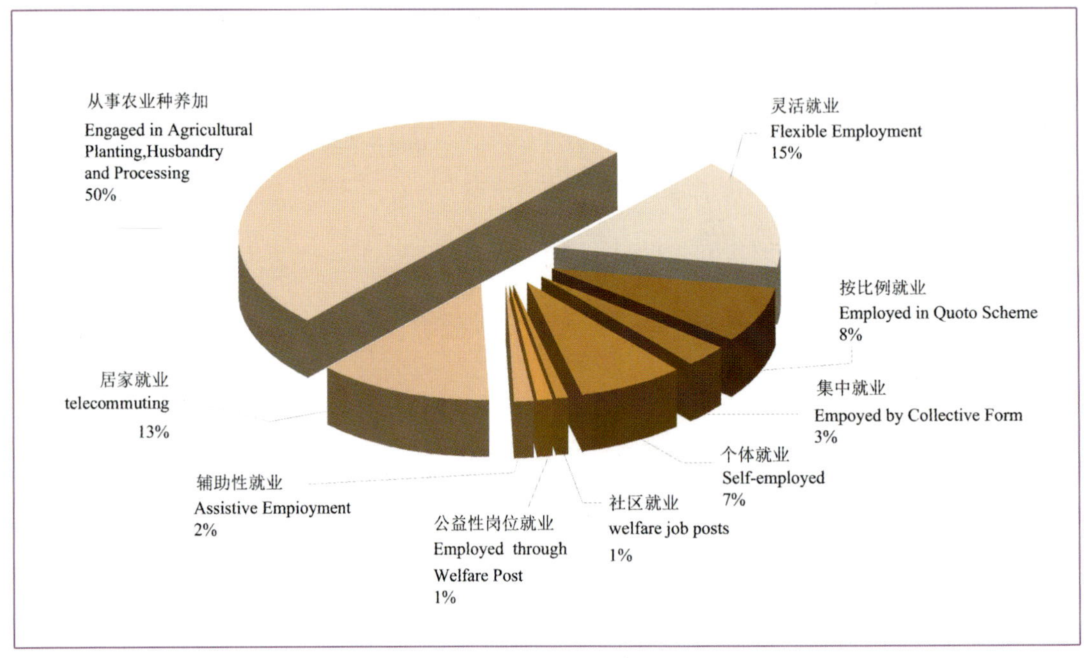

图–4 2013–2017年农村贫困残疾人危房改造情况

Chart 4 House Renovation for Poor Persons with Disabilities in Rural Areas during 2013-2017

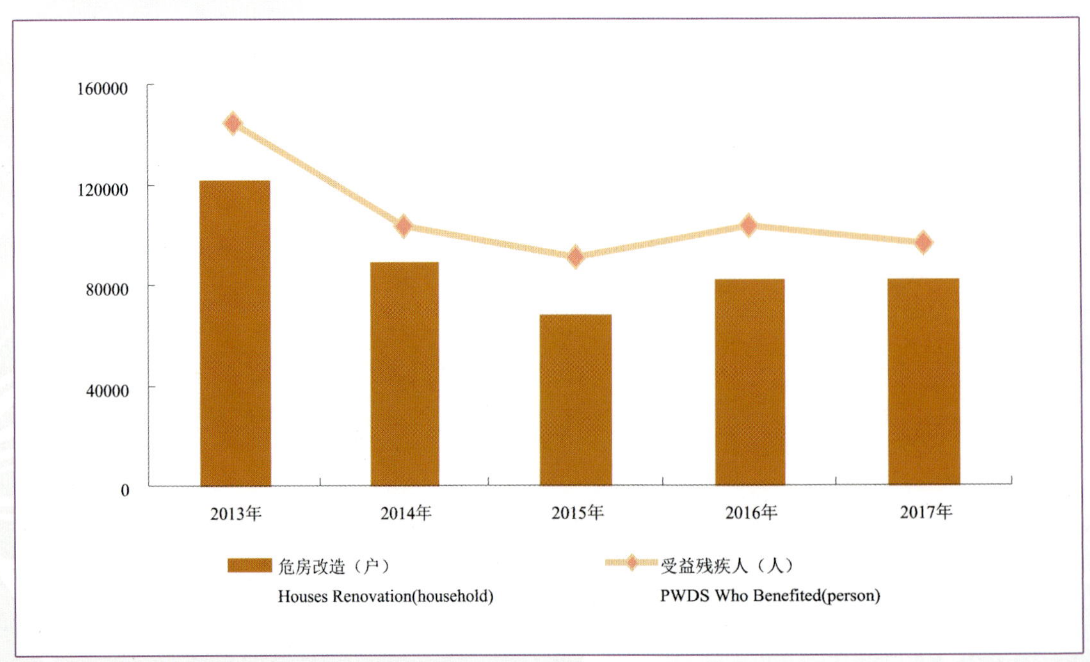

图–5 2013–2017年农村贫困残疾人扶持情况

Chart 5 Supported by Poverty Alleviation Projects for Poor Persons with Disabilities in Rural Areas during 2013-2017

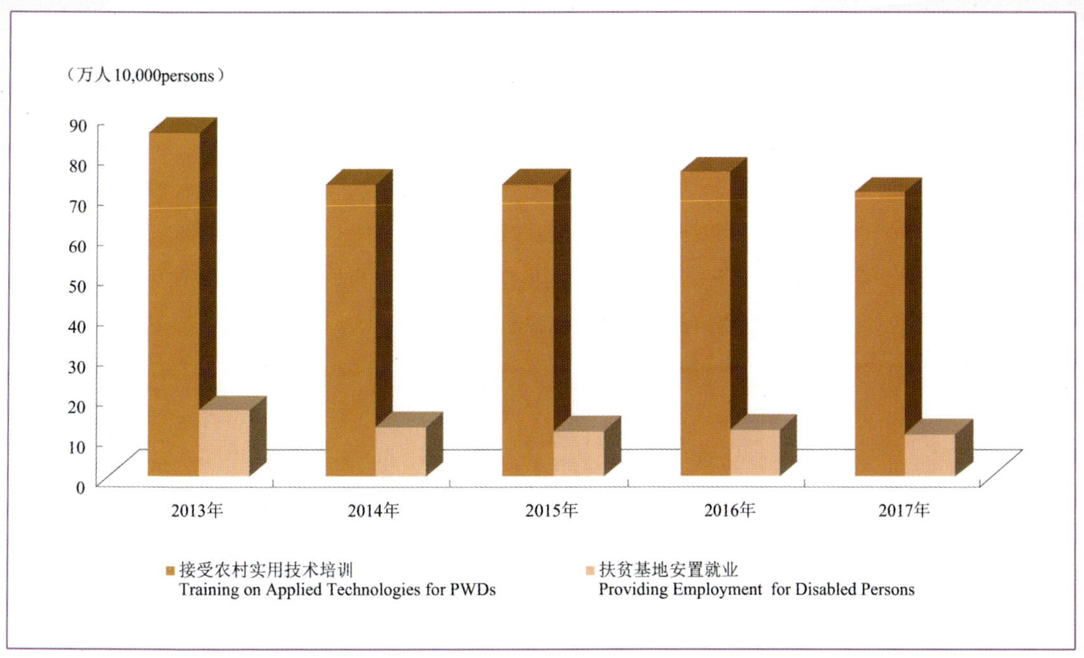

图–6 2013–2017年残疾人接受托养服务情况

Chart 6 Persons with Disabilities Receiving Fostering Service during 2013-2017

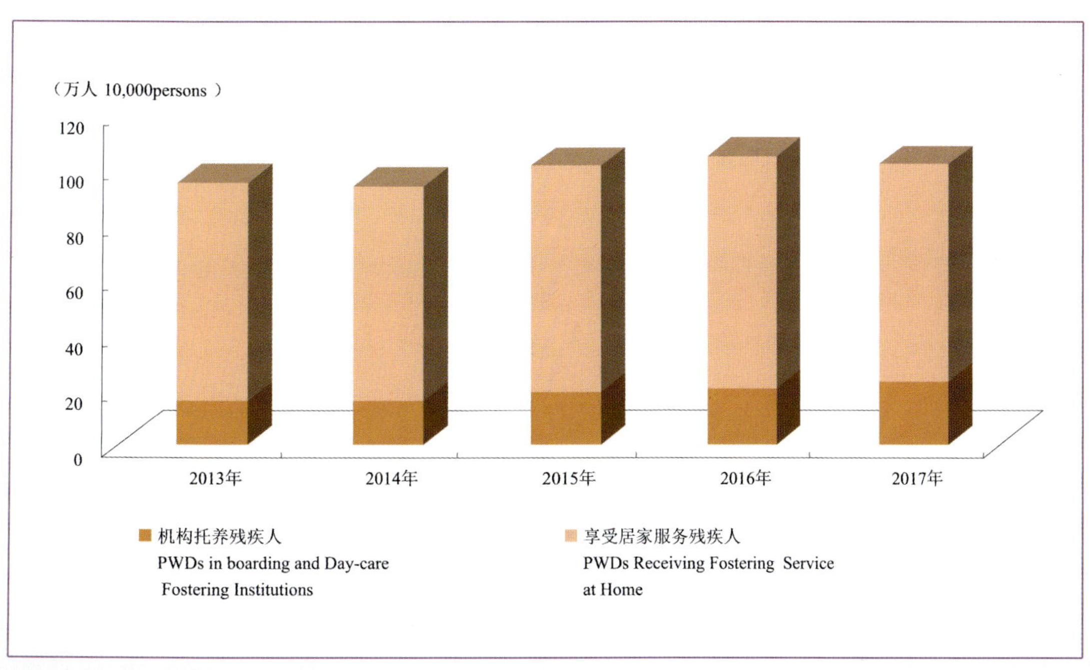

图-7 2013-2017年省、地市级电视手语栏目播出情况

Chart 7 TV Programs Displayed Sign Language at Provincial and City Levels during 2013- 2017

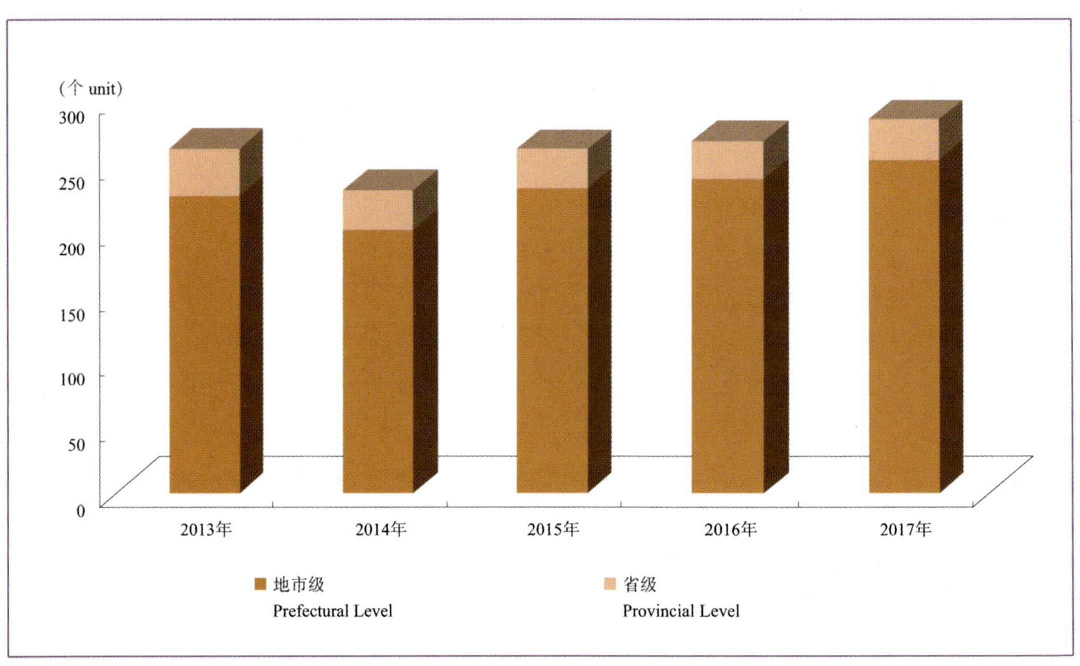

图-8 2013-2017年省、地市级残疾人体育健身指导员培养情况

Chart 8 Development of Sports and Fitness Coaches for Persons with Disabilities at Provincial and City Levels during 2013-2017

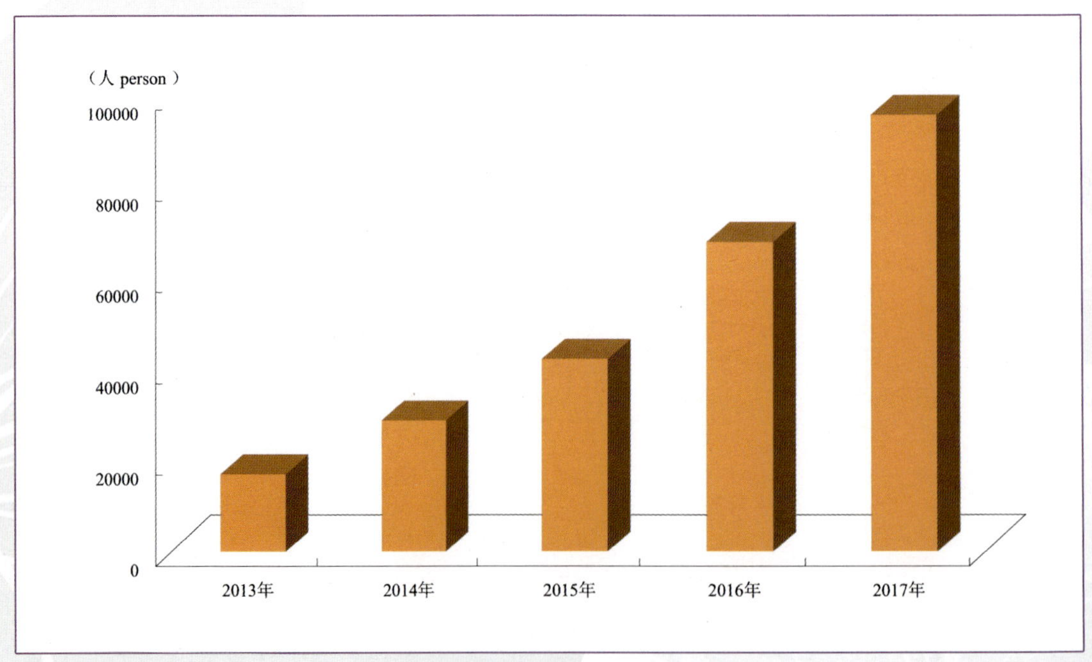

图-9 2013-2017年省、地市级残疾人体育活动示范点建设情况

Chart 9 Development of Demonstration Sports Sites at Provincial and City Levels during 2013-2017

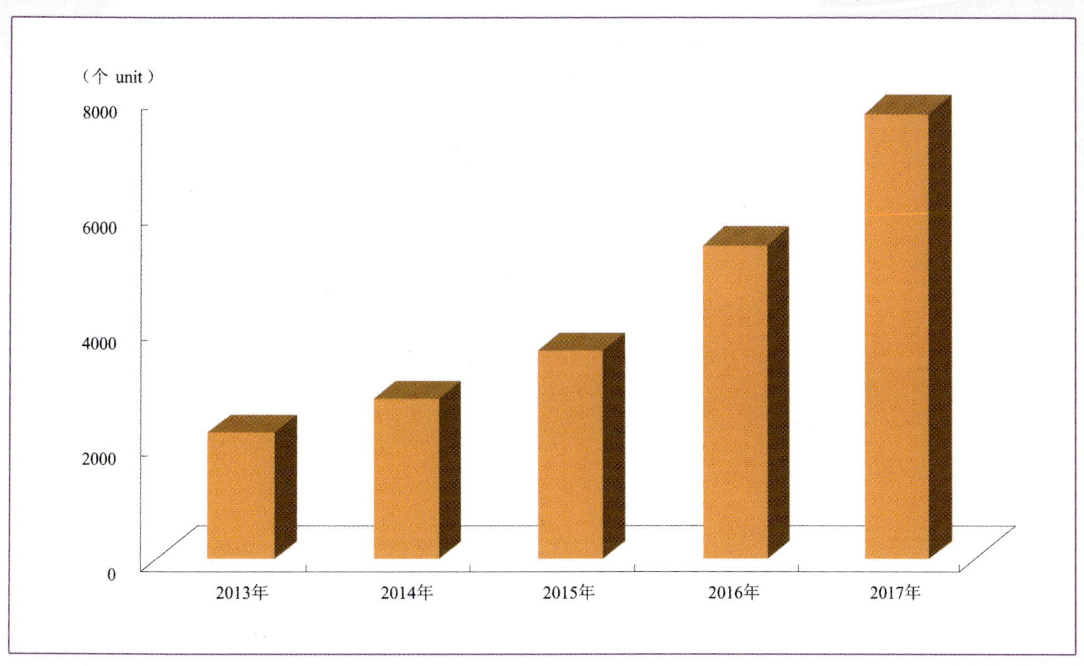

图-10 2013-2017年系统开展无障碍环境建设地市、县

Chart 10 National Systematic Construction of Accessible Environment during 2013-2017

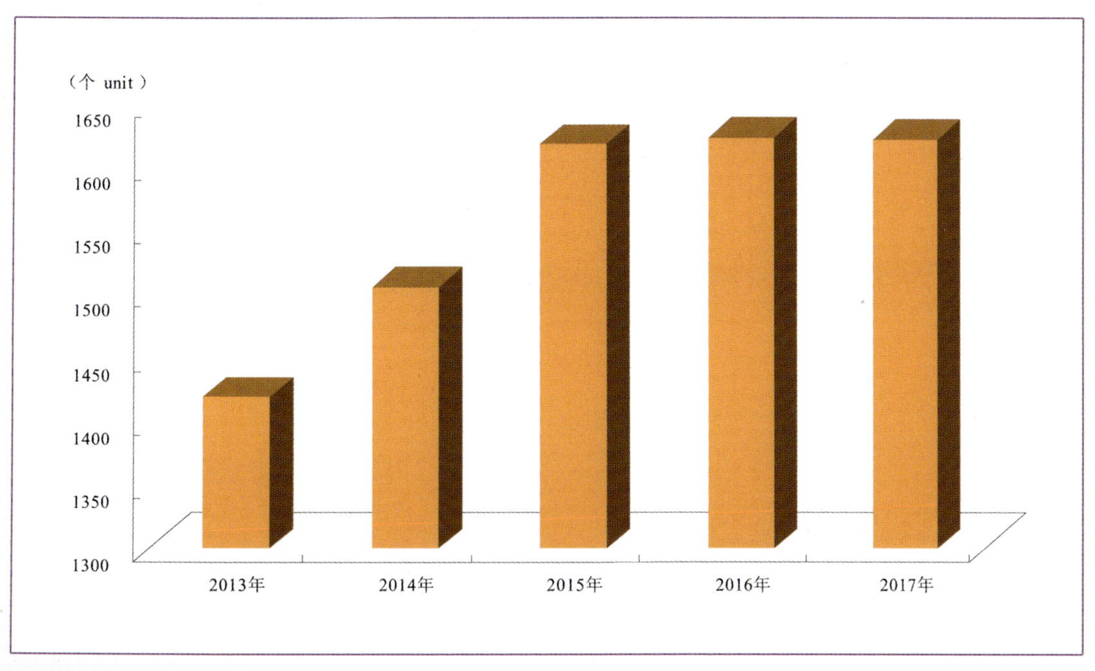

图-11 2013-2017年残疾人机动轮椅车燃油补贴发放情况

Chart 11 Subsidy for Petrol Used by Motorized Wheelchairs of Persons with Disabilities during 2013-2017

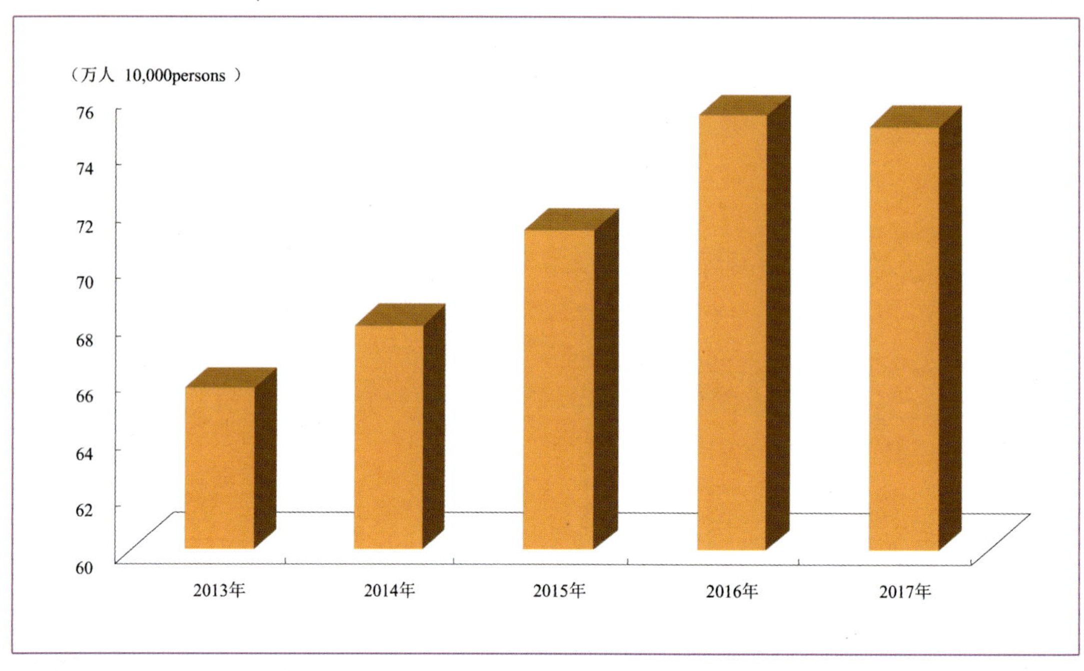

图-12 2013-2017年残疾人专职委员选聘情况

Chart 12 Full-time Workers on Disability at Grass-roots during 2013-2017

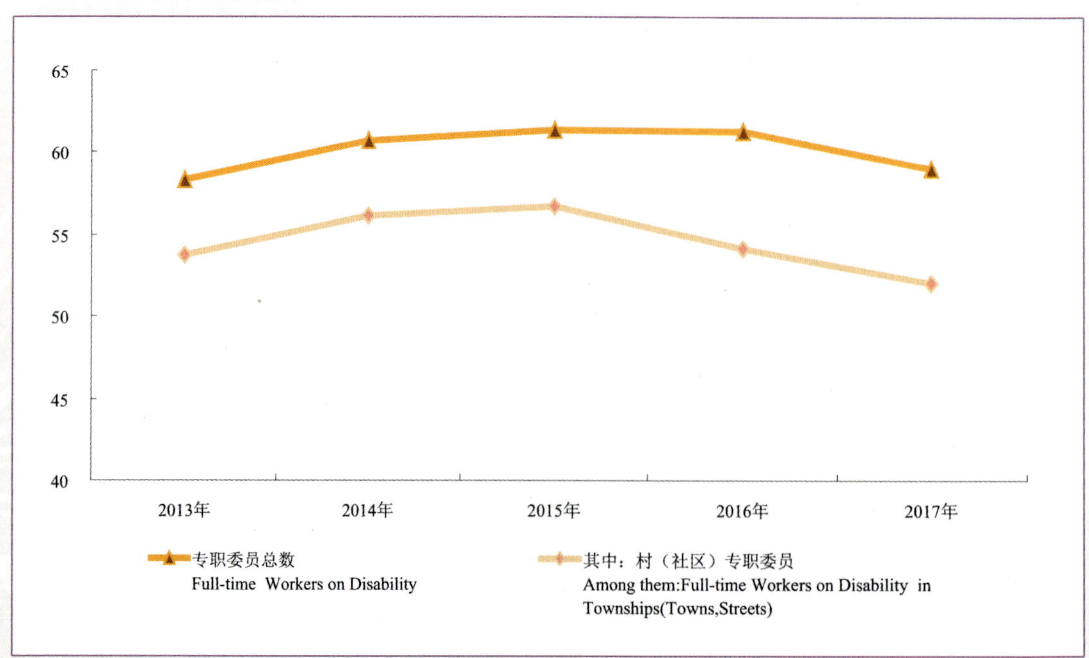

图–13 2017年残疾人服务设施建设情况

Chart 13 The Construction of Service Facilities for Persons with Disabilities in 2017

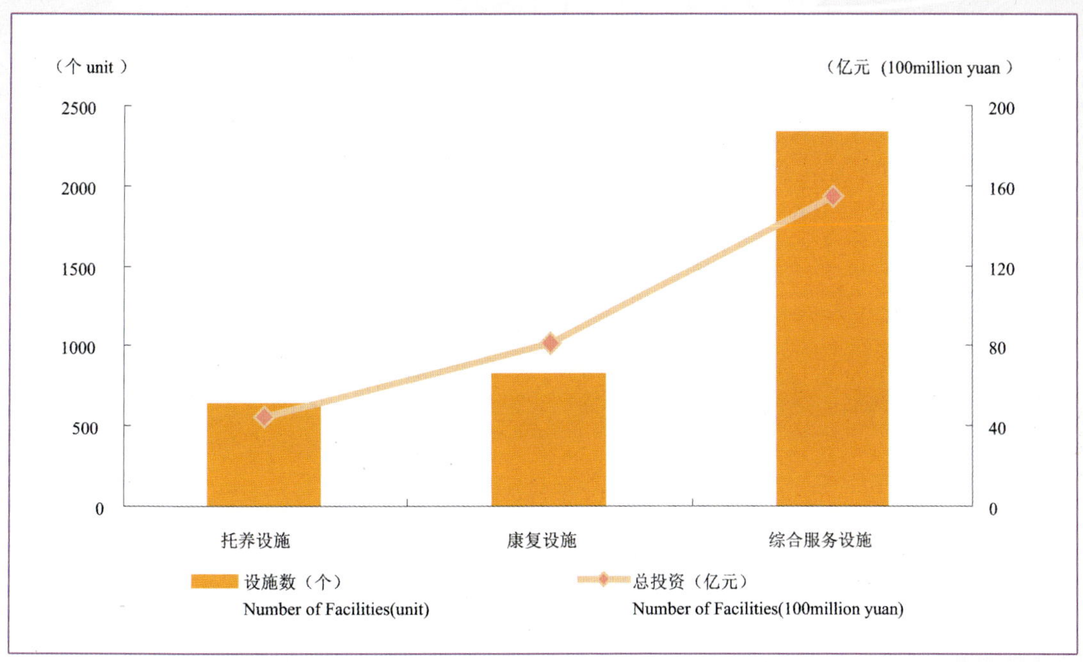

图–14 2013–2017年残疾人人口基础数据库情况

Chart 14 Development of population-based database of PWDs during 2013-2017

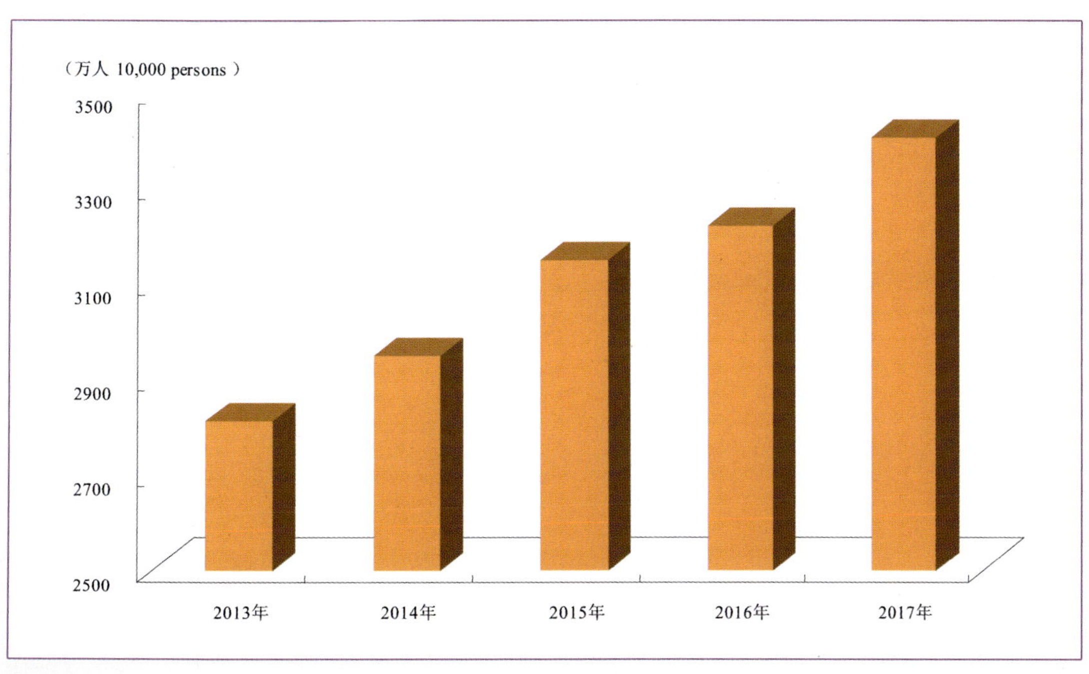

2

统计公报

Communiqué

2017 年中国残疾人事业发展统计公报

2017 年,在国务院残疾人工作委员会的指导下,全国残联系统深入学习贯彻党的十九大精神,认真贯彻落实党中央、国务院关于残疾人事业发展的一系列重要部署,主动担当,积极作为,推动残疾人事业持续健康发展。

一、康复

2017 年,854.7 万残疾儿童及持证残疾人得到基本康复服务,其中包括 0-6 岁残疾儿童 141239 人。得到康复服务的持证残疾人中,有视力残疾人 88.3 万、听力残疾人 40.7 万、言语残疾人 4.3 万、肢体残疾人 484.6 万、智力残疾人 71.3 万、精神残疾人 125.9 万、多重残疾人 35.5 万。全年共为 244.4 万残疾人提供各类辅助器具适配服务。

截至 2017 年底,全国已有残疾人康复机构 8334 个,其中,提供视力残疾康复服务的机构 1194 个,提供听力言语残疾康复服务的机构 1417 个,提供肢体残疾康复服务的机构 3088 个,提供智力残疾康复服务的机构 2659 个,提供精神残疾康复服务的机构 1695 个,提供孤独症儿童康复服务的机构 1611 个,提供辅助器具服务的机构 1866 个。康复机构在岗人员达 24.6 万人,其中,管理人员 3.1 万人,专业技术人员 16.5 万人,其他人员 5.0 万人。

二、教育

中国残联、教育部等部门制定实施《第二期特殊教育提升计划(2017-2020 年)》,与教育部正式印发《残疾人参加普通高等学校招生全国统一考试管理规定》,开展残疾人高等融合教育试点工作,将《国家通用手语常用词表》《国家通用盲文方案》纳入国家语委语言文字标准体系。残疾人受教育权得到了更好保障,进一步提高了特殊教育发展水平 。

残疾人事业专项彩票公益金助学项目的实施,为全国 1.9 万人次家庭经济困难的残疾儿童享受普惠性学前教育提供资助。各地多渠道争取资金支持,对 2971 名残疾儿童给予学前教育资助。

2017 年,全国共有特殊教育普通高中班(部)112 个,在校生 8466 人,其中聋生 7010 人,盲生 1456 人。残疾人中等职业学校(班)132 个,在校生 12968 人,毕业生 3501 人,其中 1802 人获得职业资格证书。全国有 10818 名残疾人被普通高等院校录取,1845 名残疾人进入高等特殊教育学院学习。

继续实施《"十三五"残疾青壮年文盲扫盲行动方案》。4.3 万名残疾青壮年文盲接受了扫盲教育。

三、就业

2017 年城乡持证残疾人新增就业 35.5 万人,其中,城镇新增就业 13.1 万人,农村新增就业 22.4 万人;培训城乡残疾人 62.5 万人。

全国城乡持证残疾人就业人数为 942.1 万人,其中按比例就业 72.7 万人,集中就业 30.2 万人,个体就业 70.6 万人,公益性岗位就业 9.0 万人,辅助性就业 14.4 万人,社区就业 8.0 万人,居家就业 118.9 万人,灵活就业 145.8 万人,从事农业种养殖 472.5 万人。

盲人按摩事业稳步发展,按摩机构持续增长。2017 年度,全国共培训盲人保健按摩人员 20796 名、盲人医疗按摩人员 7217 名;保健按摩机构 19257 个,医疗按摩机构 1255 个;有 54 人和 870 人分别获得盲人医疗按摩人员中级和初级职务任职资格。

四、社会保障

截至 2017 年底,城乡残疾居民参加城乡社会养老保险人数 2614.7 万;547.2 万 60 岁以下参保的重度残疾人中,有 529.5 万得到政府的参保扶助,代缴养老保险费比例 96.8%。有 282.9 万非重度残疾人享受了全额或部分代缴养老保险费的优惠政策。1042.3 万人领取养老金。

残疾人托养服务工作稳步推进,残疾人托养服务机构 7923 个,其中寄宿制托养服务机构 2560 个,日间照料机构 3076 个，综合性托养服务机构 2287 个，为 23.1 万残疾人提供了托养服务。接受居家服务的残疾人 78 万人。全年 1.9 万名托养服务管理和服务人员接受了各级各类专业培训。

五、扶贫开发

贫困残疾人脱贫攻坚取得阶段性成效，残疾人生产生活状况得到进一步改善。贫困残疾人得到有效扶持，其中 92.5 万残疾人退出建档立卡；残疾人接受实用技术培训 70.6 万人次。

康复扶贫贴息贷款扶持 2.1 万农村残疾人。6692 个残疾人扶贫基地安置 10.5 万残疾人就业，扶持带动 21.8 万户残疾人家庭。

全国共完成 8.2 万户农村贫困残疾人危房改造，各地投入危房资金 10 亿元。

六、宣传文化

2017 年，以“推进残疾预防，健康成就小康”为主题，组织第二十七次全国助残日活动，开展“残疾预防日”“国际残奥委会代表大会”“2017 年国际残疾人日”等系列宣传活动；全年组织记者采访 500 余人次，进行 20 次专题新闻发布，结合工作实际组织拍摄微视频 4 部，其中《盲人女孩》入选国家新闻出版广电总局 2017 年度“百人百部中国梦短纪录片扶持计划”。各大媒体大力宣传残疾人事业，新华社发表文章 119 篇，中央电视台《新闻联播》播发新闻 16 条，人民日报发表文章 65 篇。“两微一端”影响力持续提升，至 2017 年底，关注、订阅人数近 378 万人，总阅览量约 2391 万人次。截至 2017 年底，全国共有省级残疾人专题广播节目 25 个、电视手语栏目 31 个；地市级残疾人专题广播节目 198 个、电视手语栏目 254 个。

2017 年残疾人文化工作强化创新意识，组织开展了全国残疾人文化周等活动，中国残联、教育部、民政部、文化部及国家新闻出版广电总局共同举办第九届全国残疾人艺术汇演。截至 2017 年底，全国省地县三级公共图书馆共设立盲文及盲文有声读物阅览室 959 个，共开展残疾人文化周活动 6740 场次；全国省地两级残联共举办残疾人文化艺术类的比赛及展览 640 次，共有各类残疾人艺术团 281 个。

七、体育

积极落实国务院全民健身部际联席会议要求，努力将残疾人体育基本公共服务融入全民健身计划，全国残疾人康复体育关爱家庭服务 13.3 万户，新建 3620 个残疾人体育健身示范点，新增培养 35741 名残疾人体育健身指导员。“第七届残疾人自强健身周”列入国家体育总局 2017 年全民健身日系列活动，特奥活动融合性进一步加强，中国残联、国家体育总局、北京冬奥组委等 7 家中央单位共同组织“第二届中国残疾人冰雪运动季”活动。实现我国冬残奥会项目全覆盖。首次举办了全国残疾人高山滑雪、单板滑雪和残奥冰球锦标赛，举办第四届残疾人冰壶锦标赛。参加 21 项国际赛事，单板滑雪历史性获得一枚世界杯金牌、高山滑雪获得一个洲际杯第一名，有 64 人次进入前八名，轮椅冰壶队获得世锦赛第四名、公开赛第二名。我国获得 5 个大项 26 个平昌参赛名额，实现了参赛规模和项目翻番的目标。中国残联与冬奥组委建立了常态化工作机制，无障碍、市场开发、新闻宣传等专家分别深度参与了相关工作。

举办 23 项全国残疾人体育赛事，共有 3500 多名运动员参赛，涉及 17 项夏季残奥，3 项群体项目比赛，3 项特奥比赛，并承办 7 项国际赛事。在国际赛事中，共取得了 186 枚金牌、88 枚银牌、75 枚铜牌，创 7 项世界记录。在土耳其第二十三届夏季听障奥运会上，获得 14 枚金牌、9 枚银牌、11 枚铜牌，位列奖牌榜第 5 位，破 1 项世界记录，取得我国参加听障奥运会以来的最好成绩。参加奥地利第十一届世界冬季特奥运动会。

八、维权

各级残联维权组织建设进一步加强，残疾人事业法律法规体系更加完善，无障碍环境建设取得新成果，残疾人维权工作全面开展。

2017 年，制定或修改了关于残疾人的专门法规、规章省级 11 个、地市级 10 个；制定或修改保障残疾人权益的规范性文件省级 12 个、地市级 53 个、县级 152 个。全国县级以上人大开展《中华人民共和国残疾人保障法》执法检查和专题调研 290 次；政协开展视察和专题调研 267 次。全国开展省级普法宣传教育活动 283 次，19968 人参加；举办省级法律培训班 74 个，4810 人参加。

截至 2017 年底，全国成立残疾人法律救助工作协调机构 1987 个，建立残疾人法律救助工作站 1746 个。

残疾人参政议政工作继续开展，各地残联协助人大代表、政协委员提出议案、建议、提案 753 件，办理议案、建议、提案 993 件。

无障碍建设法规、标准进一步完善。全国共出台了 451 个省、地市、县级无障碍建设与管理法规、规章和规范性文件；系统开展无障碍建设市、县、区 1622 个；全国开展无障碍建设检查 4006 次，无障碍培训 3.2 万人次；为 89.2 万户残疾人家庭实施了无障碍改造，其中包括 10.5 万户贫困重度残疾人[①]；为 74.9 万残疾人发放了残疾人机动轮椅车燃油补贴。

九、组织建设

2017 年，全国省市县乡（除兵团、垦区外）共成立残联 4.3 万个，各省（区、市）、市（地、州）全部建立残联；93.5%的县（市、区）、98.7%的乡镇（街道）已建立残联；95.4%的社区（村）建立残协，达到 58.6 万个。

省市县乡残联工作人员达 11.3 万人，乡镇（街道）、村（社区）选聘残疾人专职委员总计 59 万人。93.5%的省级残联、67.5%的地市级残联配备了残疾人领导干部，52.7%的县级残联配备了残疾人干部。

全国共建立省级及以下各类残疾人专门协会 1.5 万余个，其中省级专门协会已建比例为 100%，市级专门协会已建比例为 96.5%，县级专门协会已建比例为 86.4%。全国助残社会组织 2520 个。

十、服务设施

残疾人服务设施建设得到全面发展。截至 2017 年底，全国已竣工并投入使用的各级残疾人综合服务设施 2340 个，总建设规模 533 万平方米，总投资 154.9 亿元；已竣工并投入使用的各级残疾人康复设施 833 个，总建设规模 261.4 万平方米，总投资 80.8 亿元；已竣工并投入使用的各级残疾人托养服务设施 649 个，总建设规模 161.2 万平方米，总投资 44.3 亿元。

十一、信息化建设

截至 2017 年底，中国残联门户网站发布稿件约 3.2 万篇，全国 31 个省、276 个地市、1197 个县级残联开通网站。全国残疾人人口基础数据库持证残疾人 3404.0 万人。积极推动残疾人证（智能化）工作，全国共有 21 个省申请智能化残疾人证试点。完成浙江省杭州、宁波市与江苏省苏州市两省三市先行发卡。同时开展残疾证电子证照建设，为“互联网+残疾人服务”应用奠定技术基础。

[①] 无障碍改造数据来源为 2017 年全国残疾人基本服务状况和需求信息数据动态更新数据。

Statistical Communiqué on the Development of Work for Persons with Disabilities in 2017

Statistical Communiqué on the Development of Work for Persons with Disabilities in 2017.

Under the leadership of the State Council Working Committee on Disability, China Disabled Persons' Federation (CDPF) has learned and implemented the guiding principles of the 19th National Congress of the Communist Party of China (CPC) in a thorough and systematic manner. It has prudently carried out new tasks and missions related to disability issues, as required by the CPC Central Committee and the State Council. It has also shouldered and performed responsibilities proactively in 2017 to promote the continuous and sound development of work on persons with disabilities (PWDs).

I. Rehabilitation

In 2017, 8.547 million registered PWDs and unregistered children with disabilities received basic rehabilitation services. Among them, 141,239 were children aged between 0 and 6 years. Of the registered PWDs, 883,000 had visual disabilities, 407,000 had hearing disabilities, 43,000 had speech disabilities, 4.846 million had physical disabilities, 713,000 had intellectual disabilities, 1.259 million had psychiatric disabilities, and 355,000 had multiple disabilities. Particularly, 2.444 million PWDs were fitted with various assistive devices.

By the end of 2017, the number of rehabilitation facilities in China reached 8,334. Among them, 1,194 provided services for persons with visual disabilities, 1,417 provided services for persons with hearing disabilities, 3,088 provided services for persons with physical disabilities, 2,659 provided services for persons with intellectual disabilities, 1,695 provided services for persons with psychiatric disabilities, 1,611 provided services for children with autism, and 1,866 provided assistive technology related services. The number of employees working in those rehabilitation institutions reached 246,000, including 31,000 administrative staff, 165,000 technical personnel, and 50,000 others.

II. Education

CDPF, the Ministry of Education and other departments formulated and implemented the *Special Education Advancement Program (Phase II) for 2017-2020. CDPF and the Ministry of Education issued the Administrative Provisions on Disabled Persons' Participation in the National College Entrance Examination.* Meanwhile, pilot projects for inclusive higher education of PWDs were launched and the National List of Common Words for Universal Sign Language and the National Scheme of Universal Braille were included in the system of National Language Standards provided by the State Language Commission. Overall, PWDs' right to education was better protected and special education was further improved.

Moreover, the education project funded by a disability-specific welfare lottery provided financial support to more than 19,000 disabled children from financially difficult families for their preschool education. Other funding channels were also explored and had provided financial support for the pre-school education of 2,971 disabled children.

In 2017, there were 112 special education classes in senior high schools nationwide, with an enrollment of 8,466 students, among whom 7,010 were deaf and 1,456 were blind. There were 132 medium-level vocational education institutions (classes), with 12,968 enrolled students and 3,501 graduates, among whom 1,802 achieved vocational certificates. Throughout the country, 10,818 students with disabilities were admitted to regular higher education institutions and 1,845 entered special higher education institutions.

The *Action Plan to Eliminate Illiteracy among Young and Middle-aged People with Disabilities during the 13th Five-Year Period* was implemented.

Under the plan, 43,000 adults with disabilities received literacy education.

III. Employment

In 2017, 355,000 registered PWDs were newly employed, including 131,000 PWDs in urban areas and 224,000 PWDs in rural areas. In addition, 625,000 PWDs in urban and rural areas received vocational training.

Throughout the country, 9.421 million registered PWDs in urban and rural areas were employed. Among them, 727,000 were employed through the quota scheme, 302,000 through concentrative placement, 706,000 through self-employment, 90,000 by welfare job posts, 144,000 through supportive employment, 80,000 through community-aided employment, 1.189 million through telecommuting, 1.458 million through flexible employment, and 4.725 million through farming and husbandry.

Massage business by blind people grew steadily, with a continuous increase in the number of massage institutions. In 2017, 20,796 healthcare massagers and 7,217 medical massagers received professional training. The number of healthcare massage institutions reached 19,257, and the number of medical massage institutions increased to 1,255. As many as 54 and 870 massagers obtained secondary- and elementary-level professional qualification respectively.

IV. Social Security

By the end of 2017, 26.147 million PWDs in rural and urban areas were covered by the pension scheme. Of the 5.472 million persons with severe disabilities under the age of 60, 5.295 million (accounting for 96.8%) received government's subsidies for paying the pension premium. Another 2.829 million persons with slight or moderate disabilities also enjoyed full or partial amount of subsidies for joining in the pension scheme. Meanwhile, 10.423 million PWDs received their pension.

Fostering services for PWDs progressed steadily. By the end of 2017, the country housed 7,923 fostering facilities catering to 231,000 PWDs. Among them, 2,560 were boarding facilities, 3,076 were day-care facilities , and 2,287 were combined fostering facilities. In addition, 780,000 PWDs received care services at home. Throughout the year, 19,000 administrative and service staff from fostering facilities received trainings of various types.

V. Poverty Alleviation

In 2017, progress was also made on poverty alleviation for PWDs, whose working and living conditions were further improved. With effective supportive measures, 925,000 PWDs were lifted out of poverty; 706,000 PWDs received training on practical skills and technologies.

Moreover, 21,000 PWDs in rural areas were granted interest-subsidized loan through poverty alleviation finance projects. A total of 6,692 poverty alleviation centers provided jobs to 105,000 PWDs and provided income sources for 218,000 households with members living with disabilities.

An amount of RMB 1 billion was invested to renovate dilapidated houses for 82,000 households with PWDs.

VI. Publicity and Cultural Activities

For the 27th National Day of Helping Persons with Disabilities, a series of activities were held under the theme of "Promoting Disability Prevention and Good Health for a Moderately Prosperous Society". Disability-related events such as the Disability Prevention Day, the IPC General Assembly meeting, and 2017 World Disabled Day were widely covered. Regarding disability affairs, more than 500 interviews were conducted by journalists and 20 pieces of featured news were released. Four fact-based micro-videos were produced, among which the Blind Girl was selected and promoted by the State Administration of Press, Publication, Radio, Film and Television (SAPPRFT) as one of the top one hundred short documentaries that best illustrated the Chinese dream for the year of 2017. Disability issues were highlighted by multiple mainstream media agencies. For example, Xinhua News Agency published 119 disability-related articles, China Central Television aired 16 pieces of news about disability, and the *People's Daily* published 65 articles pertaining to this topic.

Meanwhile, the influence of CDPF's official accounts of Sina Weibo, WeChat, and news app was increased continuously. By the end of 2017, the number of their followers and subscribers reached 3.78 million and the total number of visits approximated 23.91 million. At the provincial level, there were 25 radio programs on disability issues and 31 TV programs displaying sign language; at the prefectural level, there were 198 radio programs on disability issues and 254 TV programs with sign language.

In 2017, cultural services for PWDs showed more creativity. Events including the National Cultural Week of Persons with Disabilities were organized. CDPF, the Ministry of Education, Ministry of Civil Affairs, Ministry of Culture, and SAPPRFT jointly held the 9th National Art Festival of Persons with Disabilities. By the end of 2017, at the provincial-, prefectural- and county-level libraries nationwide, 959 reading rooms with Braille and audible reading materials were established and 6,740 activities echoing the Cultural Week of Persons with Disabilities were held. Provincial and prefectural Disabled Persons' Federation (DPFs) held 640 cultural and artistic competitions and exhibitions. Meanwhile, the number of art organizations of PWDs in the country reached 281.

VII. Sports

Following the requirements set forth by the State Council Inter-Ministerial Meeting on National Fitness Program, CDPF acted in a proactive manner to integrate basic public sports services for PWDs into the National Fitness Program. As many as 133,000 households nationwide received rehabilitative sports services for PWDs, 3,620 demonstrative fitness facilities for PWDs were newly established, and 35,741 more sports or fitness coaches for PWDs joined their peers. The 7th Fitness Week of Disabled Persons was included in the 2017 National Fitness Day events held by the General Administration of Sport of China (GASC). The inclusivity of the Special Olympics was further improved. Seven departments, including CDPF, GASC, and the Beijing Organizing Committee for the 2022 Olympic and Paralympic Winter Games, jointly organized the Second Winter Sports Season for Disabled Persons. During the 2018 Paralympic Winter Games, athletes from the Chinese delegation participated in all sports.

The First National Alpine Skiing Championships for Disabled Persons, the First National Snowboarding Championships for Disabled Persons, the First National Para Ice Hockey Championships, and the 4th Curling Championships for Disabled Persons were successfully held. Chinese athletes with disabilities took part in 21 international competitions, won a gold medal in the Snowboard World Cup, won the first place in an the Alpine Skiing Intercontinental Cup, and 64 of them managed to rank in the top eight in their competitions. The national wheelchair curling team won the fourth position in the World Wheelchair Curling Championship and the second position in the Open Wheelchair Curling Championship. During the PyeongChang 2018 Winter Paralympic Games, 26 Chinese athletes participated in all the five sports, twice as many as in the last Winter Paralympics. CDPF and the Beijing Organizing Committee for the 2022 Olympic and Paralympic Winter Games collaborated on a regular basis and had involved experts on accessibility, market development, press and publicity, etc. in their work.

A total of 23 national sports events for persons with disabilities were organized, with a participation of 3,500 athletes. Among these events, 17 were about sports in the Paralympics, 3 were for group games, and 3 were about sports in Special Olympics. In addition, China organized 7 international sports games. In international sports games, Chinese athletes won 186 gold medals, 88 silver medals and 75 bronze medals, and broke 7 world records. In the 23th Summer Deaflympics held in Turkey, Chinese athletes ranked fifth on the medal table with 14 gold medals, 9 silver medals and 11 bronze medals, breaking one world record. Chinese athletes also competed in the 11th Special Olympic World Winter Games held in Austria.

VIII. Rights Protection

DPFs at various levels continued to strengthen the rights protection of persons with disabilities. The legal and regulatory system regarding disability affairs was further improved, new achievements were made in building accessible environments, and the work on rights protection of PWDs was carried out in an all-round way.

In 2017, 11 provincial- and 10 prefectural-level disability-specific laws and regulations were formulated or amended. As many as 12 provincial-level, 53 prefectural-level, and 152 county-level regulatory documents on rights protection of PWD were formulated or amended. The People's Congress at and above the county level carried out 290 inspections and researches on the enforcement of the Law on Protection of Persons with Disabilities; the Political Consultative Conference at all levels carried out 267 inspections and researches on disability issues. Moreover, 283 events were held nationwide to publicize disability-related laws and regulations, attracting 19,968 participants, while 74 legal education sessions were organized at the provincial level and were joined by 4,810 audience. By the end of 2017, 1,987 agencies coordinating legal assistance for PWDs were established, and 1,746 legal assistance stations were set up.

PWDs continued to take active part in political affairs. With assistance from DPFs, members of the People's Congress and the Political Consultative Conferences submitted 753 and processed 993 motions and proposals.

Legislation and standardization on accessibility were further improved. As many as 451 regulations, rules, and guidelines on accessibility were issued, while 1,622 cities, counties, and districts were in the process of building accessibility facilities systematically. 4,006 accessibility inspections were carried out, and 32,000 persons received trainings on accessibility. The homes of 892,000 households with PWDs were renovated to enhance their accessibility, of which 105,000 were impoverished families with severely disabled members[①]. Meanwhile, 749,000 PWDs received subsidies to fuel their motorized wheelchairs.

IX. Organizational Development

As many as 43,000 DPFs at provincial, prefectural, county, and village levels (excluding DPFs in production and construction corps and reclamation areas) were set up in 2017. Across the country, all provinces, prefectures and cities had DPFs; 93.5% of counties (and districts) and 98.7% of townships had their DPFs in place; 95.4% communities (and villages) had disabled persons' associations, amounting to 586,000.

About 113,000 people worked in provincial-, prefectural-, county- or township-level DPFs, while 590,000 people were designated to undertake responsibilities in township DPFs and village (and community) level disabled persons' association. Around 93.5% of provincial and 67.5% of prefectural DPFs had leading members with disabilities and 52.7% of the county-level DPFs had members with disabilities playing an important role.

There were 15,000 specialized associations sorted by disability categories at the provincial level and below. In China, all provinces, 96.5% of the cities and prefectures, and 86.4% of the counties established their local specialized associations. Meanwhile, 2,520 civil organizations assisting PWDs were established nationwide.

X. Services for PWDs

Service facilities for PWDs were widely developed. By the end of 2017, 2,340 comprehensive service facilities at multiple administrative levels were completed and put into use, with a construction area of 5.33 million square meters. The total investment in this regard amounted to RMB 15.49 billion. In addition, RMB 8.08 billion was invested in building rehabilitation facilities, and 833 rehabilitation facilities were completed and put into use, with a construction area of 2.614 million square meters. Moreover, 649 fostering facilities were completed and put into use, with a total investment of RMB 4.43 billion and a construction area of1.612 million square meters.

XI. Informatization

By the end of 2017, approximately 32,000 articles were posted on the website of CDPF. Meanwhile, 31 provincial-level, 276 prefectural-level and 1,197 county-level DPFs launched their websites.

The National Basic Database of Disabled Population covered 34.04 million registered PWDs. CDPF and DPFs promoted actively the popularization of intelligent disability identification cards, and 21 provinces had applied to run pilot projects in this regard. Among them, Hangzhou and Ningbo of Zhejiang Province and Suzhou of Jiangsu Province took the initiative and had completed the issuance of the new-generation identification cards. The project of making electronic disability identification cards was also carried out, laying a technical foundation for the application of "Internet + Services for PWDs".

① Data on renovating houses to increase accessibility were retrieved from the regularly updated database Needs and Supply of Basic Services for People with Disabilities in China.

3

综合统计资料

Comprehensive Statistical Data

3-1 中国残疾人事业主要业务进展情况 (2013－2017)

指标名称		Item	
康 复		**Rehabilitation**	
1. 残疾人精准康复服务		**The Provision of Precision Rehabilitation Service**	
视力残疾人	(万人)	Visual Disability	(10,000 persons)
听力残疾人	(万人)	Hearing Disability	(10,000 persons)
言语残疾人	(万人)	Speech Disability	(10,000 persons)
肢体残疾人	(万人)	Physical Disability	(10,000 persons)
智力残疾人	(万人)	Intellectual Disability	(10,000 persons)
精神残疾人	(万人)	Psychosocial Disability	(10,000 persons)
多重残疾人	(万人)	Multiple Disabilities	(10,000 persons)
2. 残疾人辅助器具供应服务		**Provision of Assistive Devices**	
辅助器具供应	(万人)	Assistive Devices Provided	(10,000 persons)
3. 康复机构建设		**Construction of Rehabilitation institution**	
残疾人康复机构	(个)	Rehabilitation Institutions for PWDs	(unit)
康复机构在岗人员	(万人)	In-Service Personnel for Rehabilitation Institutions	(10000 persons)
4. 社区康复		**Community-based Rehabilitation (CBR)**	
开展社区康复服务的县(市、区)*	(个)	Counties and Districts Where CBR Has Been Conducted	(unit)
社区康复协调员	(万人)	CBR Coordinators at Communities	(10,000 persons)
教 育		**Education**	
1. 学前教育		**Pre-school Rehabilitation and Education**	
残疾人事业专项彩票公益金助学项目资助	(人)	Support of Educational Project Funded by Dedicated Welfare Lottery Fund	(person)
其他残疾儿童学前教育助学项目资助	(人)	Support of Other Pre-School Educational Project for Disabled Children	(person)
2. 残疾人高级中等教育		**Senior Secondary Education for PWDs**	
特教普通高中	(个)	Special Education Senior High Schools	(unit)
特教普通高中在校学生	(人)	Students at Special Education Senior High Schools	(person)
中等职业教育机构	(个)	Secondary Vocational Schools	(unit)
中等职业教育在校学生	(人)	Students at Secondary Vocational Schools	(person)
3. 残疾人高等教育		**Higher Education for PWDs**	
高等特殊教育院校	(个)	Higher Special Education Institutions	(unit)
高等特殊教育院校录取残疾考生	(人)	Disable Students Enrolled by Higher Special Education Institutions	(person)
普通高等院校录取残疾考生	(人)	Disable Students Enrolled by Ordinary Higher Education Institutions	(person)
4. 扫盲教育	**(人)**	**Anti-Illiteracy Education**	**(person)**

注：*“开展社区康复服务的县(市、区)”包含正式行政区划单位和开发区、管委会等非正式行政区划，以及新疆兵团、黑龙江垦区下属县级单位。
Counties (cities and districts) providing community rehabilitation service include formal administrative divisions and development zones, informal administrative divisions such as management committees, and county-level units subordinate to the Xinjiang Production and Construction Corps and Heilongjiang Reclamation Area.

Brief Summary on the Development of the Work for Persons with Disabilities (2013－2017)

2013-2017年完成情况 The Accomplishment (2013-2017)				
2013	2014	2015	2016	2017
-	-	-	40.0	88.3
-	-	-	18.5	40.7
-	-	-	-	4.3
-	-	-	135.7	484.6
-	-	-	23.1	71.3
-	-	-	62.6	125.9
-	-	-	-	35.5
-	-	-	132.2	244.4
6618	6914	7111	7858	8334
21.6	23.4	23.2	22.3	24.6
2915	2937	2956	2962	2988
37.9	39.2	40.6	45.4	47.9
10468	11528	12127	14412	18685
3489	2908	1767	2607	2971
194	187	109	111	112
7313	7227	7488	7686	8466
198	197	100	118	132
11350	11671	8134	11209	12968
15	18	20	21	21
1388	1678	1678	1942	1845
7538	7864	8508	9592	10818
-	-	-	**43408**	**42782**

3-1 续表 1

指 标 名 称		Item	
就 业		**Employment**	
1. 城乡持证残疾人就业状况		**Employment of PWDs in Urban and Rural Areas**	
按比例就业	(万人)	Employed in Quoto Scheme	(10,000 persons)
集中就业	(万人)	Employed by Collective Form	(10,000 persons)
个体就业	(万人)	Self-Employed	(10,000 persons)
公益性岗位就业	(万人)	Employed through Welfare Post	(10,000 persons)
辅助性就业	(万人)	Assistive Employment	(10,000 persons)
灵活就业(含社区就业、居家就业)	(万人)	Flexible Employment	(10,000 persons)
从事农业种养加	(万人)	Engaged in Agricultural Planting, Husbandry and Processing	(10,000 persons)
2. 盲人按摩		**Massage by the Blind**	
按摩人员培训		Massage Training	
保健按摩人员	(人)	Training for Health-care Masseurs	(person)
医疗按摩人员	(人)	Training for Blind Therapeutical Masseurs	(person)
按摩机构		Institutions of Blind Massage	
医疗按摩机构	(个)	Therapeutical Blind Massage Clinics	(unit)
保健按摩机构	(个)	Health-care Blind Massage Houses	(unit)
社会保障		**Social Security**	
1. 社会保险		**Social Insurance**	
残疾居民参加城乡社会养老保险	(万人)	PWDs participating urban and rural social endowment insurance	(10,000 persons)
2. 托养服务		**Fostering Service**	
托养服务机构	(个)	Fostering Services Facilities	(unit)
托养残疾人	(万人)	PWDs Receiving Fostering Service	(10,000 persons)
扶 贫		**Poverty Alleviation**	
1. 扶贫效果		**Outcome of Poverty Alleviation**	
退出建档立卡贫困残疾户	(万户)	Families of Poor Persons with Disabilities No Longer Subject to Archive Filing and Card Issuing	(10,000 households)
退出建档立卡贫困残疾人	(万人)	Poor Persons with Disabilities No Longer Subject to Archive Filing and Card Issuing	(10,000 persons)
实用技术培训	(万人次)	Training on Applied Technologies for PWDs	(10,000 person-times)
2. 残疾人扶贫资金落实情况		**Poverty Alleviation Fund for PWDs**	
贷款实际落实	(亿元)	Actual Implementation of The Loan	(100 million yuan)
项目贷款扶持贫困残疾人	(万人)	Poor Disabled Persons Supported by Loans for Project	(10,000 persons)
到户贷款扶持贫困残疾人	(万人)	Poor Disabled Persons Supported by Loans to Households	(10,000 persons)
3. 残疾人扶贫基地建设		**Poverty Alleviation Bases for PWDs in Rural Areas**	
残疾人扶贫基地	(个)	Poverty Alleviation Bases for PWDs	(unit)
安置残疾人就业	(万人)	Providing Employment for PWDs	(10,000 persons)
扶持带动贫困残疾人	(万户)	Supporting and Leading Households with PWDs	(10,000 households)
4. 农村贫困残疾人危房改造		**House Renovation for Poor PWDs in Rural Areas**	
危房改造	(万户)	Houses Renovated for PWDs	(10,000 households)
受益残疾人	(万人)	PWDs Who Benefited	(10,000 persons)
宣传文化		**Publicity and Culture**	
1. 宣传		**Publicity at Provincial and Prefectural/City Level**	
省、市级广播电台残疾人专题节目	(个)	Radio Broadcast-Special Programs on Disability	(unit)

Continued 1

2013-2017年完成情况 The Accomplishment(2013-2017)				
2013	2014	2015	2016	2017
-	-	-	66.9	72.7
-	-	-	29.3	30.2
-	-	-	63.9	70.6
-	-	-	7.9	9.0
-	-	-	13.9	14.4
-	-	-	262.9	272.6
-	-	-	451.2	472.5
20111	21296	19979	18997	20796
5694	5623	5165	5267	7217
936	1018	1025	1211	1255
14704	15609	17171	18605	19257
2039.8	2180.0	2229.6	2370.6	2614.7
5677	5917	6352	6740	7923
94.4	93.2	100.5	104.2	101.1
-	-	-	66.4	66.4
-	-	-	87.8	92.5
85.6	72.6	72.7	75.6	70.6
10.1	9.4	7.6	6.6	4.1
2.6	2.4	1.2	0.9	1.2
5.3	3.7	1.6	1.4	0.9
6201	6593	6693	7111	6692
16.4	12.4	11.4	11.6	10.5
24.6	25.8	25.0	24.9	21.8
12.2	9.0	6.9	8.2	8.2
14.4	10.3	9.1	10.4	9.6
659	258	235	223	223

3-1 续表 2

指标名称		Item	
省、市级电视手语栏目	(个)	Programmes with Sign Language on TV	(unit)
2. 文化		**Culture at Provincial and Prefectural/City Level**	
省、市级盲文及盲人有声读物阅览室	(个)	Reading Rooms with Braille and Audio Reading Materials	(unit)
省、市级残疾人文化周	(场次)	Culture Week for PWDs	(session)
省、市级残疾人文化艺术类比赛及展览	(次)	Culture or Art Competitions and Exhibitions for PWDs	(time)
体 育		**Sports**	
1. 省、市级残疾人体育健身示范点累计	**(个)**	**Sports Activity Demonstration Sites for PWDs**	**(unit)**
2. 省、市级残疾人社会体育指导员累计	**(万人)**	**Coaches for Fitness Activity for PWDs**	**(1,0000 persons)**
3. 残疾人康复体育关爱家庭服务	**(万户)**	**Sports and Caring Family Services for PWDs**	**(1,0000 households)**
维 权		**Safeguarding the Rights of PWDs**	
1. 法规体系和政策文件		**Legal System**	
制定或修改关于残疾人的专门法规、规章	(个)	Special Laws and Regulations Enacted or Reviewed for PWDs	(unit)
制定或修改保障残疾人权益的规范性文件	(个)	Policies Enacted or Reviewed for PWDs	(unit)
2. 执法检查		**Inspections on Law Performance**	
人大执法检查或专题调研	(次)	Inspections and Investigations by Officials of People's Congresses	(time)
政协视察或专题调研	(次)	Inspections and Investigations by Political Consultative Conferences	(time)
3. 法律救助		**Legal Aid**	
残疾人法律救助工作站	(个)	Legal Assistance Stations for PWDs	(unit)
4. 参政议政		**PWDs Participating in the Administration and Discussion of State Affairs**	
协助人大代表、政协委员提出议案、建议、提案	(件)	Bills, Suggestions and Proposals Submitted with the Assistance of Disabled Persons' Federations	(case)
办理人大政协议案、建议、提案	(件)	Suggestions and Proposals Handled by Disabled Persons' Federation	(case)
5. 无障碍设施建设		**Accessible Environment Building**	
无障碍设施建设法规、政府令	(个)	Regulations and Decrees on Accessible Environment Building and Management	(unit)
残疾人家庭无障碍改造	(万户)	Accessibility Renovation for Homes of Poor PWDs	(10,000 households)
6. 残疾人机动轮椅车燃油补贴	**(万人)**	**Subsidy for Petrol Used by Motorized Wheelchairs of PWDs**	**(10,000 persons)**

Continued 2

2013-2017年完成情况 the Accomplishment (2013-2017)				
2013	2014	2015	2016	2017
263	231	262	269	285
596	462	420	267	282
2212	1356	1062	1002	1037
1399	959	803	719	640
2187	**2769**	**3591**	**5433**	**7707**
1.7	**2.9**	**4.2**	**6.8**	**9.5**
-	**-**	**-**	**8.9**	**13.3**
31	18	13	19	21
543	427	338	285	217
799	649	548	392	290
746	635	565	370	267
901	1348	1542	1670	1746
1743	1538	1406	956	753
1464	1374	1238	988	993
444	451	451	451	451
13.6	14.9	14.7	93.6	89.2
65.7	**67.9**	**71.3**	**75.3**	**74.9**

3-1 续表 3

指 标 名 称		Item	
组织建设		**Organizational Structure**	
1. 省市县乡残联实有人员	(万人)	**Staff of Disabled Persons'Federations at Provincial, City, County and Township Level**	**(10,000 persons)**
2. 市级残联		**Disabled Persons'Federations at Cities and Prefectures Level**	
配备残疾人领导干部的残联	(个)	Disabled Persons' Federations Whose Leadership Include PWDs	(unit)
残疾人干部	(人)	Staff with Disability	(person)
3. 县级残联		**Disabled Persons' Federations at County Level**	
配备残疾人干部的残联	(个)	Disabled Persons' Federations Whose Leadership Include PWDs	(unit)
残疾人干部	(人)	Staff with Disability	(person)
4. 乡级残联与村级残疾人协会		**Disabled Persons' Federations in Township(Town, Street) and Villages(Communities)**	
已建乡、镇、街道残联	(万个)	Disabled Persons' Federation Established	(10,000 units)
其中：已配专兼职理事长	(万人)	Full-time(part-time) Presidents	(10,000 persons)
已建村(社区)残疾人协会	(万个)	Associations of Disabled Persons Established in Villages(Communities)	(10,000 units)
选聘残疾人专职委员	(万人)	Full-time Workers on Disability	(10,000 persons)
5. 省级以下各类专门协会		**Special Associations below Provincial Level**	
盲人协会	(个)	Associations of Persons with Visual Disability	(unit)
聋人协会	(个)	Associations of Persons with Hearing Disability	(unit)
肢残人协会	(个)	Associations of Persons with Physical Disability	(unit)
智力残疾人及亲友协会	(个)	Associations of Persons with Intellectual Disability and Their Relatives and Friends	(unit)
精神残疾人及亲友协会	(个)	Associations of Persons with Psychosocial Disability and Their Relatives and Friends	(unit)
智力残疾人及亲友协会和精神残疾人及亲友协会合一的协会	(个)	Joint Associations of people with Mental or Psychosocial Disability and Their Relatives and Friends	(unit)
残疾人服务设施建设		**Service Facilities for PWDs**	
1. 残疾人综合服务设施		**Comprehensive Service Facilities for PWDs**	
建设完成已投入使用项目	(个)	Accumulated Projects in Operation	(unit)
总建设规模	(万平米)	Construction Area	(10,000 sq.m)
2. 残疾人康复设施		**Rehabilitation Service Facilities for PWDs**	
建设完成已投入使用项目	(个)	Accumulated Projects in Operation	(unit)
总建设规模	(万平米)	Construction Area	(10,000 sq.m)
3. 残疾人托养设施		**Fostering Service Facilities for PWDs**	
建设完成已投入使用项目	(个)	Accumulated Projects in Operation	(unit)
总建设规模	(万平米)	Construction Area	(10,000 sq.m)
信息化建设		**Informatization**	
1. 残疾人人口基础库数据	(万人)	**Data of the National Basic Database of Persons with Disabilities**	**(10,000 persons)**
2. 省、市、县各级残联网站	(个)	**Websites at Provincial, City, County Level**	**(unit)**

Continued 3

2013–2017年完成情况 The Accomplishment (2013-2017)				
2013	2014	2015	2016	2017
11.1	**11.5**	**11.1**	**11.3**	**11.3**
251	246	244	235	229
433	433	423	409	418
1625	1631	1630	1584	1572
2221	2234	2211	2180	2165
4.0	4.0	4.0	4.0	4.0
3.1	2.8	2.6	2.4	2.4
58.1	59.0	58.6	58.4	58.6
58.4	60.7	61.4	61.3	59.0
3110	3128	3120	3147	3145
3097	3113	3107	3133	3130
3117	3139	3127	3159	3155
3001	2958	2953	2986	3003
3003	2954	2951	2982	3003
82	177	171	169	117
2094	2231	2281	2294	2340
424.1	460.3	491.4	504.7	533.0
542	613	682	762	833
100.7	130.0	165.7	213.4	261.4
353	442	500	566	649
78.2	101.4	115.4	129.6	161.2
2811.5	**2946.7**	**3145.7**	**3219.4**	**3404.0**
1617	**1660**	**1694**	**1634**	**1504**

3-2 全国残疾人人口基础库主要数据
Brief Data of the National Basic Information Database of Persons with Disabilities

单位：人 (截止时间：2017年12月31日) (person)

地 区	Region	已办理残疾人证 PWDs with Disabled Persons Certificate	0-14岁 Age 0-14	15-59岁 Age 15-59	60岁及以上 Age 60 and above
全 国	**Total**	**34039653**	**1005315**	**19046518**	**13987820**
北 京	Beijing	513834	6199	254695	252940
天 津	Tianjin	345939	4358	180862	160719
河 北	Hebei	1807672	51833	1001887	753952
山 西	Shanxi	926014	22523	547596	355895
内蒙古	Inner Mongolia	802934	15667	501204	286063
辽 宁	Liaoning	1016777	17500	639097	360180
吉 林	Jilin	823901	15922	517278	290701
黑龙江	Heilongjiang	1056176	17921	702812	335443
上 海	Shanghai	514568	3048	202854	308666
江 苏	Jiangsu	1559492	36790	879025	643677
浙 江	Zhejiang	1179734	23034	609737	546963
安 徽	Anhui	1655552	49016	913743	692793
福 建	Fujian	910699	28337	446706	435656
江 西	Jiangxi	1053527	43517	658241	351769
山 东	Shandong	2168439	68722	1172875	926842
河 南	Henan	2444144	92024	1344482	1007638
湖 北	Hubei	1467779	33273	864477	570029
湖 南	Hunan	1683572	52424	949812	681336
广 东	Guangdong	1443354	69528	830479	543347
广 西	Guangxi	1353767	47431	614293	692043
海 南	Hainan	169508	7660	104133	57715
重 庆	Chongqing	857468	27406	482675	347387
四 川	Sichuan	2653461	70895	1349341	1233225
贵 州	Guizhou	1166334	44616	662255	459463
云 南	Yunnan	1304627	44128	792035	468464
西 藏	Tibet	96691	8405	63883	24403
陕 西	Shaanxi	1298496	22850	649519	626127
甘 肃	Gansu	750393	25030	447523	277840
青 海	Qinghai	173616	9130	110488	53998
宁 夏	Ningxia	233123	7837	131823	93463
新 疆	Xinjiang	506091	36362	345506	124223
新疆兵团	Xinjiang Corps	66115	1420	49267	15428
黑龙江垦区	Heilongjiang Land Reclamation	35856	509	25915	9432

3-2 续表 1 Continued 1

单位：人　　(person)

地　区	Region	已办理证件残疾人 PWDs with Disabled Persons Certificate					
		性　别 Gender		残疾等级 Disability Grading			
		男　性 Male	女　性 Female	残疾一级 Grade-1	残疾二级 Grade-2	残疾三级 Grade-3	残疾四级 Grade-4
全　国	**Total**	**20055800**	**13983853**	**4579523**	**9784988**	**8900788**	**10774354**
北　京	Beijing	278867	234967	63152	112210	128997	209475
天　津	Tianjin	195840	150099	40567	102293	101869	101210
河　北	Hebei	1064714	742958	226842	490810	404896	685124
山　西	Shanxi	573117	352897	123175	240935	230005	331899
内蒙古	Inner Mongolia	479386	323548	84029	217974	231970	268961
辽　宁	Liaoning	627328	389449	132843	283693	292767	307474
吉　林	Jilin	497066	326835	98452	247028	244383	234038
黑龙江	Heilongjiang	656594	399582	130797	287386	313531	324462
上　海	Shanghai	268014	246554	76239	99192	125195	213942
江　苏	Jiangsu	866040	693452	210211	491866	465882	391533
浙　江	Zhejiang	694481	485253	157888	231702	361288	428856
安　徽	Anhui	944043	711509	216921	725121	391864	321646
福　建	Fujian	519920	390779	122361	276515	218846	292977
江　西	Jiangxi	645066	408461	118573	295634	285628	353692
山　东	Shandong	1311794	856645	314351	660413	561353	632322
河　南	Henan	1427534	1016610	333406	796832	626680	687226
湖　北	Hubei	869683	598096	226723	485678	349648	405730
湖　南	Hunan	1032777	650795	230145	588820	372723	491884
广　东	Guangdong	855442	587912	270376	501615	348508	322855
广　西	Guangxi	764413	589354	151359	331414	315434	555560
海　南	Hainan	99072	70436	64228	35722	35740	33818
重　庆	Chongqing	516844	340624	98527	234272	220432	304237
四　川	Sichuan	1554835	1098626	374173	745205	667339	866744
贵　州	Guizhou	719345	446989	129180	202327	296059	538768
云　南	Yunnan	779080	525547	156125	280417	307936	560149
西　藏	Tibet	50522	46169	12859	20281	24608	38943
陕　西	Shaanxi	735185	563311	151857	277204	498657	370778
甘　肃	Gansu	437555	312838	136722	199409	198226	216036
青　海	Qinghai	98397	75219	26105	69370	40916	37225
宁　夏	Ningxia	128501	104622	27849	81375	58624	65275
新　疆	Xinjiang	302173	203918	62902	144992	150634	147563
新疆兵团	Xinjiang Corps	39670	26445	6329	19461	19441	20884
黑龙江垦区	Heilongjiang Land Reclamation	22502	13354	4257	7822	10709	13068

3-2 续表 2 Continued 2

单位：人 (person)

地 区	Region	已办理证件残疾人 PWDs with Disabled Persons Certificate 残疾类别 Disability Category 视力残疾人 Persons with Visual Disability	听力残疾人 Persons with Hearing Disability	言语残疾人 Persons with Speech Disability	肢体残疾人 Persons with Physical Disability	智力残疾人 Persons with Intellectual Disability
全 国	**Total**	**3973235**	**2712651**	**605040**	**19218851**	**2900103**
北 京	Beijing	55490	37122	2844	290510	50654
天 津	Tianjin	29378	22026	4400	226968	30501
河 北	Hebei	168701	126324	35723	1139501	148066
山 西	Shanxi	99114	79517	20805	550281	86726
内蒙古	Inner Mongolia	84628	76573	16735	471487	65669
辽 宁	Liaoning	108001	81078	10514	561388	112913
吉 林	Jilin	91722	72858	13943	466629	72443
黑龙江	Heilongjiang	113307	86828	13938	643788	87164
上 海	Shanghai	89533	58790	4875	241210	57714
江 苏	Jiangsu	187071	106035	9593	842118	198371
浙 江	Zhejiang	120686	171669	17487	578928	116713
安 徽	Anhui	183908	105202	29645	868011	152964
福 建	Fujian	120234	115150	12465	441172	87647
江 西	Jiangxi	115812	76176	16273	582373	93811
山 东	Shandong	173630	134144	24822	1338876	196677
河 南	Henan	237200	181839	67395	1503687	228675
湖 北	Hubei	198136	99783	37119	749528	120740
湖 南	Hunan	223651	101192	32914	926986	133090
广 东	Guangdong	132311	115563	26120	707199	149594
广 西	Guangxi	176611	108007	23423	782718	83794
海 南	Hainan	17456	8053	3029	92440	15134
重 庆	Chongqing	134204	56143	14512	461841	75253
四 川	Sichuan	405968	214945	43450	1502713	177478
贵 州	Guizhou	143510	75130	25928	742031	57722
云 南	Yunnan	167720	98093	30417	772186	73572
西 藏	Tibet	16443	10420	4905	48442	2821
陕 西	Shaanxi	159328	125905	26607	723044	78778
甘 肃	Gansu	83321	64815	11948	421214	61359
青 海	Qinghai	22814	23605	3935	93100	13981
宁 夏	Ningxia	30042	24755	4517	128819	18877
新 疆	Xinjiang	70955	47385	13320	265704	41233
新疆兵团	Xinjiang Corps	8439	4811	837	34360	6534
黑龙江垦区	Heilongjiang Land Reclamation	3911	2715	602	19599	3435

3-2　续表 3　Continued 3

单位：人 (person)

地 区	Region	已办理证件残疾人 PWDs with Disabled Persons Certificate			
		残疾类别 Disability Category		户口性质 Household Register Type	
		精神残疾人 Persons with Psychosocial Disability	多重残疾人 Persons with Multiple Disabilities	农业 Rural	非农业 Non-Rural
全 国	**Total**	**3056498**	**1573275**	**25807723**	**8231930**
北 京	Beijing	51810	25404	201828	312006
天 津	Tianjin	26753	5913	136872	209067
河 北	Hebei	100775	88582	1547447	260225
山 西	Shanxi	55247	34324	745319	180695
内蒙古	Inner Mongolia	54129	33713	538148	264786
辽 宁	Liaoning	105404	37479	568843	447934
吉 林	Jilin	77549	28757	479548	344353
黑龙江	Heilongjiang	79031	32120	549243	506933
上 海	Shanghai	51296	11150	90795	423773
江 苏	Jiangsu	167128	49176	301274	1258218
浙 江	Zhejiang	136876	37375	958152	221582
安 徽	Anhui	210237	105585	1386272	269280
福 建	Fujian	86629	47402	764240	146459
江 西	Jiangxi	111329	57753	842431	211096
山 东	Shandong	197541	102749	1890435	278004
河 南	Henan	152262	73086	2155499	288645
湖 北	Hubei	180046	82427	1179894	287885
湖 南	Hunan	171924	93815	1437843	245729
广 东	Guangdong	226698	85869	1087325	356029
广 西	Guangxi	107330	71884	1219659	134108
海 南	Hainan	25651	7745	125825	43683
重 庆	Chongqing	83892	31623	657902	199566
四 川	Sichuan	215992	92915	2242589	410872
贵 州	Guizhou	49838	72175	1041571	124763
云 南	Yunnan	104617	58022	1150420	154207
西 藏	Tibet	5578	8082	89118	7573
陕 西	Shaanxi	101780	83054	1136708	161788
甘 肃	Gansu	47216	60520	632396	117997
青 海	Qinghai	5091	11090	136601	37015
宁 夏	Ningxia	15483	10630	165772	67351
新 疆	Xinjiang	37856	29638	345566	160525
新疆兵团	Xinjiang Corps	8895	2239	1579	64536
黑龙江垦区	Heilongjiang Land Reclamation	4615	979	609	35247

3-2 续表 4 Continued 4

单位：人 (person)

地 区	Region	已办理证件残疾人 PWDs with Disabled Persons Certificate					
		受教育程度 Education					
		文 盲 Illiterate	小 学 Primary School	初 中 Junior High School	高中及中专 Senior High School	大学专科及以上 Junior College and above	其 他 Other
全 国	**Total**	**6269418**	**13417026**	**10464899**	**2909825**	**568900**	**409585**
北 京	Beijing	66501	91093	199542	106996	45243	4459
天 津	Tianjin	36700	83178	132428	64386	18901	10346
河 北	Hebei	211405	730083	648640	157462	27279	32803
山 西	Shanxi	120578	316195	376035	85690	16715	10801
内蒙古	Inner Mongolia	133831	273238	284416	88592	17379	5478
辽 宁	Liaoning	108249	317782	454657	108335	21983	5771
吉 林	Jilin	91431	266871	331124	116965	13921	3589
黑龙江	Heilongjiang	87499	355474	450417	130973	22041	9772
上 海	Shanghai	46157	106794	215680	111022	34915	
江 苏	Jiangsu	509267	481719	419693	118751	29749	313
浙 江	Zhejiang	258822	518017	306873	65422	17951	12649
安 徽	Anhui	449717	674997	419216	82536	18564	10522
福 建	Fujian	166149	442328	215075	56835	10130	20182
江 西	Jiangxi	138284	451755	343787	82176	11606	25919
山 东	Shandong	381874	779120	741594	208052	30222	27577
河 南	Henan	610105	793464	771848	198324	29807	40596
湖 北	Hubei	301769	478371	489132	164323	23514	10670
湖 南	Hunan	226587	705157	536202	180915	17451	17260
广 东	Guangdong	228684	599761	424337	120051	21653	48868
广 西	Guangxi	167883	699827	367598	76334	10900	31225
海 南	Hainan	34498	53253	61186	16680	2415	1476
重 庆	Chongqing	93370	443352	241033	53163	9792	16758
四 川	Sichuan	419743	1413407	649330	132946	24587	13448
贵 州	Guizhou	340621	505432	254958	45034	12636	7653
云 南	Yunnan	343465	618710	257017	60557	17242	7636
西 藏	Tibet	55321	34489	4595	1188	542	556
陕 西	Shaanxi	250557	488356	424258	110576	16721	8028
甘 肃	Gansu	221605	284989	168874	60102	11331	3492
青 海	Qinghai	40558	89705	27156	11369	3447	1381
宁 夏	Ningxia	61002	86355	58297	18799	6483	2187
新 疆	Xinjiang	60475	208355	146024	55671	18615	16951
新疆兵团	Xinjiang Corps	4811	18017	26524	12008	3878	877
黑龙江垦区	Heilongjiang Land Reclamation	1900	7382	17353	7592	1287	342

分省统计资料

Statistical Data of Provinces

一、康复
Rehabilitation

4-1-1　社区康复
Community-Based Rehabilitation(CBR)

地　区	Region	开展社区康复服务的市辖区* Districts Where CBR Has Been Conducted	开展社区康复服务的县(市)* Counties and Cities Where CBR Has Been Conducted	社区康复协调员 Accumulative CBR Coordinators at Communities
		个 unit	个 unit	人 person
全　国	**Total**	**965**	**2023**	**478962**
北　京	Beijing	16		6118
天　津	Tianjin	16		4446
河　北	Hebei	45	127	45654
山　西	Shanxi	23	96	24300
内蒙古	Inner Mongolia	23	82	11755
辽　宁	Liaoning	63	43	14370
吉　林	Jilin	31	40	11334
黑龙江	Heilongjiang	60	62	6667
上　海	Shanghai	16		5086
江　苏	Jiangsu	59	41	19862
浙　江	Zhejiang	34	57	25398
安　徽	Anhui	47	60	15734
福　建	Fujian	27	57	12566
江　西	Jiangxi	25	78	14287
山　东	Shandong	62	87	49331
河　南	Henan	62	104	47811
湖　北	Hubei	39	62	10180
湖　南	Hunan	37	87	25327
广　东	Guangdong	69	58	22739
广　西	Guangxi	39	75	14079
海　南	Hainan	4	16	2147
重　庆	Chongqing	28	12	10914
四　川	Sichuan	34	104	24666
贵　州	Guizhou	7	78	9442
云　南	Yunnan	11	112	12636
西　藏	Tibet	3	20	87
陕　西	Shaanxi	29	83	12780
甘　肃	Gansu	18	69	11782
青　海	Qinghai	6	40	2353
宁　夏	Ningxia	9	13	1559
新　疆	Xinjiang	12	82	2987
新疆兵团	Xinjiang Corps	11	138	465
黑龙江垦区	Heilongjiang Land Reclamation		40	100

注：*“开展社区康复服务的县(市、区)”包含正式行政区划单位和开发区、管委会等非正式行政区划，以及新疆兵团、黑龙江垦区下属县级单位。

Counties (cities and districts) providing community rehabilitation service include formal administrative divisions and development zones, informal administrative divisions such as management committees, and county-level units subordinate to the Xinjiang Production and Construction Corps and Heilongjiang Reclamation Area.

4–1–2 残疾人接受基本康复服务总体情况
Rehabilitation Services Received by Various Persons with Disabilities

地 区	Region	合 计 Total	其中：0–6岁残疾儿童 Disabled children aged 0-6	视力残疾 Visual Disability	听力残疾 Hearing Disability	言语残疾 Speech Disability	肢体残疾 Physical Disability
		人 person	人 person	人 person	人 person	人 person	人 person
全 国	**Total**	**8546661**	**141239**	**882855**	**406774**	**42863**	**4845876**
北 京	Beijing	173806	970	14812	9876	26	98226
天 津	Tianjin	60764	154	4067	6256	1192	35991
河 北	Hebei	342781	5115	30048	13120	186	240847
山 西	Shanxi	281188	2503	23447	8683	52	186770
内蒙古	Inner Mongolia	104332	1262	9768	9255	203	65555
辽 宁	Liaoning	206905	2189	21218	8605	211	114598
吉 林	Jilin	154226	1684	13551	3969	85	106394
黑龙江	Heilongjiang	81732	2270	10722	2681	39	52488
上 海	Shanghai	215804	177	42777	20665	1514	99197
江 苏	Jiangsu	383743	16970	41761	15958	112	196944
浙 江	Zhejiang	564584	6102	56821	54587	3414	220650
安 徽	Anhui	709632	6525	81265	26410	5085	350723
福 建	Fujian	160540	6502	4409	4544	25	86859
江 西	Jiangxi	230997	3623	28949	10005	53	134586
山 东	Shandong	383237	11665	30490	13793	156	256730
河 南	Henan	541028	14192	53212	23408	1898	368460
湖 北	Hubei	483612	5868	75613	38211	15816	191204
湖 南	Hunan	375581	7932	50525	12995	970	209753
广 东	Guangdong	180249	9906	13144	6837	288	76381
广 西	Guangxi	224606	5530	22512	6849	405	120642
海 南	Hainan	68933	1380	7804	2063	268	30621
重 庆	Chongqing	167725	2580	21781	7345	137	74988
四 川	Sichuan	1268058	9813	78010	10198	2836	889934
贵 州	Guizhou	151538	2684	20762	7892	654	92324
云 南	Yunnan	273241	2977	35484	21101	2238	140731
西 藏	Tibet	725	27	71	42		501
陕 西	Shaanxi	249468	3189	27764	18320	1224	139130
甘 肃	Gansu	242864	2915	27095	15865	789	136346
青 海	Qinghai	63104	1246	9065	8754	1439	31052
宁 夏	Ningxia	115132	1445	15157	11720	1356	54444
新 疆	Xinjiang	63450	1693	7616	5518	191	32793
新疆兵团	Xinjiang Corps	20575	136	1962	998		9564
黑龙江垦区	Heilongjiang Land Reclamation	2501	15	1173	251	1	450

4-1-2 续表 1 Continued 1

地 区	Region	智力残疾 Intellectual Disability	精神残疾 Psychosocial Disability	多重残疾 Multiple Disabilities	0-17岁未持证残疾儿童 Disabled children without certificate aged 0-17
		人 person	人 person	人 person	人 person
全 国	**Total**	**713179**	**1259300**	**355204**	**40610**
北 京	Beijing	13785	27611	9460	10
天 津	Tianjin	5194	6511	1553	
河 北	Hebei	17549	27095	12703	1233
山 西	Shanxi	27743	25570	8221	702
内蒙古	Inner Mongolia	5923	9561	3871	196
辽 宁	Liaoning	17343	39083	5122	725
吉 林	Jilin	9116	16522	4114	475
黑龙江	Heilongjiang	3762	9199	1727	1114
上 海	Shanghai	21621	24323	5707	
江 苏	Jiangsu	35227	71846	8897	12998
浙 江	Zhejiang	88211	119311	20378	1212
安 徽	Anhui	72692	133318	39667	472
福 建	Fujian	26691	27959	7676	2377
江 西	Jiangxi	9717	38345	8942	400
山 东	Shandong	17804	46221	17070	973
河 南	Henan	38789	35976	13169	6116
湖 北	Hubei	39494	83177	38368	1729
湖 南	Hunan	20649	64773	12839	3077
广 东	Guangdong	10699	62985	7662	2253
广 西	Guangxi	21015	38669	12823	1691
海 南	Hainan	7159	17330	3607	81
重 庆	Chongqing	14803	42496	5709	466
四 川	Sichuan	101211	153247	32622	
贵 州	Guizhou	8817	11134	9719	236
云 南	Yunnan	18846	40851	13832	158
西 藏	Tibet	18	14	79	
陕 西	Shaanxi	9514	39750	12375	1391
甘 肃	Gansu	23695	18959	20002	113
青 海	Qinghai	5063	1967	5721	43
宁 夏	Ningxia	13218	11976	7032	229
新 疆	Xinjiang	5699	7753	3740	140
新疆兵团	Xinjiang Corps	2081	5247	723	
黑龙江垦区	Heilongjiang Land Reclamation	31	521	74	

4-1-3 视力残疾基本康复服务
Basic Rehabilitation Services for Persons with Visual Disability

地 区	Region	复明手术、定向行走等训练 Sight-restoring Surgeries and Orientation Mobility Training for Cataract Victims	盲杖、助视器等辅具适配服务 Allocation of Assistive Devices and Services	其他 Others
		人 person	人 person	人 person
全 国	**Total**	**114063**	**376311**	**445017**
北 京	Beijing	7885	3397	3860
天 津	Tianjin	411	2762	927
河 北	Hebei	3662	19973	7264
山 西	Shanxi	4880	12706	7105
内蒙古	Inner Mongolia	1160	6556	2457
辽 宁	Liaoning	3282	11564	8465
吉 林	Jilin	1511	8140	4704
黑龙江	Heilongjiang	1846	8653	264
上 海	Shanghai	35	763	42919
江 苏	Jiangsu	8462	25718	12948
浙 江	Zhejiang	1960	14909	50775
安 徽	Anhui	9020	18295	60314
福 建	Fujian	535	817	3338
江 西	Jiangxi	3825	25119	1352
山 东	Shandong	2573	25362	3819
河 南	Henan	7576	28668	19090
湖 北	Hubei	3680	9389	61211
湖 南	Hunan	8103	37328	7036
广 东	Guangdong	3180	8782	1835
广 西	Guangxi	3813	14023	7504
海 南	Hainan	834	769	6662
重 庆	Chongqing	2574	10181	10183
四 川	Sichuan	6473	24231	57552
贵 州	Guizhou	4082	10317	7134
云 南	Yunnan	4526	10973	21751
西 藏	Tibet	8	35	34
陕 西	Shaanxi	6232	12023	5432
甘 肃	Gansu	6752	10567	10706
青 海	Qinghai	831	2261	6307
宁 夏	Ningxia	2304	4458	10614
新 疆	Xinjiang	1032	5517	1313
新疆兵团	Xinjiang Corps	1015	874	142
黑龙江垦区	Heilongjiang Land Reclamation	1	1181	

4-1-4　听力残疾基本康复服务
Basic Rehabilitation Services for Persons with Hearing Disability

地　区	Region	人工耳蜗植入手术及服务、助听器适配 Artificial Cochlea Implant Surgeries and Allocation of Hearing Aids and Services	听觉言语功能训练 Hearing and Speech Trainings	其他 Others
		人 person	人 person	人 person
全　国	**Total**	**306063**	**10068**	**268119**
北　京	Beijing	3891	120	8263
天　津	Tianjin	4496	2	3001
河　北	Hebei	16711	399	1798
山　西	Shanxi	8168	165	1924
内蒙古	Inner Mongolia	9970	44	665
辽　宁	Liaoning	8098	201	2269
吉　林	Jilin	4299	61	445
黑龙江	Heilongjiang	3097	33	36
上　海	Shanghai	388		23028
江　苏	Jiangsu	12791	1673	6235
浙　江	Zhejiang	29222	668	35610
安　徽	Anhui	17239	464	30931
福　建	Fujian	4409	637	990
江　西	Jiangxi	12743	283	670
山　东	Shandong	15957	1014	1867
河　南	Henan	22423	911	9274
湖　北	Hubei	4963	331	74834
湖　南	Hunan	17064	478	2099
广　东	Guangdong	5557	1422	1095
广　西	Guangxi	6145	305	3533
海　南	Hainan	1140	14	2422
重　庆	Chongqing	9204	99	1098
四　川	Sichuan	6762		8647
贵　州	Guizhou	9509	197	2508
云　南	Yunnan	19273	78	10477
西　藏	Tibet	55		
陕　西	Shaanxi	14450	238	4013
甘　肃	Gansu	24473	71	2748
青　海	Qinghai	1930	30	12842
宁　夏	Ningxia	3802	97	14101
新　疆	Xinjiang	6335	28	643
新疆兵团	Xinjiang Corps	1233	5	24
黑龙江垦区	Heilongjiang Lan Reclamation	266		29

4-1-5 肢体残疾基本康复服务
Basic Rehabilitation Services for Persons with Physical Disability

地 区	Region	矫治手术、运动功能训练等 Orthopedic Surgeries Conducted and Motor Function Trainings	假肢、矫形器等辅具适配服务 Allocation of Assistive Devices and Services	其他 Others
		人 person	人 person	人 person
全 国	**Total**	**616678**	**1684794**	**2903288**
北 京	Beijing	33322	16461	51602
天 津	Tianjin	4252	11990	19540
河 北	Hebei	75226	109546	66695
山 西	Shanxi	25197	87474	96740
内蒙古	Inner Mongolia	9340	37794	21695
辽 宁	Liaoning	21650	57928	47974
吉 林	Jilin	12800	51125	47791
黑龙江	Heilongjiang	26522	24014	3028
上 海	Shanghai	52	1245	100500
江 苏	Jiangsu	21532	123846	63830
浙 江	Zhejiang	6920	45166	246484
安 徽	Anhui	22633	45904	312048
福 建	Fujian	3300	9354	80899
江 西	Jiangxi	17196	114130	9010
山 东	Shandong	45939	162692	65624
河 南	Henan	78726	154666	153162
湖 北	Hubei	10203	36607	134150
湖 南	Hunan	37152	150767	30289
广 东	Guangdong	15013	32704	33199
广 西	Guangxi	15939	57417	63384
海 南	Hainan	931	2657	28873
重 庆	Chongqing	10415	32773	37119
四 川	Sichuan	21790	74288	878930
贵 州	Guizhou	8288	39265	47921
云 南	Yunnan	18534	40524	90111
西 藏	Tibet	17	239	307
陕 西	Shaanxi	23110	68959	35265
甘 肃	Gansu	25260	49276	69665
青 海	Qinghai	1814	7433	22530
宁 夏	Ningxia	11720	17286	33577
新 疆	Xinjiang	6989	17668	9498
新疆兵团	Xinjiang Corps	4829	3217	1826
黑龙江垦区	Heilongjiang Land Reclamation	67	379	22

4-1-6 智力残疾基本康复服务
Basic Rehabilitation Services for Persons with Intellectual Disability

	认知及适应训练 Recognition and Adaptive Trainings	其他 Others
	人 person	人 person
全 国 Total	**128905**	**680769**
北 京 Beijing	4802	10685
天 津 Tianjin	178	5224
河 北 Hebei	6766	12801
山 西 Shanxi	3179	27869
内蒙古 Inner Mongolia	1559	4861
辽 宁 Liaoning	5550	13811
吉 林 Jilin	1123	8426
黑龙江 Heilongjiang	2554	2008
上 海 Shanghai	68	22336
江 苏 Jiangsu	12696	27799
浙 江 Zhejiang	2553	105404
安 徽 Anhui	6950	76385
福 建 Fujian	2704	27163
江 西 Jiangxi	6074	5096
山 东 Shandong	7914	13112
河 南 Henan	13770	30712
湖 北 Hubei	3274	37316
湖 南 Hunan	11486	14165
广 东 Guangdong	5482	6912
广 西 Guangxi	3862	21052
海 南 Hainan	530	7534
重 庆 Chongqing	3203	12734
四 川 Sichuan	798	110495
贵 州 Guizhou	2572	7571
云 南 Yunnan	3407	18154
西 藏 Tibet	2	25
陕 西 Shaanxi	4096	6854
甘 肃 Gansu	7154	19915
青 海 Qinghai	341	4940
宁 夏 Ningxia	1291	13618
新 疆 Xinjiang	1945	4532
新疆兵团 Xinjiang Corps	1006	1243
黑龙江垦区 Heilongjiang Land Reclamation	16	17

4-1-7 精神残疾基本康复服务
Basic Rehabilitation Services for Persons with Intellectual Disability

地区	Region	孤独症沟通及适应训练 Communication and Adaptive Trainings for Autistic Children	药物治疗及作业疗法训练 Medical Teratment and Occupational Therapy for Mental Disorder	其他 Others
		人 person	人 person	人 person
全国	**Total**	**21139**	**688766**	**621057**
北京	Beijing	250	17206	11642
天津	Tianjin		3868	2955
河北	Hebei	456	19090	8913
山西	Shanxi	150	7418	19877
内蒙古	Inner Mongolia	258	5893	3789
辽宁	Liaoning	666	22250	26555
吉林	Jilin	404	8655	8692
黑龙江	Heilongjiang	834	6846	1999
上海	Shanghai	1	303	673
江苏	Jiangsu	2951	58900	15102
浙江	Zhejiang	1095	62779	14126
安徽	Anhui	1101	62137	85850
福建	Fujian	1713	15475	14414
江西	Jiangxi	720	35746	4982
山东	Shandong	2042	35317	13004
河南	Henan	567	17470	19520
湖北	Hubei	268	21356	56939
湖南	Hunan	1455	57461	11097
广东	Guangdong	4063	52727	13898
广西	Guangxi	340	12394	27223
海南	Hainan	190	8563	12521
重庆	Chongqing	266	33541	11000
四川	Sichuan	104	53639	154339
贵州	Guizhou	231	5211	6689
云南	Yunnan	176	22113	20617
西藏	Tibet			17
陕西	Shaanxi	426	20601	24986
甘肃	Gansu	191	7384	12647
青海	Qinghai	1	164	1779
宁夏	Ningxia	103	4113	11330
新疆	Xinjiang	74	5547	2554
新疆兵团	Xinjiang Corps	42	4073	1327
黑龙江垦区	Heilongjiang Land Reclamation	1	526	1

4-1-8 辅助器具供应服务
Provision of Assistive Devices

地 区	Region	接受辅助器具适配服务的残疾人 Providing and fitting assistive devices for persons with disablities	接受盲杖及助视器适配服务 Providing and fitting canes and visual aids	接受人工耳蜗及助听器适配服务 Providing and fitting cochlears and hearing aids	接受假肢、矫形器、轮椅等主要肢体残疾辅助器具适配服务 Providing and fitting prosthetics, orthoses, wheelchairs, and other mobility aids	接受其他各类辅助器具适配服务 Providing and fitting other assistive devices
		人 person	人次 person-time	人次 person-time	人次 person-time	人次 person-time
全 国	**Total**	**2443665**	**200847**	**179645**	**1373140**	**1168207**
北 京	Beijing	25009	1144	1640	5813	15435
天 津	Tianjin	19601	1399	607	6508	7575
河 北	Hebei	147690	12954	9258	58169	64216
山 西	Shanxi	108163	7895	5084	41132	54088
内蒙古	Inner Mongolia	54420	3573	7765	24860	17513
辽 宁	Liaoning	77250	2540	4265	30012	44922
吉 林	Jilin	63417	3404	1759	26311	32441
黑龙江	Heilongjiang	35748	4843	3069	25063	4723
上 海	Shanghai	55767	7699	4653	17088	29211
江 苏	Jiangsu	162773	11807	6040	81738	74421
浙 江	Zhejiang	88788	4634	19069	24000	35183
安 徽	Anhui	81665	5824	4496	27072	36418
福 建	Fujian	15398	317	3779	6023	5201
江 西	Jiangxi	150870	11919	6537	53899	83613
山 东	Shandong	211064	13065	8280	99972	88348
河 南	Henan	206256	16757	12123	93291	82527
湖 北	Hubei	54333	3814	2715	18571	28980
湖 南	Hunan	205118	20259	11615	70699	104275
广 东	Guangdong	46831	2725	4034	25836	21129
广 西	Guangxi	78643	7845	4409	31171	38727
海 南	Hainan	4611	238	538	2205	1120
重 庆	Chongqing	51964	4945	5594	17110	24923
四 川	Sichuan	104418	24230	6955	445332	98834
贵 州	Guizhou	58818	4609	4681	15397	32117
云 南	Yunnan	70773	4375	10072	19895	30581
西 藏	Tibet	328	6	17	153	116
陕 西	Shaanxi	102292	5790	9277	47222	47489
甘 肃	Gansu	84797	5060	12921	28461	30418
青 海	Qinghai	14780	1005	2883	6338	5694
宁 夏	Ningxia	25405	2048	1232	11574	11059
新 疆	Xinjiang	29543	3079	3453	10133	14129
新疆兵团	Xinjiang Corps	5309	318	559	1748	2227
黑龙江垦区	Heilongjiang Land Reclamation	1823	727	266	344	554

4-1-9 康复机构
Rehabilitation Institutions

地 区	Region	残疾人康复机构 Rehabilitation Institutions for Persons with Disabilities	各类康复机构 Various Rehabilitation Institutions		
			视力残疾康复机构 Rehabilitation Institution for Persons with Visual Disabilities	听力言语残疾康复机构 Rehabilitation Institutions for Hearing and Speech	肢体残疾康复机构 Rehabilitation Institutions for Persons with Physical Disabilities
		个 unit	个 unit	个 unit	个 unit
全 国	**Total**	**8334**	**1194**	**1417**	**3088**
北 京	Beijing	130	13	27	26
天 津	Tianjin	71	8	7	11
河 北	Hebei	439	40	102	189
山 西	Shanxi	308	68	54	133
内蒙古	Inner Mongolia	223	43	47	91
辽 宁	Liaoning	362	59	47	135
吉 林	Jilin	213	54	34	80
黑龙江	Heilongjiang	165	36	37	67
上 海	Shanghai	1081	79	42	326
江 苏	Jiangsu	421	82	74	151
浙 江	Zhejiang	190	25	45	82
安 徽	Anhui	228	13	84	79
福 建	Fujian	253	27	35	62
江 西	Jiangxi	204	8	40	51
山 东	Shandong	552	65	77	227
河 南	Henan	364	40	109	154
湖 北	Hubei	220	16	37	64
湖 南	Hunan	374	52	70	88
广 东	Guangdong	570	72	76	181
广 西	Guangxi	220	32	37	78
海 南	Hainan	34	4	5	18
重 庆	Chongqing	262	44	43	87
四 川	Sichuan	263	50	58	111
贵 州	Guizhou	185	46	50	63
云 南	Yunnan	240	47	45	70
西 藏	Tibet	5	1	1	4
陕 西	Shaanxi	316	64	47	190
甘 肃	Gansu	123	38	33	54
青 海	Qinghai	35	12	12	20
宁 夏	Ningxia	29	7	6	21
新 疆	Xinjiang	134	36	24	73
新疆兵团	Xinjiang Corps	50	13	12	42
黑龙江垦区	Heilongjiang Land Reclamation	70			60

4-1-9　续表 1　Continued 1

地　区	Region	各类康复机构 Various Rehabilitation Institutions			
		智力残疾康复机构 Rehabilitation Institutions for Persons with Intellectual Disabilities	精神残疾康复机构 Rehabilitation Institutions for Persons with Mental Illness	孤独症儿童康复机构 Rehabilitation Institutions for Children with Autism	辅助器具服务机构 Assistive Device Services Providers
		个 unit	个 unit	个 unit	个 unit
全　国	**Total**	**2659**	**1695**	**1611**	**1866**
北　京	Beijing	40	20	28	12
天　津	Tianjin	20	10	28	14
河　北	Hebei	152	92	67	70
山　西	Shanxi	129	69	36	59
内蒙古	Inner Mongolia	55	24	35	70
辽　宁	Liaoning	98	86	67	116
吉　林	Jilin	40	38	37	40
黑龙江	Heilongjiang	54	18	43	17
上　海	Shanghai	312	242	61	263
江　苏	Jiangsu	120	79	104	71
浙　江	Zhejiang	92	39	79	58
安　徽	Anhui	127	7	102	42
福　建	Fujian	71	46	81	63
江　西	Jiangxi	62	64	30	28
山　东	Shandong	156	96	127	82
河　南	Henan	141	88	86	65
湖　北	Hubei	69	64	32	52
湖　南	Hunan	112	70	71	107
广　东	Guangdong	201	96	195	86
广　西	Guangxi	80	63	31	91
海　南	Hainan	11	6	10	4
重　庆	Chongqing	67	48	31	39
四　川	Sichuan	117	81	58	68
贵　州	Guizhou	60	56	37	44
云　南	Yunnan	70	63	29	92
西　藏	Tibet	2			5
陕　西	Shaanxi	67	57	32	62
甘　肃	Gansu	45	24	32	67
青　海	Qinghai	21	6	15	16
宁　夏	Ningxia	22	5	17	7
新　疆	Xinjiang	32	19		26
				8	
新疆兵团	Xinjiang Corps	14	16	2	16
黑龙江垦区	Heilongjiang Land Reclamation		3		14

4-1-10 康复人才
Rehabilitation Professionals

地 区	Region	康复机构在岗人员 Staff of Rehabilitation Institutions	业务人员 Professionals	管理人员 Managerial Personnels	其他人员 Other Staff Members
		人 person	人 person	人 person	人 person
全 国	**Total**	**245822**	**164264**	**31185**	**50373**
北 京	Beijing	3928	2925	503	500
天 津	Tianjin	3292	1885	516	891
河 北	Hebei	13071	8900	1744	2427
山 西	Shanxi	10306	7417	1186	1703
内蒙古	Inner Mongolia	5859	3997	1037	825
辽 宁	Liaoning	12038	8115	1542	2381
吉 林	Jilin	9050	6014	1417	1619
黑龙江	Heilongjiang	4750	3333	524	893
上 海	Shanghai	9030	4273	1559	3198
江 苏	Jiangsu	11377	7788	1309	2280
浙 江	Zhejiang	5735	3970	656	1109
安 徽	Anhui	5914	4424	704	786
福 建	Fujian	6212	3848	824	1540
江 西	Jiangxi	5184	3525	800	859
山 东	Shandong	25505	18472	3190	3843
河 南	Henan	16328	11444	1726	3158
湖 北	Hubei	9123	6493	1178	1452
湖 南	Hunan	11682	8106	1230	2346
广 东	Guangdong	18037	12195	2038	3804
广 西	Guangxi	6868	4620	713	1535
海 南	Hainan	1258	919	129	210
重 庆	Chongqing	7952	4835	952	2165
四 川	Sichuan	11394	6995	1354	3045
贵 州	Guizhou	8273	5502	989	1782
云 南	Yunnan	7173	4018	815	2340
西 藏	Tibet	78	38	12	28
陕 西	Shaanxi	9468	5908	1240	2320
甘 肃	Gansu	2474	1564	394	516
青 海	Qinghai	489	258	91	140
宁 夏	Ningxia	585	424	87	74
新 疆	Xinjiang	1955	1156	470	329
新疆兵团	Xinjiang Corps	1037	679	145	213
黑龙江垦区	Heilongjiang Land Reclamation	397	224	111	62

4-1-10 续表 1 Continued 1

地 区	Region	康复机构在岗人员 Staff of Rehabilitation Institutions 视力残疾康复在岗人员 In-Service Personal for Rehabilitation of Persons with Visual Disabilities	业务人员 Professionals	管理人员 Managerial Personnels	其他人员 Other Staff Members
		人 person	人 person	人 person	人 person
全 国	**Total**	**22790**	**15002**	**3107**	**4681**
北 京	Beijing	140	110	26	4
天 津	Tianjin	61	49	11	1
河 北	Hebei	546	314	79	153
山 西	Shanxi	1110	712	179	219
内蒙古	Inner Mongolia	811	534	162	115
辽 宁	Liaoning	2161	1304	307	550
吉 林	Jilin	1817	1221	288	308
黑龙江	Heilongjiang	313	232	41	40
上 海	Shanghai	429	314	77	38
江 苏	Jiangsu	1487	915	254	318
浙 江	Zhejiang	70	40	22	8
安 徽	Anhui	349	204	53	92
福 建	Fujian	312	209	81	22
江 西	Jiangxi	57	23	6	28
山 东	Shandong	4327	3563	364	400
河 南	Henan	657	371	123	163
湖 北	Hubei	391	79	20	292
湖 南	Hunan	1299	735	147	417
广 东	Guangdong	1135	805	126	204
广 西	Guangxi	578	485	31	62
海 南	Hainan	57	37	5	15
重 庆	Chongqing	1014	602	143	269
四 川	Sichuan	1173	662	144	367
贵 州	Guizhou	617	346	85	186
云 南	Yunnan	615	435	67	113
西 藏	Tibet	3	2	1	
陕 西	Shaanxi	537	279	133	125
甘 肃	Gansu	312	180	52	80
青 海	Qinghai	68	32	9	27
宁 夏	Ningxia	23	15	5	3
新 疆	Xinjiang	260	155	54	51
新疆兵团	Xinjiang Corps	61	38	12	11
黑龙江垦区	Heilongjiang Land Reclamation				

4-1-10 续表 2 Continued 2

地 区	Region	康复机构在岗人员 Staff of Rehabilitation Institutions			
		听力言语康复在岗人员 In-Service Personnel for Hearing and Speech Rehabilitation	业务人员 Professionals	管理人员 Managerial Personnels	其他人员 Other Staff Members
		人 person	人 person	人 person	人 person
全 国	**Total**	**16498**	**10971**	**2349**	**3178**
北 京	Beijing	339	245	56	38
天 津	Tianjin	82	67	9	6
河 北	Hebei	1356	981	216	159
山 西	Shanxi	527	331	90	106
内蒙古	Inner Mongolia	373	277	61	35
辽 宁	Liaoning	511	348	61	102
吉 林	Jilin	578	342	97	139
黑龙江	Heilongjiang	327	208	61	58
上 海	Shanghai	231	139	49	43
江 苏	Jiangsu	923	666	117	140
浙 江	Zhejiang	389	269	58	62
安 徽	Anhui	800	607	118	75
福 建	Fujian	572	379	75	118
江 西	Jiangxi	401	281	52	68
山 东	Shandong	1117	827	128	162
河 南	Henan	1629	1199	208	222
湖 北	Hubei	359	275	46	38
湖 南	Hunan	913	605	130	178
广 东	Guangdong	1156	813	119	224
广 西	Guangxi	438	271	48	119
海 南	Hainan	103	62	12	29
重 庆	Chongqing	552	305	125	122
四 川	Sichuan	564	370	80	114
贵 州	Guizhou	466	279	74	113
云 南	Yunnan	688	139	68	481
西 藏	Tibet	10	6	1	3
陕 西	Shaanxi	588	360	90	138
甘 肃	Gansu	193	123	40	30
青 海	Qinghai	49	24	13	12
宁 夏	Ningxia	78	67	8	3
新 疆	Xinjiang	162	100	26	36
新疆兵团	Xinjiang Corps	24	6	13	5
黑龙江垦区	Heilongjiang Land Reclamation				

4-1-10 续表 3 Continued 3

地 区	Region	康复机构在岗人员 Staff of Rehabilitation Institutions			
		肢体残疾康复在岗人员 In-Service Personnel for Rehabilitation of Persons with Physical Disabilities	业务人员 Professionals	管理人员 Managerial Personnels	其他人员 Other Staff Members
		人 person	人 person	人 person	人 person
全 国	**Total**	**62012**	**44621**	**6459**	**10932**
北 京	Beijing	714	580	76	58
天 津	Tianjin	435	325	33	77
河 北	Hebei	3608	2505	399	704
山 西	Shanxi	3347	2560	195	592
内蒙古	Inner Mongolia	1153	960	103	90
辽 宁	Liaoning	2443	1692	246	505
吉 林	Jilin	1273	954	166	153
黑龙江	Heilongjiang	1539	1238	119	182
上 海	Shanghai	4347	2244	480	1623
江 苏	Jiangsu	3255	2530	261	464
浙 江	Zhejiang	2022	1543	156	323
安 徽	Anhui	2020	1636	189	195
福 建	Fujian	1054	765	93	196
江 西	Jiangxi	504	394	60	50
山 东	Shandong	8297	5875	1226	1196
河 南	Henan	3935	2844	402	689
湖 北	Hubei	1836	1477	143	216
湖 南	Hunan	2137	1678	169	290
广 东	Guangdong	3438	2473	368	597
广 西	Guangxi	1682	1341	116	225
海 南	Hainan	259	200	29	30
重 庆	Chongqing	1832	1183	195	454
四 川	Sichuan	1930	1373	246	311
贵 州	Guizhou	2105	1531	190	384
云 南	Yunnan	1562	877	92	593
西 藏	Tibet	33	17	4	12
陕 西	Shaanxi	3019	2296	371	352
甘 肃	Gansu	584	422	55	107
青 海	Qinghai	150	84	17	49
宁 夏	Ningxia	158	117	23	18
新 疆	Xinjiang	697	472	110	115
新疆兵团	Xinjiang Corps	337	257	42	38
黑龙江垦区	Heilongjiang Land Reclamation	307	178	85	44

4-1-10 续表 4 Continued 4

地 区	Region	康复机构在岗人员 Staff of Rehabilitation Institutions			
		智力残疾康复在岗人员 In-Service Personnel for Rehabilitation of Persons with Intellectual Disabilities	业务人员 Professionals	管理人员 Managerial Personnels	其他人员 Other Staff Members
		人 person	人 person	人 person	人 person
全 国	**Total**	**38645**	**27410**	**4198**	**7037**
北 京	Beijing	815	614	123	78
天 津	Tianjin	340	242	42	56
河 北	Hebei	3335	2322	411	602
山 西	Shanxi	1876	1539	138	199
内蒙古	Inner Mongolia	640	509	86	45
辽 宁	Liaoning	1162	852	117	193
吉 林	Jilin	422	304	60	58
黑龙江	Heilongjiang	731	527	78	126
上 海	Shanghai	1578	553	387	638
江 苏	Jiangsu	1528	1096	162	270
浙 江	Zhejiang	778	513	99	166
安 徽	Anhui	1578	1204	146	228
福 建	Fujian	1024	677	146	201
江 西	Jiangxi	811	579	104	128
山 东	Shandong	3221	2411	311	499
河 南	Henan	3441	2525	285	631
湖 北	Hubei	1311	972	132	207
湖 南	Hunan	2054	1624	184	246
广 东	Guangdong	2536	1793	271	472
广 西	Guangxi	943	723	82	138
海 南	Hainan	155	134	10	11
重 庆	Chongqing	1365	959	121	285
四 川	Sichuan	2561	1541	230	790
贵 州	Guizhou	944	648	58	238
云 南	Yunnan	978	562	119	297
西 藏	Tibet	6	1	2	3
陕 西	Shaanxi	1301	1122	92	87
甘 肃	Gansu	481	396	50	35
青 海	Qinghai	112	76	14	22
宁 夏	Ningxia	119	83	19	17
新 疆	Xinjiang	384	225	103	56
新疆兵团	Xinjiang Corps	115	84	16	15
黑龙江垦区	Heilongjiang Land Reclamation				

4-1-10　续表 5　Continued 5

地区	Region	康复机构在岗人员 Staff of Rehabilitation Institutions			
		精神残疾康复在岗人员 In-Service Personnel for Rehabilitation of Persons with Mental Illness	业务人员 Professionals	管理人员 Managerial Personnels	其他人员 Other Staff Members
		人 person	人 person	人 person	人 person
全　国	**Total**	**76518**	**49001**	**9644**	**17873**
北　京	Beijing	1311	955	145	211
天　津	Tianjin	1713	737	313	663
河　北	Hebei	2930	1931	416	583
山　西	Shanxi	2914	2002	471	441
内蒙古	Inner Mongolia	2272	1401	500	371
辽　宁	Liaoning	4403	3096	538	769
吉　林	Jilin	4299	2741	687	871
黑龙江	Heilongjiang	1107	693	99	315
上　海	Shanghai	1092	522	249	321
江　苏	Jiangsu	2344	1455	221	668
浙　江	Zhejiang	1508	975	154	379
安　徽	Anhui	260	208	27	25
福　建	Fujian	1666	878	176	612
江　西	Jiangxi	2812	1923	442	447
山　东	Shandong	5953	4186	672	1095
河　南	Henan	5407	3822	464	1121
湖　北	Hubei	4462	3242	710	510
湖　南	Hunan	3912	2650	335	927
广　东	Guangdong	5651	3634	558	1459
广　西	Guangxi	2555	1547	266	742
海　南	Hainan	444	288	49	107
重　庆	Chongqing	2514	1465	252	797
四　川	Sichuan	4276	2541	467	1268
贵　州	Guizhou	3508	2350	434	724
云　南	Yunnan	2857	1804	336	717
西　藏	Tibet				
陕　西	Shaanxi	3043	1233	380	1430
甘　肃	Gansu	391	205	67	119
青　海	Qinghai	13	3	6	4
宁　夏	Ningxia	99	78	10	11
新　疆	Xinjiang	297	128	133	36
新疆兵团	Xinjiang Corps	440	270	54	116
黑龙江垦区	Heilongjiang Land Reclamation	65	38	13	14

4-1-10 续表 6 Continued 6

地 区	Region	康复机构在岗人员 Staff of Rehabilitation Institutions			
		孤独症儿童康复在岗人员 In-Service Personnel for Rehabilitation Institutions of Children with Autism	业务人员 Professionals	管理人员 Managerial Personnels	其他人员 Other Staff Members
		人 person	人 person	人 person	人 person
全 国	**Total**	**21043**	**13765**	**2943**	**4335**
北 京	Beijing	510	362	63	85
天 津	Tianjin	624	458	88	78
河 北	Hebei	1002	718	146	138
山 西	Shanxi	240	172	45	23
内蒙古	Inner Mongolia	321	188	43	90
辽 宁	Liaoning	872	577	129	166
吉 林	Jilin	385	298	46	41
黑龙江	Heilongjiang	662	417	102	143
上 海	Shanghai	615	191	68	356
江 苏	Jiangsu	1301	843	193	265
浙 江	Zhejiang	793	560	114	119
安 徽	Anhui	748	476	126	146
福 建	Fujian	1271	779	168	324
江 西	Jiangxi	479	285	102	92
山 东	Shandong	2085	1439	284	362
河 南	Henan	936	541	146	249
湖 北	Hubei	540	364	68	108
湖 南	Hunan	952	647	115	190
广 东	Guangdong	3362	2364	392	606
广 西	Guangxi	334	170	47	117
海 南	Hainan	213	182	19	12
重 庆	Chongqing	453	237	50	166
四 川	Sichuan	507	317	86	104
贵 州	Guizhou	467	300	79	88
云 南	Yunnan	255	150	45	60
西 藏	Tibet				
陕 西	Shaanxi	606	433	85	88
甘 肃	Gansu	297	181	53	63
青 海	Qinghai	49	16	16	17
宁 夏	Ningxia	89	54	17	18
新 疆	Xinjiang	47	32	7	8
新疆兵团	Xinjiang Corps	28	14	1	13
黑龙江垦区	Heilongjiang Land Reclamation				

4-1-10　续表 7　Continued 7

地　区	Region	康复机构在岗人员 Staff of Rehabilitation Institutions				培训康复管理人员 Rehabilitation Managerial Staff Trained	培训康复业务人员 Rehabilitation Professionals Trained
		辅助器具残疾康复在岗人员 In-Service Personnel for Assistive Device Services	业务人员 Professionals	管理人员 Managerial Personnels	其他人员 Other Staff Members		
		人 person	人 person	人 person	人 person	人 person	人 person
全　国	**Total**	**8316**	**3494**	**2485**	**2337**	**53434**	**247121**
北　京	Beijing	99	59	14	26	1380	4447
天　津	Tianjin	37	7	20	10	356	934
河　北	Hebei	294	129	77	88	2189	12982
山　西	Shanxi	292	101	68	123	1247	3295
内蒙古	Inner Mongolia	289	128	82	79	970	3746
辽　宁	Liaoning	486	246	144	96	3474	11574
吉　林	Jilin	276	154	73	49	1026	5144
黑龙江	Heilongjiang	71	18	24	29	503	2079
上　海	Shanghai	738	310	249	179	3129	13229
江　苏	Jiangsu	539	283	101	155	3395	15326
浙　江	Zhejiang	175	70	53	52	1553	12855
安　徽	Anhui	159	89	45	25	1408	6874
福　建	Fujian	313	161	85	67	836	4803
江　西	Jiangxi	120	40	34	46	681	2102
山　东	Shandong	505	171	205	129	4065	24042
河　南	Henan	323	142	98	83	3370	12022
湖　北	Hubei	224	84	59	81	1257	6509
湖　南	Hunan	415	167	150	98	1507	5778
广　东	Guangdong	759	313	204	242	4465	25943
广　西	Guangxi	338	83	123	132	2136	19140
海　南	Hainan	27	16	5	6	361	1550
重　庆	Chongqing	222	84	66	72	2624	9508
四　川	Sichuan	383	191	101	91	2848	11918
贵　州	Guizhou	166	48	69	49	1723	7439
云　南	Yunnan	218	51	88	79	1670	10064
西　藏	Tibet	26	12	4	10	10	43
陕　西	Shaanxi	374	185	89	100	2159	6458
甘　肃	Gansu	216	57	77	82	1847	3003
青　海	Qinghai	48	23	16	9	173	406
宁　夏	Ningxia	19	10	5	4	160	715
新　疆	Xinjiang	108	44	37	27	479	2343
新疆兵团	Xinjiang Corps	32	10	7	15	346	601
黑龙江垦区	Heilongjiang Land Reclamation	25	8	13	4	87	249

二、教育
Education

4-2-1 学前教育阶段
Pre-school Education

地 区	Region	残疾人事业专项彩票公益金助学项目资助 Support of Educational Project Funded by Dedicated Welfare Lottery Fund in 2017	视力残疾 Children with Visual Disability	听力残疾 Children with Hearing Disability	言语残疾 Children with Speech Disability	肢体残疾 Children with Physical Disability
		人 person	人 person	人 person	人 person	人 person
全 国	**Total**	**18685**	**351**	**3553**	**837**	**3532**
北 京	Beijing	6		1		
天 津	Tianjin					
河 北	Hebei	1000	11	142	20	110
山 西	Shanxi	911	26	235	56	135
内蒙古	Inner Mongolia	264	7	35	15	82
辽 宁	Liaoning	975	2	138	18	126
吉 林	Jilin	240		2	4	39
黑龙江	Heilongjiang	507	12	43	15	52
上 海	Shanghai					
江 苏	Jiangsu	779	28	207	25	140
浙 江	Zhejiang	522	16	157	4	71
安 徽	Anhui	835	15	245	22	175
福 建	Fujian	411	17	88	14	126
江 西	Jiangxi	500	2	69	12	50
山 东	Shandong	944	9	187	17	207
河 南	Henan	1607	35	300	83	353
湖 北	Hubei	750	14	113	64	117
湖 南	Hunan	910	8	186	55	100
广 东	Guangdong	1403	40	213	74	368
广 西	Guangxi	1220	8	266	58	151
海 南	Hainan	345	5	60	11	55
重 庆	Chongqing	374	3	34	47	55
四 川	Sichuan	1004	8	195	48	87
贵 州	Guizhou	582	25	79	46	225
云 南	Yunnan	465	23	119	35	123
西 藏	Tibet	107	7	14	25	22
陕 西	Shaanxi	223	2	75	9	31
甘 肃	Gansu	1178	11	211	28	344
青 海	Qinghai	201	6	44	11	94
宁 夏	Ningxia	177	6	31	6	41
新 疆	Xinjiang	195	5	48	14	34
新疆兵团	Xinjiang Corps	33		8		13
黑龙江垦区	Heilongjiang Land Reclamation	17		8	1	6

4-2-1 续表 Continued

地区	Region	智力残疾 Chidren with Intellectual Disability	精神残疾 Children with Psychosocial Disability	多重残疾 Children with Multi-disabilities	其他残疾儿童学前教育助学项目资助 Support of Other Pre-School Educational Project for Disabled Children in 2017
		人 person	人 person	人 person	人 person
全 国	**Total**	**5953**	**1756**	**2703**	**2971**
北 京	Beijing	3	1	1	292
天 津	Tianjin				45
河 北	Hebei	431	95	191	
山 西	Shanxi	271	79	109	2
内蒙古	Inner Mongolia	52	45	28	39
辽 宁	Liaoning	306	234	151	30
吉 林	Jilin	60	108	27	60
黑龙江	Heilongjiang	170	188	27	
上 海	Shanghai				
江 苏	Jiangsu	211	48	120	357
浙 江	Zhejiang	167	67	40	348
安 徽	Anhui	212	77	89	278
福 建	Fujian	95	25	46	119
江 西	Jiangxi	241	34	92	
山 东	Shandong	286	73	165	157
河 南	Henan	620	90	126	
湖 北	Hubei	279	71	92	
湖 南	Hunan	380	76	105	776
广 东	Guangdong	372	103	233	119
广 西	Guangxi	467	42	228	8
海 南	Hainan	94	82	38	6
重 庆	Chongqing	175	18	42	38
四 川	Sichuan	368	87	211	182
贵 州	Guizhou	67	28	112	3
云 南	Yunnan	103	10	52	11
西 藏	Tibet	6	3	30	
陕 西	Shaanxi	31	10	65	10
甘 肃	Gansu	299	51	234	10
青 海	Qinghai	40		6	16
宁 夏	Ningxia	62	9	22	11
新 疆	Xinjiang	74		20	33
新疆兵团	Xinjiang Corps	10	1	1	21
黑龙江垦区	Heilongjiang Land Reclamation	1	1		

4-2-2 高中教育阶段
Senior High Education

地区	Region	特殊教育普通高中学校(班) Special Education Senior High Schools/classes				学生 Students		
			盲普通高中 Senior High Schools for Blind Students	聋普通高中 Senior High Schools for Deaf Students	其他 Others	招生 Newly Enrolled Students with Disabilities	盲 Students with Visual Disability	聋 Students with Hearing Disability
		个 unit	个 unit	个 unit	个 unit	人 person	人 person	人 person
全国	**Total**	**112**	**12**	**84**	**16**	**2782**	**476**	**2306**
北京	Beijing	2	1	1		65	48	17
天津	Tianjin	2	1	1		37	11	26
河北	Hebei	10		5	5	137	42	95
山西	Shanxi	10	1	9		174	19	155
内蒙古	Inner Mongolia	6	1	4	1	205	58	147
辽宁	Liaoning	5		5		39		39
吉林	Jilin	6		6		42		42
黑龙江	Heilongjiang	1		1		30		30
上海	Shanghai	1	1			7	7	
江苏	Jiangsu	4		3	1	238	29	209
浙江	Zhejiang	5	1	4		142	14	128
安徽	Anhui	2		1	1	130		130
福建	Fujian	3		3		107		107
江西	Jiangxi	2		2		111		111
山东	Shandong	7	1	6		183	43	140
河南	Henan	4	1	3		56	7	49
湖北	Hubei	7	1	5	1	205	36	169
湖南	Hunan	4		4		134		134
广东	Guangdong	6	1	4	1	115	21	94
广西	Guangxi	2		2		17		17
海南	Hainan	1		1		30		30
重庆	Chongqing	3	1	2		70	36	34
四川	Sichuan	4		4		100		100
贵州	Guizhou	5		3	2	262	70	192
云南	Yunnan	1			1	28	5	23
西藏	Tibet							
陕西	Shaanxi	3		2	1	47	13	34
甘肃	Gansu	3		2	1	19	1	18
青海	Qinghai	1	1			15	15	
宁夏	Ningxia	1			1	37	1	36
新疆	Xinjiang	1		1				
新疆兵团	Xinjiang Corps							
黑龙江垦区	Heilongjiang Land Reclamation							

4-2-2　续表 1　Continued 1

地区	Region	学生 Students					
		在校生 Students at Schools	盲 Students with Visual Disability	聋 Students with Hearing Disability	毕业生 Graduates	盲 Students with Visual Disability	聋 Students with Hearing Disability
		人 person	人 person	人 person	人 person	人 person	人 person
全　国	**Total**	**8466**	**1456**	**7010**	**1992**	**337**	**1655**
北　京	Beijing	296	112	184	51	21	30
天　津	Tianjin	115	32	83	36	8	28
河　北	Hebei	518	160	358	190	50	140
山　西	Shanxi	502	35	467	116	15	101
内蒙古	Inner Mongolia	283	57	226	174	58	116
辽　宁	Liaoning	262		262	40		40
吉　林	Jilin	223		223	36		36
黑龙江	Heilongjiang	8		8			
上　海	Shanghai	175	175				
江　苏	Jiangsu	762	92	670	178	19	159
浙　江	Zhejiang	744	262	482	80	19	61
安　徽	Anhui	386	7	379	56		56
福　建	Fujian	139		139	27		27
江　西	Jiangxi	287		287	15		15
山　东	Shandong	461	128	333	232	43	189
河　南	Henan	234	19	215	86	16	70
湖　北	Hubei	697	93	604	77		77
湖　南	Hunan	349		349	79		79
广　东	Guangdong	462	53	409	166	15	151
广　西	Guangxi	44		44	12		12
海　南	Hainan	90		90	60		60
重　庆	Chongqing	131	97	34	59	59	
四　川	Sichuan	100		100	33		33
贵　州	Guizhou	384	70	314	42		42
云　南	Yunnan	272	40	232	35	6	29
西　藏	Tibet						
陕　西	Shaanxi	102	13	89	28		28
甘　肃	Gansu	168	10	158	42		42
青　海	Qinghai						
宁　夏	Ningxia	37	1	36	19	8	11
新　疆	Xinjiang	235		235	23		23
新疆兵团	Xinjiang Corps						
黑龙江垦区	Heilongjiang Land Reclamation						

4-2-2 续表 2 Continued 2

地 区	Region	残疾人中等职业学校(班) Secondary Vocational Schools/classes for PWDs	教育部门办 Established by Education Administrative Departments	残联部门办 Established by Disabled Persons' Federations	其他 Others
		个 unit	个 unit	个 unit	个 unit
全 国	**Total**	**132**	**115**	**11**	**6**
北 京	Beijing	3	3		
天 津	Tianjin				
河 北	Hebei	4	3		1
山 西	Shanxi				
内蒙古	Inner Mongolia	2	1	1	
辽 宁	Liaoning	6	6		
吉 林	Jilin	4	3	1	
黑龙江	Heilongjiang	5	5		
上 海	Shanghai	17	16		1
江 苏	Jiangsu	12	11	1	
浙 江	Zhejiang	13	13		
安 徽	Anhui	3	2	1	
福 建	Fujian	6	6		
江 西	Jiangxi	5	4		1
山 东	Shandong	5	4	1	
河 南	Henan	7	7		
湖 北	Hubei	5	4		1
湖 南	Hunan	7	6	1	
广 东	Guangdong	10	9	1	
广 西	Guangxi	1	1		
海 南	Hainan	1	1		
重 庆	Chongqing	1	1		
四 川	Sichuan	3	3		
贵 州	Guizhou	1		1	
云 南	Yunnan	4	3	1	
西 藏	Tibet				
陕 西	Shaanxi	3	1	1	1
甘 肃	Gansu	2	1		1
青 海	Qinghai				
宁 夏	Ningxia				
新 疆	Xinjiang	2	1	1	
新疆兵团	Xinjiang Corps				
黑龙江垦区	Heilongjiang Land Reclamation				

4-2-2　续表 3　Continued 3

地　区	Region	残疾人中等职业学校(班)学生 Students of Secondary Vocational Schools/classes for PWDs			
		招生 Newly Enrolled Students	盲 Students with Visual Disability	聋 Students with Hearing Disability	肢残 Students with Physical Disability
		人 person	人 person	人 person	人 person
全　国	**Total**	**5611**	**1276**	**1746**	**948**
北　京	Beijing	85		12	
天　津	Tianjin				
河　北	Hebei	224	35	24	22
山　西	Shanxi				
内蒙古	Inner Mongolia	24	19	2	3
辽　宁	Liaoning	100	61	19	
吉　林	Jilin	330	97	113	42
黑龙江	Heilongjiang	78	21	36	
上　海	Shanghai	235	6	22	1
江　苏	Jiangsu	272	79	87	39
浙　江	Zhejiang	227		61	2
安　徽	Anhui	811	249	216	189
福　建	Fujian	59		13	
江　西	Jiangxi	378	9	166	
山　东	Shandong	138	49	26	32
河　南	Henan	158	25	97	
湖　北	Hubei	152	47	34	32
湖　南	Hunan	433	99	189	134
广　东	Guangdong	498	109	132	57
广　西	Guangxi	63	10	53	
海　南	Hainan	40		30	
重　庆	Chongqing	28		28	
四　川	Sichuan	86	11	67	
贵　州	Guizhou	180	60	30	60
云　南	Yunnan	286	56	123	99
西　藏	Tibet				
陕　西	Shaanxi	494	177	83	194
甘　肃	Gansu	64	12	50	
青　海	Qinghai				
宁　夏	Ningxia				
新　疆	Xinjiang	168	45	33	42
新疆兵团	Xinjiang Corps				
黑龙江垦区	Heilongjiang Land Reclamation				

4-2-2 续表 4 Continued 4

地 区	Region	残疾人中等职业学校(班)学生 Students of Secondary Vocational Schools/classes for PWDs			
		在校学生 Students at Schools	盲 Students with Visual Disability	聋 Students with Hearing Disability	肢残 Students with Physical Disability
		人 person	人 person	人 person	人 person
全 国	**Total**	**12968**	**2588**	**4717**	**2178**
北 京	Beijing	241		43	
天 津	Tianjin				
河 北	Hebei	315	37	92	21
山 西	Shanxi				
内蒙古	Inner Mongolia	37	19	5	5
辽 宁	Liaoning	615	188	184	
吉 林	Jilin	758	149	294	134
黑龙江	Heilongjiang	248	53	145	
上 海	Shanghai	516	162	89	1
江 苏	Jiangsu	1164	306	558	130
浙 江	Zhejiang	497		135	2
安 徽	Anhui	934	199	272	296
福 建	Fujian	148		44	
江 西	Jiangxi	517	150	164	
山 东	Shandong	393	41	147	97
河 南	Henan	487	61	356	
湖 北	Hubei	578	113	157	154
湖 南	Hunan	833	220	293	302
广 东	Guangdong	1547	269	407	190
广 西	Guangxi	219	54	165	
海 南	Hainan	120		90	
重 庆	Chongqing	77		77	
四 川	Sichuan	215	53	140	
贵 州	Guizhou	80	25	25	30
云 南	Yunnan	819	119	441	200
西 藏	Tibet				
陕 西	Shaanxi	1104	308	206	415
甘 肃	Gansu	155	34	119	
青 海	Qinghai				
宁 夏	Ningxia				
新 疆	Xinjiang	351	28	69	201
新疆兵团	Xinjiang Corps				
黑龙江垦区	Heilongjiang Land Reclamation				

4-2-2　续表 5　Continued 5

地　区	Region	残疾人中等职业学校(班)学生 Students of Secondary Vocational Schools/classes for PWDs			
		毕业生 Graduates	盲 Students with Visual Disability	聋 Students with Hearing Disability	肢残 Students with Physical Disability
		人 person	人 person	人 person	人 person
全　国	**Total**	**3501**	**790**	**1334**	**639**
北　京	Beijing	66		14	
天　津	Tianjin				
河　北	Hebei	149	30	8	13
山　西	Shanxi				
内蒙古	Inner Mongolia	27	26		1
辽　宁	Liaoning	82	31	38	
吉　林	Jilin	78	25	53	
黑龙江	Heilongjiang	71	13	53	
上　海	Shanghai	98	6	30	
江　苏	Jiangsu	336	83	180	45
浙　江	Zhejiang	152		63	
安　徽	Anhui	255	63	92	60
福　建	Fujian	62		20	
江　西	Jiangxi	97	22	60	
山　东	Shandong	120	38	17	53
河　南	Henan	182	75	106	1
湖　北	Hubei	141	32	16	55
湖　南	Hunan	284	79	89	108
广　东	Guangdong	399	79	102	83
广　西	Guangxi	62	5	57	
海　南	Hainan	40		30	
重　庆	Chongqing	25		25	
四　川	Sichuan	72	12	55	
贵　州	Guizhou				
云　南	Yunnan	229	34	110	85
西　藏	Tibet				
陕　西	Shaanxi	282	91	52	105
甘　肃	Gansu	41		41	
青　海	Qinghai				
宁　夏	Ningxia				
新　疆	Xinjiang	151	46	23	30
新疆兵团	Xinjiang Corps				
黑龙江垦区	Heilongjiang Land Reclamation				

4-2-2 续表 6 Continued 6

地 区	Region	残疾人中等职业学校(班)学生 Students of Secondary Vocational Schools/classes for PWDs			
		毕业生获得职业资格证书 Graduates Who were Issued Professional Qualification Certificates	盲 Students with Visual Disability	聋 Students with Hearing Disability	肢残 Students with Physical Disability
		人 person	人 person	人 person	人 person
全 国	**Total**	**1802**	**506**	**718**	**356**
北 京	Beijing				
天 津	Tianjin				
河 北	Hebei	35	6	2	4
山 西	Shanxi				
内蒙古	Inner Mongolia	18	17		1
辽 宁	Liaoning	35	29	6	
吉 林	Jilin	73	25	48	
黑龙江	Heilongjiang	14		14	
上 海	Shanghai	44	6	15	
江 苏	Jiangsu	294	81	157	45
浙 江	Zhejiang	82		63	
安 徽	Anhui	57	20	15	2
福 建	Fujian	19		19	
江 西	Jiangxi	41		41	
山 东	Shandong	49	14	7	23
河 南	Henan	118	72	45	1
湖 北	Hubei	60	25	3	29
湖 南	Hunan	139	56	6	77
广 东	Guangdong	53		23	10
广 西	Guangxi				
海 南	Hainan	40		30	
重 庆	Chongqing				
四 川	Sichuan	54	5	47	
贵 州	Guizhou				
云 南	Yunnan	215	34	96	85
西 藏	Tibet				
陕 西	Shaanxi	170	70	17	49
甘 肃	Gansu	41		41	
青 海	Qinghai				
宁 夏	Ningxia				
新 疆	Xinjiang	151	46	23	30
新疆兵团	Xinjiang Corps				
黑龙江垦区	Heilongjiang Land Reclamation				

4-2-3 高等教育
Higher Education

地区	Region	高等特殊教育学院 Higher Special Education Institutions						
		机构 Institutions	录取残疾考生 Newly Enrolled Students					
				研究生 Postgraduates	盲 Students with Visual Disability	本科 Under-graduates	盲 Students with Visual Disability	聋 Students with Hearing Disability
		个 unit	人 person	人 person	人 person	人 person	人 person	人 person
全　国	**Total**	**21**	**1845**	**2**	**2**	**787**	**141**	**563**
北　京	Beijing	1	141	2	2	139	36	102
天　津	Tianjin	1	112			112		112
河　北	Hebei							
山　西	Shanxi							
内蒙古	Inner Mongolia							
辽　宁	Liaoning	1	72					
吉　林	Jilin	1	204			204	86	118
黑龙江	Heilongjiang	1	79			79		74
上　海	Shanghai	1	13			13		11
江　苏	Jiangsu	3	183			100	2	88
浙　江	Zhejiang	1	330					
安　徽	Anhui							
福　建	Fujian	1	27					
江　西	Jiangxi							
山　东	Shandong	2	161			17	17	
河　南	Henan	3	332			112		47
湖　北	Hubei							
湖　南	Hunan	1	104					
广　东	Guangdong	2	76					
广　西	Guangxi							
海　南	Hainan							
重　庆	Chongqing	1	11			11		11
四　川	Sichuan							
贵　州	Guizhou							
云　南	Yunnan							
西　藏	Tibet							
陕　西	Shaanxi	1						
甘　肃	Gansu							
青　海	Qinghai							
宁　夏	Ningxia							
新　疆	Xinjiang							
新疆兵团	Xinjiang Corps							
黑龙江垦区	Heilongjiang Land Reclamation							

4-2-3 续表 1 Continued 1

地区	Region	普通高等院校 Ordinary Higher Education Institutions						
		专科(高职) Postsecondary Specialised College Students (Vocational College Students)	盲 Students with Visual Disability	聋 Students with Hearing Disability	残疾考生达到录取分数线 Students who Passed the Admission Line	录取人数 Students Enrolled	研究生 Postgraduates	盲 Students with Visual Disability
		人 person	人 person	人 person	人 person	人 person	人 person	人 person
全 国	**Total**	**1056**	**211**	**631**	**13939**	**10818**	**146**	**15**
北 京	Beijing				90	89		
天 津	Tianjin				46	46		
河 北	Hebei				344	343	3	
山 西	Shanxi				418	375		
内蒙古	Inner Mongolia				455	455	6	
辽 宁	Liaoning	72	11	31	298	298	3	
吉 林	Jilin				284	283	5	1
黑龙江	Heilongjiang				199	199	2	
上 海	Shanghai				70	70		
江 苏	Jiangsu	83	23	60	375	375	14	1
浙 江	Zhejiang	330	40	252	391	384	3	1
安 徽	Anhui				501	496	17	
福 建	Fujian	27		27	208	205	3	1
江 西	Jiangxi				327	327	1	
山 东	Shandong	144	15	99	604	587	36	3
河 南	Henan	220	100	48	626	626	11	2
湖 北	Hubei				369	369	16	2
湖 南	Hunan	104		60	379	369	6	1
广 东	Guangdong	76	22	54	560	550		
广 西	Guangxi				317	315	1	1
海 南	Hainan				722	83		
重 庆	Chongqing				319	317	7	
四 川	Sichuan				1288	682	7	1
贵 州	Guizhou				1479	612		
云 南	Yunnan				1298	917	1	
西 藏	Tibet				40	36		
陕 西	Shaanxi				423	224	2	
甘 肃	Gansu				523	523		
青 海	Qinghai				146	135		
宁 夏	Ningxia				154	151		
新 疆	Xinjiang				325	316	2	1
新疆兵团	Xinjiang Corps				352	52		
黑龙江垦区	Heilongjiang Land Reclamation				9	9		

4-2-3 续表 2 Continued 2

地区	Region	普通高等院校 Ordinary Higher Education Institutions					
		聋 Students with Hearing Disability	肢残 Students with Physical Disability	本科 Undergraduates	盲 Students with Visual Disability	聋 Students with Hearing Disability	肢残 Students with Physical Disability
		人 person	人 person	人 person	人 person	人 person	人 person
全 国	**Total**	**16**	**103**	**5198**	**686**	**836**	**3203**
北 京	Beijing			64	7	18	32
天 津	Tianjin			38	1	16	21
河 北	Hebei		3	197	20	37	126
山 西	Shanxi			155	13	19	119
内蒙古	Inner Mongolia		6	185	28	24	113
辽 宁	Liaoning	1	2	169	9	42	103
吉 林	Jilin	1	2	175	29	46	81
黑龙江	Heilongjiang	1		112	14	23	69
上 海	Shanghai			45	4	22	19
江 苏	Jiangsu	2	10	185	21	47	102
浙 江	Zhejiang		2	187	18	63	95
安 徽	Anhui	4	11	256	21	47	148
福 建	Fujian		2	102	12	16	60
江 西	Jiangxi	1		139	21	15	88
山 东	Shandong	3	30	286	32	63	152
河 南	Henan	1	7	313	32	44	215
湖 北	Hubei		10	177	28	33	101
湖 南	Hunan	1	3	158	15	22	96
广 东	Guangdong			185	19	28	127
广 西	Guangxi			125	22	7	83
海 南	Hainan			41	4	6	26
重 庆	Chongqing		7	174	42	20	93
四 川	Sichuan	1	4	343	57	39	216
贵 州	Guizhou			330	48	13	245
云 南	Yunnan		1	357	50	37	254
西 藏	Tibet			15	5	2	8
陕 西	Shaanxi		2	147	19	26	89
甘 肃	Gansu			204	41	15	116
青 海	Qinghai			64	7	6	44
宁 夏	Ningxia			89	20	12	50
新 疆	Xinjiang		1	155	22	26	95
新疆兵团	Xinjiang Corps			21	4	2	14
黑龙江垦区	Heilongjiang Land Reclamation			5	1		3

4−2−3 续表 3 Continued 3

地 区	Region	普通高等院校 Ordinary Higher Education Institutions 录取残疾考生 Students Enrolled 专科(高职) Postsecondary Specialised College Students (Vocational College Students) 人 person	盲 Students with Visual Disability 人 person	聋 Students with Hearing Disability 人 person	肢残 Students with Physical Disability 人 person
全 国	**Total**	**5474**	**632**	**626**	**3571**
北 京	Beijing	25	1	6	14
天 津	Tianjin	8		3	4
河 北	Hebei	143	18	17	95
山 西	Shanxi	220	16	19	166
内蒙古	Inner Mongolia	264	31	33	166
辽 宁	Liaoning	126	9	15	94
吉 林	Jilin	103	11	17	56
黑龙江	Heilongjiang	85	11	9	57
上 海	Shanghai	25	2	5	15
江 苏	Jiangsu	176	16	27	118
浙 江	Zhejiang	194	20	41	115
安 徽	Anhui	223	11	23	146
福 建	Fujian	100	5	19	64
江 西	Jiangxi	187	24	20	117
山 东	Shandong	265	36	39	151
河 南	Henan	302	35	38	188
湖 北	Hubei	176	21	31	100
湖 南	Hunan	205	22	23	140
广 东	Guangdong	365	40	39	265
广 西	Guangxi	189	23	18	123
海 南	Hainan	42	7	3	22
重 庆	Chongqing	136	14	14	83
四 川	Sichuan	332	41	43	213
贵 州	Guizhou	282	55	17	180
云 南	Yunnan	559	74	33	412
西 藏	Tibet	21	4	1	16
陕 西	Shaanxi	75	8	7	49
甘 肃	Gansu	319	41	30	194
青 海	Qinghai	71	11	8	42
宁 夏	Ningxia	62	5	5	40
新 疆	Xinjiang	159	15	15	111
新疆兵团	Xinjiang Corps	31	5	7	12
黑龙江垦区	Heilongjiang Land Reclamation	4		1	3

三、就业
Employment

4-3-1 残疾人就业状况
Employment of Persons with Disabilities

地 区	Region	就业合计 Employed PWDs	按比例就业 Employed in Quoto Scheme	集中就业 Employed by Collective Form	个体就业 Self-Employed	社区就业 community-aided employment
		人 person	人 person	人 person	人 person	人 person
全 国	**Total**	**9421039**	**727277**	**302205**	**705844**	**79572**
北 京	Beijing	107020	39527	5161	4535	4661
天 津	Tianjin	82427	46914	560	12922	56
河 北	Hebei	618533	16656	7440	18902	2126
山 西	Shanxi	291156	5500	6020	9849	1174
内蒙古	Inner Mongolia	237209	10791	6990	24260	2676
辽 宁	Liaoning	291315	41431	16309	17596	361
吉 林	Jilin	194770	5159	5236	22517	785
黑龙江	Heilongjiang	241326	15347	6937	27547	1905
上 海	Shanghai	88790	40158	19193	832	
江 苏	Jiangsu	464019	25199	8762	2141	1746
浙 江	Zhejiang	331005	86484	46724	48803	1649
安 徽	Anhui	500543	12469	7217	37022	3076
福 建	Fujian	215453	15444	6005	24666	2937
江 西	Jiangxi	352422	12482	21389	47590	8576
山 东	Shandong	577488	66050	21154	31350	7304
河 南	Henan	566373	27220	14406	112828	4088
湖 北	Hubei	421105	33624	23989	27015	4801
湖 南	Hunan	413075	25631	15038	36618	2954
广 东	Guangdong	278333	58746	7321	12911	3958
广 西	Guangxi	322419	9034	1995	14600	1270
海 南	Hainan	34330	4825	406	1186	823
重 庆	Chongqing	248840	15001	11096	20296	3055
四 川	Sichuan	893011	21269	12772	55675	9390
贵 州	Guizhou	335327	7758	5745	18599	2070
云 南	Yunnan	450019	18370	7703	17132	989
西 藏	Tibet	18228	368	294	616	57
陕 西	Shaanxi	262540	12530	4678	13989	2171
甘 肃	Gansu	267339	7638	2083	18317	1909
青 海	Qinghai	44893	1660	2005	2773	245
宁 夏	Ningxia	58342	7041	1805	4912	345
新 疆	Xinjiang	179791	21327	4442	13673	2166
新疆兵团	Xinjiang Corps	23558	11267	109	3041	63
黑龙江垦区	Heilongjiang Land Reclamation	10040	4357	1221	1131	186

4-3-1　续表 1　Continued 1

地　区	Region	公益性岗位就业 Employed through Welfare Post	辅助性就业 Assistive Employment	居家就业 telecommuting	从事农业种养加 Engaged in Agricultural Planting, Husbandry and Processing	灵活就业 Flexible Employment
		人 person	人 person	人 person	人 person	人 person
全　国	**Total**	**89694**	**143927**	**1189185**	**4725594**	**1457741**
北　京	Beijing	2728	1468	3159	17069	28712
天　津	Tianjin	1300	1	10	20646	18
河　北	Hebei	1434	3403	70897	437864	59811
山　西	Shanxi	1069	1009	15229	230667	20639
内蒙古	Inner Mongolia	1621	1186	19388	127616	42681
辽　宁	Liaoning	7204	8428	2984	156924	40078
吉　林	Jilin	2545	1134	11185	116766	29443
黑龙江	Heilongjiang	6447	2389	20515	108270	51969
上　海	Shanghai	3326	6417		6310	12554
江　苏	Jiangsu	1225	3645	6620	44599	370082
浙　江	Zhejiang	5314	7097	9166	59770	65998
安　徽	Anhui	2698	10762	91889	279050	56360
福　建	Fujian	2428	4276	26304	98570	34823
江　西	Jiangxi	6949	7977	60021	117605	69833
山　东	Shandong	2893	4610	42192	351250	50685
河　南	Henan	3868	17212	37869	334292	14590
湖　北	Hubei	3912	7889	61417	194204	64254
湖　南	Hunan	2332	5797	72766	196494	55445
广　东	Guangdong	4981	4606	35193	129367	21250
广　西	Guangxi	2018	2487	39700	226523	24792
海　南	Hainan	419	206	3355	20643	2467
重　庆	Chongqing	2081	3147	28525	125286	40353
四　川	Sichuan	7295	17351	326658	346408	96193
贵　州	Guizhou	1398	3055	48944	202785	44973
云　南	Yunnan	973	5064	44788	306197	48803
西　藏	Tibet	111	62	7657	6731	2332
陕　西	Shaanxi	3837	5669	37503	150294	31869
甘　肃	Gansu	2677	4145	35012	167573	27985
青　海	Qinghai	848	573	4667	23426	8696
宁　夏	Ningxia	607	1223	12238	23169	7002
新　疆	Xinjiang	2678	1297	12606	93902	27700
新疆兵团	Xinjiang Corps	337	324	77	3192	3339
黑龙江垦区	Heilongjiang Land Reclamation	141	18	651	2132	2012

四、社会保障
Social Security

4-4-1　残疾人参加社会保险情况
Persons with Disabilities Covered by Social Insurance

地　区	Region	残疾居民参加城乡社会养老保险 Residents with Disabilities Covered by Pension Insurance	享受养老保金 PWDs Covered by the Insurance Pension	重度残疾人 Persons with Severe Disability
		万人 10,000 persons	万人 10,000 persons	万人 10,000 persons
全　国	**Total**	**2614.7**	**1042.3**	**331.1**
北　京	Beijing	9.6	1.9	0.6
天　津	Tianjin	7.6	5.0	2.0
河　北	Hebei	146.3	45.3	14.1
山　西	Shanxi	105.5	49.8	8.4
内蒙古	Inner Mongolia	41.2	18.6	6.5
辽　宁	Liaoning	39.9	18.3	6.5
吉　林	Jilin	30.5	9.3	2.8
黑龙江	Heilongjiang	37.3	17.2	3.3
上　海	Shanghai	6.6	1.8	0.4
江　苏	Jiangsu	140.4	62.3	15.7
浙　江	Zhejiang	63.4	28.1	10.1
安　徽	Anhui	131.0	48.7	22.5
福　建	Fujian	68.7	34.7	12.3
江　西	Jiangxi	84.5	32.0	9.4
山　东	Shandong	153.9	60.8	24.7
河　南	Henan	330.9	137.5	29.1
湖　北	Hubei	126.3	49.3	15.2
湖　南	Hunan	172.8	66.7	25.7
广　东	Guangdong	96.5	38.3	19.4
广　西	Guangxi	112.3	59.2	16.8
海　南	Hainan	16.0	5.7	2.3
重　庆	Chongqing	52.7	20.1	7.8
四　川	Sichuan	222.9	72.9	29.0
贵　州	Guizhou	76.6	38.2	8.6
云　南	Yunnan	86.3	31.0	10.9
西　藏	Tibet	2.0	0.9	0.4
陕　西	Shaanxi	77.3	27.0	6.8
甘　肃	Gansu	103.9	34.3	8.8
青　海	Qinghai	12.5	4.9	2.4
宁　夏	Ningxia	21.1	10.2	5.0
新　疆	Xinjiang	35.8	11.7	3.2
新疆兵团	Xinjiang Corps	2.4	0.3	0.2
黑龙江垦区	Heilongjiang Land Reclamation			

4-4-1 续表 Continued

地区	Region	残疾居民参加城乡社会养老保险 Residents with Disabilities Covered by Pension Insurance				
		60周岁以下参保残疾人 PWDs under Age 60	重度残疾人 Persons with Severe Disability	全部或部分代缴 Paid by Subsidy Totally or Partially	其他残疾人 Other PWDs	全部或部分代缴 Paid by Subsidy Totally or Partially
		万人 10,000 persons	万人 10,000 persons	万人 10,000 persons	万人 10,000 persons	万人 10,000 persons
全国	**Total**	**1572.5**	**547.2**	**529.5**	**1025.3**	**282.9**
北京	Beijing	7.7	4.4	4.4	3.3	2.8
天津	Tianjin	2.6	2.0	2.0	0.5	0.5
河北	Hebei	101.0	26.9	26.6	74.1	25.0
山西	Shanxi	55.7	16.6	16.0	39.1	6.7
内蒙古	Inner Mongolia	22.6	9.4	8.3	13.1	4.9
辽宁	Liaoning	21.6	7.6	7.1	14.0	2.4
吉林	Jilin	21.2	9.1	8.6	12.1	6.4
黑龙江	Heilongjiang	20.1	5.6	5.3	14.5	3.5
上海	Shanghai	4.8	3.8	3.8	1.0	0.5
江苏	Jiangsu	78.1	24.2	23.7	53.9	19.7
浙江	Zhejiang	35.4	13.6	13.2	21.7	15.6
安徽	Anhui	82.3	34.9	34.6	47.4	5.5
福建	Fujian	34.0	16.1	16.0	17.9	16.2
江西	Jiangxi	52.5	17.3	17.0	35.2	11.7
山东	Shandong	93.2	37.0	35.5	56.1	11.1
河南	Henan	193.3	65.3	62.5	128.1	3.8
湖北	Hubei	77.0	29.3	27.8	47.7	19.4
湖南	Hunan	106.1	33.1	32.8	73.1	9.4
广东	Guangdong	58.2	31.6	30.3	26.5	7.9
广西	Guangxi	53.1	17.6	16.6	35.4	9.6
海南	Hainan	10.3	5.0	5.0	5.3	0.6
重庆	Chongqing	32.6	12.8	12.7	19.8	3.3
四川	Sichuan	150.0	41.7	40.4	108.3	26.3
贵州	Guizhou	38.3	9.9	8.8	28.4	6.1
云南	Yunnan	55.3	18.1	17.4	37.1	19.0
西藏	Tibet	1.1	0.3	0.3	0.8	0.6
陕西	Shaanxi	50.3	13.4	13.4	36.9	18.2
甘肃	Gansu	69.6	23.5	23.0	46.1	8.1
青海	Qinghai	7.6	3.9	3.9	3.6	3.0
宁夏	Ningxia	10.9	5.0	5.0	5.9	3.3
新疆	Xinjiang	24.1	7.1	6.7	17.0	11.3
新疆兵团	Xinjiang Corps	2.1	0.9	0.9	1.3	0.3
黑龙江垦区	Heilongjiang Land Reclamation					

4-4-2　托养服务
Fostering Service

地　区	Region	托养服务机构合计 Fostering Institutions	寄宿制托养服务 Boarding Fostering Services	日间照料托养服务机构 Day-Care Fostering Service	综合托养服务机构 Combined Fostering Services Facilities	托养残疾人 PWDs in the Institutions	寄宿制机构中托养残疾人 PWDs Fostered in the Form of Boarding
		个 unit	个 unit	个 unit	个 unit	人 person	人 person
全　国	**Total**	**7923**	**2560**	**3076**	**2287**	**1010975**	**69762**
北　京	Beijing	108	87		21	128939	756
天　津	Tianjin	73	19	53	1	40764	458
河　北	Hebei	233	111	37	85	19411	3881
山　西	Shanxi	92	30	25	37	4057	710
内蒙古	Inner Mongolia	136	85	4	47	12048	2535
辽　宁	Liaoning	219	115	58	46	27403	5392
吉　林	Jilin	69	53	6	10	6801	1586
黑龙江	Heilongjiang	98	60	2	36	8554	1775
上　海	Shanghai	819	387	407	25	34686	5723
江　苏	Jiangsu	1425	112	536	777	49752	3120
浙　江	Zhejiang	1112	461	378	273	315337	8639
安　徽	Anhui	243	154	18	71	16401	2493
福　建	Fujian	119	44	46	29	20456	1096
江　西	Jiangxi	41	13	19	9	7528	1085
山　东	Shandong	519	234	87	198	26203	6634
河　南	Henan	195	88	22	85	20325	3504
湖　北	Hubei	236	78	102	56	16038	1896
湖　南	Hunan	147	36	67	44	21755	1143
广　东	Guangdong	1017	39	875	103	41132	1380
广　西	Guangxi	55	23	26	6	28792	1610
海　南	Hainan	14	11		3	21642	877
重　庆	Chongqing	80	24	37	19	30153	761
四　川	Sichuan	167	50	76	41	31732	1924
贵　州	Guizhou	26	8	3	15	8446	797
云　南	Yunnan	74	33	8	33	15633	965
西　藏	Tibet	1	1			721	13
陕　西	Shaanxi	143	80	13	50	16138	4455
甘　肃	Gansu	85	28	19	38	15201	1071
青　海	Qinghai	46	15	10	21	2609	273
宁　夏	Ningxia	69	15	46	8	5875	551
新　疆	Xinjiang	191	36	86	69	8716	1183
新疆兵团	Xinjiang Corps	60	22	9	29	7133	1072
黑龙江垦区	Heilongjiang Land Reclamation	11	8	1	2	594	404

4-4-2 续表 1 Continued 1

地 区	Region	托养残疾人 PWDs in the Institutions							
		智力残疾人 Persons with Intellectual Disability	精神残疾人 Persons with Psychosocial Disability	重度肢体残疾人 Persons with Severe Physical Disability	日间照料机构中托养残疾人 PWDs Fostered in the Form of Day Care	智力残疾人 Persons with Intellectual Disability	精神残疾人 Persons with Psychosocial Disability	重度肢体残疾人 Persons with Severe Physical Disability	综合托养服务机构中托养残疾人 PWDs in Combined Fostering Services Facilities
		人 person	人 person	人 person	人 person	人 person	人 person	人 person	人 person
全 国	**Total**	**16404**	**25721**	**14063**	**77645**	**32689**	**20730**	**12241**	**83807**
北 京	Beijing	332	63	138					687
天 津	Tianjin	213	34	172	746	539	117	50	36
河 北	Hebei	796	1853	590	2754	769	692	512	4213
山 西	Shanxi	217	260	138	1024	317	150	369	878
内蒙古	Inner Mongolia	360	156	621	228	206	1	7	1218
辽 宁	Liaoning	1479	1885	918	1180	940	126	92	2090
吉 林	Jilin	217	1022	302	149	39	38	71	543
黑龙江	Heilongjiang	421	626	370	14	14			1931
上 海	Shanghai	2395	2024	1107	10865	6769	3843	16	581
江 苏	Jiangsu	1158	258	876	9124	3355	1709	1725	17020
浙 江	Zhejiang	2066	2750	2562	8373	4216	2703	646	12317
安 徽	Anhui	358	1385	437	675	164	183	248	3065
福 建	Fujian	113	273	306	1057	567	140	45	1349
江 西	Jiangxi	289	88	102	853	441	193	149	525
山 东	Shandong	1710	2255	1506	3779	1218	523	494	6730
河 南	Henan	561	1870	572	754	170	237	342	5116
湖 北	Hubei	583	733	217	2846	1313	585	600	3662
湖 南	Hunan	353	300	249	2428	963	766	567	2159
广 东	Guangdong	424	551	149	22000	7828	6407	4016	3479
广 西	Guangxi	60	1488	45	1482	615	430	297	268
海 南	Hainan	38	823	2					466
重 庆	Chongqing	63	516	51	473	114	109	210	817
四 川	Sichuan	206	1323	244	1769	842	283	305	2411
贵 州	Guizhou	69	523	34	75	22	31	11	1176
云 南	Yunnan	124	551	36	742	126	149	369	473
西 藏	Tibet	3							
陕 西	Shaanxi	976	806	1255	332	96	78	72	3584
甘 肃	Gansu	179	189	291	367	73	98	93	2384
青 海	Qinghai	39	12	93	267	47	30	52	874
宁 夏	Ningxia	144	152	107	1485	245	693	388	366
新 疆	Xinjiang	295	167	395	1503	557	272	469	2140
新疆兵团	Xinjiang Corps	121	508	127	291	124	144	16	1190
黑龙江垦区	Heilongjiang Land Reclamation	42	277	51	10			10	59

4-4-2　续表 2　Continued 2

地　区	Region	托养残疾人　PWDs in the Institutions								
		以寄宿制方式托养的残疾人 PWDs Fostered in the Form of Boarding	智力残疾人 Persons with Intellectual Disability	精神残疾人 Persons with Psychosocial Disability	重度肢体残疾人 Persons with Severe Physical Disability	以日间照料方式托养的残疾人 PWDs Fostered in the Form of Day Care	智力残疾人 Persons with Intellectual Disability	精神残疾人 Persons with Psychosocial Disability	重度肢体残疾人 Persons with Severe Physical Disability	享受居家托养服务残疾人 PWDs Recieving Fostering Service at Home
		人 person	人 person	人 person	人 person	人 person	人 person	人 person	人 person	人 person
全　国	**Total**	**37537**	**9668**	**9543**	**8994**	**46270**	**13454**	**11166**	**12041**	**779761**
北　京	Beijing	570	184	263	79	117	62	23	20	127496
天　津	Tianjin	29	12	4	13	7	6	1		39524
河　北	Hebei	1683	319	431	345	2530	433	452	940	8563
山　西	Shanxi	233	59	91	39	645	151	189	187	1445
内蒙古	Inner Mongolia	612	118	55	195	606	88	96	147	8067
辽　宁	Liaoning	1535	353	620	348	555	206	168	106	18741
吉　林	Jilin	322	158	5	82	221	54	71	89	4523
黑龙江	Heilongjiang	1113	141	572	359	818	583	72	124	4834
上　海	Shanghai	287	127	160		294	133	160		17517
江　苏	Jiangsu	6955	2797	1036	1787	10065	3440	1576	2384	20488
浙　江	Zhejiang	4508	991	1203	1340	7809	2485	2230	2229	286008
安　徽	Anhui	1806	337	240	474	1259	258	270	278	10168
福　建	Fujian	915	222	91	39	434	230	164	30	16954
江　西	Jiangxi	174	34	88	38	351	135	97	107	5065
山　东	Shandong	3655	895	682	1067	3075	733	488	865	9060
河　南	Henan	2536	427	709	684	2580	437	639	996	10951
湖　北	Hubei	1382	255	406	206	2280	603	672	497	7634
湖　南	Hunan	974	242	393	158	1185	413	403	221	16025
广　东	Guangdong	1293	529	266	211	2186	646	657	430	14273
广　西	Guangxi	218	11	118	75	50	18	10	22	25432
海　南	Hainan	217	12	203		249	12	235		20299
重　庆	Chongqing	347	63	130	3	470	146	302	20	28102
四　川	Sichuan	1099	276	333	317	1312	427	388	328	25628
贵　州	Guizhou	542	53	380	12	634	131	360	40	6398
云　南	Yunnan	289	35	139	36	184	14	73	89	13453
西　藏	Tibet									708
陕　西	Shaanxi	1570	332	285	419	2014	441	418	666	7767
甘　肃	Gansu	1081	328	255	132	1303	308	260	176	11379
青　海	Qinghai	271	63	24	105	603	124	76	275	1195
宁　夏	Ningxia	133	46	5	36	233	64	30	81	3473
新　疆	Xinjiang	646	131	175	236	1494	425	352	545	3890
新疆兵团	Xinjiang Corps	489	99	161	148	701	248	234	143	4580
黑龙江垦区	Heilongjiang Land Reclamation	53	19	20	11	6			6	121

五、扶贫
Poverty Alleviation

4-5-1 农村贫困残疾人扶持效果
Poverty Alleviation for Persons with Disabilities in Rural Areas

地 区	Region	本年度退出建档立卡贫困残疾户 Families of Poor Persons with Disabilities No Longer Subject to Archive Filing and Card Issuing in 2017	本年度退出建档立卡贫困残疾人 Poor Persons with Disabilities No Longer Subject to Archive Filing and Card Issuing in 2017	本年返贫 Reimpoverished PWDs in 2017	残疾人实用技术培训 Training on Applied Technologies for PWDs		
					本年度培训残疾人 Training on Applied Technologies for PWDs in 2017	扫盲教育 Anti-Illiteracy Education	本年度培训投入经费 Fund for Training on Applied Technologies for PWDs in 2017
		万户 10,000 households	万人 10,000 persons	万人 10,000 persons	万人次 10,000 person-times	人 person	万元 10,000 yuan
全 国	**Total**	**66.37**	**92.54**	**3.40**	**70.63**	**42782**	**22570.81**
北 京	Beijing				0.71	138	19.57
天 津	Tianjin						
河 北	Hebei	2.61	3.59	0.24	4.25	948	1462.74
山 西	Shanxi	1.50	2.35	0.04	1.06	506	396.55
内蒙古	Inner Mongolia	0.69	0.82	0.08	2.30	870	613.16
辽 宁	Liaoning	2.44	3.37	0.02	1.16	336	502.97
吉 林	Jilin	1.58	1.93	0.25	1.06	2208	371.00
黑龙江	Heilongjiang	2.35	2.81	0.00	1.08	708	439.88
上 海	Shanghai				0.19	213	73.81
江 苏	Jiangsu				1.02	2576	299.40
浙 江	Zhejiang				1.40	2539	451.75
安 徽	Anhui	5.13	6.86	0.14	2.47	1161	882.24
福 建	Fujian	1.85	2.18	0.02	0.87	1175	796.90
江 西	Jiangxi	3.44	5.17	0.03	1.08	839	618.79
山 东	Shandong	4.56	7.04	0.08	2.62	1541	873.29
河 南	Henan	3.75	5.35	0.08	5.02	1373	1403.51
湖 北	Hubei	5.60	9.39	0.03	2.39	1021	652.65
湖 南	Hunan	5.67	7.61	0.31	2.09	1353	2171.19
广 东	Guangdong	1.64	1.83		1.57	2345	391.57
广 西	Guangxi	4.64	8.11	0.54	2.99	1186	1758.01
海 南	Hainan	0.43	0.55	0.00	0.62	1024	271.24
重 庆	Chongqing	1.25	1.39	0.06	1.98	2134	724.80
四 川	Sichuan	4.29	5.22	0.10	15.41	3951	3194.74
贵 州	Guizhou	3.36	4.21	0.23	1.16	1419	292.80
云 南	Yunnan	3.47	4.34	0.52	3.52	3560	1037.53
西 藏	Tibet	0.06	0.08		0.14	425	186.88
陕 西	Shaanxi	2.54	3.71	0.28	4.13	966	789.64
甘 肃	Gansu	1.75	2.23	0.22	3.28		698.15
青 海	Qinghai	0.35	0.53	0.02	0.72	890	106.06
宁 夏	Ningxia	0.62	0.81	0.03	0.69	1822	132.27
新 疆	Xinjiang	0.63	0.81	0.07	2.17	2436	477.12
新疆兵团	Xinjiang Corps	0.18	0.25	0.01	1.34	1105	406.37
黑龙江垦区	Heilongjiang Land Reclamation				0.14	14	74.23

4-5-2 扶贫资金与残疾人扶贫贷款
Poverty Alleviation Fund and Loans

地 区	Region	扶贫资金 Poverty Alleviation Fund		残疾人扶贫贷款 Poverty Alleviation Fund and Loans		
				康复扶贫贴息贷款 Interest-subsidized Loans for Rehabilitation		
		省级财政投入 Poverty Alleviation Fund from the Provincial Budget	社会募集 Fund Raised From Society	本年度贷款实际落实 Actually Allocated Loans in 2017	本年度贷款财政贴息资金数额 Amount of interest subsidy by government finance for loans in 2017	本年度项目贷款扶持贫困残疾人 Poor PWDs Supported by Loans for Project in 2017
		万元 10,000 yuan	万元 10,000 yuan	万元 10,000 yuan	万元 10,000 yuan	人 person
全 国	**Total**	**42294.1**	**1178.8**	**40921.3**	**1545.9**	**12155**
北 京	Beijing	1714.6				
天 津	Tianjin	220.0				
河 北	Hebei	1888.7	6.6	829.9	57.8	3
山 西	Shanxi	334.2		2.0	0.2	
内蒙古	Inner Mongolia	3.5	1.0	4499.9	298.0	8382
辽 宁	Liaoning	1049.8	6.5			
吉 林	Jilin			75.5	4.6	
黑龙江	Heilongjiang	479.4	37.6			
上 海	Shanghai					
江 苏	Jiangsu	1570.6	57.1	3201.5	125.7	13
浙 江	Zhejiang	8529.6	133.0	9910.7		873
安 徽	Anhui	5472.0		1595.0	93.5	234
福 建	Fujian	190.0	12.0	124.4	3.8	103
江 西	Jiangxi	1543.0	410.0	131.2	9.4	30
山 东	Shandong	1088.0				
河 南	Henan	1310.0				
湖 北	Hubei	893.0	32.5	312.5	18.5	513
湖 南	Hunan	93.4	153.6			
广 东	Guangdong	434.4		1998.8	110.0	337
广 西	Guangxi	4534.1				
海 南	Hainan	230.7				
重 庆	Chongqing	2875.0	21.0	1573.0	92.0	303
四 川	Sichuan	3673.8	56.5			
贵 州	Guizhou		7.2	4340.4	235.3	454
云 南	Yunnan	338.1	60.0	159.0	5.8	
西 藏	Tibet					
陕 西	Shaanxi	3150.0				
甘 肃	Gansu	272.8	184.3			
青 海	Qinghai					
宁 夏	Ningxia	391.0		2502.5	151.4	602
新 疆	Xinjiang			328.1	32.2	152
新疆兵团	Xinjiang Corps	14.5		9336.9	307.6	156
黑龙江垦区	Heilongjiang Land Reclamation					

4-5-3 社会帮扶与残疾人扶贫基地建设
Social Assistance and Construction of Poverty Alleviation Bases

地 区	Region	社会帮扶 Social Assistance for Needy PWDs	残疾人扶贫基地建设 Poverty Alleviation bases for PWDs		
		结对帮扶受益残疾人 Individuals who Assisted PWDs in One-to-one way	残疾人扶贫基地 Poverty Alleviation Bases for PWDs	安置残疾人就业 Providing Employment for Disabled Persons	扶持带动贫困残疾人 Supporting and Leading Disabled Persons
		人 person	个 unit	人 person	户 household
全 国	**Total**	**467658**	**6692**	**104620**	**218187**
北 京	Beijing		27	1012	1090
天 津	Tianjin	360	148	1163	3750
河 北	Hebei	4666	248	4481	12343
山 西	Shanxi	6543	118	2019	2451
内蒙古	Inner Mongolia	6447	153	1934	2792
辽 宁	Liaoning	6262	35	957	3412
吉 林	Jilin	4882	246	2572	6598
黑龙江	Heilongjiang	6810	105	2828	4814
上 海	Shanghai	156	198	4761	3839
江 苏	Jiangsu	21351	324	8305	11594
浙 江	Zhejiang	25693	1042	7614	18497
安 徽	Anhui	55374	166	2059	3062
福 建	Fujian	12422	136	2307	3161
江 西	Jiangxi	16967	391	2700	3275
山 东	Shandong	9802	566	9871	15211
河 南	Henan	27583	289	9099	16544
湖 北	Hubei	38895	80	2888	6376
湖 南	Hunan	14945	325	6237	11192
广 东	Guangdong	3096	103	3291	5682
广 西	Guangxi	24297	132	3347	15755
海 南	Hainan		41	220	300
重 庆	Chongqing	12468	115	1145	1513
四 川	Sichuan	43330	385	6564	11873
贵 州	Guizhou	19325	200	1840	3583
云 南	Yunnan	18386	385	3263	25410
西 藏	Tibet	894			
陕 西	Shaanxi	13730	168	3067	7115
甘 肃	Gansu	53897	167	2419	5563
青 海	Qinghai	6108	64	892	1311
宁 夏	Ningxia	4669	55	1106	2704
新 疆	Xinjiang	2989	218	3564	5747
新疆兵团	Xinjiang Corps	5264	58	1078	1626
黑龙江垦区	Heilongjiang Land Reclamation	47	4	17	4

4-5-4 农村贫困残疾人危房改造
House Renovation for Poor Persons with Disabilities in Rural Areas

地 区	Region	本年度危房改造实际完成 Houses Renovated for PWDs in 2017	本年度危房改造项目受益贫困残疾人 Poor PWDs who Benefited by House Renovation Project in 2017	本年度投入资金 Fund Input in Houses Renovation in 2017	省级投入资金 Fund from the Provincial Budgets	地市级投入资金 Fund from the Prefectural/ City Level Budgets	县级投入资金 Fund from the County Level Budgets
		户 household	人 person	万元 10,000 yuan	万元 10,000 yuan	万元 10,000 yuan	万元 10,000 yuan
全 国	**Total**	**82213**	**96494**	**100812.2**	**63026.9**	**7740.7**	**30044.6**
北 京	Beijing	381	406	415.2	19.2		396.0
天 津	Tianjin	249	249	498.0	240.4		257.6
河 北	Hebei	3536	3611	4927.6	3744.9	406.1	776.6
山 西	Shanxi	405	435				
内蒙古	Inner Mongolia	392	409	368.1	261.5		106.6
辽 宁	Liaoning	3122	3189	3543.1	1010.0	752.2	1781.0
吉 林	Jilin	337	376	129.3	118.3	2.0	9.0
黑龙江	Heilongjiang	8759	11294	9599.7	9095.5	149.4	354.9
上 海	Shanghai	180	194	216.0	22.5	41.3	152.2
江 苏	Jiangsu	847	992	905.8	573.6	6.8	325.4
浙 江	Zhejiang	2346	2726	2275.9	229.9	246.8	1799.3
安 徽	Anhui	11245	12440	12825.7	9021.2	122.0	3682.4
福 建	Fujian	2518	2966	3554.4	1759.8	548.0	1246.6
江 西	Jiangxi	2583	2794	2790.9	2361.0	33.7	396.2
山 东	Shandong	645	646	579.0		366.4	212.6
河 南	Henan	2526	4465	1790.1	967.0	204.6	618.5
湖 北	Hubei	497	605	469.3	344.6		124.7
湖 南	Hunan	13695	16276	13027.5	5500.4	1769.6	5757.5
广 东	Guangdong	3656	3956	7518.5	4866.8	1278.5	1373.2
广 西	Guangxi	2207	3400	2431.4	1004.3	288.2	1138.8
海 南	Hainan	297	297	901.0	161.5		739.5
重 庆	Chongqing	3550	3849	5882.2	2025.0		3857.2
四 川	Sichuan	2985	3480	3034.2	1009.2	124.0	1900.9
贵 州	Guizhou	353	412	232.0	90.0	13.0	129.0
云 南	Yunnan	3317	4112	2242.2	17.5	1028.0	1196.7
西 藏	Tibet						
陕 西	Shaanxi	418	429	232.9		182.9	50.0
甘 肃	Gansu	9115	9619	16407.0	15508.9	10.8	887.3
青 海	Qinghai	557	1354	1759.9	1580.0	9.3	170.6
宁 夏	Ningxia	178	189	489.0	341.0		148.0
新 疆	Xinjiang	1182	1184	1221.8	622.1	157.3	442.5
新疆兵团	Xinjiang Corps	127	132	542.9	529.0		13.9
黑龙江垦区	Heilongjiang Land Reclamation	8	8	1.8	1.8		

六、专门协会
Special Associations

4-6-1 省(自治区、直辖市)专门协会建立情况
Establishment of Special Associations at Provincial Level

地 区	Region	盲人协会 Associations of Persons with Visual Disability Established	聋人协会 Associations of Persons with Hearing Disability Established	肢残人协会 Associations of Persons with Physical Disability Established	智力残疾人及亲友协会 Associations of Persons with Intellectual Disability and Their Relatives and Friends Established	精神残疾人及亲友协会 Associations of Persons with Psychosocial Disability and Their Relatives and Friends Established
		个 unit	个 unit	个 unit	个 unit	个 unit
全 国	**Total**	**33**	**33**	**33**	**32**	**32**
北 京	Beijing	1	1	1	1	1
天 津	Tianjin	1	1	1	1	1
河 北	Hebei	1	1	1	1	1
山 西	Shanxi	1	1	1	1	1
内蒙古	Inner Mongolia	1	1	1	1	1
辽 宁	Liaoning	1	1	1	1	1
吉 林	Jilin	1	1	1	1	1
黑龙江	Heilongjiang	1	1	1	1	1
上 海	Shanghai	1	1	1	1	1
江 苏	Jiangsu	1	1	1	1	1
浙 江	Zhejiang	1	1	1	1	1
安 徽	Anhui	1	1	1	1	1
福 建	Fujian	1	1	1	1	1
江 西	Jiangxi	1	1	1	1	1
山 东	Shandong	1	1	1	1	1
河 南	Henan	1	1	1	1	1
湖 北	Hubei	1	1	1	1	1
湖 南	Hunan	1	1	1	1	1
广 东	Guangdong	1	1	1	1	1
广 西	Guangxi	1	1	1	1	1
海 南	Hainan	1	1	1	1	1
重 庆	Chongqing	1	1	1	1	1
四 川	Sichuan	1	1	1	1	1
贵 州	Guizhou	1	1	1	1	1
云 南	Yunnan	1	1	1	1	1
西 藏	Tibet	1	1	1		
陕 西	Shaanxi	1	1	1	1	1
甘 肃	Gansu	1	1	1	1	1
青 海	Qinghai	1	1	1	1	1
宁 夏	Ningxia	1	1	1	1	1
新 疆	Xinjiang	1	1	1	1	1
新疆兵团	Xinjiang Corps	1	1	1	1	1
黑龙江垦区	Heilongjiang Land Reclamation	1	1	1	1	1

4-6-2 市(地、州、盟)专门协会建立情况
Establishment of Special Associations at Prefectural / City Level

地 区	Region	盲人协会 Associations of Persons with Visual Disability Established	聋人协会 Associations of Persons with Hearing Disability Established	肢残人协会 Associations of Persons with Physical Disability Established	智力残疾人及亲友协会 Associations of Persons with Intellectual Disability and Their Relatives and Friends Established	精神残疾人及亲友协会 Associations of Persons with Psychosocial Disability and Their Relatives and Friends Established	智力残疾人及亲友协会和精神残疾人及亲友协会合一的协会 Associations of Persons with Intellectual Disability and Psychosocial Disability and Their Relatives and Friends Established
		个 unit	个 unit	个 unit	个 unit	个 unit	个 unit
全 国	**Total**	**344**	**344**	**345**	**338**	**336**	**6**
北 京	Beijing						
天 津	Tianjin						
河 北	Hebei	11	11	11	11	11	
山 西	Shanxi	11	11	11	11	11	
内蒙古	Inner Mongolia	12	12	12	12	12	
辽 宁	Liaoning	14	14	14	14	14	
吉 林	Jilin	10	10	10	10	10	
黑龙江	Heilongjiang	13	13	13	13	13	
上 海	Shanghai						
江 苏	Jiangsu	13	13	13	13	13	
浙 江	Zhejiang	11	11	11	11	11	
安 徽	Anhui	15	15	15	15	15	
福 建	Fujian	9	9	9	9	9	
江 西	Jiangxi	11	11	11	11	11	
山 东	Shandong	17	17	17	15	15	1
河 南	Henan	18	18	18	18	18	
湖 北	Hubei	13	13	13	13	13	
湖 南	Hunan	14	14	14	14	14	
广 东	Guangdong	21	21	21	21	21	
广 西	Guangxi	14	14	14	14	14	
海 南	Hainan	3	3	3	3	3	
重 庆	Chongqing						
四 川	Sichuan	21	21	21	21	21	
贵 州	Guizhou	6	6	6	7	6	
云 南	Yunnan	16	16	16	16	15	
西 藏	Tibet						
陕 西	Shaanxi	10	10	10	10	10	
甘 肃	Gansu	15	15	15	15	15	
青 海	Qinghai	8	8	8	8	8	
宁 夏	Ningxia	5	5	5	5	5	
新 疆	Xinjiang	14	14	13	12	12	2
新疆兵团	Xinjiang Corps	10	10	12	7	7	3
黑龙江垦区	Heilongjiang Land Reclamation	9	9	9	9	9	

4-6-3 县(县级市、市辖区)专门协会建立情况
Establishment of Special Associations at County Level

地 区	Region	盲人协会 Associations of Persons with Visual Disability Established	聋人协会 Associations of Persons with Hearing Disability Established	肢残人协会 Associations of Persons with Physical Disability Established	智力残疾人及亲友协会 Associations of Persons with Intellectual Disability and Their Relatives and Friends Established	精神残疾人及亲友协会 Associations of Persons with Psychosocial Disability and Their Relatives and Friends Established	智力残疾人及亲友协会和精神残疾人及亲友协会合一的协会 Associations of Persons with Intellectual Disability and Psychosocial Disability and Their Relatives and Friends Established
		个 unit	个 unit	个 unit	个 unit	个 unit	个 unit
全 国	**Total**	**2801**	**2786**	**2810**	**2665**	**2667**	**111**
北 京	Beijing	16	16	16	16	16	
天 津	Tianjin	16	16	16	16	16	
河 北	Hebei	168	168	168	164	164	4
山 西	Shanxi	116	116	116	109	111	6
内蒙古	Inner Mongolia	103	103	103	87	87	16
辽 宁	Liaoning	102	102	102	102	102	
吉 林	Jilin	63	63	63	62	62	
黑龙江	Heilongjiang	132	132	132	132	132	
上 海	Shanghai	17	17	17	17	17	
江 苏	Jiangsu	98	98	98	88	88	10
浙 江	Zhejiang	89	87	90	73	73	14
安 徽	Anhui	95	96	99	89	88	6
福 建	Fujian	83	81	83	73	73	10
江 西	Jiangxi	81	81	81	80	80	
山 东	Shandong	132	127	130	123	124	2
河 南	Henan	159	158	159	158	158	
湖 北	Hubei	94	91	94	80	81	10
湖 南	Hunan	122	121	124	114	115	3
广 东	Guangdong	119	119	119	112	113	6
广 西	Guangxi	111	111	111	111	111	
海 南	Hainan	18	18	18	17	17	1
重 庆	Chongqing	39	39	39	38	38	1
四 川	Sichuan	175	173	176	170	170	4
贵 州	Guizhou	74	74	75	72	71	2
云 南	Yunnan	126	126	126	119	119	7
西 藏	Tibet						
陕 西	Shaanxi	108	107	108	106	108	
甘 肃	Gansu	86	86	86	86	86	
青 海	Qinghai	46	46	46	46	46	
宁 夏	Ningxia	20	20	20	18	18	2
新 疆	Xinjiang	90	91	92	84	80	7
新疆兵团	Xinjiang Corps						
黑龙江垦区	Heilongjiang Land Reclamation	103	103	103	103	103	

七、盲人按摩
Massage by the Blind

4-7-1 盲人按摩
Massage by the Blind

地 区	Region	保健按摩人员本年度培训 Blind Health-care Masseurs Trained in 2017	医疗按摩人员本年度培训 Blind Therapeutical Masseurs Trained in 2017	按摩机构 Institutions of Blind Massage	
				医疗按摩机构 Therapeutical Blind Massage Clinics	保健按摩机构 Health-care Blind Massage Houses
		人 person	人 person	人 person	人 person
全 国	**Total**	**20796**	**7217**	**1255**	**19257**
北 京	Beijing	223	105	4	484
天 津	Tianjin	23	30	4	162
河 北	Hebei	1117	573	67	531
山 西	Shanxi	777	852	59	587
内蒙古	Inner Mongolia	843	136	96	422
辽 宁	Liaoning	732	124	32	857
吉 林	Jilin	680	465	86	912
黑龙江	Heilongjiang	404	101	55	318
上 海	Shanghai	209	76	1	87
江 苏	Jiangsu	819	224	27	1018
浙 江	Zhejiang	346	240	89	971
安 徽	Anhui	1692	217	71	552
福 建	Fujian	361	245	33	322
江 西	Jiangxi	134	61	75	473
山 东	Shandong	1280	656	103	1401
河 南	Henan	2645	1134	111	928
湖 北	Hubei	426	49	43	912
湖 南	Hunan	1804	278	28	1334
广 东	Guangdong	469	397	10	734
广 西	Guangxi	540	56	5	324
海 南	Hainan	145	17	4	227
重 庆	Chongqing	139	255	18	874
四 川	Sichuan	994	63	57	1727
贵 州	Guizhou	710	171	26	717
云 南	Yunnan	1437	399	4	855
西 藏	Tibet	13	4		4
陕 西	Shaanxi	484	30	72	450
甘 肃	Gansu	774	137	29	341
青 海	Qinghai	145	24	5	234
宁 夏	Ningxia	328	65	11	309
新 疆	Xinjiang	94	27	22	161
新疆兵团	Xinjiang Corps	9	2	7	27
黑龙江垦区	Heilongjiang Land Reclamation		4	1	2

4-7-1 续表 Continued

地 区	Region	盲人医疗按摩人员专业技术职务任职资格评审 Vocational Qualification Appraisal for the Blind Therapeutical Masseurs		盲人保健按摩人员就业 Employed Blind Health-care Masseurs	盲人医疗按摩人员就业 Employed Blind Therapeutical Masseurs
		中级 Middle Level Blind Therapeutical Masseurs	初级 Junior Level Blind Therapeutical Masseurs		
		人 person	人 person	人 person	人 person
全 国	**Total**	**54**	**870**	**26879**	**3156**
北 京	Beijing		14	290	18
天 津	Tianjin			475	25
河 北	Hebei		104	1342	191
山 西	Shanxi	6	9	472	48
内蒙古	Inner Mongolia		39	590	217
辽 宁	Liaoning	6	16	767	73
吉 林	Jilin	3	22	693	209
黑龙江	Heilongjiang	3	44	559	134
上 海	Shanghai		7	110	25
江 苏	Jiangsu		28	893	99
浙 江	Zhejiang	1	60	1281	184
安 徽	Anhui	5	68	1626	167
福 建	Fujian		16	343	94
江 西	Jiangxi	10	23	1076	77
山 东	Shandong		62	1316	255
河 南	Henan		10	1329	241
湖 北	Hubei		25	448	181
湖 南	Hunan		41	1662	282
广 东	Guangdong	1	13	1325	48
广 西	Guangxi			1194	38
海 南	Hainan	1	7	778	9
重 庆	Chongqing			830	82
四 川	Sichuan		52	3374	88
贵 州	Guizhou		82	1412	95
云 南	Yunnan		23	538	9
西 藏	Tibet		2	6	
陕 西	Shaanxi		53	648	43
甘 肃	Gansu		11	501	93
青 海	Qinghai	2	9	194	29
宁 夏	Ningxia	6	2	685	84
新 疆	Xinjiang	6	15	107	16
新疆兵团	Xinjiang Corps		8	10	2
黑龙江垦区	Heilongjiang Land Reclamation	4	5	5	

八、宣传文化
Publicity and Cultural Activities

4-8-1　宣传文化
Publicity and Culture

地　区	Region	宣传 Publicity 省级 At Provincial Level 组织新闻发布会 Organizing Press Conferences	广播电台残疾人专题栏目 Radio Broadcast Special Programs on Disability	电视手语栏目 Sign Language TV Programmes
		次 time	个 unit	个 unit
全　国	**Total**	**173**	**25**	**31**
北　京	Beijing	7	1	2
天　津	Tianjin	2	1	2
河　北	Hebei	18	1	
山　西	Shanxi	5	1	1
内蒙古	Inner Mongolia			1
辽　宁	Liaoning	4	1	1
吉　林	Jilin	1		1
黑龙江	Heilongjiang	1	1	2
上　海	Shanghai	28	1	1
江　苏	Jiangsu		1	2
浙　江	Zhejiang	2	1	3
安　徽	Anhui	1	1	1
福　建	Fujian			1
江　西	Jiangxi	1		
山　东	Shandong	2	1	
河　南	Henan		1	1
湖　北	Hubei		1	
湖　南	Hunan			
广　东	Guangdong	26	1	1
广　西	Guangxi	40	1	1
海　南	Hainan	10	1	1
重　庆	Chongqing	3	1	1
四　川	Sichuan	2	1	1
贵　州	Guizhou		3	1
云　南	Yunnan	1		1
西　藏	Tibet			
陕　西	Shaanxi		1	1
甘　肃	Gansu	1	1	1
青　海	Qinghai		1	2
宁　夏	Ningxia	18	1	
新　疆	Xinjiang			
新疆兵团	Xinjiang Corps			1
黑龙江垦区	Heilongjiang Land Reclamation			

4-8-1 续表 1 Continued 1

地 区	Region	宣传 Publicity			
		省级 At Provincial Level			
		新促会 Societies for Promoting News Relating to PWDs	官方微博 Official Blog	官方微信 Official WeChat	入驻政务客户端平台 Housed Politic Client-End Platforms
		个 unit	个 unit	个 unit	个 unit
全 国	**Total**	**22**	**15**	**24**	**9**
北 京	Beijing	1	3	1	1
天 津	Tianjin		2	2	1
河 北	Hebei	1	1	1	
山 西	Shanxi				
内蒙古	Inner Mongolia				
辽 宁	Liaoning	1		1	
吉 林	Jilin	1	1	1	1
黑龙江	Heilongjiang	1			
上 海	Shanghai	1		1	
江 苏	Jiangsu	1		1	
浙 江	Zhejiang	1		1	
安 徽	Anhui			1	
福 建	Fujian				
江 西	Jiangxi	1	1	1	
山 东	Shandong	1			
河 南	Henan	1		1	
湖 北	Hubei	1		1	1
湖 南	Hunan	1			
广 东	Guangdong	1		1	
广 西	Guangxi	1	1	1	1
海 南	Hainan	1	2	2	1
重 庆	Chongqing	1	1	1	1
四 川	Sichuan	1	2	1	1
贵 州	Guizhou			1	
云 南	Yunnan	1		1	
西 藏	Tibet		1	1	
陕 西	Shaanxi			1	
甘 肃	Gansu	1			
青 海	Qinghai	1			
宁 夏	Ningxia	1			
新 疆	Xinjiang			1	1
新疆兵团	Xinjiang Corps				
黑龙江垦区	Heilongjiang Land Reclamation				

4-8-1 续表 2 Continued 2

地区 Region		宣传 Publicity			
		地市级 At Prefectural/City Level			
		组织新闻发布会 Organizing Press Conferences	广播电台残疾人专题栏目 Radio Broadcast Special Programs on Disability	电视手语栏目 Sign Language TV Programmes	新促会 Societies for Promoting News Relating to PWDs
		次 time	个 unit	个 unit	个 unit
全国	**Total**	**445**	**198**	**254**	**109**
北京	Beijing			3	1
天津	Tianjin		1	4	1
河北	Hebei	2	8	10	6
山西	Shanxi	26	9	5	3
内蒙古	Inner Mongolia		3	8	1
辽宁	Liaoning	6	8	13	3
吉林	Jilin	1	1	8	5
黑龙江	Heilongjiang		8	6	3
上海	Shanghai	1	2	14	3
江苏	Jiangsu	8	14	15	8
浙江	Zhejiang	3	12	11	7
安徽	Anhui	2	12	16	4
福建	Fujian		5	8	2
江西	Jiangxi	1	7	5	
山东	Shandong	2	14	10	7
河南	Henan		13	8	14
湖北	Hubei	1	6	8	1
湖南	Hunan	21	9	3	4
广东	Guangdong	230	14	11	10
广西	Guangxi	42	3	6	
海南	Hainan			1	
重庆	Chongqing	16	6	25	1
四川	Sichuan	6	6	7	3
贵州	Guizhou		4	6	3
云南	Yunnan	2	6	10	9
西藏	Tibet				
陕西	Shaanxi			8	2
甘肃	Gansu	74	22	13	6
青海	Qinghai			4	
宁夏	Ningxia	1	2	4	
新疆	Xinjiang		3	4	2
新疆兵团	Xinjiang Corps				
黑龙江垦区	Heilongjiang Land Reclamation				

4-8-1 续表 3 Continued 3

地 区	Region	文化 Culture 省级 At Provincial Level 公共图书馆盲文及盲人有声读物图书室 Reading Rooms with Braille and Audio Reading Materials in Public Library 个 unit	残疾人文化周 Culture Week for PWDs 场次 time	残疾人文化艺术类比赛及展览 Cultural or Art Competitions and Exhibitions of PWDs 次 time	残疾人艺术团 PWDs' Performing Art Troupes 个 unit
全 国	**Total**	**27**	**133**	**91**	**25**
北 京	Beijing		1	5	1
天 津	Tianjin	2	4	2	4
河 北	Hebei	1	11	4	
山 西	Shanxi	1	1	1	
内蒙古	Inner Mongolia	1	1		2
辽 宁	Liaoning	1	7	3	1
吉 林	Jilin	2	11	2	
黑龙江	Heilongjiang	1	2	2	1
上 海	Shanghai	1	17	6	1
江 苏	Jiangsu	1	4	5	
浙 江	Zhejiang	1	1	4	1
安 徽	Anhui	1	1	3	
福 建	Fujian	2	1	4	1
江 西	Jiangxi		1	7	
山 东	Shandong		1	1	1
河 南	Henan	1	1	4	1
湖 北	Hubei	1	5	2	1
湖 南	Hunan		2	5	
广 东	Guangdong	1	4	5	1
广 西	Guangxi	1		1	1
海 南	Hainan	1	4	1	2
重 庆	Chongqing	1	4	6	1
四 川	Sichuan		30	1	1
贵 州	Guizhou	1	4	1	
云 南	Yunnan	1	1	1	
西 藏	Tibet			2	
陕 西	Shaanxi	1	1	2	1
甘 肃	Gansu	1	6	7	1
青 海	Qinghai	1	1	1	1
宁 夏	Ningxia	1	1		
新 疆	Xinjiang		3	3	1
新疆兵团	Xinjiang Corps		1		
黑龙江垦区	Heilongjiang Land Reclamation		1		

4-8-1　续表 4　Continued 4

地区	Region	文化 Culture					
		地市级 At Prefectural/City Level				县级 At County Level	
		公共图书馆盲文及盲人有声读物图书室 Reading Rooms with Braille and Audio Reading Materials in Public Library	残疾人文化周 Culture Week for PWDs	残疾人文化艺术类比赛及展览 Cultural or Art Competitions and Exhibitions of PWDs	残疾人艺术团 PWDs' Performing Art Troupes	公共图书馆盲文及盲人有声读物图书室 Reading Rooms with Braille and Audio Reading Materials in Public Library	残疾人文化周 Culture Week for PWDs
		个 unit	场次 time	次 time	个 unit	个 unit	场次 time
全　国	**Total**	**255**	**904**	**549**	**256**	**677**	**5703**
北　京	Beijing					7	453
天　津	Tianjin					5	26
河　北	Hebei	15	22	29	8	10	281
山　西	Shanxi	4	15	10	6	6	182
内蒙古	Inner Mongolia	8	17	11	5	16	64
辽　宁	Liaoning	16	92	62	16	32	406
吉　林	Jilin	9	17	17	8	37	124
黑龙江	Heilongjiang	11	19	28	12	24	168
上　海	Shanghai					36	310
江　苏	Jiangsu	17	64	39	18	33	425
浙　江	Zhejiang	12	31	26	25	58	573
安　徽	Anhui	15	29	11	6	36	178
福　建	Fujian	6	8	13	6	33	58
江　西	Jiangxi	7	9	10	7	16	80
山　东	Shandong	11	33	35	30	42	250
河　南	Henan	16	53	14	4	43	116
湖　北	Hubei	8	31	25	7	15	77
湖　南	Hunan	5	79	68	26	5	149
广　东	Guangdong	17	76	39	34	26	170
广　西	Guangxi	9	20	11	5	9	60
海　南	Hainan	1					9
重　庆	Chongqing					41	193
四　川	Sichuan	16	13	17	8	24	182
贵　州	Guizhou	6	20	3	2	16	175
云　南	Yunnan	11	40	12	8	16	226
西　藏	Tibet						
陕　西	Shaanxi	7	89	10	6	33	123
甘　肃	Gansu	14	35	24	4	36	166
青　海	Qinghai	4	12	12	1	6	66
宁　夏	Ningxia	5	7	16	2	10	27
新　疆	Xinjiang	4	48	3	2	6	161
新疆兵团	Xinjiang Corps	1	20	4			196
黑龙江垦区	Heilongjiang Land Reclamation		5				29

九、体育
Sports

4-9-1 体 育
Sports

地 区	Region	省级 At Provincial Level					
		残疾人群众体育健身活动 Massive Sports and Fitness Activities for PWDs	残疾人群众体育健身活动参加人次 Participation in Mass Sports and Fitness Activities for PWDs	新增残疾人健身示范点 Sports Activity Demonstration Sites for PWDs in 2017	新增残疾人社会体育指导员 Coaches for Fitness Activity for PWDs in 2017	残疾人体育比赛 Sports Events for PWDs	参赛残疾人运动员 Disabled Athletes who Participated in the Sports Events
		次 time	人次 person-time	个 unit	人 person	次 time	人次 person-time
全 国	**Total**	**190**	**146680**	**1665**	**21170**	**228**	**19995**
北 京	Beijing	25	7000	18	1730	22	200
天 津	Tianjin	8	6000	100	1125	10	102
河 北	Hebei	14	2431	253	4055	31	1230
山 西	Shanxi	3	200	40	690	2	305
内蒙古	Inner Mongolia	1	134		56	6	43
辽 宁	Liaoning	3	500	10	1735	2	128
吉 林	Jilin	5	1500	82	504	4	810
黑龙江	Heilongjiang	2	2000	60	420	1	20
上 海	Shanghai	25	9474	171	938	23	8674
江 苏	Jiangsu	2	415	78	478	2	299
浙 江	Zhejiang	2	100000	20	200	10	200
安 徽	Anhui	3	279	2	1235	4	441
福 建	Fujian	13	2800	155	1531	7	612
江 西	Jiangxi	2	309	30	12	23	491
山 东	Shandong	1	63	1			
河 南	Henan	5	300	76	300	1	500
湖 北	Hubei	2	300	30	1150	1	100
湖 南	Hunan	5	753	93	405	2	411
广 东	Guangdong	10	900	196	494	4	591
广 西	Guangxi	1	130	3	130		
海 南	Hainan	6	300	5	400	15	600
重 庆	Chongqing	4	2000	110	179	12	731
四 川	Sichuan			5	60		
贵 州	Guizhou	3	1000	37	200	1	200
云 南	Yunnan	2	180	5	602		
西 藏	Tibet	6	32		1		
陕 西	Shaanxi	18	2100	7	2314	23	1600
甘 肃	Gansu	4	2650	69	120	1	187
青 海	Qinghai	6	2300		70	8	910
宁 夏	Ningxia	6	300	4	10	12	80
新 疆	Xinjiang	1	60	4	11	1	530
新疆兵团	Xinjiang Corps	2	270	1	15		
黑龙江垦区	Heilongjiang Land Reclamation						

4-9-1 续表 Continued

地区	Region	省级 At Provincial Level 残疾人体育训练基地 Sports Training Bases for PWDs	省级 At Provincial Level 聘任教练员 Stable Coaches	地市级 At Prefectural/City Level 残疾人群众体育健身活动 Massive Sports and Fitness Activities for PWDs	地市级 At Prefectural/City Level 残疾人群众体育健身活动参加人数 Participation in Mass Sports and Fitness Activities for PWDs	地市级 At Prefectural/City Level 新增残疾人体育健身示范点 Sports Activity Demonstration Sites for PWDs in 2017	地市级 At Prefectural/City Level 新增残疾人社会体育指导员 Coaches for Fitness Activity for PWDs in 2017	残疾人康复体育关爱家庭服务 Sports and Caring Family Services for the Rehabilitation of Persons with Disabilities
		个 unit	人 person	次 time	人次 person-time	个 unit	人 person	户 household
全 国	**Total**	**224**	**786**	**5416**	**150020**	**609**	**6387**	**132753**
北 京	Beijing	6	42					3100
天 津	Tianjin	2	15					9680
河 北	Hebei	10	31	4820	91844			10200
山 西	Shanxi		18	9	485	17	47	7250
内蒙古	Inner Mongolia	1	1	3	242	12	68	
辽 宁	Liaoning	31	58	33	3413	6	47	1000
吉 林	Jilin	16	20	58	6575	64	378	3400
黑龙江	Heilongjiang	5	12	5	450	2	33	1000
上 海	Shanghai	5	160					1360
江 苏	Jiangsu	2	38	45	3645	39	265	7128
浙 江	Zhejiang	7	50	28	4181	27	427	2500
安 徽	Anhui	1	15	27	6085	24	141	1000
福 建	Fujian	15	22	16	1341	15	66	
江 西	Jiangxi	11	17	12	500	14	28	8000
山 东	Shandong	4	32	79	4799	171	1177	850
河 南	Henan	6	25	27	925	43	380	2000
湖 北	Hubei	4	11	19	1900	3	20	1500
湖 南	Hunan	4	9	34	1676	63	450	3600
广 东	Guangdong	8	30	102	11872	90	2078	2650
广 西	Guangxi	1	20	10	744		101	
海 南	Hainan	13	25				5	50
重 庆	Chongqing	8	8					10000
四 川	Sichuan	16	50	2	775	1	236	46000
贵 州	Guizhou	6	12	6	572	5	4	
云 南	Yunnan	1	20	1	25	4	104	1000
西 藏	Tibet							
陕 西	Shaanxi	31	16	20	2100	1	7	1435
甘 肃	Gansu	3	15	46	4867	2	314	5000
青 海	Qinghai	1	2	4	139	2	2	1500
宁 夏	Ningxia	1	6	8	700	2	3	1000
新 疆	Xinjiang	5	6	1	45	2	5	550
新疆兵团	Xinjiang Corps			1	120		1	
黑龙江垦区	Heilongjiang Land Reclamation							

十、维权
Rights Protection

4-10-1 法规体系
Legal System

地 区	Region	制定或修改关于残疾人的专门法规、规章 Special Laws and Regulations Enacted or Reviewed for PWDs	省级 At Provincial Level	地市级 At Prefectural/ City Level	制定或修改保障残疾人权益的规范性文件 Polices Enacted or Reviewed for PWDs	省级 At Provincial Level	地市级 At Prefectural/ City Level	县级 At County Level
		个 unit	个 unit	个 unit	个 unit	个 unit	个 unit	个 unit
全 国	**Total**	**21**	**11**	**10**	**217**	**12**	**53**	**152**
北 京	Beijing							
天 津	Tianjin				5	5		
河 北	Hebei				11	2	2	7
山 西	Shanxi				3			3
内蒙古	Inner Mongolia				2		1	1
辽 宁	Liaoning	1	1		4		2	2
吉 林	Jilin	1		1	3	1	2	
黑龙江	Heilongjiang				1		1	
上 海	Shanghai							
江 苏	Jiangsu				9		2	7
浙 江	Zhejiang				21		2	19
安 徽	Anhui				25		4	21
福 建	Fujian	3	1	2	11		6	5
江 西	Jiangxi	2	1	1	6		3	3
山 东	Shandong	3	1	2	9		3	6
河 南	Henan				7		5	2
湖 北	Hubei				4		2	2
湖 南	Hunan	1	1		9		1	8
广 东	Guangdong	1		1	8	1	5	2
广 西	Guangxi							
海 南	Hainan	1		1	3		1	2
重 庆	Chongqing				6			6
四 川	Sichuan				8		1	7
贵 州	Guizhou				14	2	1	11
云 南	Yunnan				2			2
西 藏	Tibet							
陕 西	Shaanxi				1			1
甘 肃	Gansu	8	6	2	39	1	9	29
青 海	Qinghai				4			4
宁 夏	Ningxia				1			1
新 疆	Xinjiang				1			1
新疆兵团	Xinjiang Corps							
黑龙江垦区	Heilongjiang Land Reclamation							

4-10-2 执法检查
Inspections on Law Enforcement

地 区	Region	人大执法检查或专题调研 Inspections and Investigations by People's Congresses	省级 At Provincial Level	地市级 At Prefectural/City Level	县级 At County Level
		次 time	次 time	次 time	次 time
全 国	**Total**	**290**	**7**	**51**	**232**
北 京	Beijing	2	1		1
天 津	Tianjin	1			1
河 北	Hebei	17		2	15
山 西	Shanxi	9		2	7
内蒙古	Inner Mongolia	1			1
辽 宁	Liaoning	8	1	2	5
吉 林	Jilin	4		1	3
黑龙江	Heilongjiang	16		3	13
上 海	Shanghai	2	1		1
江 苏	Jiangsu	14	1	5	8
浙 江	Zhejiang	47	1	5	41
安 徽	Anhui	12		1	11
福 建	Fujian	3			3
江 西	Jiangxi	9		1	8
山 东	Shandong	22		1	21
河 南	Henan	13		5	8
湖 北	Hubei	10		4	6
湖 南	Hunan	20		6	14
广 东	Guangdong	11		5	6
广 西	Guangxi	3			3
海 南	Hainan	3			3
重 庆	Chongqing	9			9
四 川	Sichuan	13	1	2	10
贵 州	Guizhou	7	1		6
云 南	Yunnan	6			6
西 藏	Tibet				
陕 西	Shaanxi	1			1
甘 肃	Gansu	22		4	18
青 海	Qinghai	3		2	1
宁 夏	Ningxia	2			2
新 疆	Xinjiang				
新疆兵团	Xinjiang Corps				
黑龙江垦区	Heilongjiang Land Reclamation				

4-10-2 续表 Continued

地 区	Region	政协视察或专题调研 Inspections and Investigations by People's Political Consultative Conferences	省级 At Provincial Level	地市级 At Prefectural/City Level	县级 At County Level
		次 time	次 time	次 time	次 time
全 国	**Total**	**267**	**9**	**46**	**212**
北 京	Beijing	2	1		1
天 津	Tianjin	1			1
河 北	Hebei	18		1	17
山 西	Shanxi	9		3	6
内蒙古	Inner Mongolia				
辽 宁	Liaoning	9		3	6
吉 林	Jilin	3			3
黑龙江	Heilongjiang	9		1	8
上 海	Shanghai				
江 苏	Jiangsu	12		4	8
浙 江	Zhejiang	50	3	6	41
安 徽	Anhui	14	2	2	10
福 建	Fujian	3			3
江 西	Jiangxi	7		1	6
山 东	Shandong	21	1	3	17
河 南	Henan	7		2	5
湖 北	Hubei	10		3	7
湖 南	Hunan	22		5	17
广 东	Guangdong	13		8	5
广 西	Guangxi	2			2
海 南	Hainan				
重 庆	Chongqing	13			13
四 川	Sichuan	9	1	1	7
贵 州	Guizhou	7			7
云 南	Yunnan	4			4
西 藏	Tibet				
陕 西	Shaanxi				
甘 肃	Gansu	18		3	15
青 海	Qinghai	3	1		2
宁 夏	Ningxia	1			1
新 疆	Xinjiang				
新疆兵团	Xinjiang Corps				
黑龙江垦区	Heilongjiang Land Reclamation				

4-10-3　法制宣传
Publicity on Laws

地　区	Region	省级 At Provincial Level			
		普法宣传教育活动 Activities for Laws Publicity and Education	普法宣传教育活动参加人数 Participipants of Activities for Laws Publicity and Education	残疾人工作者法律培训班 Training Courses on Laws	法律培训班参加人数 Trainees of Laws Courses
		次 time	人 person	个 unit	人 person
全　国	**Total**	**283**	**19968**	**74**	**4810**
北　京	Beijing	200	5000	40	1455
天　津	Tianjin	3	280	2	120
河　北	Hebei	2	2000		
山　西	Shanxi	5	1100	3	230
内蒙古	Inner Mongolia				
辽　宁	Liaoning	14	1300		
吉　林	Jilin			1	100
黑龙江	Heilongjiang	1	237	1	170
上　海	Shanghai	2	221	2	78
江　苏	Jiangsu	1	90		
浙　江	Zhejiang	1	189	1	130
安　徽	Anhui	4	420	1	126
福　建	Fujian	3	326	1	43
江　西	Jiangxi	7	402	2	160
山　东	Shandong	4	551		
河　南	Henan				
湖　北	Hubei	2	200	1	200
湖　南	Hunan			6	600
广　东	Guangdong	1	315		
广　西	Guangxi				
海　南	Hainan	4	506	4	374
重　庆	Chongqing	3	640	1	103
四　川	Sichuan	2	300	1	80
贵　州	Guizhou	2	400	2	400
云　南	Yunnan				
西　藏	Tibet	3	21		
陕　西	Shaanxi				
甘　肃	Gansu	4	3000	3	270
青　海	Qinghai	7	1800	1	96
宁　夏	Ningxia	5	430	1	75
新　疆	Xinjiang	2	120		
新疆兵团	Xinjiang Corps				
黑龙江垦区	Heilongjiang Land Reclamation	1	120		

4-10-4 法律救助
Legal Aid

地 区	Region	建立残疾人法律救助协调组织 Legal Assistance and Coordination Organization for PWDs			
		建立残疾人法律救助工作协调机构 Legal Assistance and Coordination Organization for PWDs	省级 At Provincial Level	地市级 At Prefectural/ City Level	县级 At County Level
		个 unit	个 unit	个 unit	个 unit
全 国	**Total**	**1987**	**25**	**252**	**1710**
北 京	Beijing	14	1		13
天 津	Tianjin	17	1		16
河 北	Hebei	152	1	11	140
山 西	Shanxi	18	1	4	13
内蒙古	Inner Mongolia	86		4	82
辽 宁	Liaoning	80	1	14	65
吉 林	Jilin	68	1	9	58
黑龙江	Heilongjiang	20	1	3	16
上 海	Shanghai	18	1		17
江 苏	Jiangsu	96	1	12	83
浙 江	Zhejiang	102	1	11	90
安 徽	Anhui	42	1	10	31
福 建	Fujian	64	1	9	54
江 西	Jiangxi	54	1	7	46
山 东	Shandong	82		11	71
河 南	Henan	137	1	18	118
湖 北	Hubei	112	1	11	100
湖 南	Hunan	106	1	14	91
广 东	Guangdong	57	1	14	42
广 西	Guangxi	45	1	9	35
海 南	Hainan	17		3	14
重 庆	Chongqing	29			29
四 川	Sichuan	115	1	13	101
贵 州	Guizhou	74	1	6	67
云 南	Yunnan	35	1	8	26
西 藏	Tibet				
陕 西	Shaanxi	99	1	9	89
甘 肃	Gansu	102	1	15	86
青 海	Qinghai	39		6	33
宁 夏	Ningxia	13		2	11
新 疆	Xinjiang	82	1	9	72
新疆兵团	Xinjiang Corps	6		5	1
黑龙江垦区	Heilongjiang Land Reclamation	6	1	5	

4-10-4 续表 1 Continued 1

地 区	Region	残疾人法律救助工作站 Legal Assistance Stations for PWDs			
		残疾人法律救助工作站 Legal Assistance Stations for PWDs	省级 At Provincial Level	地市级 At Prefectural/ City Level	县级 At County Level
		个 unit	个 unit	个 unit	个 unit
全 国	**Total**	**1746**	**19**	**227**	**1500**
北 京	Beijing	9			9
天 津	Tianjin	17	1		16
河 北	Hebei	151	1	11	139
山 西	Shanxi	14		3	11
内蒙古	Inner Mongolia	70		4	66
辽 宁	Liaoning	73	1	14	58
吉 林	Jilin	64		9	55
黑龙江	Heilongjiang	12		2	10
上 海	Shanghai	17	1		16
江 苏	Jiangsu	89	1	12	76
浙 江	Zhejiang	102	1	11	90
安 徽	Anhui	36		8	28
福 建	Fujian	56	1	9	46
江 西	Jiangxi	41	1	6	34
山 东	Shandong	83		11	72
河 南	Henan	110	1	14	95
湖 北	Hubei	59	1	10	48
湖 南	Hunan	105	1	14	90
广 东	Guangdong	47	1	12	34
广 西	Guangxi	43	1	8	34
海 南	Hainan	21		3	18
重 庆	Chongqing	29			29
四 川	Sichuan	93	1	11	81
贵 州	Guizhou	64	1	4	59
云 南	Yunnan	32	1	8	23
西 藏	Tibet				
陕 西	Shaanxi	91	1	9	81
甘 肃	Gansu	102	1	15	86
青 海	Qinghai	36		5	31
宁 夏	Ningxia	9		2	7
新 疆	Xinjiang	66	1	8	57
新疆兵团	Xinjiang Corps	5		4	1
黑龙江垦区	Heilongjiang Land Reclamation				

4-10-4 续表 2 Continued 2

地 区	Region	残疾人法律救助工作站 Legal Assistance Stations for PWDs			
		残疾人法律救助工作站办理的案件 Cases Handled by the Legal Assistance Stations for PWDs	省级 At Provincial Level	地市级 At Prefectural/ City Level	县级 At County Level
		件 case	件 case	件 case	件 case
全 国	**Total**	**3649**	**206**	**527**	**2916**
北 京	Beijing	108			108
天 津	Tianjin	409	118		291
河 北	Hebei	107	1	19	87
山 西	Shanxi	36			36
内蒙古	Inner Mongolia	95		33	62
辽 宁	Liaoning	250	5	103	142
吉 林	Jilin	57		6	51
黑龙江	Heilongjiang	11			11
上 海	Shanghai	129			129
江 苏	Jiangsu	140	8	46	86
浙 江	Zhejiang	434	1	40	393
安 徽	Anhui	13		10	3
福 建	Fujian	90	11	7	72
江 西	Jiangxi	29		1	28
山 东	Shandong	172		46	126
河 南	Henan	139		76	63
湖 北	Hubei	140	2	13	125
湖 南	Hunan	197	9	34	154
广 东	Guangdong	66	2	32	32
广 西	Guangxi	67	1	15	51
海 南	Hainan	28		6	22
重 庆	Chongqing	234			234
四 川	Sichuan	141	3	8	130
贵 州	Guizhou	74	2	1	71
云 南	Yunnan	79	12	5	62
西 藏	Tibet				
陕 西	Shaanxi	78	29	17	32
甘 肃	Gansu	180		1	179
青 海	Qinghai	58		4	54
宁 夏	Ningxia	44		2	42
新 疆	Xinjiang	44	2	2	40
新疆兵团	Xinjiang Corps				
黑龙江垦区	Heilongjiang Land Reclamation				

4-10-5 参政议政
Persons with Disabilities Participating in the Administration and Discussion of State Affairs

地 区	Region	残联协助提出建议、议案和提案 Bills Suggestions and Proposals Submitted with the Assistance of Disabled Persons' Federations		残联办理人大政协建议、提案 Suggestions and Proposals Handled by Disabled Persons' Federations	
		协助人大代表提出议案、建议 Bills and Suggestions Submitted to People's Congresses	协助政协委员提出提案 Proposals Submitted to People's Political Consultative Conferences	办理人大建议 Suggestions of People's Congresses Handled	办理政协提案 Proposals of People's Political Consultative Conferences Handled
		件 case	件 case	件 case	件 case
全 国	**Total**	**225**	**528**	**355**	**638**
北 京	Beijing	3	7	4	11
天 津	Tianjin			8	3
河 北	Hebei	12	22	9	10
山 西	Shanxi	5	13	6	12
内蒙古	Inner Mongolia	5	11	2	2
辽 宁	Liaoning	20	34	22	24
吉 林	Jilin	3	6	1	4
黑龙江	Heilongjiang	3	9	7	11
上 海	Shanghai	1	6	4	11
江 苏	Jiangsu	8	20	25	48
浙 江	Zhejiang	60	88	81	104
安 徽	Anhui	4	20	8	35
福 建	Fujian	3	13	9	27
江 西	Jiangxi	12	28	4	12
山 东	Shandong	4	23	10	48
河 南	Henan	4	9	6	16
湖 北	Hubei	12	22	42	25
湖 南	Hunan	8	24	11	20
广 东	Guangdong	5	23	42	78
广 西	Guangxi	4	8	2	4
海 南	Hainan		7		1
重 庆	Chongqing	16	25	11	25
四 川	Sichuan	5	33	13	46
贵 州	Guizhou		5	2	7
云 南	Yunnan	11	23	14	5
西 藏	Tibet				
陕 西	Shaanxi	6	2	1	13
甘 肃	Gansu	6	21	4	17
青 海	Qinghai	2	7	3	3
宁 夏	Ningxia	1	13	2	8
新 疆	Xinjiang	2	5	2	7
新疆兵团	Xinjiang Corps		1		1
黑龙江垦区	Heilongjiang Land Reclamation				

4-10-6 无障碍环境建设与残疾人机动轮椅车燃油补贴
Accessible Environment Building and Subsidy for Petrol Used by Motorized Wheelchairs of Disabled Persons

地 区	Region	无障碍建设与管理法规、政府令 Regulations and Decrees on Accessible Environment Building and Management	无障碍建设领导协调组织 Leading and Coordinating Bodies for Building Accessible Environment	系统开展无障碍建设市、县 Cities and Counties that Systematic Accessibility Construction has been Carried out	地市级 At Prefectural/City Level	县级 At County Level
		个 unit	个 unit	个 unit	个 unit	个 unit
全 国	**Total**	**451**	**1121**	**1622**	**219**	**1403**
北 京	Beijing	1	17	16		16
天 津	Tianjin	9	17	16		16
河 北	Hebei	44	129	180	11	169
山 西	Shanxi	11	36	72	11	61
内蒙古	Inner Mongolia	5	22	64	6	58
辽 宁	Liaoning	6	49	5	4	1
吉 林	Jilin	14	29	13	4	9
黑龙江	Heilongjiang	4	12	36	8	28
上 海	Shanghai	5	32	16		16
江 苏	Jiangsu	23	67	54	13	41
浙 江	Zhejiang	22	47	76	11	65
安 徽	Anhui	6	25	80	16	64
福 建	Fujian	25	51	48	9	39
江 西	Jiangxi	7	13	111	11	100
山 东	Shandong	32	57	57	6	51
河 南	Henan	31	38	58	5	53
湖 北	Hubei	7	19	84	17	67
湖 南	Hunan	23	35	6	6	
广 东	Guangdong	30	28	145	21	124
广 西	Guangxi	11	36	125	14	111
海 南	Hainan		4	2	2	
重 庆	Chongqing	9	32	38		38
四 川	Sichuan	25	70	37	7	30
贵 州	Guizhou	15	20	26	2	24
云 南	Yunnan	18	49	74	5	69
西 藏	Tibet					
陕 西	Shaanxi	10	19	43	3	40
甘 肃	Gansu	40	64	101	15	86
青 海	Qinghai		39	11	3	8
宁 夏	Ningxia	6	17	23	5	18
新 疆	Xinjiang	10	33	3	2	1
新疆兵团	Xinjiang Corps		1			
黑龙江垦区	Heilongjiang Land Reclamation	2	14	2	2	

4-10-6 续表 Continued

地 区	Region	残疾人家庭无障碍改造 Accessibility Renovation for Homes of Poor Disabled Persons	无障碍建设检查 Inspections on Accessibility	无障碍培训 Training on Accessibility	残疾人机动轮椅车燃油补贴 Subsidy for Petrol Used by Motorized Wheelchairs of Disabled Persons
		户 household	次 time	人次 person-time	人 person
全 国	**Total**	**892447**	**4006**	**32059**	**748559**
北 京	Beijing	31306	38	3609	24110
天 津	Tianjin	14812	61	828	21492
河 北	Hebei	26585	48	175	15239
山 西	Shanxi	12544	39	860	8057
内蒙古	Inner Mongolia	28011	50	327	26293
辽 宁	Liaoning	22928	90	4400	15336
吉 林	Jilin	5593	25	259	13515
黑龙江	Heilongjiang	16016	8	218	15908
上 海	Shanghai	42969	1791	2949	19577
江 苏	Jiangsu	41071	142	2412	22723
浙 江	Zhejiang	130635	395	2226	11238
安 徽	Anhui	45611	36	818	27137
福 建	Fujian	11876	35	961	5268
江 西	Jiangxi	20039	23	117	22459
山 东	Shandong	120139	91	736	21432
河 南	Henan	40411	126	442	62017
湖 北	Hubei	32778	36	264	51255
湖 南	Hunan	40694	83	760	92348
广 东	Guangdong	25881	283	1054	29416
广 西	Guangxi	17618	43	169	17689
海 南	Hainan	3539	4	304	6682
重 庆	Chongqing	13976	55	1642	4410
四 川	Sichuan	10856	279	5073	27995
贵 州	Guizhou	30100	25	76	35649
云 南	Yunnan	20807	52	414	28376
西 藏	Tibet	1312	1		4026
陕 西	Shaanxi	36036	18	320	12977
甘 肃	Gansu	11610	48	114	29976
青 海	Qinghai	2944	28	51	18064
宁 夏	Ningxia	3806	27	119	14057
新 疆	Xinjiang	28085	23	222	33621
新疆兵团	Xinjiang Corps	356	2	15	8630
黑龙江垦区	Heilongjiang Land Reclamation	1503	1	125	1587

4-10-7 残疾人信访
Complaints by Letter and Visit

地 区	Region	来信 Complaint Letter					
		总计 Subtotal	涉法涉诉类 Complaints Related with Legal Lawsuit	医疗康复类 Medical Rehabilitation	教育类 Education	就业扶贫类 Employment and Poverty Alleviation	社会保障类 Social Security
		件 case	件 case	件 case	件 case	件 case	件 case
全 国	**Total**	**40525**	**2538**	**6503**	**2317**	**6864**	**9833**
北 京	Beijing	7705	470	960	205	1591	1736
天 津	Tianjin	248	5	10	1	19	78
河 北	Hebei	590	3	130	60	200	108
山 西	Shanxi	1426	33	388	67	182	384
内蒙古	Inner Mongolia	1470	1	304	184	225	239
辽 宁	Liaoning	529	38	43	39	65	118
吉 林	Jilin	523	3	152	36	107	128
黑龙江	Heilongjiang	308	23	58	40	66	43
上 海	Shanghai	973	40	108	47	146	162
江 苏	Jiangsu	698	17	52	24	112	161
浙 江	Zhejiang	1908	135	193	25	125	787
安 徽	Anhui	395	4	54	17	78	100
福 建	Fujian	627	74	54	39	105	178
江 西	Jiangxi	1160	80	299	99	199	295
山 东	Shandong	539	59	49	24	55	93
河 南	Henan	745	185	49	23	79	162
湖 北	Hubei	2523	101	241	54	421	1012
湖 南	Hunan	4664	1052	659	251	802	904
广 东	Guangdong	2306	35	362	291	365	493
广 西	Guangxi	643	13	282	44	92	108
海 南	Hainan	214	7	33	14	43	96
重 庆	Chongqing	981	15	116	42	78	100
四 川	Sichuan	2509	63	299	188	591	559
贵 州	Guizhou	497	2	193	34	56	128
云 南	Yunnan	2410	13	609	198	370	737
西 藏	Tibet						
陕 西	Shaanxi	1142	22	205	43	306	353
甘 肃	Gansu	1016	10	311	109	107	184
青 海	Qinghai	19				2	15
宁 夏	Ningxia	215	3	69	12	7	100
新 疆	Xinjiang	1494	29	215	101	260	260
新疆兵团	Xinjiang Corps	48	3	6	6	10	12
黑龙江垦区	Heilongjiang Land Reclamation						

4-10-7　续表 1　Continued 1

地　区	Region	来信 Complaint Letter				
		权益保障类 Right and Interest Protection	控告检举类 Complaints	意见建议类 Opinions and Suggestions	非残类 Non-Disable Related	其他类 Others
		件 case	件 case	件 case	件 case	件 case
全　国	**Total**	**3581**	**348**	**1718**	**1678**	**5145**
北　京	Beijing	74	76	32	1224	1337
天　津	Tianjin	45	35	12	4	39
河　北	Hebei	52	2	32		3
山　西	Shanxi	118	4	43	34	173
内蒙古	Inner Mongolia	145		30	53	289
辽　宁	Liaoning	44	3	11	4	164
吉　林	Jilin	37		27		33
黑龙江	Heilongjiang	30	4	10	5	29
上　海	Shanghai	210	7	131	28	94
江　苏	Jiangsu	109	34	86	15	88
浙　江	Zhejiang	310	18	54	9	252
安　徽	Anhui	93	1	5	2	41
福　建	Fujian	71	6	9	2	89
江　西	Jiangxi	50	14	74	15	35
山　东	Shandong	57	6	30	8	158
河　南	Henan	128	1	39	1	78
湖　北	Hubei	145	13	79	34	423
湖　南	Hunan	444	31	285	42	194
广　东	Guangdong	360	32	179	16	173
广　西	Guangxi	47	1	33	6	17
海　南	Hainan	12				9
重　庆	Chongqing	91	7	112	6	414
四　川	Sichuan	478	31	156	13	131
贵　州	Guizhou	61	1	11	2	9
云　南	Yunnan	107	1	71	40	264
西　藏	Tibet					
陕　西	Shaanxi	39		8	13	153
甘　肃	Gansu	102	12	124	13	44
青　海	Qinghai					2
宁　夏	Ningxia	8	3	1	1	11
新　疆	Xinjiang	107	5	33	87	397
新疆兵团	Xinjiang Corps	7		1	1	2
黑龙江垦区	Heilongjiang Land Reclamation					

4-10-7 续表 2 Continued 2

地 区	Region	来访 Complaint Visit					
		总计 Subtotal	涉法涉诉类 Complaints Related with Legal Lawsuit	医疗康复类 Medical Rehabilitation	教育类 Education	就业扶贫类 Employment and Poverty Alleviation	社会保障类 Social Security
		人次 person-time	人次 person-time	人次 person-time	人次 person-time	人次 person-time	人次 person-time
全 国	**Total**	**209483**	**8321**	**37505**	**12208**	**33859**	**55898**
北 京	Beijing	4544	832	272	92	359	1012
天 津	Tianjin	1633	258	124	58	192	423
河 北	Hebei	4953	104	1282	316	1198	1023
山 西	Shanxi	13253	188	3253	395	2974	4927
内蒙古	Inner Mongolia	1951	44	306	216	325	669
辽 宁	Liaoning	9773	666	1067	206	1092	2925
吉 林	Jilin	2694	124	379	59	428	647
黑龙江	Heilongjiang	2943	126	343	250	713	690
上 海	Shanghai	3420	169	223	189	583	602
江 苏	Jiangsu	3507	71	385	142	639	570
浙 江	Zhejiang	17080	847	1753	1658	1906	4645
安 徽	Anhui	6423	87	1090	468	1256	1405
福 建	Fujian	4913	129	934	377	909	1306
江 西	Jiangxi	6789	117	1141	356	1784	1763
山 东	Shandong	3902	509	428	270	531	1179
河 南	Henan	5027	168	585	347	851	1442
湖 北	Hubei	15063	441	1921	797	2166	4574
湖 南	Hunan	18896	2072	2622	1091	3176	4698
广 东	Guangdong	8186	207	2096	648	1286	1784
广 西	Guangxi	9147	242	3099	554	1237	2561
海 南	Hainan	365	12	50	20	65	121
重 庆	Chongqing	4607	175	454	163	846	1091
四 川	Sichuan	18936	239	3935	861	2493	4297
贵 州	Guizhou	7259	46	1266	204	562	3354
云 南	Yunnan	13766	145	2830	1223	2231	3399
西 藏	Tibet	4				1	2
陕 西	Shaanxi	6627	132	1521	367	1675	1889
甘 肃	Gansu	3532	82	945	306	568	744
青 海	Qinghai	265	7	44	35	62	52
宁 夏	Ningxia	3966	23	2075	156	669	597
新 疆	Xinjiang	3227	55	656	148	574	572
新疆兵团	Xinjiang Corps	2530	4	407	233	468	817
黑龙江垦区	Heilongjiang Land Reclamation	302		19	3	40	118

4-10-7 续表 3 Continued 3

地 区	Region	来访 Complaint Visit				
		权益保障类 Right and Interest Protection	控告检举类 Complaints	意见建议类 Opinions and Suggestions	非残类 Non-Disable Related	其他类 Others
		人次 person-time	人次 person-time	人次 person-time	人次 person-time	人次 person-time
全 国	**Total**	**25142**	**1156**	**8348**	**2066**	**24980**
北 京	Beijing	1028	38	124	128	659
天 津	Tianjin	96	15	36	4	427
河 北	Hebei	694	15	163	17	141
山 西	Shanxi	338	3	199	84	892
内蒙古	Inner Mongolia	131	1	23	9	227
辽 宁	Liaoning	1576	103	641	183	1314
吉 林	Jilin	507	4	35	6	505
黑龙江	Heilongjiang	279	6	85	35	416
上 海	Shanghai	672	34	613	30	305
江 苏	Jiangsu	727	66	290	129	488
浙 江	Zhejiang	2149	318	867	76	2861
安 徽	Anhui	1180	13	273	43	608
福 建	Fujian	715	27	48	14	454
江 西	Jiangxi	1069	15	222	69	253
山 东	Shandong	482	17	36	14	436
河 南	Henan	596	12	307	91	628
湖 北	Hubei	1290	53	1136	97	2588
湖 南	Hunan	2746	175	679	111	1526
广 东	Guangdong	995	64	212	40	854
广 西	Guangxi	669		271	77	437
海 南	Hainan	18		6	12	61
重 庆	Chongqing	842	24	246	37	729
四 川	Sichuan	2139	72	682	159	4059
贵 州	Guizhou	809	15	501	233	269
云 南	Yunnan	1370	25	138	124	2281
西 藏	Tibet	1				
陕 西	Shaanxi	347	10	163	34	489
甘 肃	Gansu	545	27	150	47	118
青 海	Qinghai	21		2		42
宁 夏	Ningxia	214	1	55	97	79
新 疆	Xinjiang	360	3	57	27	775
新疆兵团	Xinjiang Corps	417		88	39	57
黑龙江垦区	Heilongjiang Land Reclamation	120				2

十一、组织建设
Disabled Person's Organizations

4-11-1 省(自治区、直辖市)级残联
Disabled Persons' Federations in Provinces, Autonomous Regions and Municipalities

地 区	Region	省市县乡残联实有人员 Actual Total Staff of Disabled Persons' Federations at Provincial,City, County and Township Level	省级残联机关 Disabled Persons' Federations at Provincial Level		省级残联事业单位 Affiliated Institutions at Provincial Level		
			实有人员 Actual Staff	残疾人干部 Staff with Disability	单位 Institu-tions	实有人员 Actual Total Staff	残疾人 Persons with Disability
		人 person	人 person	人 person	个 unit	人 person	人 person
全 国	**Total**	**113369**	**1571**	**155**	**158**	**7190**	**272**
北 京	Beijing	1242	71	11	11	254	19
天 津	Tianjin	945	47	4	9	173	31
河 北	Hebei	5676	51	2	4	149	7
山 西	Shanxi	4392	62	6	8	234	7
内蒙古	Inner Mongolia	3091	32	4	4	99	2
辽 宁	Liaoning	3918	40	6	5	270	5
吉 林	Jilin	3010	38	6	4	395	17
黑龙江	Heilongjiang	3181	43	7	3	595	3
上 海	Shanghai	1089	42	6	7	211	12
江 苏	Jiangsu	4951	53	7	5	145	16
浙 江	Zhejiang	4872	42	5	6	456	11
安 徽	Anhui	3697	47	5	4	211	10
福 建	Fujian	2645	37	4	4	176	14
江 西	Jiangxi	4000	51	2	6	118	
山 东	Shandong	6308	49	3	5	262	7
河 南	Henan	8145	57	7	3	155	5
湖 北	Hubei	3446	49	2	6	51	2
湖 南	Hunan	4906	44	3	6	116	3
广 东	Guangdong	7714	52	7	5	276	15
广 西	Guangxi	3352	55	4	5	121	5
海 南	Hainan	734	69	3	2	83	3
重 庆	Chongqing	1975	38	1	3	158	5
四 川	Sichuan	9180	50	10	2	609	4
贵 州	Guizhou	3221	55	8	3	113	7
云 南	Yunnan	3767	59	9	8	253	26
西 藏	Tibet	293	25	3	2	80	7
陕 西	Shaanxi	4211	65	2	7	390	3
甘 肃	Gansu	4148	77	5	9	617	
青 海	Qinghai	1234	41	4	2	77	1
宁 夏	Ningxia	822	51	3	2	159	6
新 疆	Xinjiang	2873	59	5	5	166	17
新疆兵团	Xinjiang Corps	110	12	1	2	14	1
黑龙江垦区	Heilongjiang Land Reclamation	221	8		1	4	1

4-11-1 续表 Continued

地 区	Region	干部队伍综合培训情况 Training of Staff						志愿者助残情况 Volunteer	
		省级举办综合培训班 Provincial-level General Training Courses	参加省级综合培训人次 Trainees on Provincial-level Training Courses	省级举办残疾人干部培训班 Provincial-level Training Courses for Staff with Disability	参加省级残疾人干部培训人次 Trainees on Provincial-level Training Courses for Staff with Disability	参加全国培训人次 Trainees on State-level Training Courses	参加全国残疾人干部培训人次 Trainees on Stats-level Training Courses for Staff with Disability	志愿者登记在册 Registered Volunteer	受助残疾人 PWDs Helped by Volunteers
		期 course	人次 person-time	期 course	人次 person-time	人次 person-time	人次 person-time	人 person	人 person
全 国	**Total**	**100**	**10583**	**28**	**1785**	**166**	**79**	**7732**	**102095**
北 京	Beijing	5	700	3	150				
天 津	Tianjin	1	275	2	112				
河 北	Hebei	1	40					796	781
山 西	Shanxi	1	160			2	1	21	21
内蒙古	Inner Mongolia	1	32	1	26				
辽 宁	Liaoning	12	1080						
吉 林	Jilin	1	38	1	60			315	3780
黑龙江	Heilongjiang	10	1485						
上 海	Shanghai	3	650	2	150			259	67608
江 苏	Jiangsu	7	630			1			
浙 江	Zhejiang	2	420	1	130	32	70		
安 徽	Anhui	1	169						
福 建	Fujian	11	1400						
江 西	Jiangxi	1	200	2	80	50	2		
山 东	Shandong								
河 南	Henan	1	400	1	70			108	1245
湖 北	Hubei	2	150	2	100	39	1	5708	22600
湖 南	Hunan	1	186	1	92				
广 东	Guangdong	5	150	1	30	10	3		
广 西	Guangxi	10	600	2	140				
海 南	Hainan	2	160						
重 庆	Chongqing	1	80	1	80				
四 川	Sichuan	10	700	6	500				
贵 州	Guizhou	3	223				2		
云 南	Yunnan								
西 藏	Tibet							25	60
陕 西	Shaanxi								
甘 肃	Gansu	1	39						
青 海	Qinghai	3	252						
宁 夏	Ningxia	1	40	1	40			500	6000
新 疆	Xinjiang	1	64	1	25	32			
新疆兵团	Xinjiang Corps								
黑龙江垦区	Heilongjiang Land Reclamation	2	260						

4-11-2 地市级残联
Disabled Persons' Federations in Cities and Prefectures

地区	Region	残联 Disabled Persons' Federations	配备了残疾人领导干部的残联 Disabled Persons' Federations whose Leadership Include PWDs	残联机关 Disabled Persons' Federations		
				实有人员 Actual Staff	残疾人领导干部 Leaders with Disability	残疾人干部 Ordinary Staff with Disability
		个 unit	个 unit	人 person	人 person	人 person
全 国	**Total**	**361**	**229**	**5049**	**246**	**418**
北 京	Beijing					
天 津	Tianjin					
河 北	Hebei	11	10	247	10	10
山 西	Shanxi	11	6	158	6	10
内蒙古	Inner Mongolia	12	11	184	13	29
辽 宁	Liaoning	14	14	296	15	28
吉 林	Jilin	10	4	156	4	10
黑龙江	Heilongjiang	13	9	170	9	16
上 海	Shanghai					
江 苏	Jiangsu	13	7	302	7	17
浙 江	Zhejiang	11	10	163	11	20
安 徽	Anhui	16	8	187	8	11
福 建	Fujian	9	8	135	8	12
江 西	Jiangxi	11	7	130	7	13
山 东	Shandong	17	14	308	14	18
河 南	Henan	18	9	284	10	14
湖 北	Hubei	13	5	141	6	11
湖 南	Hunan	14	8	182	8	14
广 东	Guangdong	21	14	334	16	21
广 西	Guangxi	15	11	175	11	15
海 南	Hainan	3	1	45	2	3
重 庆	Chongqing					
四 川	Sichuan	21	12	273	12	23
贵 州	Guizhou	10	8	128	9	11
云 南	Yunnan	16	12	196	14	23
西 藏	Tibet	7	2	73	2	5
陕 西	Shaanxi	10	10	176	12	17
甘 肃	Gansu	15	13	246	15	22
青 海	Qinghai	8	1	84	1	11
宁 夏	Ningxia	5	3	45	3	5
新 疆	Xinjiang	14	11	171	12	26
新疆兵团	Xinjiang Corps	14	1	42	1	3
黑龙江垦区	Heilongjiang Land Reclamation	9		18		

4-11-2　续表　Continued

地　区	Region	事业单位 Affiliated Institutions 单位 Institutions	实有人员 Actual Total of Staff	残疾人 Persons with Disability	干部队伍综合培训情况 Training of Cadre 地市级举办综合培训班 City-level General Training Courses	参加地市级培训人次 Trainees on City-level General Training Courses	地市级举办残疾人干部培训班 City-level Training Courses for Staff with Disability	参加地市级残疾人干部培训人次 Trainees on City-level Training Courses for Staff with Disability	志愿者助残情况 Volunteer 志愿者登记在册 Registered Volunteer	受助残疾人 PWDs Helped by Volunteers
		个 unit	人 person	人 person	期 course	人次 person-time	期 course	人次 person-time	人 person	人 person
全　国	**Total**	**723**	**9956**	**562**	**826**	**50950**	**343**	**20121**	**83042**	**440949**
北　京	Beijing									
天　津	Tianjin									
河　北	Hebei	24	385	17	20	1668	29	987	2552	5143
山　西	Shanxi	39	461	31	24	1166	11	650	50	750
内蒙古	Inner Mongolia	24	142	11	13	1158	4	279	52	365
辽　宁	Liaoning	42	419	36	58	3942	31	1301	4047	5196
吉　林	Jilin	22	291	19	17	938	7	312	4217	16031
黑龙江	Heilongjiang	24	200	8	27	3801	14	398	409	161
上　海	Shanghai									
江　苏	Jiangsu	33	488	20	23	1643	11	677	3541	40329
浙　江	Zhejiang	25	599	25	13	919	9	724	3030	36461
安　徽	Anhui	29	279	9	41	2252	10	370	321	3733
福　建	Fujian	24	242	16	11	962			25645	4219
江　西	Jiangxi	17	91	6	20	871	14	303	88	6443
山　东	Shandong	41	768	68	36	1726	18	1345	385	1591
河　南	Henan	45	757	17	38	2517	22	959	35317	244277
湖　北	Hubei	27	204	20	16	257	4	162	73	1987
湖　南	Hunan	32	162	10	39	1979	11	437	173	4691
广　东	Guangdong	76	2672	103	119	1901	13	739	1628	36787
广　西	Guangxi	33	341	19	20	781	6	210	137	2547
海　南	Hainan	4	36	3	1	500			371	18062
重　庆	Chongqing									
四　川	Sichuan	34	325	22	149	13190	59	5807	65	3307
贵　州	Guizhou	16	72	5	9	212	2	16	69	649
云　南	Yunnan	27	121	12	24	2036	14	1314	156	442
西　藏	Tibet	4	12		1	11			1	
陕　西	Shaanxi	16	153	7	26	1393	17	885		
甘　肃	Gansu	24	505	59	33	3234	21	1910	134	1320
青　海	Qinghai	6	40		14	570	5	85	14	150
宁　夏	Ningxia	6	67	3	11	614	1	80	100	886
新　疆	Xinjiang	18	94	11	17	491	5	130		
新疆兵团	Xinjiang Corps	11	30	5	2	90	1	12	372	4081
黑龙江垦区	Heilongjiang Land Reclamation				4	128	4	29	95	1341

4-11-3 县(县级市、市辖区)级残联

Disabled Persons' Federations in Counties, County-Level Cities and Districts under Cities

地区	Region	残联 Disabled Persons' Federations	配备了残疾人干部的残联 Disabled Persons' Federations with Disabled Staff	残联机关 Disabled Persons' Federations	
				实有人员 Actual Staff	残疾人干部 Ordinary Staff with Disability
		个 unit	个 unit	人 person	人 person
全　国	**Total**	**3076**	**1572**	**27301**	**2165**
北　京	Beijing	16	13	190	21
天　津	Tianjin	16	11	148	20
河　北	Hebei	170	158	1514	174
山　西	Shanxi	120	73	1289	98
内蒙古	Inner Mongolia	108	59	932	97
辽　宁	Liaoning	102	90	690	103
吉　林	Jilin	71	28	725	42
黑龙江	Heilongjiang	132	32	566	37
上　海	Shanghai	16	7	163	8
江　苏	Jiangsu	102	44	1269	54
浙　江	Zhejiang	92	57	1218	73
安　徽	Anhui	117	65	830	77
福　建	Fujian	84	29	527	32
江　西	Jiangxi	111	49	907	83
山　东	Shandong	158	61	1794	69
河　南	Henan	168	93	2306	121
湖　北	Hubei	106	40	915	52
湖　南	Hunan	125	73	1342	97
广　东	Guangdong	137	44	1188	55
广　西	Guangxi	114	48	829	62
海　南	Hainan	20	8	167	8
重　庆	Chongqing	40	22	326	38
四　川	Sichuan	189	96	1554	132
贵　州	Guizhou	88	59	881	96
云　南	Yunnan	134	89	1287	149
西　藏	Tibet	74	9	100	9
陕　西	Shaanxi	113	59	1130	96
甘　肃	Gansu	86	70	1059	125
青　海	Qinghai	46	13	287	26
宁　夏	Ningxia	21	12	169	13
新　疆	Xinjiang	97	57	808	92
新疆兵团	Xinjiang Corps				
黑龙江垦区	Heilongjiang Land Reclamation	103	4	191	6

4-11-3　续表　Continued

地　区	Region	事业单位 Affiliated Institutions			干部队伍综合培训情况 Training of Cadre		志愿者助残情况 Volunteer	
		单位 Institutions	实有人员 Actual Total of Staff	残疾人 Persons with Disability	县级举办综合培训班累计 County-level General Training Courses	参加县级培训 Trainees on County-level General Training Courses	志愿者登记在册 Registered Volunteer	受助残疾人 PWDs Helped by Volunteers
		个 unit	人 person	人 person	期 course	人次 person-time	人 person	人 person
全　国	**Total**	**2516**	**14061**	**1105**	**6341**	**231536**	**630910**	**6316582**
北　京	Beijing	40	358	35	51	4394	269	28931
天　津	Tianjin	26	202	22	74	3744	2367	23312
河　北	Hebei	94	667	38	327	10575	36556	239401
山　西	Shanxi	136	584	29	224	7245	2729	39309
内蒙古	Inner Mongolia	51	242	42	191	8245	3507	40439
辽　宁	Liaoning	99	502	32	272	12587	9112	63932
吉　林	Jilin	62	352	12	158	5868	79558	900623
黑龙江	Heilongjiang	73	284	49	154	4465	105533	716522
上　海	Shanghai	22	206	24	73	3767	1169	123691
江　苏	Jiangsu	134	949	62	422	10874	18070	171021
浙　江	Zhejiang	138	772	57	430	11067	18858	532704
安　徽	Anhui	46	294	14	231	11906	6333	145503
福　建	Fujian	137	374	39	236	11020	41908	289604
江　西	Jiangxi	73	372	26	187	4604	2172	23868
山　东	Shandong	105	720	37	365	8332	16413	172692
河　南	Henan	179	1397	53	240	8322	79378	826494
湖　北	Hubei	116	586	43	195	3965	4268	57272
湖　南	Hunan	134	790	30	206	5206	2798	59725
广　东	Guangdong	180	1100	57	236	9437	6380	161113
广　西	Guangxi	99	408	60	185	8435	6296	114091
海　南	Hainan	11	72	14	17	591	2386	32302
重　庆	Chongqing	43	217	29	126	8029	22408	354095
四　川	Sichuan	108	607	34	577	24716	17967	338014
贵　州	Guizhou	60	242	24	129	5179	1838	55857
云　南	Yunnan	109	347	46	218	10374	1832	36400
西　藏	Tibet	2	3	1	6	76		
陕　西	Shaanxi	87	642	46	287	12511	8641	94018
甘　肃	Gansu	52	155	44	201	9023	119061	539166
青　海	Qinghai	29	129	21	74	1990	503	7137
宁　夏	Ningxia	7	88	7	44	1197	1851	6332
新　疆	Xinjiang	64	400	78	198	3764	7251	81476
新疆兵团	Xinjiang Corps						2260	28317
黑龙江垦区	Heilongjiang Land Reclamation				7	28	1238	13221

4-11-4 乡(镇、街道)残联
Disabled Persons' Federations in Townships (Towns, Streets)

地区	Region	乡(镇、街道)已建残联 Disabled Persons' Federations Established in Townships (Towns, Streets)	残联机关 Disabled Persons' Federation			
			实有人员 Actual Staff	专职残联理事长 Full-time Presidents	兼职残联理事长 Part-time Presidents	残疾人专职委员 Full-time Workers on Disability
		个 unit	人 person	人 person	人 person	人 person
全　国	**Total**	**39847**	**48241**	**11811**	**12172**	**69838**
北　京	Beijing	326	369	257	58	1284
天　津	Tianjin	242	375	242		232
河　北	Hebei	2300	2663	595	955	3830
山　西	Shanxi	1464	1604	85	704	3666
内蒙古	Inner Mongolia	1128	1460	247	370	1656
辽　宁	Liaoning	1515	1701	398	1122	2512
吉　林	Jilin	907	1053	234	566	941
黑龙江	Heilongjiang	1291	1323	103	389	2110
上　海	Shanghai	219	467	61	114	1092
江　苏	Jiangsu	1339	1745	921	152	2215
浙　江	Zhejiang	1374	1622	1247	51	2807
安　徽	Anhui	1562	1849	481	310	2030
福　建	Fujian	1108	1154	371	382	1451
江　西	Jiangxi	1626	2331	398	555	2498
山　东	Shandong	1825	2407	542	387	1805
河　南	Henan	2407	3189	993	945	8025
湖　北	Hubei	1221	1500	297	265	1874
湖　南	Hunan	2010	2270	661	500	5449
广　东	Guangdong	1640	2092	390	345	2069
广　西	Guangxi	1249	1423	305	513	2957
海　南	Hainan	223	262	2	146	298
重　庆	Chongqing	1023	1236	522	378	1086
四　川	Sichuan	4514	5762	586	1570	8686
贵　州	Guizhou	1425	1730	538	250	1091
云　南	Yunnan	1405	1504	460	470	1430
西　藏	Tibet					3
陕　西	Shaanxi	1401	1655	235	124	3093
甘　肃	Gansu	1379	1489	541	326	1638
青　海	Qinghai	410	576	16	61	548
宁　夏	Ningxia	242	243	14	8	463
新　疆	Xinjiang	1061	1175	68	155	883
新疆兵团	Xinjiang Corps	11	12	1	1	60
黑龙江垦区	Heilongjiang Land Reclamation					56

4-11-4 续表 Continued

地 区	Region	干部队伍综合培训情况 Training of Staff		志愿者助残情况 Volunteer	
		乡镇级举办综合培训班 Township-level General Training Courses	参加乡镇级培训人次 Trainees on Township-level Training	志愿者登记在册 Registered Volunteer	受助残疾人 PWDs Helped by Volunteers
		期 course	人次 person-time	万人 10,000 persons	万人 10,000 persons
全 国	**Total**	**25102**	**377878**	**138.1**	**1024.6**
北 京	Beijing	760	13684	0.5	20.9
天 津	Tianjin	226	3279	7.6	21.6
河 北	Hebei	1075	9973	14.6	59.5
山 西	Shanxi	793	12514	0.4	1.3
内蒙古	Inner Mongolia	405	4879	1.3	8.0
辽 宁	Liaoning	880	12629	1.9	9.9
吉 林	Jilin	385	4470	5.9	40.9
黑龙江	Heilongjiang	383	2154	16.6	85.7
上 海	Shanghai	331	2205	0.2	68.9
江 苏	Jiangsu	1566	19246	4.8	56.3
浙 江	Zhejiang	729	15450	1.3	26.3
安 徽	Anhui	1121	13824	0.8	8.2
福 建	Fujian	413	7103	4.4	22.0
江 西	Jiangxi	840	5663	0.7	5.6
山 东	Shandong	1576	36879	3.4	30.8
河 南	Henan	1048	8478	19.9	214.2
湖 北	Hubei	791	9733	0.5	5.7
湖 南	Hunan	312	3628	2.1	10.2
广 东	Guangdong	1014	9954	22.1	13.3
广 西	Guangxi	470	5750	0.5	5.6
海 南	Hainan	72	1451	0.4	3.1
重 庆	Chongqing	1241	38837	3.5	87.3
四 川	Sichuan	4812	69053	4.8	47.4
贵 州	Guizhou	549	7450	0.2	1.7
云 南	Yunnan	594	8892	0.4	7.3
西 藏	Tibet				
陕 西	Shaanxi	1335	24313	1.0	5.3
甘 肃	Gansu	803	17516	17.4	152.2
青 海	Qinghai	96	1986	0.1	0.2
宁 夏	Ningxia	65	807	0.5	1.4
新 疆	Xinjiang	409	5709	0.3	2.9
新疆兵团	Xinjiang Corps	8	369	0.1	0.8
黑龙江垦区	Heilongjiang Land Reclamation			0.0	0.0

4-11-5 村(社区)残疾人组织
Disabled Persons' Federations in Villages and Communities

地 区	Region	已建残协 Associations of PWDs Established		残协情况 Associations		
		村 In Villages	社区 In Communities	已建残疾人活动室 Entertainment Rooms for PWDs Established	村 In Villages	社区 In Communities
		个 unit	个 unit	个 unit	个 unit	个 unit
全 国	**Total**	**517768**	**68624**	**267051**	**227403**	**39648**
北 京	Beijing	3825	2190	3439	2230	1209
天 津	Tianjin	3365	1233	4595	3365	1230
河 北	Hebei	48321	3171	37122	34390	2732
山 西	Shanxi	21590	1746	8434	7636	798
内蒙古	Inner Mongolia	11423	1861	3161	2427	734
辽 宁	Liaoning	11774	3892	14434	10814	3620
吉 林	Jilin	9444	1580	5415	4587	828
黑龙江	Heilongjiang	6944	2058	3472	2331	1141
上 海	Shanghai	1289	2811	3118	1202	1916
江 苏	Jiangsu	15644	4756	17408	13252	4156
浙 江	Zhejiang	21140	2577	17806	15562	2244
安 徽	Anhui	14154	2125	5741	4774	967
福 建	Fujian	14130	1939	4872	4314	558
江 西	Jiangxi	15780	2300	8663	7423	1240
山 东	Shandong	57063	4138	23310	21231	2079
河 南	Henan	43945	3405	28861	26024	2837
湖 北	Hubei	21521	2701	6359	5502	857
湖 南	Hunan	28092	2902	12644	11189	1455
广 东	Guangdong	18772	5157	7564	4727	2837
广 西	Guangxi	14658	1513	3996	3581	415
海 南	Hainan	2323	260	349	263	86
重 庆	Chongqing	8927	2059	5224	3858	1366
四 川	Sichuan	42405	4033	15894	14267	1627
贵 州	Guizhou	14648	1012	2050	1909	141
云 南	Yunnan	12651	1513	4968	4275	693
西 藏	Tibet					
陕 西	Shaanxi	24483	1954	5303	4886	417
甘 肃	Gansu	16104	1139	10373	9642	731
青 海	Qinghai	4173	369	368	336	32
宁 夏	Ningxia	1667	370	201	66	135
新 疆	Xinjiang	7513	1786	1907	1340	567
新疆兵团	Xinjiang Corps		6			
黑龙江垦区	Heilongjiang Land Reclamation		68			

4-11-5　续表　Continued

地　区	Region	残协情况 Associations			志愿者助残情况 Volunteers	
		残疾人专职委员选聘情况 Full-time Workers on Disability			志愿者登记在册 Registered Volunteers	受助残疾人 PWDs Assisted by Volunteers
		残疾人专职委员 Full-time Workers on Disability	村 In Villages	社区 In Communties		
		人 person	人 person	人 person	万人 10,000 persons	万人 10,000 persons
全　国	**Total**	**520421**	**454695**	**65726**	**123.1**	**845.9**
北　京	Beijing	5080	3540	1540	0.4	15.8
天　津	Tianjin	4050	2994	1056	7.1	15.2
河　北	Hebei	49633	46582	3051	10.6	40.6
山　西	Shanxi	20913	19090	1823	0.3	3.4
内蒙古	Inner Mongolia	12574	10780	1794	0.8	3.7
辽　宁	Liaoning	14894	11006	3888	3.6	23.1
吉　林	Jilin	10754	9090	1664	7.4	39.9
黑龙江	Heilongjiang	4734	2038	2696	12.0	60.1
上　海	Shanghai	3670	1320	2350	0.1	13.2
江　苏	Jiangsu	19764	15485	4279	6.1	53.0
浙　江	Zhejiang	21087	17917	3170	0.8	19.0
安　徽	Anhui	16802	14499	2303	1.6	17.7
福　建	Fujian	15964	14032	1932	1.5	10.9
江　西	Jiangxi	14322	12338	1984	0.5	3.3
山　东	Shandong	61937	55834	6103	3.2	20.6
河　南	Henan	41989	38566	3423	22.6	247.4
湖　北	Hubei	19147	17147	2000	1.2	26.0
湖　南	Hunan	21190	18900	2290	2.5	18.1
广　东	Guangdong	22567	18560	4007	13.1	6.2
广　西	Guangxi	14496	13139	1357	0.7	8.0
海　南	Hainan	2743	2496	247	0.3	2.3
重　庆	Chongqing	10304	8213	2091	3.4	47.3
四　川	Sichuan	36710	33524	3186	6.8	43.9
贵　州	Guizhou	15268	13651	1617	0.4	2.0
云　南	Yunnan	13591	12106	1485	0.6	3.9
西　藏	Tibet					
陕　西	Shaanxi	24766	22766	2000	1.3	11.9
甘　肃	Gansu	16022	14983	1039	12.5	81.1
青　海	Qinghai	1697	1435	262	0.1	0.3
宁　夏	Ningxia	1116	878	238	0.4	1.2
新　疆	Xinjiang	2547	1782	765	1.0	5.9
新疆兵团	Xinjiang Corps	58	3	55	0.0	0.6
黑龙江垦区	Heilongjiang Land Reclamation	32	1	31	0.0	0.1

十二、残疾人服务设施建设
Service Facilities for Persons with Disabilities

4-12-1 残疾人综合服务设施
Comprehensive Service Facilities for Persons with Disabilities

地区	Region	已投入使用项目 Projects in Operation		
		本年度新投入使用项目 Projects Getting into Operation in 2017		
		项目个数 Number of Projects	建设规模 Construction Area	总投资 Total Investment
		个 unit	平方米 square meter	万元 10,000 yuan
全国	**Total**	**73**	**318401**	**121402.5**
北京	Beijing			
天津	Tianjin			
河北	Hebei			
山西	Shanxi	1	2500	500.0
内蒙古	Inner Mongolia			
辽宁	Liaoning			
吉林	Jilin			
黑龙江	Heilongjiang			
上海	Shanghai			
江苏	Jiangsu	3	25853	20160.0
浙江	Zhejiang	6	29039	13706.9
安徽	Anhui	3	6692	1600.0
福建	Fujian	5	22572	6522.0
江西	Jiangxi	3	7173	1678.6
山东	Shandong	2	20246	9686.4
河南	Henan	1	1060	115.0
湖北	Hubei	2	2135	1050.0
湖南	Hunan	2	1310	393.0
广东	Guangdong	7	127800	45765.2
广西	Guangxi			
海南	Hainan			
重庆	Chongqing	1	1100	168.0
四川	Sichuan	11	24437	7044.5
贵州	Guizhou	1	4135	830.0
云南	Yunnan	2	3552	1344.2
西藏	Tibet	15	18200	6086.0
陕西	Shaanxi	2	8500	1300.0
甘肃	Gansu			
青海	Qinghai	1	1000	394.0
宁夏	Ningxia	1	3060	1024.8
新疆	Xinjiang	4	8038	2034.0
新疆兵团	Xinjiang Corps			
黑龙江垦区	Heilongjiang Land Reclamation			

4-12-1 续表 1 Continued 1

地 区	Region	已投入使用项目 Projects in Operation		
		累计已投入使用项目 Accumulated Projects in Operation		
		项目个数 Number of Projects	建设规模 Construction Area	总投资 Total Investment
		个 unit	平方米 square meter	万元 10,000 yuan
全 国	**Total**	**2340**	**5330030**	**1549095.3**
北 京	Beijing	6	70776	45323.5
天 津	Tianjin	23	87282	46446.3
河 北	Hebei	138	139942	26739.2
山 西	Shanxi	53	126255	34429.7
内蒙古	Inner Mongolia	67	86642	20369.9
辽 宁	Liaoning	120	268219	93334.9
吉 林	Jilin	46	84435	21539.9
黑龙江	Heilongjiang	98	113753	36836.4
上 海	Shanghai	15	21870	11453.5
江 苏	Jiangsu	81	522784	193961.0
浙 江	Zhejiang	95	567848	214432.3
安 徽	Anhui	85	191555	42683.4
福 建	Fujian	85	201089	64713.3
江 西	Jiangxi	73	74337	17650.9
山 东	Shandong	126	321720	76672.1
河 南	Henan	144	226045	39272.9
湖 北	Hubei	88	182795	34661.2
湖 南	Hunan	101	127243	24257.9
广 东	Guangdong	104	544207	158774.1
广 西	Guangxi	101	145134	25680.1
海 南	Hainan	10	13022	3919.0
重 庆	Chongqing	27	79819	23289.2
四 川	Sichuan	141	338226	96067.9
贵 州	Guizhou	58	62035	11527.2
云 南	Yunnan	127	164455	31714.4
西 藏	Tibet	28	32637	10542.0
陕 西	Shaanxi	77	161881	35469.5
甘 肃	Gansu	90	94071	29617.9
青 海	Qinghai	22	41105	13647.7
宁 夏	Ningxia	17	31252	7757.3
新 疆	Xinjiang	78	195464	54703.0
新疆兵团	Xinjiang Corps	10	7183	999.0
黑龙江垦区	Heilongjiang Land Reclamation	6	4949	608.6

4-12-1 续表 2 Continued 2

地 区	Region	在建项目 Projects under Construction		
		项目个数 Number of Projects	建设规模 Construction Area	总投资 Total Investment
		个 unit	平方米 square meter	万元 10,000 yuan
全 国	**Total**	**152**	**1095336**	**392997.5**
北 京	Beijing	2	24945	18556.7
天 津	Tianjin	2	31356	17207.6
河 北	Hebei	2	1600	190.0
山 西	Shanxi	6	17299	4440.8
内蒙古	Inner Mongolia	5	49431	21008.6
辽 宁	Liaoning	3	18489	7236.0
吉 林	Jilin	2	2893	2022.0
黑龙江	Heilongjiang	4	2942	485.0
上 海	Shanghai			
江 苏	Jiangsu	2	14000	12500.0
浙 江	Zhejiang	6	122049	71270.5
安 徽	Anhui	11	71472	17526.8
福 建	Fujian	8	68368	24764.6
江 西	Jiangxi	7	22685	5122.0
山 东	Shandong	5	19530	5389.0
河 南	Henan	4	117882	31074.0
湖 北	Hubei	4	49419	10990.0
湖 南	Hunan	2	14000	2680.0
广 东	Guangdong	6	90670	29537.0
广 西	Guangxi	5	11747	2025.8
海 南	Hainan	4	18826	6888.1
重 庆	Chongqing			
四 川	Sichuan	30	121239	36242.6
贵 州	Guizhou	4	56930	22615.4
云 南	Yunnan	5	17316	3530.0
西 藏	Tibet	5	3660	1750.0
陕 西	Shaanxi	3	16300	3980.0
甘 肃	Gansu	2	7398	1677.5
青 海	Qinghai	6	48000	15180.0
宁 夏	Ningxia			
新 疆	Xinjiang	6	38891	7907.7
新疆兵团	Xinjiang Corps			
黑龙江垦区	Heilongjiang Land Reclamation	1	16000	9200.0

4-12-1　续表 3　Continued 3

地　区	Region	筹建项目 Projects under Discussion and Preparation		
		项目个数 Number of Projects	建设规模 Construction Area	总投资 Total Investment
		个 unit	平方米 square meter	万元 10,000 yuan
全　国	**Total**	**45**	**259246**	**100657.8**
北　京	Beijing			
天　津	Tianjin			
河　北	Hebei	1	500	200.0
山　西	Shanxi	5	13336	4277.0
内蒙古	Inner Mongolia	1	1000	300.0
辽　宁	Liaoning	1	3000	570.0
吉　林	Jilin			
黑龙江	Heilongjiang	2	1100	290.0
上　海	Shanghai			
江　苏	Jiangsu			
浙　江	Zhejiang	1	4342	1603.0
安　徽	Anhui	1	4000	660.0
福　建	Fujian	1	500	150.0
江　西	Jiangxi			
山　东	Shandong			
河　南	Henan	3	2300	256.0
湖　北	Hubei	2	2416	865.8
湖　南	Hunan	5	20142	7870.0
广　东	Guangdong	10	136766	62316.0
广　西	Guangxi			
海　南	Hainan	2	16828	6557.0
重　庆	Chongqing			
四　川	Sichuan	1	20071	3200.0
贵　州	Guizhou			
云　南	Yunnan	1	801	200.0
西　藏	Tibet	1	1000	330.0
陕　西	Shaanxi	2	11097	4950.0
甘　肃	Gansu	4	4082	1003.0
青　海	Qinghai	1	15965	5060.0
宁　夏	Ningxia			
新　疆	Xinjiang			
新疆兵团	Xinjiang Corps			
黑龙江垦区	Heilongjiang Land Reclamation			

4-12-2 残疾人康复设施
Rehabilitation Service Facilities for Persons with Disabilities

地区	Region	已投入使用项目 Projects in Operation		
		本年度新投入使用项目 Projects Getting into Operation in 2017		
		项目个数 Number of Projects	建设规模 Construction Area	总投资 Total Investment
		个 unit	平方米 square meter	万元 10,000 yuan
全国	**Total**	**73**	**475108**	**150108.4**
北京	Beijing			
天津	Tianjin			
河北	Hebei	1	200	
山西	Shanxi			
内蒙古	Inner Mongolia	6	52823	15058.0
辽宁	Liaoning	3	17421	5731.2
吉林	Jilin	2	11560	5402.0
黑龙江	Heilongjiang	1	8000	2400.0
上海	Shanghai			
江苏	Jiangsu	1	12680	7750.0
浙江	Zhejiang	3	10730	3028.0
安徽	Anhui	3	30995	11558.0
福建	Fujian	2	3800	1230.0
江西	Jiangxi			
山东	Shandong	8	50647	18385.0
河南	Henan	3	18879	3651.0
湖北	Hubei	2	23665	11234.4
湖南	Hunan	5	41373	9416.0
广东	Guangdong	4	18101	5360.0
广西	Guangxi	1	8084	3169.0
海南	Hainan	1	2085	504.7
重庆	Chongqing	2	26200	13593.1
四川	Sichuan	4	32490	12403.0
贵州	Guizhou	3	28703	4570.0
云南	Yunnan	3	6450	1009.0
西藏	Tibet	5	6343	2428.0
陕西	Shaanxi	2	10000	1560.0
甘肃	Gansu	1	4984	1020.0
青海	Qinghai	1	4000	1300.0
宁夏	Ningxia			
新疆	Xinjiang	4	25895	5148.0
新疆兵团	Xinjiang Corps	1	15000	2400.0
黑龙江垦区	Heilongjiang Land Reclamation	1	4000	800.0

4-12-2 续表 1 Continued 1

地 区	Region	已投入使用项目 Projects in Operation		
		累计已投入使用项目 Accumulated Projects in Operation		
		项目个数 Number of Projects	建设规模 Construction Area	总投资 Total Investment
		个 unit	平方米 square meter	万元 10,000 yuan
全 国	**Total**	**833**	**2614410**	**807973.0**
北 京	Beijing	3	13221	8273.7
天 津	Tianjin	9	9720	2186.0
河 北	Hebei	8	39607	9750.1
山 西	Shanxi	39	97935	23508.8
内蒙古	Inner Mongolia	14	66067	18607.0
辽 宁	Liaoning	22	100321	23956.5
吉 林	Jilin	10	39502	15758.0
黑龙江	Heilongjiang	5	13465	3000.8
上 海	Shanghai	5	100462	44601.0
江 苏	Jiangsu	60	207511	70774.3
浙 江	Zhejiang	38	252009	96941.7
安 徽	Anhui	17	63500	28909.4
福 建	Fujian	217	39712	12112.6
江 西	Jiangxi	5	49179	9020.0
山 东	Shandong	94	562864	155213.2
河 南	Henan	15	94518	19961.6
湖 北	Hubei	16	59758	18774.4
湖 南	Hunan	40	86207	18942.5
广 东	Guangdong	55	167478	44902.7
广 西	Guangxi	5	22301	6324.0
海 南	Hainan	2	2205	524.7
重 庆	Chongqing	9	52814	22363.1
四 川	Sichuan	38	162617	71837.0
贵 州	Guizhou	6	42225	10190.0
云 南	Yunnan	3	6450	1009.0
西 藏	Tibet	13	22369	8358.0
陕 西	Shaanxi	39	80231	19539.7
甘 肃	Gansu	7	29901	7974.7
青 海	Qinghai	3	14625	3680.0
宁 夏	Ningxia	3	15141	5060.0
新 疆	Xinjiang	19	35600	8458.0
新疆兵团	Xinjiang Corps	10	40394	12560.5
黑龙江垦区	Heilongjiang Land Reclamation	4	24500	4900.0

4-12-2 续表 2 Continued 2

地 区	Region	在建项目 Projects under Construction		
		项目个数 Number of Projects	建设规模 Construction Area	总投资 Total Investment
		个 unit	平方米 square meter	万元 10,000 yuan
全 国	**Total**	**282**	**2351232**	**731828.5**
北 京	Beijing			
天 津	Tianjin	1	9000	8700.0
河 北	Hebei	3	90134	47703.0
山 西	Shanxi	8	44383	13525.5
内蒙古	Inner Mongolia	13	70450	19725.0
辽 宁	Liaoning	1	11517	2800.0
吉 林	Jilin	4	38070	10828.9
黑龙江	Heilongjiang	6	42300	8740.0
上 海	Shanghai			
江 苏	Jiangsu	7	74454	35020.3
浙 江	Zhejiang	4	83270	49294.2
安 徽	Anhui	10	96188	19185.0
福 建	Fujian	4	25193	5461.3
江 西	Jiangxi	21	172988	33124.0
山 东	Shandong	26	227069	64545.1
河 南	Henan	19	145396	39053.7
湖 北	Hubei	16	137003	57004.3
湖 南	Hunan	11	101950	20230.0
广 东	Guangdong	9	86747	42340.2
广 西	Guangxi	16	99475	24045.1
海 南	Hainan	2	4624	1500.4
重 庆	Chongqing	12	110836	34727.0
四 川	Sichuan	7	53883	15408.0
贵 州	Guizhou	17	124716	30698.6
云 南	Yunnan	10	100118	27701.7
西 藏	Tibet	1	920	380.0
陕 西	Shaanxi	6	54008	15437.0
甘 肃	Gansu	16	115931	25565.5
青 海	Qinghai	5	27333	8137.0
宁 夏	Ningxia	15	114571	41402.8
新 疆	Xinjiang	8	44107	9745.0
新疆兵团	Xinjiang Corps	4	44600	19800.0
黑龙江垦区	Heilongjiang Land Reclamation			

4-12-2 续表 3 Continued 3

地 区	Region	筹建项目 Projects under Discussion and Preparation		
		项目个数 Number of Projects	建设规模 Construction Area	总投资 Total Investment
		个 unit	平方米 square meter	万元 10,000 yuan
全 国	**Total**	**44**	**352329**	**128405.2**
北 京	Beijing			
天 津	Tianjin			
河 北	Hebei	3	11810	2644.0
山 西	Shanxi	1	3640	728.0
内蒙古	Inner Mongolia	1	2000	600.0
辽 宁	Liaoning			
吉 林	Jilin			
黑龙江	Heilongjiang			
上 海	Shanghai			
江 苏	Jiangsu	1	3000	300.0
浙 江	Zhejiang	1	35841	19372.0
安 徽	Anhui			
福 建	Fujian			
江 西	Jiangxi			
山 东	Shandong	1	5000	1600.0
河 南	Henan	2	7800	1400.0
湖 北	Hubei	6	45188	13148.0
湖 南	Hunan	6	56039	15248.0
广 东	Guangdong	6	14608	3611.2
广 西	Guangxi	4	18320	3866.0
海 南	Hainan	1	5976	2778.0
重 庆	Chongqing	1	82583	46303.0
四 川	Sichuan			
贵 州	Guizhou	3	17844	3886.2
云 南	Yunnan	2	14237	4155.0
西 藏	Tibet	3	14772	5965.9
陕 西	Shaanxi			
甘 肃	Gansu	1	8000	1600.0
青 海	Qinghai			
宁 夏	Ningxia			
新 疆	Xinjiang	1	5670	1200.0
新疆兵团	Xinjiang Corps			
黑龙江垦区	Heilongjiang Land Reclamation			

4-12-3 残疾人托养设施
Fostering Service Facilities for Persons with Disabilities

地 区	Region	已投入使用项目 Projects in Operation		
		本年度新投入使用项目 Projects Getting into Operation in 2017		
		项目个数 Number of Projects	建设规模 Construction Area	总投资 Total Investment
		个 unit	平方米 square meter	万元 10,000 yuan
全 国	**Total**	**97**	**295119**	**97402.2**
北 京	Beijing			
天 津	Tianjin	1	1000	29.0
河 北	Hebei	1	3000	450.0
山 西	Shanxi	2	4500	1100.0
内蒙古	Inner Mongolia	2	5000	1200.0
辽 宁	Liaoning	3	42459	28100.0
吉 林	Jilin	2	4000	950.0
黑龙江	Heilongjiang	4	8000	1200.0
上 海	Shanghai			
江 苏	Jiangsu	3	17117	4630.0
浙 江	Zhejiang	4	36335	16781.0
安 徽	Anhui	1	2000	400.0
福 建	Fujian	4	17820	5300.0
江 西	Jiangxi	5	13042	2900.0
山 东	Shandong	3	3296	1020.0
河 南	Henan	10	29156	6150.0
湖 北	Hubei	4	11185	2013.6
湖 南	Hunan	4	4530	738.0
广 东	Guangdong	8	2270	270.0
广 西	Guangxi	2	3988	600.0
海 南	Hainan			
重 庆	Chongqing	1	5900	1510.0
四 川	Sichuan			
贵 州	Guizhou	5	25244	7140.0
云 南	Yunnan	5	11714	3522.2
西 藏	Tibet	2	8409	2415.0
陕 西	Shaanxi	2	7367	1177.0
甘 肃	Gansu	2	4000	800.0
青 海	Qinghai	4	8001	2360.0
宁 夏	Ningxia	1	2000	440.0
新 疆	Xinjiang	9	7786	2426.4
新疆兵团	Xinjiang Corps	1	2000	350.0
黑龙江垦区	Heilongjiang Land Reclamation	2	4000	1430.0

4-12-3 续表 1 Continued 1

地 区	Region	已投入使用项目 Projects in Operation		
		累计已投入使用项目 Accumulated Projects in Operation		
		项目个数 Number of Projects	建设规模 Construction Area	总投资 Total Investment
		个 unit	平方米 square meter	万元 10,000 yuan
全 国	**Total**	**649**	**1611861**	**442853.7**
北 京	Beijing			
天 津	Tianjin	17	11413	3896.0
河 北	Hebei	16	61719	12951.7
山 西	Shanxi	5	10900	2407.0
内蒙古	Inner Mongolia	12	21234	4358.6
辽 宁	Liaoning	26	86274	37454.8
吉 林	Jilin	8	22169	5429.0
黑龙江	Heilongjiang	11	25479	5956.5
上 海	Shanghai	12	7260	1593.0
江 苏	Jiangsu	58	303670	101765.6
浙 江	Zhejiang	26	182964	74482.7
安 徽	Anhui	8	19469	6078.3
福 建	Fujian	45	64178	11375.6
江 西	Jiangxi	14	45336	10344.0
山 东	Shandong	37	112590	32834.0
河 南	Henan	17	49711	9678.0
湖 北	Hubei	21	41006	7697.6
湖 南	Hunan	51	51934	6855.5
广 东	Guangdong	47	69919	13057.1
广 西	Guangxi	7	11315	1780.3
海 南	Hainan			
重 庆	Chongqing	2	5968	1707.9
四 川	Sichuan	21	39889	11138.7
贵 州	Guizhou	9	34877	9122.0
云 南	Yunnan	5	11714	3522.2
西 藏	Tibet	3	11109	3415.0
陕 西	Shaanxi	50	114889	15176.0
甘 肃	Gansu	9	18929	4500.3
青 海	Qinghai	28	53545	15131.2
宁 夏	Ningxia	1	2000	440.0
新 疆	Xinjiang	28	27878	6707.4
新疆兵团	Xinjiang Corps	51	80005	15220.9
黑龙江垦区	Heilongjiang Land Reclamation	4	12521	6777.0

4-12-3 续表 2 Continued 2

地 区	Region	在建项目 Projects under Construction		
		项目个数 Number of Projects	建设规模 Construction Area	总投资 Total Investment
		个 unit	平方米 square meter	万元 10,000 yuan
全 国	**Total**	**401**	**1312191**	**354788.6**
北 京	Beijing			
天 津	Tianjin			
河 北	Hebei	16	38987	7442.9
山 西	Shanxi	14	35007	9301.7
内蒙古	Inner Mongolia	17	46551	11953.0
辽 宁	Liaoning	6	12700	2860.0
吉 林	Jilin	3	10935	4378.0
黑龙江	Heilongjiang	18	47134	10193.5
上 海	Shanghai			
江 苏	Jiangsu	4	49438	13760.0
浙 江	Zhejiang	25	201327	78191.5
安 徽	Anhui	8	27880	6620.6
福 建	Fujian	2	10726	3627.0
江 西	Jiangxi	21	44080	6888.0
山 东	Shandong	9	30402	6932.8
河 南	Henan	25	84721	18703.0
湖 北	Hubei	12	40438	7758.0
湖 南	Hunan	16	54195	20646.9
广 东	Guangdong	6	25550	10848.0
广 西	Guangxi	18	47936	8239.5
海 南	Hainan	3	7080	3043.6
重 庆	Chongqing	8	25058	8681.0
四 川	Sichuan	11	31326	8576.0
贵 州	Guizhou	60	202653	48710.9
云 南	Yunnan	23	55580	14286.5
西 藏	Tibet	1	5748	2095.0
陕 西	Shaanxi	9	22925	5175.0
甘 肃	Gansu	21	54820	12213.1
青 海	Qinghai	4	8688	2552.9
宁 夏	Ningxia	10	26634	8289.0
新 疆	Xinjiang	17	38770	7410.2
新疆兵团	Xinjiang Corps	14	24900	5411.0
黑龙江垦区	Heilongjiang Land Reclamation			

4-12-3　续表 3　Continued 3

地　区	Region	筹建项目 Projects under Discussion and Preparation		
		项目个数 Number of Projects	建设规模 Construction Area	总投资 Total Investment
		个 unit	平方米 square meter	万元 10,000 yuan
全　国	**Total**	**44**	**209821**	**68053.8**
北　京	Beijing			
天　津	Tianjin			
河　北	Hebei	4	13392	2935.0
山　西	Shanxi	1	1500	150.0
内蒙古	Inner Mongolia	5	11984	2830.0
辽　宁	Liaoning	1	1200	600.0
吉　林	Jilin	1	5193	1550.0
黑龙江	Heilongjiang			
上　海	Shanghai			
江　苏	Jiangsu			
浙　江	Zhejiang	2	23674	12498.0
安　徽	Anhui	1	4022	600.0
福　建	Fujian	1	1000	275.0
江　西	Jiangxi			
山　东	Shandong	1	66667	28300.0
河　南	Henan	1	2000	300.0
湖　北	Hubei	1	2000	419.2
湖　南	Hunan	9	20848	5262.8
广　东	Guangdong	1	200	10.0
广　西	Guangxi	1	9800	1200.0
海　南	Hainan	1	3000	825.0
重　庆	Chongqing	2	10709	2845.0
四　川	Sichuan	1	4280	1200.0
贵　州	Guizhou	3	6000	1176.0
云　南	Yunnan	3	10682	2476.0
西　藏	Tibet			
陕　西	Shaanxi			
甘　肃	Gansu	2	6000	1571.85
青　海	Qinghai			
宁　夏	Ningxia			
新　疆	Xinjiang	2	5670	1030
新疆兵团	Xinjiang Corps			
黑龙江垦区	Heilongjiang Land Reclamation			

十三、信息化建设
Informatization

4-13-1 残疾人事业信息化建设
Informationzation on the Work for Persons with Disabilities

地区	Region	门户网站 Websites	省级 At Provincial Level	地市级 At Prefectural/ City Level	县级 At County Level	本年度省级统计工作培训情况 Training for Statistics and Management at Provincial Level in 2017: 举办统计工作培训班 Training Course for Statistics and Management	本年度省级统计工作培训情况 Training for Statistics and Management at Provincial Level in 2017: 参加统计工作培训班 Participants of Training Course
		个 unit	个 unit	个 unit	个 unit	期 course	人次 person-time
全　国	**Total**	**1504**	**31**	**276**	**1197**	**34**	**2132**
北　京	Beijing	17	1		16	2	130
天　津	Tianjin	8	1		7	1	100
河　北	Hebei	62	1	10	51	1	50
山　西	Shanxi	49	1	8	40	1	45
内蒙古	Inner Mongolia	62	1	10	51	1	50
辽　宁	Liaoning	64	1	14	49	1	41
吉　林	Jilin	39	1	10	28	1	30
黑龙江	Heilongjiang	16	1	5	10		
上　海	Shanghai	17	1		16	1	150
江　苏	Jiangsu	100	1	13	86	1	50
浙　江	Zhejiang	88	1	11	76	1	110
安　徽	Anhui	81	1	15	65	1	50
福　建	Fujian	98	1	9	88	1	30
江　西	Jiangxi	41	1	8	32	2	90
山　东	Shandong	74	1	16	57	1	27
河　南	Henan	59	1	15	43	1	55
湖　北	Hubei	45	1	12	32	1	85
湖　南	Hunan	57	1	14	42	1	100
广　东	Guangdong	79	1	21	57	1	65
广　西	Guangxi	88	1	15	72	1	150
海　南	Hainan	16	1	3	12	1	40
重　庆	Chongqing	28	1		27	1	50
四　川	Sichuan	88	1	19	68		
贵　州	Guizhou	25	1	3	21	1	29
云　南	Yunnan	33	1	11	21	1	60
西　藏	Tibet	1	1			1	80
陕　西	Shaanxi	58	1	10	47	1	38
甘　肃	Gansu	56	1	10	45	1	30
青　海	Qinghai	11	1	3	7	1	73
宁　夏	Ningxia	15	1	3	11	2	104
新　疆	Xinjiang	28	1	7	20	1	120
新疆兵团	Xinjiang Corps	1		1		1	60
黑龙江垦区	Heilongjiang Land Reclamation					1	40

分省统计报告

Statistical Report of Provinces

2017 年北京市残疾人事业发展统计公报

2017 年，全市各级残联以习近平新时代中国特色社会主义思想为指引，深入学习贯彻党的十九大精神，认真落实市委、市政府关于残疾人事业决策部署，紧紧抓住“服务首都城市战略定位”和“加快推进残疾人小康进程”两条主线，开拓创新，务实进取，开创了首都残疾人事业发展新局面。

一、康复

残疾预防和康复服务得到全面提升。经市政府同意，《北京市残疾预防行动计划（2017—2020 年）》颁布实施，明确全行业、全人群、全生命周期的残疾风险综合防控措施，22 项指标全国首创或领先。残疾儿童康复服务全覆盖，严重精神障碍患者救治救助无盲区，千名康复人才接受专业培训，精准康复比例达到 81.6%。

2017 年，173806 名持证残疾人得到基本康复服务，其中视力残疾人 14812 名、听力残疾人 9876 名、言语残疾人 26 名、肢体残疾人 98226 名、智力残疾人 13785 名、精神残疾人 27611 名、多重残疾人 9460 名。截至 2017 年底，全市已有残疾人专门康复机构 130 个。

二、教育

融合教育成效突出。推动制定第二期《特殊教育提升计划》，努力实现“一人一案”。开展随班就读“全员随访”，适龄残疾孩子入园难、入学难得到初步缓解，残疾学生随班就读率达到 66.6%，残疾学生高考录取率达到 95.5%，且 81%学生实现在普通高校就学。开展学前阶段和高等院校融合教育试点，覆盖全学段融合教育体系逐步建立。

继续实施中国残疾人事业专项彩票公益金助学项目，各级残联多渠道争取资金支持，共为 298 名残疾儿童给予学前教育资助。

全市共有特殊教育普通高中班（部）在校生 296 人，其中聋生 184 人，盲生 112 人。残疾人中等职业学校（班）在校生 241 人，毕业生 66 人。全市共有 89 名残疾人被普通高等院校录取，141 名残疾人进入特殊教育学院学习。138 名残疾青壮年文盲接受了扫盲教育。

三、就业

精准就业有所突破。将农村低收入残疾人增收纳入全市统筹。率先将盲人医疗按摩人员职称评审、继续教育、执业备案纳入卫生技术人员统一管理，盲人医疗按摩实现了质的跨越。贯彻落实残疾人职业技能提升计划，将残疾人职业培训纳入终身职业技能培训制度，残疾人就业能力得到提升。

截至 2017 年 12 月 31 日，就业实名制库显示：城乡持证残疾人就业人数为 107020 人，其中按比例就业 39527 人，集中就业 5161 人，个体就业 4535 人，社区就业 4661 人，公益性岗位就业 2728 人，辅助性就业 1468 人，居家就业 3159 人，从事农业种养加 17069 人，灵活就业 28712 人。

培训盲人保健按摩人员 223 名、盲人医疗按摩人员 105 名；保健按摩机构 484 个，医疗按摩机构 4 个；有 14 人通过专业技术职务资格评审获得初级职称评审。

四、扶贫

坚决落实好中央、市委市政府部署的扶贫帮扶任务，不让一名残疾人掉队。贯彻落实市委市政府关于扶持产业帮扶一批、促进就业帮扶一批、山区搬迁帮扶一批、生态建设帮扶一批、社会保障兜底一批、社会力量帮扶一批的总体要求，力争从全市层面解决好低保、低收入残疾人家庭帮扶任务。

2017 年，接受实用技术培训的残疾人达到 7092 人次。

全市共建设 27 个残疾人扶贫基地，安置 1012 名残疾人就业，扶持带动 1090 名残疾人户。

完成 381 户农村贫困残疾人危房改造，各地投入危房资金 4151500 元。

五、社会保障

残疾人基本生活保障实现全覆盖。全面落实“两项补贴”制度，13.24 万人享有生活补贴，19.74 万人获得护理补贴。残疾人作为五类重点人群之一纳入基本公共卫生服务，91 个康复项目纳入基本医疗保障范围，残疾人参加城乡居民医疗保险获得全额资助。完善养护照料体系，居家服务、喘息式托养、机构托养相结合，一户多残、老残一体、重度残疾人及其家庭生活质量得到改善。制定精准帮扶“1+6”行动计划，努力确保全面小康残疾人“一个不能少”。

截至 2017 年底，全市城乡残疾居民参加城乡居民社会养老保险人数达到 95710 名，60 周岁以下参保残疾居民 77025 人，领取待遇的 18685 人。44356 名 60 周岁以下的重度残疾人参保，其中 44351 名得到了政府的参保扶助。32669 名 60 周岁以下的非重度残疾人参保，其中 27796 名非重度残疾人也享受了全额或部分代缴养老保险费的优惠政策。

残疾人托养服务工作稳步推进，残疾人托养服务机构达到 108 个，其中寄宿制托养服务机构 87 个，综合性托养服务机构 21 个，为 1443 名残疾人提供了托养服务。接受居家服务的残疾人达到 127496 人。全年有 255 名托养服务管理和服务人员接受了各级各类专业培训。

六、宣传文化

残疾人广泛参与社会文化生活。全市残疾人在第九届全国残疾人艺术汇演中获得 3 个一等奖，打造“薪火相传”文化品牌，600 名残疾人参加非遗文化传承培训，3000 余名残疾人书画艺术爱好者走进基层，为广大市民送去艺术享受。残疾人文化周、外语游园会、棋牌赛等群众性文体活动蓬勃开展，生动反映出残疾人参与社会的热情和渴望。

残疾人在国际交往活动中更加活跃。残疾人事务纳入“一带一路”合作框架，全市轮椅篮球女队为“一带一路”沿线国家提供体育技术援助。承担亚太残疾人十年中期审查高级别政府间会议服务保障工作及才艺展示任务，市区残联服务机构多次接待外国领导人和国际组织代表访问，展现首都水准。残疾人日益成为推动包容发展、服务国家外交的重要力量。

截至 2017 年底，开设市级残疾人专题广播节目 1 个、电视手语栏目 2 个；区级电视手语栏目 3 个。市、区两级公共图书馆共设立盲文及盲文有声读物阅览室 7 个，共开展残疾人文化周活动 454 场次。

七、体育

积极参与 2022 年冬残奥会筹办。根据国际残奥委会对无障碍环境的要求及北京承诺，与规划国土委“双牵头”，明确任务清单和指南。制定《残疾人冬残奥会行动计划》，在城市无障碍环境建设、残疾人冰雪运动项目推动、冰雪运动产业发展、群众性宣传文化活动推广以及冬残奥会志愿者培养等方面，提出总体思路、目标任务和具体举措。组建 5 支冰雪运动队伍，23 人成功入选国家集训队。在冰壶锦标赛、越野滑雪锦标赛、国际网联轮椅网球团体世界杯赛获得冠军，在残疾人世界田径锦标赛、北欧滑雪世界杯赛、乒乓球亚锦赛上创造历史最好成绩，充分展现了首都残疾人顽强拼搏、超越自我的精神风貌。着力普及残疾人冰雪运动，开展冰雪体验季系列活动，1 万人次残疾人走出家门，尽享冰雪运动的欢乐。

截止 2017 年底，落实残疾人康复体育关爱家庭计划共计服务 3100 户，建设残疾人体育健身示范点 75 个，培养健身指导员 2379 名。

八、维权

残疾人维权工作得到加强。法治残联建设的 17 项重点任务全部完成，推荐 336 名同志担任区级或乡镇级人大代表和政协委员，代理残疾人法律救助案件 127 件，为残疾人挽回直接经济损失 32 万元，房产等间接利益 700 多万元，为残疾人提供法律服务 5005 人次，办理残疾人来信、来访、来电及网上咨询共计 1.7 万件次，信访结案率达到 99%。大力加强无障碍环境建设，协调完成中国盲人图书馆周边无障碍改造工作，推动 235 辆无障碍出租车上路运营，为 1.3 万户残疾人居家环境进行无障碍改造，试点对 10 户残疾人家庭单元门内台阶以安装升降平台的方式进行无障碍改造，对 44 处大型交通枢纽、123 条公交线路、173 家市区社区三级医院及周边进行无障碍体验活动，协调解决了北京西站等 6 处无障碍建设问题，开展地面公交、村镇、宾馆无障碍调研，完成《无障碍出行手册—宾馆篇》。

2017年，全市各级人大开展《中华人民共和国残疾人保障法》执法检查和专题调研2次；政协开展视察和专题调研2次。开展市级普法宣传教育活动200次，5000人参加；举办市级法律培训班40个，1455人参加。

截至2017年底，成立残疾人法律救助工作协调机构14个，建立残疾人法律救助工作站9个。

残疾人参政议政工作稳步开展，协助人大代表、政协委员提出议案、建议、提案10件，办理议案、建议、提案15件。

大力加强无障碍环境建设工作，开展无障碍建设检查38次，无障碍培训3609人次。

九、组织建设

需求渠道更加畅通。专项调查实名制掌握了所有持证残疾人基本需求及社区（村）服务设施，区残联“一口受理”试点得到巩固，12385服务热线功能得以拓展，入户调查、窗口申报、电话申报、网络申报相结合，残疾人需求正在从“端菜”到“点菜”。

温馨家园呈现活起来、实起来、强起来的良好势头，街道和社区助残微创投试点运行良好，志愿助残服务向社区和家庭延伸，着力解决好残疾人“最后一公里”问题。

高度重视专门协会作用发挥。完善协会意见建议响应机制，39项意见建议按期办结。深化业务融合，围绕重点工作召开80余次座谈会，对接需求，形成合力。开展第三届“植根基层、精准服务”主题活动，举办残疾人老物件征集和京津冀三地专门协会交流，品牌效应进一步提升。积极稳妥推进各区专门协会法人登记，实施优秀人才“百人工程”，一大批优秀残疾人进入各级专门协会，为可持续发展提供了重要保障。

2017年，市、区、乡（街镇）共建立残联342个，其中区残联16个，乡、镇（街道）残联326个；社区（村）残协6015个。

市、区、乡（街镇）残联实有人员达1242人，乡镇（街道）、村（社区）选聘残疾人专职委员总计6364名。各区残联共配备了残疾人干部21人。

全市共建立各类残疾人专门协会85个，其中市级专门协会5个，区级专门协会80个。全市登记在册的助残社会组织共有184个。

十、服务设施

着力推进全市残疾人职业康复和托养服务中心建设，打造成为展示残疾人事业发展成就以及冬残奥会的重要宣传展示窗口。

截至2017年底，已竣工并投入使用的各级残疾人综合服务设施6个，总建设规模70776平方米，总投资45324万元；已竣工并投入使用的各级残疾人康复设施3个，总建设规模13221平方米，总投资8274万元。

十一、信息化

扩大第三代残疾人证（智能化）应用范围，与10余个委办局25类200余项数据实现交换共享，实现11个残疾人服务事项网上办理，全市累计刷卡记录达2.2亿条，获取外部共享数据2400多万条，变“群众跑腿”为“信息跑路”，变“群众来回跑”为“部门协同办”。其中，残疾人辅具申请、评估、审批、购买实现“一键式”服务，像“网购”一样方便，还能实时“报销”，受到市政府肯定，并作为北京市选报的两个试点案例之一纳入“国家政务信息系统整合共享应用试点”，成为全国首批上线的5个试点之一。

截至2017年底，全市共开通市、区两级残联网站17个。

2017 年天津市残疾人事业发展统计公报

2017 年，在市委、市政府的正确领导和中国残联的有力指导下，在各区、各部门和社会各界的共同支持下，天津市全面完成了残疾人事业各项工作的年度任务，积极推进残疾人社会保障、康复、教育、培训、就业、扶贫、维权、无障碍环境建设、托养、重残护理、文化体育、福利基金、组织建设、服务设施和信息化建设等工作，取得了新的成效和新的突破，残疾人物质和文化生活状况得到进一步改善，各领域服务水平得到进一步提升，现根据 2017 年度残疾人事业统计数据和实际情况，进行分析，并公报如下：

一、残疾人康复工作稳步提升

积极推进残疾人社区康复工作。截至 2017 年底，在 16 个市辖区开展了社区康复工作，为 272693 名残疾人建立了康复服务档案，全市共有社区康复协调员 4446 人，本年度接受康复服务 78365 人。

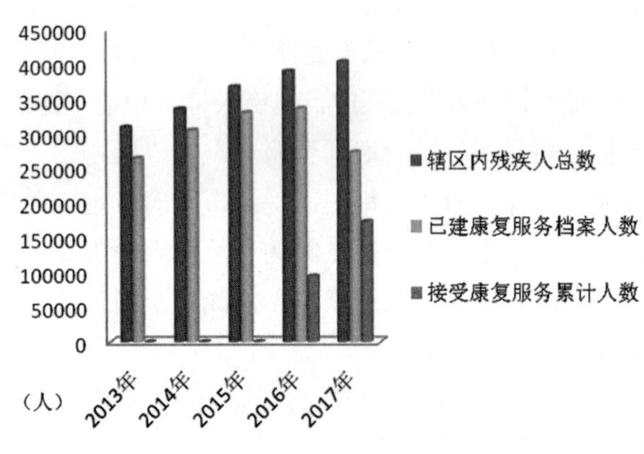

图 1　2013-2017 年社区康复情况

2017 年，制定实施了天津市残疾人精准康复实施方案和残疾预防行动计划，全年共有 60764 名残疾人得到了基本康复服务，使各类别残疾人得到了不同程度的康复。

1．在得到基本康复服务的残疾人中视力残疾人约占 7%，共 4067 人。接受复明手术、定向行走等训练 411 人；接受盲杖、助视器等辅具适配服务 2762 人。

2．在得到基本康复服务的残疾人中听力残疾人为 6256 人、言语残疾人为 1192 人，两个类别共约占 12%。接受人工耳蜗、助听器适配服务 4496 人。

3．在得到基本康复服务的残疾人中肢体残疾人约占 59%，共 35991 人。有 4252 名肢体残疾人接受矫治手术、运动功能训练等服务；接受假肢、矫形器等辅具适配服务 11990 人。

4．在得到基本康复服务的残疾人中智力残疾人约占 9%，共 5194 人。接受认知及适应性训练 178 人。

5．在得到基本康复服务的残疾人中精神残疾人约占 11%，共 6511 人。接受药物治疗及作业疗法训练 3868 人。

6．在得到基本康复服务的残疾人中多重残疾人约占 2%，共 1553 人。

7．截止 2017 年底，全市共建立残疾人康复服务机构 71 个，按机构属性划分：残联办最多，共计 19 个；按残疾类别划分，智力康复机构最多，共计 20 个。

二、残疾人教育工作进展良好

2017 年，为接受各阶段教育的残疾学生和贫困残疾人在校健全子女发放助学金，残疾人整体素质有所提高。全市各特教学校义务教育阶段对残疾学生继续实施“三免一补”（免交杂费、教科书费、住宿费，补贴生活费）政策，实现义务教育阶段免费教育。残疾人特殊教育事业发展稳定。开办特殊教育普通高中 2 所，在校生 115 人。高等特殊教育机构 1 所,录取残疾考生 112 人。有 46 名残疾考生被普通高等院校录取。

三、残疾人就业工作稳步提高

2017 年，城乡残疾人就业总人数为 82427 人。就业形式主要集中在按比例就业、个体就业和农村种植养殖加工业，其中：按比例就业为 46914 人，个体就业为 12922 人，农村种植养殖加工业为 20646 人。

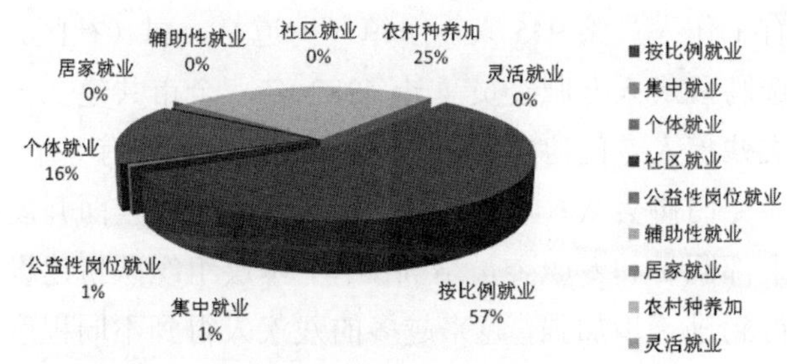

图 2　2017 年就业状况

本年培训盲人保健按摩人员 23 人，培养盲人医疗按摩人员 30 人；保健按摩机构 162 个，医疗按摩机构 4 个。

四、残疾人社会保障工作成效显著

2017 年，全市实际参保的残疾居民为 75582 人，较 2016 年增加了 2608 人。其中领取待遇的有 49960 人，较 2016 年增加了 2397 人。60 周岁以下参保残疾居民 25622 人，较 2016 年增加了 211 人。残疾人托养服务工作稳步推进，残疾人托养服务机构达到 73 个，托养残疾人总数 40764 人，较 2016 年增加了 4487 人，其中享受居家托养服务残疾人 39524 人，较 2016 年增加了 4597 人。

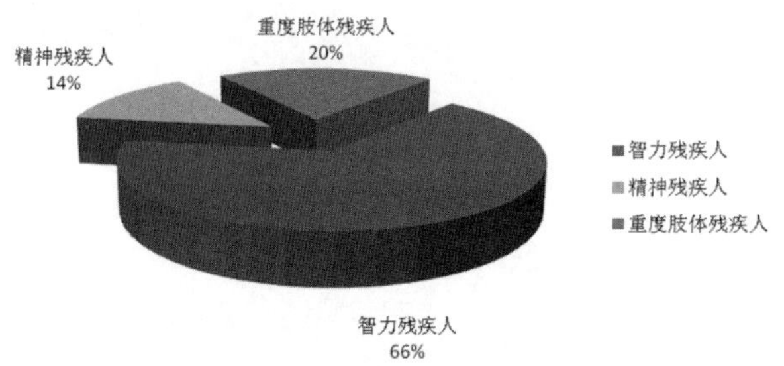

图 3　2017 年在托养服务机构中托养的残疾人情况

五、残疾人扶贫工作快速精准

2017 年，积极动员机关、企事业单位、志愿者组织及党员、干部、学生、街坊邻里等社会各界，采取多种形式，进行“帮、包、带、扶”，并充分发挥工会、共青团、妇联等团体和组织在残疾人扶贫工作中的作用。贫困残疾人生产生活状况得到进一步改善，社会帮扶效果显著，结对帮扶受益残疾人 360 人。扩大农村残疾人精准扶贫范围，提高精准扶贫工作实效，建立残疾人扶贫基地 148 个，安置 1163 名残疾人就业，辐射带动残疾人户共计 3750 户。本年度完成 249 户农村贫困残疾人危房改造，投入危房改造资金 498 万元。

六、残疾人维权工作迈出新步伐

2017 年，制定或修改保障残疾人权益的规范性文件 5 个；各级人大、政协的检查或专题调研 2 次，对残疾人保障法的贯彻实施起到了重要的推动作用。

已建立残疾人法律救助工作协调机构 17 个；建立残疾人法律救助工作站 17 个，办理案件 409 件。残联办理人大建议、政协提案 11 件，残疾人参政议政工作得到加强。

认真做好《天津市无障碍环境建设管理办法》立法调研、修订工作。截止 2017 年底，建立无障碍环境建设领导协调组织 17 个；全市 16 个区全部系统开展无障碍建设。大力实施各类无障碍建设项目，全市大多数新建主要城市道路、公共建筑物、居住建筑都建设了相应的无障碍设施，同时加强了无障碍改造和对已建无障碍设施的管理，我市城市无障碍设施建设得到进一步加强，大大方便了广大残疾人、老年人、妇女、儿童、伤病人和全体社会成员参与社会生活。

2017 年，全市各级残联信访部门共处理来信 248 件，接待来访 1633 人次。完善天津市“助残一键通”和法规政策信息平台建设，残疾人 12385 维权热线运转良好，拓宽残疾人诉求表达渠道，为残疾人维护自身合法权益提供便捷途径，接听和解答残疾人来电 8437 通。

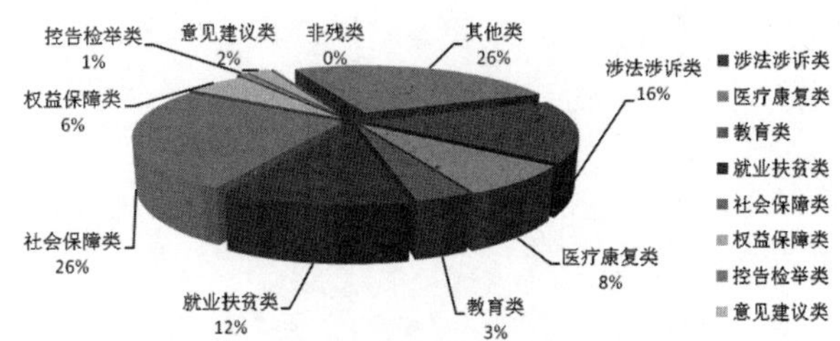

图 4　2017 年残疾人来信（件）情况

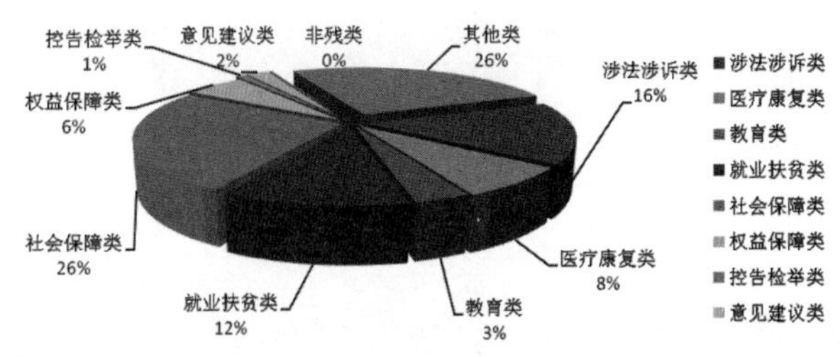

图 5　2017 年残疾人来访（人次）情况

七、宣传文化体育工作广泛深入

2017 年,组织新闻发布会 2 次。开展丰富多彩的群众性残疾人文化活动，举办残疾人文化周活动 30 场次，残疾人参加文化活动 13514 人次。举办残疾人群众体育健身活动 53 次；已建设完成的残疾人体育健身示范点 139 个；组织残疾人体育比赛 10 次，参赛残疾人运动员 102 人次。

八、残疾人组织建设进一步加强

天津市共有各类残疾人 57 万，其中持证残疾人 32 万，占残疾人总数的 56%。截至 2017 年底，全市共建立残联 258 个，其中：已建区残联 16 个，乡镇（街道）残联 242 个；已建村（社区）残协 4598 个，已建残疾人活动室 4595 个。全市残联系统实有工作人员共 945 人，乡镇（街道）、村（社区）选聘残疾人专职委员总计 4282 名。全市共建立各类残疾人专门协会 85 个，助残社会组织共有 8 个。各专门协会认真履行职责，各级残联组织全面开展干部职工和专职委员培训工作，基层组织队伍建设得到进一步加强，越来越多的残疾人得到不同程度的帮助。

九、残疾人工作信息化建设稳步推进

残疾人信息化建设队伍不断壮大，全市各级残联均配备统计工作人员。各级残联独立建立网站 6 个，搭载上级残联、同级政府网站 2 个。重点加大信息化基础设施建设、技术保障和安全投入，提高了残疾人工作信息化水平。

2017年河北省残疾人事业发展统计公报

2017年，在省委、省政府的正确领导和中国残联的精心指导下，省残联坚持以习近平新时代中国特色社会主义思想为指导，深入学习贯彻党的十九大精神和习近平总书记重要讲话精神、关于群团工作重要指示，牢固树立“四个意识”，坚定“四个自信”，认真履行“代表、服务、管理”职能，紧紧围绕残疾人需求，扎实推进残疾人工作，牢牢把握发展大局，夯实基层基础，残疾人事业取得新发展新进步。

一、康复

2017年，342781名残疾儿童及持证残疾人得到基本康复服务,其中包括0-6岁残疾儿童5115人。得到康复服务的持证残疾人中，有视力残疾人30048名、听力残疾人13120名、言语残疾人186名、肢体残疾人240847名、智力残疾人17549名、精神残疾人27095名、多重残疾人12703名。

截至2017年底，全省已有残疾人康复机构439个，其中，提供视力残疾康复服务的机构40个，提供听力言语残疾康复服务的机构102个，提供肢体残疾康复服务的机构189个，提供智力残疾康复服务的机构152个，提供精神残疾康复服务的机构92个，提供孤独症儿童康复服务的机构67个，提供辅助器具服务的机构70个。康复机构在岗人员达13071人，其中，管理人员1744人，专业技术人员8900人，其他人员2427人。

二、教育

实施残疾人事业专项彩票公益金助学项目，为1000人次家庭经济困难的残疾儿童享受普惠性学前教育提供资助。主动协调省财政厅、省教育厅将当年考上高等院校研究生专业和本科专业的贫困残疾学生资助（一次性补助）标准由3000元分别提高为6000元、5000元，有效缓解了贫困残疾学生上学压力，有力保障了困难残疾学生受教育权利,残疾人受教育权得到了更好保障。

全省共有特殊教育普通高中班（部）10个，在校生518人，其中聋生358人，盲生160人。残疾人中等职业学校（班）4个，在校生315人，毕业生149人，其中35人获得职业资格证书。有343名残疾人被普通高等院校录取。

继续实施《“十三五”残疾青壮年文盲扫盲行动方案》，948名残疾青壮年文盲接受了扫盲教育。

三、就业

截止2017年底，全省城乡持证残疾人就业人数为618533人，其中按比例就业16656人，其中本年新增717人；集中就业7440人，本年新增155人；个体就业18902人，本年新增481人；社区就业2126人，本年新增40人；公益性岗位就业1434人，本年新增32人；辅助性就业3403人，本年新增85人；居家就业70897人，本年新增681人；从事农业种养加437864人，本年新增8070人；灵活就业59811人，本年新增2550人。

全年共培训盲人保健按摩人员1117名、盲人医疗按摩人员573名；保健按摩机构达到531个，医疗按摩机构达到67个；在专业技术职务资格评审中，有104人通过医疗按摩人员初级职称评审。

四、扶贫

会同省委组织部等24个部门和单位联合出台《河北省贫困残疾人脱贫攻坚行动计划（2017-2020年）》，明确部门职责，通过实施九个一批、开展残疾人扶贫十项专项重点行动，精准帮扶每一名贫困残疾人脱贫。出台《河北省建档立卡贫困村残疾人辅助器具适配方案》，为3000多人提供了辅助器具服务。

2017年，贫困残疾人得到有效扶持，其中35862人通过扶贫开发实现脱贫；接受实用技术培训的残疾人达到42463人次。

康复扶贫贴息贷款扶持 235 名农村残疾人。截止 2017 年底，全省残疾人扶贫基地达到 248 个，安置 4481 名残疾人就业，扶持带动 12343 名残疾人户。

完成 3536 户农村贫困残疾人家庭危房改造，各地投入危房改造资金 49275666 元。

五、社会保障

截至 2017 年底，城乡残疾居民参加城乡社会养老保险人数达到 1463301 名，269009 名 60 岁以下的重度残疾人参保，其中 265660 名得到了政府的参保扶助，代缴养老保险费比例达到 98.8%。有 249539 名非重度残疾人也享受了全额或部分代缴养老保险费的优惠政策。452954 人领取养老金。

经省政府批准，省财政厅、省民政厅、省残联联合发文，从 2018 年开始，将困难残疾人生活补贴标准和重度残疾人护理补贴标准由每人每月 55 元、50 元分别调高到每人每月 66 元、60 元，有力促进残疾人生活改善。

残疾人托养服务工作稳步推进。残疾人托养服务机构达到 233 个，其中寄宿制托养服务机构 111 个，日间照料机构 37 个，综合性托养服务机构 85 个，为 10848 名残疾人提供了托养服务。接受居家服务的残疾人达到 8563 人。全年 358 名托养服务管理和服务人员接受了各级各类专业培训。

六、宣传文化

组织开展了“美丽河北 最美残疾人”推选展示活动， 140 多万人次关注并投票，推选出 9 名最美残疾人和 20 名优秀残疾人。截至 2017 年底，共有省级残疾人专题广播节目 1 个；市级残疾人专题广播节目 8 个、电视手语栏目 10 个。

截至 2017 年底，省市县三级公共图书馆共设立盲文及盲文有声读物阅览室 26 个，共开展残疾人文化周活动 314 场次；省市两级残联共举办残疾人文化艺术类的比赛及展览 33 次，共有各类残疾人艺术团 8 个。

七、体育

全省残疾人康复体育关爱家庭服务 10200 户，建设残疾人体育健身示范点 253 个，培养健身指导员 4055 名。举办残疾人群众体育健身活动 14 次，2431 人次参加了残疾人群众体育健身活动。举办第二届“冰雪河北 快乐你我”省残疾人冰雪运动季活动，带动近 9 万人次残疾人参与冰雪运动。

认真做好冬季项目运动员后备人才的选拔、培养、试训、输送，目前，省级注册冬季项目运动员共计 191 人（全国占比 34%），省级冬季项目在训运动员 136 人，输送中国残联训练营参训 118 人，入选国家队运动员 52 人。2017 年度，组队参加了 5 项全国冬季项目锦标赛，共获得 33 金 23 银 20 铜，并在平昌冬残奥会等国际比赛中实现成绩突破，为备战 2022 年冬残奥会奠定了坚实的基础。

组织参加了 12 项全国夏季项目锦标赛，共取得 87 金、42 银、30 铜的好成绩。组队参加了 2017 年 11 项国际赛事，获得 41 枚金牌、9 枚银牌、8 枚铜牌、破 2 项世界纪录的好成绩。在第二十三届听障奥运会上，我省运动员王萌一人夺三金，刷新了我省最好成绩，为国家和家乡赢得了荣誉。

八、维权

2017 年，制定或修改保障残疾人权益的规范性文件省级 2 个、地市级 2 个、县级 7 个。县级以上人大开展《中华人民共和国残疾人保障法》执法检查和专题调研 17 次；政协开展视察和专题调研 18 次。开展省级普法宣传教育活动 2 次，2000 人参加。

截至 2017 年底，成立残疾人法律救助工作协调机构 152 个，建立残疾人法律救助工作站 151 个。建立“12385 残疾人服务热线”。残疾人通过热线咨询范围涉及残疾人办证、残疾人政策、心理疏导以及投诉、求助和建议等多个方面内容，省残联建立了督办反馈机制。截至 2017 年底，共接服务热线 7 千多人次，经过各级残联共同努力，残疾人的合理需求均得到了很好的解决，热线拉近了省残联与残疾人距离。

残疾人参政议政工作稳步开展，各地残联协助人大代表、政协委员提出议案、建议、提案 34 件，办理议案、建议、提案 19 件。

无障碍建设法规、标准进一步完善。系统开展无障碍建设市、县、区 180 个；开展无障碍建设检查 48 次，无障碍培训 175 人次。

九、组织建设

2017 年，市县乡共建立残联 2481 个，各市已建残联 11 个，县（市、区）残联已建 170 个，乡镇（街道）残联已建 2300 个；已建社区（村）残协 51492 个。

省市县乡残联实有人员达 5676 人，乡镇（街道）、村（社区）选聘残疾人专职委员总计 53463 名。市级残联配备了残疾人领导干部 10 人，县级残联配备了残疾人干部 174 人。

共建立省级及以下各类残疾人专门协会 896 个，其中省级专门协会已建 5 个，市级专门协会已建 55 个，县级专门协会已建 836 个。全省各级助残社会组织共有 29 个。

十、综合服务设施建设

截至 2017 年底，已竣工并投入使用的各级残疾人综合服务设施 138 个，总建设规模 139942 平方米，总投资 26739 万元；已竣工并投入使用的各级残疾人康复设施 8 个，总建设规模 39607 平方米，总投资 9750 万元；已竣工并投入使用的各级残疾人托养服务设施 16 个，总建设规模 61719 平方米，总投资 12952 万元。

十一、信息化建设

截至 2017 年底，10 个市、51 个县级残联开通网站。

2017年山西省残疾人事业发展统计公报

2017年，在省委、省政府的坚强领导和中国残联的正确指导下，认真贯彻党的十九大精神和习近平总书记视察山西重要讲话精神，围绕一条主线，办好两件实事，突出三个重点，主动担当，积极作为，扎实工作，推动残疾人事业持续健康发展。

一、康复

2017年，28.1万名残疾儿童及持证残疾人得到基本康复服务。得到康复服务的持证残疾人中，有视力残疾人2.3万名、听力残疾人8683名、言语残疾人52名、肢体残疾人18.7万名、智力残疾人2.8万名、精神残疾人2.6万名、多重残疾人8221名。

截至2017年底，全省已有残疾人康复机构308个，其中，提供视力残疾康复服务的机构68个，提供听力言语残疾康复服务的机构54个，提供肢体残疾康复服务的机构133个，提供智力残疾康复服务的机构129个，提供精神残疾康复服务的机构69个，提供孤独症儿童康复服务的机构36个，提供辅助器具服务的机构59个。康复机构在岗人员达1.0万人，其中，管理人员1186人，专业技术人员7417人，其他人员1703人。

二、教育

实施残疾人事业专项彩票公益金助学项目，为911人次家庭经济困难的残疾儿童享受普惠性学前教育提供资助。各地也积极多渠道争取资金支持，对2名残疾儿童给予学前教育资助。

省彩票公益金助学项目资助183名残疾大学生、23名残疾研究生、239名残疾人家庭子女大学生。

共有特殊教育普通高中班（部）10个，在校生502人，其中：聋生467人，盲生35人。有375名残疾人被普通高等院校录取。

506名残疾青壮年文盲接受了扫盲教育。

三、就业

城乡持证残疾人就业人数为29.1万人，其中：按比例就业5500人，集中就业6020人，个体就业9849人，社区就业1174人，公益性岗位就业1069人，辅助性就业1009人，居家就业15229人。从事农业种养加23.1万人，灵活就业2.1万人。

培训盲人保健按摩人员777名、盲人医疗按摩人员852名。保健按摩机构达到587个，医疗按摩机构达到59个。在专业技术职务资格评审中，分别有6人和9人通过医疗按摩人员中级和初级职称评审。

四、扶贫

2017年，贫困残疾人得到有效扶持，2.4万人通过扶贫开发实际脱贫；接受实用技术培训的残疾人达到1.1万人次。

康复扶贫贴息贷款扶持60名农村残疾人。残疾人扶贫基地达到118个，安置2019名残疾人就业，扶持带动2451名残疾人户。

完成405户农村贫困残疾人危房改造。

基层党组织扶贫助残行动，帮扶3000户建档立卡贫困残疾人。

五、社会保障

截至2017年底，城乡残疾居民参加城乡社会养老保险人数达到105.5万名，16.6万名60岁以下的重度残疾人参保，其中16.0万名得到了政府的参保扶助，代缴养老保险费比例达到96.3%。有6.7万名非重度残疾人也享受了全额或部分代缴养老保险费的优惠政策。49.8万人领取养老金。

残疾人托养服务工作稳步推进，残疾人托养服务机构达到92个，其中：寄宿制托养服务机构30个、日间照料机构25个、综合性托养服务机构37个，为2612名残疾人提供了托养服务。接受居家服务的残疾人达到1445人。全年58名托养服务管理和服务人员接受了各级各类专业培训。

六、宣传文化

截至2017年底，共有省级残疾人专题广播节目

1 个、电视手语栏目 1 个；地市级残疾人专题广播节目 9 个、电视手语栏目 5 个。

截至 2017 年底，省市县三级公共图书馆共设立盲文及盲文有声读物阅览室 11 个，共开展残疾人文化周活动 198 场次；省市两级残联共举办残疾人文化艺术类的比赛及展览 11 次，共有各类残疾人艺术团 6 个。

七、体育

全省残疾人康复体育关爱家庭服务 7250 户，建设残疾人体育健身示范点 85 个，培养健身指导员 812 名。

八、维权

2017 年，制定或修改保障残疾人权益的规范性文件县级 3 个。县级以上人大开展《中华人民共和国残疾人保障法》执法检查和专题调研 9 次；政协开展视察和专题调研 9 次。开展省级普法宣传教育活动 5 次，1100 人参加；举办省级法律培训班 3 个，230 人参加。

截至 2017 年底，成立残疾人法律救助工作协调机构 18 个，建立残疾人法律救助工作站 14 个。

残疾人参政议政工作稳步开展，各地残联协助人大代表、政协委员提出议案、建议、提案 18 件，办理议案、建议、提案 18 件。

无障碍建设法规、标准进一步完善。系统开展无障碍建设市、县、区 72 个；开展无障碍建设检查 39 次，无障碍培训 860 人次。

开展家庭无障碍改造扶贫助残行动，对 1600 户贫困残疾人家庭进行了无障碍改造。

九、组织建设

2017 年，市县乡共建立残联 1595 个，各市已建残联 11 个，县（市、区）残联已建 120 个，乡镇（街道）残联已建 1464 个；已建社区（村）残协 2.3 万个。

省市县乡残联实有人员达 4392 人，乡镇（街道）、村（社区）选聘残疾人专职委员总计 2.5 万名。市级残联配备了残疾人领导干部 10 人，县级残联配备了残疾人干部 98 人。

共建立省级及以下各类残疾人专门协会 634 个，其中：省级专门协会已建 5 个、市级专门协会已建 55 个、县级专门协会已建 574。助残社会组织共有 10 个。

十、服务设施

截至 2017 年底，已竣工并投入使用的各级残疾人综合服务设施 53 个，总建设规模 12.6 万平方米，总投资 34430 万元；已竣工并投入使用的各级残疾人康复设施 39 个，总建设规模 9.8 万平方米，总投资 23509 万元；已竣工并投入使用的各级残疾人托养服务设施 5 个，总建设规模 1.1 万平方米，总投资 2407 万元。

十一、信息化建设

截至 2017 年底，8 个地市、40 个县级残联开通网站。

2017年内蒙古自治区残疾人事业发展统计公报

2017年，在自治区党委、政府的坚强领导和中国残联的精心指导下，在相关部门和社会各界的大力支持下，在各级残联共同努力下，全区残疾人工作以深入学习宣传贯彻党的十九大精神为主线，紧紧围绕推进残疾人小康进程、全面小康不让一个残疾人掉队这个关键，主动担当、积极作为，推动残疾人各项工作深入开展，促进了残疾人事业的进步和残疾人民生的改善。

一、康复

2017年，全区104332名残疾儿童及持证残疾人得到基本康复服务,其中包括0-6岁残疾儿童1262人。得到康复服务的持证残疾人中，有视力残疾人9768名、听力残疾人9255名、言语残疾人203名、肢体残疾人65555名、智力残疾人5923名、精神残疾人9561名、多重残疾人3871名。

截至2017年底，全区有残疾人康复机构223个，其中，提供视力残疾康复服务的机构43个，提供听力言语残疾康复服务的机构47个，提供肢体残疾康复服务的机构91个，提供智力残疾康复服务的机构55个，提供精神残疾康复服务的机构24个，提供孤独症儿童康复服务的机构35个，提供辅助器具服务的机构70个。康复机构在岗人员达5859人，其中：管理人员1037人，专业技术人员3997人，其他人员825人。

二、教育

实施残疾人事业专项彩票公益金助学项目，为264人次家庭经济困难的残疾儿童享受普惠性学前教育提供资助。各地也积极多渠道争取资金支持，对39名残疾儿童给予学前教育资助。

全区共有特殊教育普通高中班（部）6个，在校生283人，其中：聋生226人、盲生57人。残疾人中等职业学校（班）2个，在校生37人、毕业生27人，其中18人获得职业资格证书。有455名残疾人被普通高等院校录取。有870名残疾青壮年文盲接受了扫盲教育。

三、就业

截止2017年底，城乡持证残疾人就业人数累计237209人，其中：按比例就业10791人，集中就业6990人，个体就业24260人，社区就业2676人，公益性岗位就业1621人，辅助性就业1186人，居家就业19388人，从事农业种养加127616人，灵活就业42681人。

2017年，培训盲人保健按摩人员843名、盲人医疗按摩人员136名；保健按摩机构达到422个，医疗按摩机构达到96个；在专业技术职务资格评审中，39人通过医疗按摩人员初级职称评审。

四、扶贫

2017年，通过各部门的相互协调配合，全区贫困残疾人脱贫攻坚取得了阶段性成效，残疾人的生活状况得到进一步改善。贫困残疾人得到有效扶持，其中8177人通过扶贫开发实际脱贫；接受实用技术培训的残疾人达到2.3万人次。

康复扶贫贴息贷款扶持1万名农村残疾人。全区153个残疾人扶贫基地，安置1934名残疾人就业，扶持带动2792名残疾人户。

全区共完成392户农村贫困残疾人危房改造，各地投入危房资金368.14万元。

五、社会保障

截至2017年底，全区城乡残疾居民参加城乡社会养老保险人数达到41.15万名，9.4万名60岁以下的重度残疾人参保，其中8.3万名得到了政府的参保扶助，代缴养老保险费比例达到87.7%。有4.9万名非重度残疾人也享受了全额或部分代缴养老保险费的优惠政策。18.6万人领取养老金。

残疾人托养服务工作稳步推进，残疾人托养服务机构达到136个，其中寄宿制托养服务机构85个，日间照料机构4个，综合性托养服务机构47个，为

3981名残疾人提供了托养服务。接受居家服务的残疾人达到8067人。全年22名托养服务管理和服务人员接受了各级各类专业培训。

六、宣传文化

截至2017年底，共有自治区级电视手语栏目1个；地市级残疾人专题广播节目3个、电视手语栏目8个。

截至2017年底，自治区、盟市、旗县（市区）三级公共图书馆共设立盲文及盲文有声读物阅览室25个，开展残疾人文化周活动82场次；自治区和各盟市共举办残疾人文化艺术类的比赛及展览11次，共有各类残疾人艺术团7个。

“全国第27次助残日”期间，与自治区党委宣传部共同成功举办了“心手相牵、守望相助”公益慈善晚会和轮椅捐赠、慰问等系列活动。参加第九届全国残疾人艺术汇演，我区选送6个节目分别获得1个评委特别奖、2个二等奖和3个三等奖的好成绩。实施了“文化进社区”、“文化进家庭五个一”、“残疾人文化周”、推进盲人数字阅读等活动。

七、体育

全区建设残疾人体育健身示范点23个，培养健身指导员139名。注重并推动残疾人康复体育、健身体育与竞技体育协调发展，举办了“残疾人健身周”、“内蒙古自治区残疾人冰雪运动季”、“全国特奥日”等活动。参加全国举重锦标赛和第十一届世界冬季特奥运动会，我区4名运动员夺得了2金、2银、1铜的好成绩。积极筹备2018年第五届全区残疾人残运会，经积极协调争取实现了与自治区全运会同城同步举办。

八、维权

各级残联维权组织建设进一步加强，残疾人维权工作全面开展。

2017年，制定或修改保障残疾人权益的规范性文件地市级1个、县级1个。县级以上人大开展《中华人民共和国残疾人保障法》执法检查和专题调研1次。

截至2017年底，成立残疾人法律救助工作协调机构86个，建立残疾人法律救助工作站70个。

残疾人参政议政工作稳步开展，各地残联协助人大代表、政协委员提出议案、建议、提案16件，办理议案、建议、提案4件。

无障碍建设法规、标准进一步完善。系统开展无障碍建设市、县、区64个；开展无障碍建设检查50次，无障碍培训327人次。

九、组织建设

2017年，全区盟市、旗县（市区）、乡镇（街道）共建立残联1248个，各盟市已建残联12个，旗县（市区）残联已建108个，乡镇（街道）残联已建1128个；已建村（社区）残协13284个。

全区各级残联实有人员达3091人，乡镇（街道）、村（社区）选聘残疾人专职委员总计1.4万名。各盟市残联配备了残疾人领导干部29人，各旗县（市区）残联配备了残疾人干部97人。

全区共建立自治区级及以下各类残疾人专门协会564个，其中自治区级专门协会已建5个，盟市级专门协会已建60个，旗县（市区）级专门协会已建499。助残社会组织共有30个。

十、服务设施

残疾人服务设施建设得到全面发展。截至2017年底，全区已竣工并投入使用的各级残疾人综合服务设施67个，总建设规模8.66万平方米，总投资2.04亿元；已竣工并投入使用的各级残疾人康复设施14个，总建设规模6.6万平方米，总投资1.86亿元；已竣工并投入使用的各级残疾人托养服务设施12个，总建设规模2.1万平方米，总投资4359万元。

十一、信息化

截至2017年底，10个盟市、51个旗县（市区）残联开通门户网站。

2017 年辽宁省残疾人事业发展统计公报

2017 年，辽宁省残联贯彻省委、省政府和中国残联的决策部署，主动履职尽责，聚焦脱贫攻坚和小康进程，着力推动残疾人状况改善和全面发展，促进残疾人平等参与社会生活。

一、康复

加大残疾预防和精准康复服务。推动残疾人精准康复与公共卫生服务对接，与健康扶贫工程同步实施，优先覆盖残疾人。

全年会同有关部门联合出台了 11 个政策性文件，以制度性保障推进康复工作。牵头制定《辽宁省残疾预防行动计划（2017—2020 年）》（辽政办发〔2017〕87 号），由省政府办公厅发至全省执行。会同省财政、省卫计委、省物价局等 7 个部门出台《辽宁省残疾人基本康复服务项目实施方案》。

2017 年，全省有 63 个市辖区、43 个县（市）开展了社区康复服务。截至 2017 年 12 月 20 日，全省已累计有 20.7 万名残疾儿童及持证残疾人得到基本康复服务。得到康复服务的持证残疾人中，有视力残疾人 21218 名、听力残疾人 8605 名、言语残疾人 211 名、肢体残疾人 114598 名、智力残疾人 17343 名、精神残疾人 39083 名、多重残疾人 5122 名。

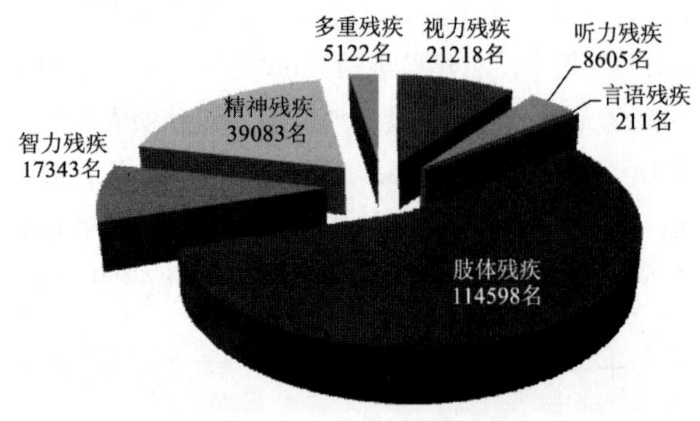

图 1　2017 年残疾人接受康复服务情况（单位：人）

截至 2017 年底，全省已有残疾人康复机构 362 个，其中，提供视力残疾康复服务的机构 59 个，提供听力言语残疾康复服务的机构 47 个，提供肢体残疾康复服务的机构 135 个，提供智力残疾康复服务的机构 98 个，提供精神残疾康复服务的机构 86 个，提供孤独症儿童康复服务的机构 67 个，提供辅助器具服务的机构 116 个。康复机构在岗人员达 1.2 万人，其中，管理人员 1542 人，专业技术人员 8115 人，其他人员 2381 人。我省高度重视康复人才培养，全年培训康复业务人员及管理人员分别为 11574 人次及 3474 人次。

二、教育

加强残疾人教育服务。参与制定《辽宁省第二期特殊教育提升计划实施方案（2017—2020 年）》，确保每一个残疾孩子都能接受合适的教育。

实施残疾人事业专项彩票公益金助学项目，为全省 975 人次家庭经济困难的残疾儿童享受普惠性学前教育提供资助。各地多渠道争取资金支持，资助新入园儿童 447 人，其他残疾儿童学前教育助学项目资助 30 人。

共有特殊教育普通高中班（部）5 个，在校生 262 人。残疾人中等职业学校（班）6 个，招生 100 人，在校生 615 人，毕业生 82 人，其中 35 人获得职业资格证书。全省有 298 名残疾考生达到普通高等院校录取分数线，并全部被录取，72 名残疾考生进入特殊教育学院学习。

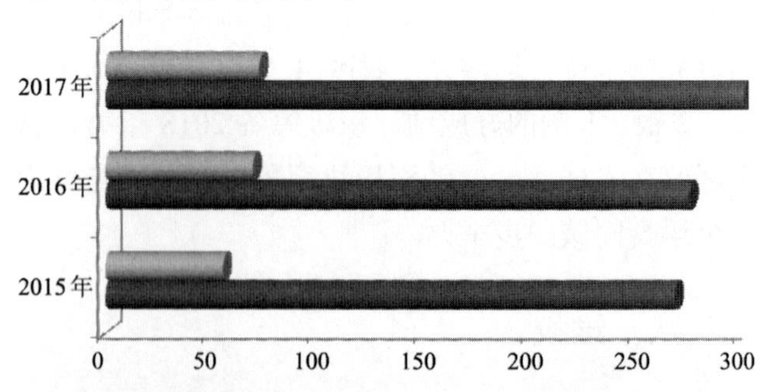

图 2　2015-2017 年高等院校录取残疾考生情况（单位：人）

336 名残疾青壮年文盲接受了扫盲教育。

三、就业

出台《辽宁省超比例安排残疾人就业奖励办

法》和《辽宁省扶持残疾人辅助性就业实施办法》，进一步完善残疾人就业奖励和扶持机制，开展全省首届残疾人电商创业之星大赛、首届高校残疾人毕业生网络招聘会、“启动互联网+，开辟残疾人就业创业新蓝海”为主题的全省残疾人就业促进日等活动，并与省人社厅、省生命学会联合举办辽宁省首届茶艺技能大赛暨全国残疾人岗位精英职业技能竞赛辽宁选拔赛，促进残疾人提升职业技能，实现就业创业。

城乡持证残疾人就业人数为29.1万人，其中按比例就业41431人，集中就业16309人，个体就业17596人，社区就业361人，公益性岗位就业7204人，辅助性就业8428人，居家就业2984人，从事农业种养加156924人，灵活就业40078人。

培训盲人保健按摩人员732名，医疗按摩人员124名；保健按摩机构达到857个，医疗按摩机构达到32个；在专业技术职务资格评审中，分别有6人和16人通过医疗按摩人员中级和初级职称评审。安排盲人保健按摩人员、医疗按摩人员就业人数分别为767人和73人。

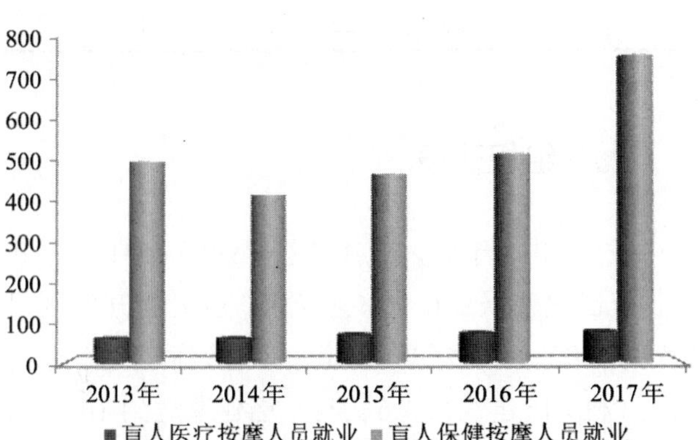

图3 2013-2017年安排盲人按摩就业情况（单位：人）

四、社会保障

强化贫困残疾人兜底保障。截至2017年底，城乡残疾居民参加城乡社会养老保险人数达到39.9万名，60岁以下的参保残疾人中有7.1万名重度残疾人得到了政府的参保扶助，代缴养老保险费比例达到92.8%。有2.4万名非重度残疾人也享受了全额或部分代缴养老保险费的优惠政策。领取养老金待遇的人数达到18.3万人。

残疾人托养服务工作稳步推进，残疾人托养服务机构达到219个，其中寄宿制托养服务机构115个，日间照料机构58个，综合性托养服务机构46个，共为8662名残疾人提供了托养服务。接受居家服务的残疾人达到18741人。全年共有1403名托养服务管理和服务人员接受了各级各类专业培训。

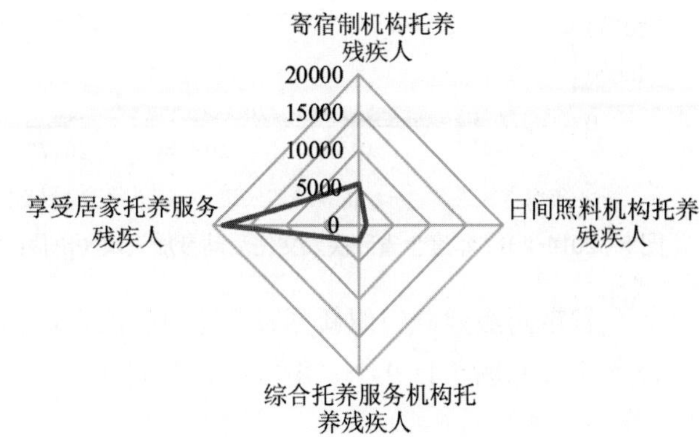

图4 2017年残疾人接受托养服务情况（单位：人）

五、扶贫

残疾人脱贫攻坚工作纳入各级党委政府工作大局。《中共辽宁省委办公厅辽宁省人民政府办公厅转发省残联等27部门和单位关于<贫困残疾人脱贫攻坚行动计划（2017-2020年）>的通知》，提出“到2020年，稳定实现贫困残疾人及其家庭不愁吃、不愁穿，义务教育、基本医疗、住房安全有保障，有效扩大基本康复服务和家庭无障碍改造覆盖面，现行标准下建档立卡贫困残疾人如期稳定脱贫”的总体目标。

2017年，贫困残疾人得到有效扶持，其中3.4万人通过扶贫开发实际脱贫。接受实用技术培训的残疾人达到1.2万人次。残疾人扶贫基地35个，安置957名残疾人就业，扶持带动3412户残疾人。结对帮扶受益残疾人6262名。贫困残疾人家庭优先纳入危房改造计划，推动住建、扶贫部门完成危房改造3122户。

六、宣传文化

强化宣传文化工作。以助残日等残疾人纪念日为节点，围绕残疾人事业重点工作和重大项目，打造立体化宣传格局。

2017年，省市县三级公共图书馆共设立盲文及盲文有声读物阅览室49个，共开展残疾人文化周活动505场次，5.6万人次参加；省市两级残联共举办残疾人文化艺术类的比赛及展览65次，共有各类残疾人艺术团17个。

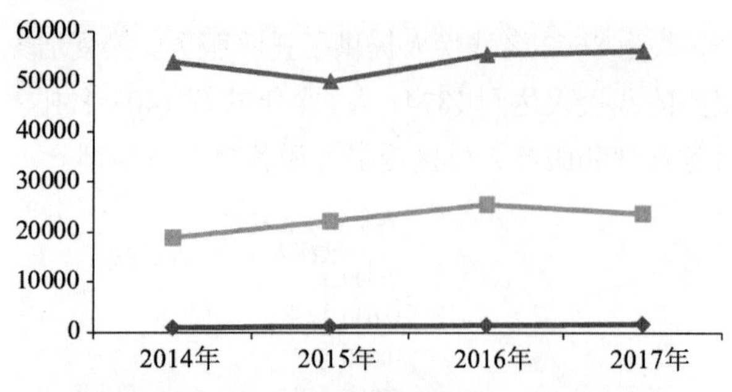

图5 2014-2017年度全省残疾人文化活动参加人次（单位：人）

省市两级残联组织新闻发布会10次、广播电台残疾人专题节目9个、电视手语栏目14个。

七、体育

全省残疾人康复体育关爱家庭服务1000户，建设残疾人体育健身示范点48个，培养健身指导员1889名。

截至2017年底，全省共组织残疾人体育健身活动751次，2.1万人次参加。

八、维权

加大残疾人权益维护力度。进一步加强残疾人法律救助工作站建设，为残疾人提供优先优质法律服务，基本做到"应援尽援"。截至2017年底，全省成立残疾人法律救助工作协调机构80个，建立残疾人法律救助工作站73个，办理案件250件。

省及14个市全部开通12385残疾人维权服务热线，启动辽宁省全国残疾人信访信息系统和民心网"网络回应人"制度，建立领导班子定期接访制度，形成立体化、多方位信访服务格局。帮助解决残疾人合理合法诉求，确保残疾人群体基本稳定。

2017年，出台了《辽宁省无障碍环境建设管理规定》，修改了《辽宁省实施<中华人民共和国残疾人保障法>办法》。县级以上人大开展《中华人民共和国残疾人保障法》执法检查和专题调研8次；政协开展视察和专题调研9次。开展省级普法宣传教育活动14次，1300人参加。

残疾人参政议政工作稳步开展，各级残联协助人大代表、政协委员提出议案、建议、提案54件，残联办理议案、建议、提案46件。

无障碍建设法规、标准进一步完善。全省系统开展无障碍建设市、县、区5个；开展无障碍环境建设检查90次，无障碍培训4400人次。

表1 2017年度全省残疾人法律救助情况

级　别	法律救助协调机构（个）	法律救助	
		工作站（个）	办理案件（件）
省　级	1	1	5
地市级	14	14	103
县　级	65	58	142
总　计	80	73	250

表2 2017年度全省残疾人参政议政情况

级　别	人大			政协		
	人大代表（人）	协助人大代表提出议案、建议（件）	办理人大建议（件）	政协委员（人）	协助政协委员提出提案（件）	办理政协提案（件）
省　级	1	6	5	1	6	7
地市级	10	10	16	30	22	15
县　级	119	4	1	106	6	2
总　计	130	20	22	137	34	24

九、组织建设

截至2017年底，市县乡建立残联1631个，其中各市已建残联14个，县（市、区）含开发区已建残联102个，乡镇（街道）已建残联1515个；社区（村）已建残协1.6万个。已建率达到100%。

省市县乡残联实有人员3918人，乡镇（街道）、村（社区）选聘残疾人专职委员总计1.7万名。地市级残联配备残疾人干部28人，县级残联配备残疾人干部103人。全省共有助残志愿者6.7万人，受助残疾人39.9万人次。

共建立各类残疾人专门协会585个。其中，省级专门协会5个，市级专门协会70个，县级专门协会510个。助残社会组织共有36个。广泛开展志愿助残服务活动和募捐资助工作。志愿助残服务队伍不断壮大，项目不断拓展。

十、服务设施

推进残疾人服务设施和政府购买服务工作。截至 2017 年底，全省已竣工并投入使用的各级残疾人综合服务设施120个，总建设规模26.8万平方米，总投资 9.3 亿元；已竣工并投入使用的各级残疾人康复设施 22 个，总建设规模 10 万平方米，总投资 2.4 亿元；已竣工并投入使用的各级残疾人托养服务设施 26 个，总建设规模 8.6 万平方米，总投资 3.7 亿元。

十一、信息化建设

会同有关厅局出台《辽宁省残疾人事业信息化建设“十三五”实施方案》，残疾人事业信息化建设得到加强。残疾人事业统计工作进一步规范。省残联公众信息无障碍网站稳步运行，对推进政府部门网站无障碍建设起到引领示范作用。

截止 2017 年底，辽宁省残联门户网站发布稿件 6790 篇，已建立省级门户网站 1 个，市级 14 个，县级 49 个，在政务公开和为残疾人提供在线服务方面发挥积极作用。

2017 年吉林省残疾人事业发展统计公报

2017 年，在吉林省委、省政府关心重视下，在中国残联的正确指导下，省残联认真贯彻落实中共中央、国务院和省委、省政府关于发展残疾人事业的重大决策和部署，把残疾人事业融入全省经济社会发展和民生改善的大局，以全面从严治党引领残联工作健康发展，以加快残疾人小康进程为主题，以残疾人脱贫攻坚为重点，坚持把工作重心下移，推动各项重点工作任务落实，残疾人事业实现了新的发展。

一、康复

2017 年，全省围绕“为有需求的残疾儿童和持证残疾人提供基本康复服务的比例达到 50%以上”的目标，坚持保基本、强基础、建机制的基本原则，全面加强新阶段残疾人康复政策与机制建设，深入推动精准康复服务行动，努力在改善残疾人康复服务状况，提升残疾人获得感上实现新进展。

2017 年，154226 名残疾儿童及持证残疾人得到基本康复服务，其中国家建档立卡贫困残疾人 18009 名，因病致（返）贫残疾人 20470 名。得到康复服务的持证残疾人中，有视力残疾人 13551 名、听力残疾人 3969 名、言语残疾人 85 名、肢体残疾人 106394 名、智力残疾人 9116 名、精神残疾人 16522 名、多重残疾人 4114 名。

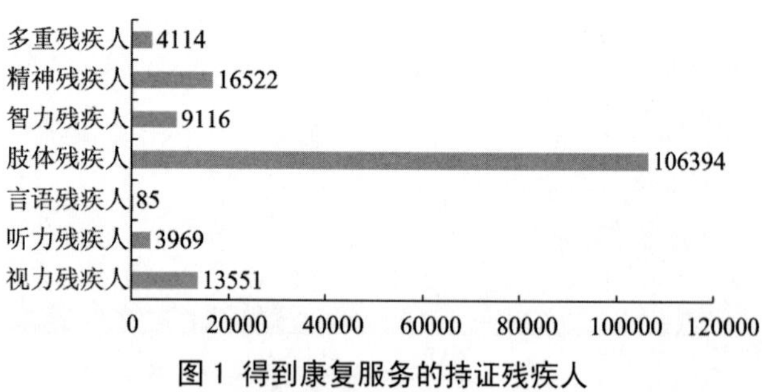

图 1 得到康复服务的持证残疾人

全年为 63915 人次残疾人提供各类辅助器具适配服务，其中，提供助视器、盲杖等适配服务 3404 人次，提供人工耳蜗及助听器验配服务 1759 人次，提供假肢、矫形器、轮椅等适配服务 26311 人次，提供其他各类辅助器具适配服务 32441 人次。

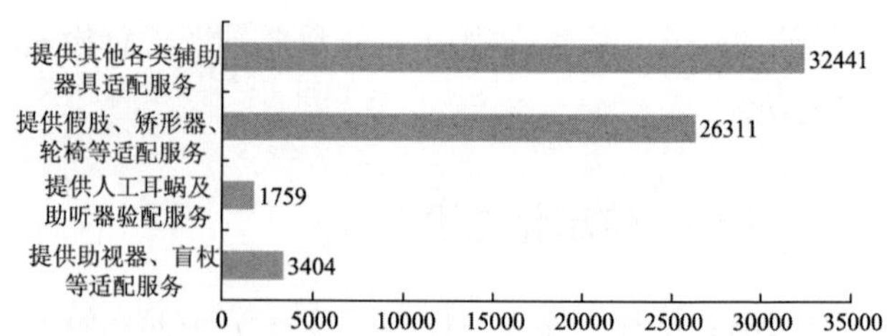

图 2 全年为残疾人提供各类辅助器具适配服务

截至 2017 年底，全省已有残疾人康复机构 213 个，其中，提供视力残疾康复服务的机构 54 个，提供听力言语残疾康复服务的机构 34 个，提供肢体残疾康复服务的机构 80 个，提供智力残疾康复服务的机构 40 个，提供精神残疾康复服务的机构 38 个，提供孤独症儿童康复服务的机构 37 个，提供辅助器具服务的机构 40 个。康复机构在岗人员达 9050 人，其中，管理人员 1417 人，专业技术人员 6014 人，其他人员 1619 人。

31 个市辖区和 40 个县（市）开展社区康复工作，配备 11334 名社区康复协调员。

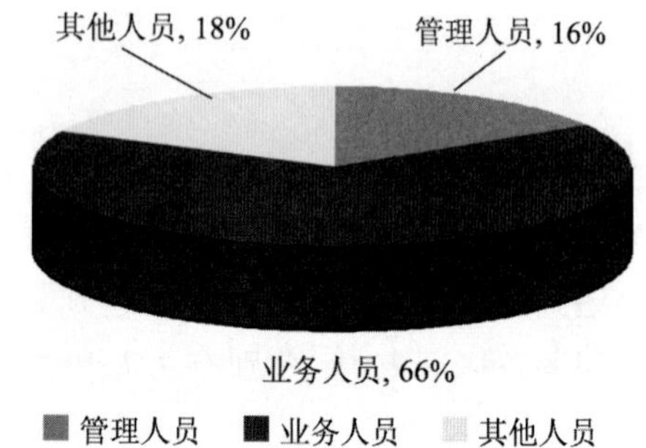

图 3 2017 年残疾人康复机构在岗人员情况

二、教育

实施残疾人事业专项彩票公益金助学项目，省市各地共为 300 人次家庭经济困难的残疾儿童享受普惠性学前教育提供资助。

全省共有特殊教育普通高中班（部）6 个，在校生 223 人，均为聋生。残疾人中等职业学校（班）4 个，在校生 758 人，毕业生 78 人，其中 73 人获得职业资格证书。有 283 名残疾人被普通高等院校录取，204 名残疾人进入特殊教育学院学习。 2208 名残疾青壮年文盲接受了扫盲教育。

为588名残疾人、1000名残疾人子女发放扶残助学金，共计794万元。

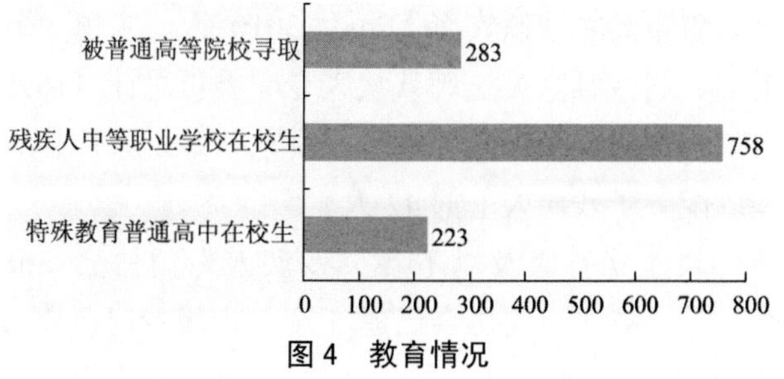

图4　教育情况

三、就业

2017年，城乡持证残疾人就业人数为194770人，其中按比例就业5159人，集中就业5236人，个体就业22517人，社区就业785人，公益性岗位就业2545人，辅助性就业1134人，居家就业11185人，从事农业种养加116766人，灵活就业29443人。

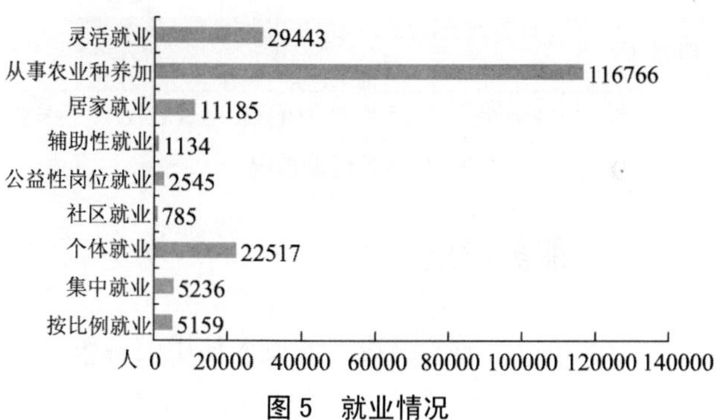

图5　就业情况

盲人按摩事业稳步发展，全省共培训盲人保健按摩人员680名、盲人医疗按摩人员465名；保健按摩机构达到912个，医疗按摩机构达到86个；在专业技术职务资格评审中，分别有3人和22人通过医疗按摩人员中级和初级职称评审。

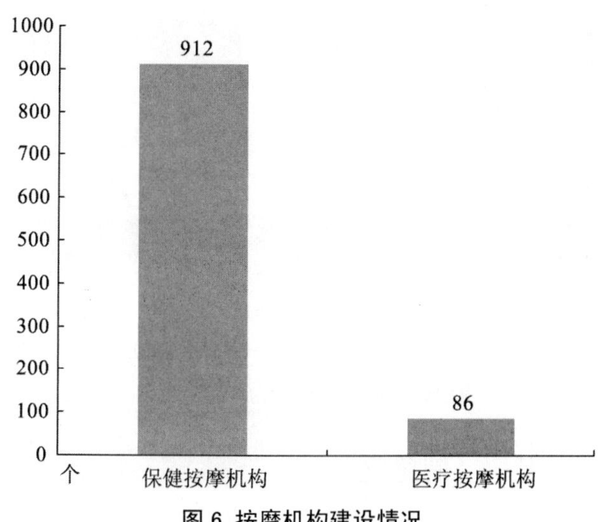

图6 按摩机构建设情况

四、扶贫

全国残疾人脱贫攻坚取得阶段性成果，贫困残疾人得到有效扶持，其中19302人通过扶贫开发实际脱贫；接受实用技术培训的残疾人达到10565人次。

康复扶贫贴息贷款扶持39名农村残疾人。全省246个残疾人扶贫基地，安置2572名残疾人就业，扶持带动6598户残疾人家庭。

各地投入危房改造资金1293226元，完成337户农村贫困残疾人危房改造。

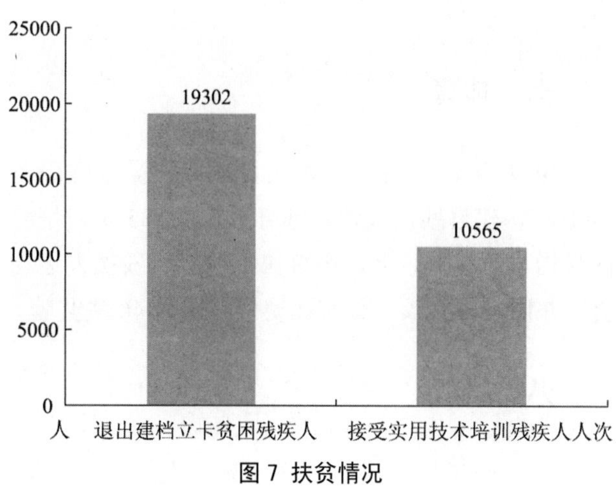

图7 扶贫情况

五、社会保障

截至2017年底，城乡残疾居民参加城乡社会养老保险人数达到304921名，91068名60岁以下的重度残疾人参保，其中85870名得到了政府的参保扶助，代缴养老保险费比例达到94.3%。有63989名非重度残疾人也享受了全额或部分代缴养老保险费的优惠政策。93131人领取养老金。

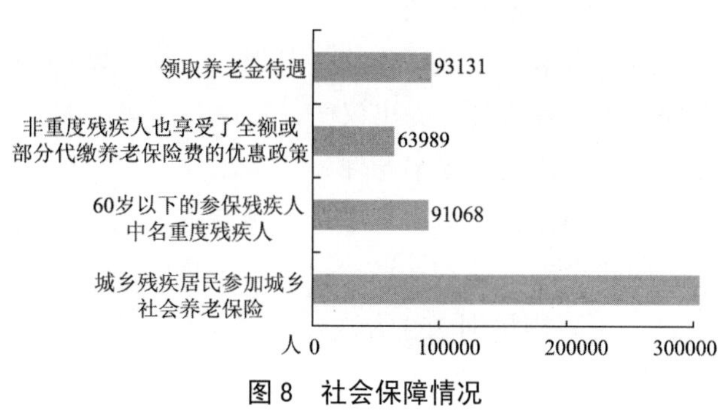

图8　社会保障情况

残疾人托养服务工作稳步推进，残疾人托养服务机构达到69个，其中寄宿制托养服务机构53个，日间照料机构6个，综合性托养服务机构10个，为2278名残疾人提供了托养服务。接受居家服务的残疾人达到4523人。全年17名托养服务管理和服务人员接受了各级各类专业培训。

六、宣传文化

开通省级电视台手语栏目 1 个；市州级残疾人专题广播节目 1 个、电视手语栏目 8 个。

截至 2017 年底，省市县三级公共图书馆共设立盲文及盲文有声读物阅览室 48 个，共开展残疾人文化周活动 152 场次；省市两级残联共举办残疾人文化艺术类的比赛及展览 19 次，现有各类残疾人艺术团 8 个，省残联自办媒体影响力持续提升。

七、体育

2017 年，全省残疾人康复体育关爱家庭服务 3400 户，建设残疾人体育健身示范点 235 个，培养健身指导员 1341 名，举办第二届全省残疾人运动会，在国内外残疾人体育比赛中共获得 46 块奖牌。

八、维权

2017 年，制定或修改了关于残疾人的专门法规、规章市州级 1 个；制定或修改保障残疾人权益的规范性文件省级 1 个、市州级 2 个。县级以上人大开展《残疾人保障法》执法检查和专题调研 4 次；政协开展视察和专题调研 3 次。举办省级法律培训班 1 个，100 人参加。

截至 2017 年底，成立残疾人法律救助工作协调机构 68 个，建立残疾人法律救助工作站 64 个，各级人大代表政协委员中共有残疾人及残疾人工作者 106 名，办理案件 57 件。

残疾人参政议政工作稳步开展，各地残联协助人大代表、政协委员提出议案、建议、提案 9 件，办理议案、建议、提案 5 件。

无障碍建设法规、标准进一步完善。系统开展无障碍建设市、县、区 13 个；开展无障碍建设检查 25 次，无障碍培训 259 人次。

各级残联共处理残疾人来信 523 件，接待来访 2694 人次，其中集体访 47 批次、720 人次，来电 201 次，网上投诉 119 件。

九、组织建设

2017 年，市县乡共建立残联 988 个，各地市已建残联 10 个，县（市、区）残联已建 71 个，乡镇（街道）残联已建 907 个；已建社区（村）残协 11024 个。

省市县乡残联实有人员达 3010 人，乡镇（街道）、村（社区）选聘残疾人专职委员总计 11695 名。地市级残联配备了残疾人领导干部 4 人，县级残联配备了残疾人干部 42 人。

共建立省级及以下各类残疾人专门协会 368 个，其中省级专门协会已建 5 个，市级专门协会已建 50 个，县级专门协会已建 313。助残社会组织共有 63 个。

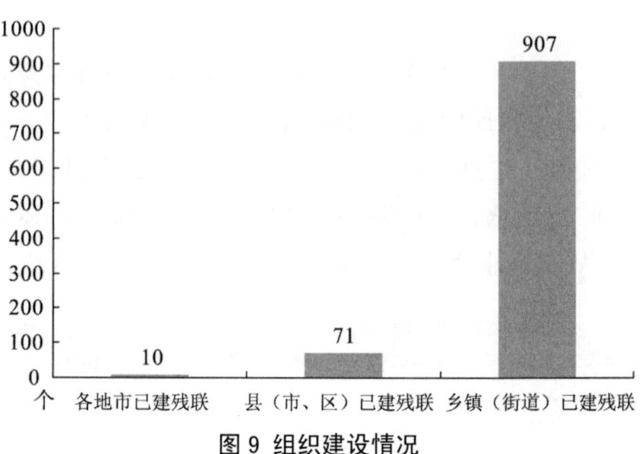

图 9 组织建设情况

十、服务设施

截至 2017 年底，已竣工并投入使用的各级残疾人综合服务设施 46 个，总建设规模 84435 平方米，总投资 21540 万元；已竣工并投入使用的各级残疾人康复设施 10 个，总建设规模 39502 平方米，总投资 15758 万元；已竣工并投入使用的各级残疾人托养服务设施 8 个，总建设规模 22169 平方米，总投资 5429 万元。

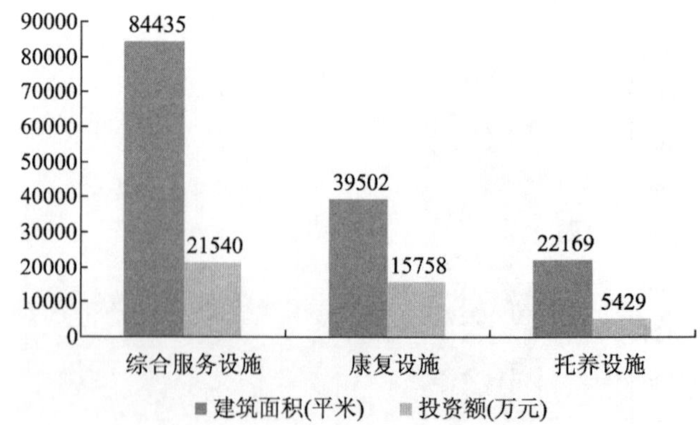

图 10 残疾人服务设施建设情况

十一、信息化

截至 2017 年底，10 个地市、28 个县级残联开通网站。省残联网站获得 2017 年度全国省级残联网站测评第二名。省残联网站组织了“吉林省第二届残疾人运动会”“第六届吉林省残疾人优秀作品（产品）展示（展销）”等多个高水平专题报道，全年发布各类信息 5870 条，微博发布各类信息 2249 条，公众微信发布各类信息 1283 条。发布政策解读信息 40 次，互联网线上接收回答网友各类提问、政策咨询 1494 次。

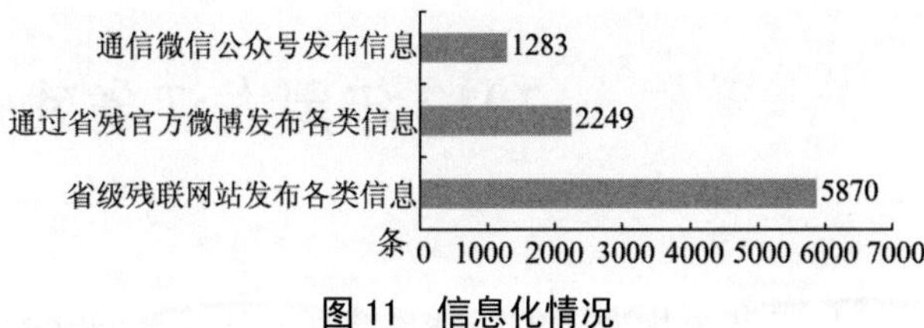

图 11 信息化情况

2017年黑龙江省残疾人事业发展统计公报

2017年，黑龙江省残联系统深入学习贯彻党的十九大精神，认真贯彻落实关于残疾人事业发展的一系列重要部署，在省委、省政府的高度关注下，在中国残联的业务指导下，全力推进我省残疾人事业发展。

一、康复

通过实施精准康复服务，全省有81732名残疾儿童及持证残疾人得到基本康复服务，其中包括0-6岁残疾儿童2270人。得到康复服务的持证残疾人中，有视力残疾人10722名、听力残疾人2681名、言语残疾人39名、肢体残疾人52488名、智力残疾人3762名、精神残疾人9199名、多重残疾人1727名。

截至2017年底，全省已有残疾人康复机构165个，其中，残联办康复机构24个，卫生办康复机构62个，民政办康复机构5个，教育办康复机构24个，民办康复机构39个，其他康复机构11个。全省已有提供视力残疾康复服务的机构36个，提供听力言语残疾康复服务的机构37个，提供肢体残疾康复服务的机构67个，提供智力残疾康复服务的机构54个，提供精神残疾康复服务的机构18个，提供孤独症儿童康复服务的机构43个，提供辅助器具服务的机构17个。全省各类残疾人康复机构在岗人员达4750人，其中，管理人员524人，专业技术人员3333人，其他人员893人。

全省有60个市辖区和62个县（市）开展社区康复工作，配备社区康复协调员6667名，为72074人次提供社区康复服务。

二、教育

实施残疾人事业专项彩票公益金助学项目，为507人次家庭经济困难的残疾儿童享受普惠性学前教育提供资助。

全省共有特殊教育普通高中班（部）1个，在校生8人。残疾人中等职业学校（班）5个，在校生248人，毕业生71人，其中14人获得职业资格证书。全省有199名残疾人被普通高等院校录取，79名残疾人进入特殊教育学院学习。

全省有708名残疾青壮年文盲接受了扫盲教育。

三、就业

全省城乡持证残疾人就业人数241326人，其中按比例就业15347人，集中就业6937人，个体就业27547人，社区就业1905人，公益性岗位就业6447人，辅助性就业2389人，居家就业20515人，从事农业种养加108270人，灵活就业51969人。

全省保健按摩机构318个，医疗按摩机构55个；全年培训盲人保健按摩人员404名、盲人医疗按摩人员101名；在专业技术职务资格评审中，分别有3人和44人通过医疗按摩人员中级和初级职称评审。

四、扶贫

全省贫困残疾人得到有效扶持，有28130名贫困残疾人退出建档立卡。接受实用技术培训的残疾人10758人次。残疾人扶贫基地达到105个，安置2828名残疾人就业，扶持带动残疾人户4814户。完成8759户农村贫困残疾人危房改造，各地投入危房资金9599.7万元。

五、社会保障

截至2017年底，城乡残疾居民参加城乡社会养老保险人数372917人，60岁以下参保的200673名残疾居民中，有55751名重度残疾人，其中52854名得到了政府的参保扶助，代缴养老保险费比例达到94.8%。有34909名非重度残疾人也享受了全额或部分代缴养老保险费的优惠政策。领取养老金待遇的人数172244人。

全省残疾人托养服务工作稳步推进，残疾人托养服务机构98个，其中寄宿制托养服务机构60个，日间照料机构2个，综合性托养服务机构36个。全省共托养残疾人8554人，其中，托养服务机构中托养残疾人3720人，托养服务机构之外享受居家托养服务残疾人 4834 人。全年共有 231 名托养服务管理和服务人员接受了各级各类专业培训。

六、宣文体育

全省共有省级残疾人专题广播节目 1 个、电视手语栏目 2 个；地市级残疾人专题广播节目 8 个、电视手语栏目 6 个。

全省各级公共图书馆共设立盲文及盲文有声读物阅览室 36 个，全年共开展残疾人文化周活动 189 场次，共举办残疾人文化艺术类的比赛及展览 30 次，全省共有各类残疾人艺术团 13 个。

全省建立省级残疾人体育训练基地 5 个，聘任教练员 12 人。全年组织省级残疾人体育比赛 1 次，参赛残疾人运动员 20 人次。通过实施《残疾人康复体育关爱家庭计划》，全省已为 1000 户重度残疾人家庭提供康复体育服务。

七、维权

2017 年，全省地市级制定或修改保障残疾人权益的规范性文件 1 个。全省县级以上人大开展《中华人民共和国残疾人保障法》执法检查和专题调研 16 次；政协开展视察和专题调研 9 次。全省开展省级普法宣传教育活动 1 次，参加人数 237 人；举办省级法律培训班 1 个，参加人数 170 人。

截至 2017 年底，全省成立残疾人法律救助工作协调机构 20 个，建立残疾人法律救助工作站 12 个。

残疾人参政议政工作稳步开展，各地残联协助人大代表、政协委员提出议案、建议、提案 12 件，办理议案、建议、提案 18 件。

全省开展无障碍建设检查 8 次，无障碍培训 218 人次。

八、组织建设

2017 年，全省省市县乡共成立残联 1437 个，各地市已建残联 13 个，县（市、区）残联已建 132 个，乡镇（街道）残联已建 1291 个；已建社区（村）残协 9002 个。

全省省市县乡残联实有人员 3181 人，乡镇（街道）、村（社区）选聘残疾人专职委员总计 6844 名。地市级残联配备了残疾人干部 16 人，县级残联配备了残疾人干部 37 人。

全省共建立省级及以下各类残疾人专门协会 730 个，其中，省级已建专门协会 5 个，市级已建专门协会 65 个，县级已建专门协会 660 个。全省共建立助残社会组织 12 个。

九、服务设施

全省残疾人服务设施建设得到全面发展。截至 2017 年底，已竣工并投入使用的各级残疾人综合服务设施 98 个，总建设规模 113753 平方米，总投资 36836 万元；已竣工的各级残疾人康复设施 5 个，总建设规模 13465 平方米，总投资 3001 万元；已竣工并投入使用的各级残疾人托养服务设施 11 个，总建设规模 25479 平方米，总投资 5956 万元。

十、信息化

省级残疾人综合业务管理平台建成，平台涵盖动态更新、残疾人证管理、精准康复、精准扶贫、就业保障金年审等业务，各业务系统之间实现了数据共享与业务协同，为推进“互利网+助残服务”建设奠定了技术基础。全省残疾人人口基础数据库持证残疾人 105.27 万人。

2017 年，黑龙江省残联开通官方微信公众平台，用户总数持续增加，微信公众平台发布稿件约 68 篇；黑龙江省残联门户网站全新改版上线，网站发布稿件约 527 篇。

截至 2017 年底，全省 5 个地市、10 个县级残联开通网站。

2017年上海市残疾人事业发展统计公报

2017年，在上海市委、市政府的坚强领导和中国残联的具体指导下，上海市残疾人工作紧贴需求优化服务，突出重点优质保障，协调各方主动作为，推动了残疾人事业持续健康发展。

一、康复

通过实施康复服务，全年有21.6万名残疾儿童及持证残疾人得到基本康复服务。得到康复服务的持证残疾人中，视力残疾人有4.3万名，听力残疾有2.1万名，肢体残疾有9.9万名，智力残疾有2.2万名，精神残疾有2.4万名，多重残疾的有0.6万名。全年为9.4万名残疾人提供17.3万余件各类辅助器具适配服务。

截至2017年底，全市已有残疾人康复机构1081个，其中，提供视力残疾康复服务的机构79个，提供听力言语残疾康复服务的机构42个，提供肢体残疾康复服务的机构326个，提供智力残疾康复服务的机构312个，提供精神残疾康复服务的机构242个，提供孤独症儿童康复服务的机构61个，提供辅助器具服务的机构263个。康复机构在岗人员达9030人，其中，管理人员1559人，专业技术人员4273人，其他人员3198人，培训康复管理和业务类人员共计1.6万人。

二、教育

上海市教委、市残联联合印发了《关于加强特殊职业教育管理的实施意见》（沪教委基〔2017〕11号），市级设置2个、各区设置1个特殊职业教育办学点，进一步完善特殊教育体系，加快特殊职业教育发展，建立健全特殊职业教育管理机制，使残疾学生享有优质的职业教育。

全市设立了18个特殊职业教育办学点，其中1个特殊教育普通高中学校（班），在校盲生175人。残疾人中等职业学校（班）17个，在校生516人，毕业98人，其中有44人获得职业资格证书。全年有13名残疾人被特殊高等教育机构录取，70名残疾人进入普通高等院校学习。全年有1659名残疾人学生和生活困难残疾人家庭子女获得助学补贴。

上海开放大学残疾人教育学院开设本科、专科和中专学历教学，2017年有834名残疾人在校就读。

三、就业与扶贫

2017年，全市持证残疾人新增就业6397人次，其中城镇就业新增5506人次，农村城镇就业人数新增891人次。

全市持证残疾人就业人数为7.9万人，其中，按比例就业残疾人3.9万人，约占总人数的49.1%；集中就业残疾人1.8万人，约占总人数的22.5%；从事农村种植、养殖0.5万人，约占总人数5.7%；公益性岗位就业、个体就业、辅助性就业及其它形式就业残疾人1.8万人，约占总人数的22.7%。

全年培训盲人保健按摩人员209人、盲人医疗按摩人员76人，有7人获得初级专业技术职称。全市共有医疗按摩机构1家，保健按摩机构87家。

实施贫困残疾人群体精准扶贫就业，大力开展“帮扶5000名农村困难残疾人劳动增收”实事项目，积极扶持涉残涉农经济组织，全市有198个残疾人扶贫基地，1866名残疾人得到实用技术培训，安置4761名残疾人就业。年投入资金215.9万余元，改造农村困难残疾人家庭180户。

四、社会保障

截至2017年底，城乡残疾居民参加城乡社会养老保障人数达到6.6万名，60周岁以下的参保残疾人中有3.8万名重度残疾人。

落实残疾人“三项补贴”制度，享受“两项补贴”的26.4万人，享受困难残疾人生活补贴7.7万人。

截至2017年底，残疾人托养机构达到819个，其中寄宿制托养服务机构387个，日间照料托养服务机构407个。有3.5万名残疾人接受了托养服务，其中寄宿制机构中托养残疾人0.6人，日间照料机构中托养残疾人1.1万人，综合托养服务机构中托养服务享受居家托养服务残疾人 1.8 万人。全市分别有 222 个阳光之家、214 个阳光心园，共托养残疾人 1.1 万余人次。全年有 3209 名托养服务管理员和服务人员接受专业培训。

五、宣传文化

举办第 27 次“全国助残日”、第 18 个“上海助残周”、首个全国“残疾预防日”、国际残疾人日暨“特奥十年”等系列活动；全年共组织媒体采访 56 次，《新民周刊》“一个不能少”的宣传影响深远广泛，选送的 5 件新闻类作品分获全国残疾人事业新闻一、二、三等奖。截至 2017 年底，全市有残疾人专题广播节目 1 个、电视手语栏目 1 个；区级残疾人专题广播节目 2 个、电视手语栏目 16 个。

专项扶持公共图书馆盲人阅览室建设、残疾人艺术人才培养基地建设。截至 2017 年底，全市共设立 37 个盲文盲人有声读物图书馆，录制（播）无障碍电影 45 部，开展残疾人文化周活动 310 场次，商业影院放映 212 场无障碍电影，全年有 6.6 万多人次参加各级各类文化活动。

六、体育

坚持将残疾人体育基本公共服务融入全民健身计划，全国残疾人康复体育关爱家庭服务 1360 户，新建 171 个残疾人体育健身示范点，配备 938 名残疾人体育健身指导员。举办上海市第九届残疾人运动会，共设田径等 13 个大项，全市 16 个区、5 大类别残疾人报名组团参赛，参赛运动员达到 5000 人。全年共举办残疾人体育比赛 23 次，组织市级残疾人群众体育健身活动 25 次，残疾人参加人数达到 8674 人次。

截至 2017 年底，全市共有 5 个残疾人体育训练基地，在训残疾人运动员达到 186 名。全年在全国各项锦标赛上取得 26 金、30 银、20 铜，在国际赛事上获得 7 金、6 银、1 铜的成绩。

七、维权

通过完善残疾人事业法规体系、强化市区两级残联维权组织、优化无障碍环境建设，残疾人维权工作全面展开。

2017 年，《上海市基本公共服务“十三五”规划》残疾人服务专章得以落地，18 项基本公共服项目纳入政府服务项目清单；梳理残联成立以来的 228 个规范性文件，清理 111 条失效政策。市级人大开展执法检查 1 次；开展普法宣传教育活动 2 次，221 人次参加；举办法律工作培训班 2 个，78 人次参加。

截至 2017 年底，全市成立残疾人法律救助工作协调机构 18 个，建立残疾人法律救助工作站 17 个；创设全国首个手语视频服务的政府服务热线，浦东新区等 5 个区设置视频服务网点。全年共受理残疾人群众来信 973 件，接待残疾人群众来访 3420 人次（含集体访），均得到妥善处理。

2017 年，各级残联协助人大代表、政协委员提出议案、建议、提案共计 7 件，办理议案、建议和提案 15 件。

2017 年，共出台 1 个市、区级无障碍建设与管理法规、政府令；开展无障碍建设检查 1791 次，无障碍培训 2949 人次；全年为 2239 户残疾人家庭进行无障碍改造，为 1.83 万名残疾人发放机动轮椅车燃油补贴。连续实施“为农村困难残疾人家庭实施无障碍改造”市政府实事项目，截至 2017 年底，完成 1001 户农村困难残疾人家庭无障碍改造。

八、组织建设

规范基层组织建设，全市 220 个街镇(乡)残联完成换届，16 个区社区助残劳动公益性组织完成转制工作，举办 2 期助残志愿者、1 期助残社会组织负责人培训班。加快 21 项政府购买助残服务项目落地，全年投入 1.8 亿资金购买助残服务项目 297 个。

全市已建区级残联 16 个，乡镇（街道）残联 219 个；已建社区（村）残协 1289 个。

全市残联系统实有人员达 1089 人，乡镇（街道）、村（社区）选聘残疾人专职委员总计 4762 名，区级残联配备残疾人干部 8 人。

共建立市级及以下各类残疾人专门协会 90 个，其中市级专门协会已建 5 个，区级专门协会已建 85 个，助残社会组织 147 个。

九、服务设施建设

截至 2017 年底，全市累计投入使用的各级残疾人综合服务设施 15 个，总建设规模为 2.2 万平方米，总投资 1.1 亿元；已竣工并投入使用的各级残疾人托养设施 12 个，总建设规模为 7260 平方米，总投资为 1593 万元；已竣工并投入使用的各级残疾人康复设施 5 个，总建设规模为 10 万平方米，总投资 4.5 亿元。

十、信息化建设

截至 2017 年底，市残联门户网站发布工作动态 472 条、年访问量 20.8 万次，全市建立局域网 1 个、16 个网站，1 个 OA 办公系统。圆满完成残疾人基本服务状况和需求信息数据动态更新，实名制获取了 489530 名持证残疾人、6119 个社区（村）动态信息，信息采集入户率为 97.01%。全市残疾人人口基础数据库持证残疾人 512863 人，新增持证残疾人 5.9 万人。在闵行区残联试点第三代残疾人证工作。连续 3 年对 1010 户残疾人实施小康状况动态监测。开发构建含图形展示、数据手册等 7 大类的“上海市残疾人数据资源中心”，搭建为残疾人服务的智能化数据平台。

2017年江苏省残疾人事业发展统计公报

2017年，省残联认真贯彻执行中央各项大政方针，服从服务于省委、省政府中心工作，落实中国残联主席团会议和全国残联工作会议要求，围绕年初全省残联工作会议和第五次全省残疾人事业工作会议明确的目标，以打赢残疾人脱贫攻坚战为首要任务，创新实干，较好地完成了各项工作。

一、康复

2017年全省全面推进精准康复服务，残疾人康复服务覆盖率进一步提高；全面落实辅具补贴制度，提高辅具服务机构服务能力；部署实施《残疾预防和残疾人康复条例》，形成《江苏省残疾预防和残疾人康复实施办法》初稿；推进残疾预防综合试验区创建工作，确定总体目标和年度工作目标；建立实训基地机制，加强康复专业人才培养。

2017年，383743名残疾儿童及持证残疾人得到基本康复服务，其中包括0-6岁残疾儿童16970人。得到康复服务的持证残疾人中，有视力残疾人41761名、听力残疾人15958名、言语残疾人112名、肢体残疾人196944名、智力残疾人35227名、精神残疾人71846名、多重残疾人8897名。全年共为16.3万残疾人提供各类辅助器具适配服务。

截至2017年底，全省已有残疾人康复机构421个，其中，提供视力残疾康复服务的机构82个，提供听力言语残疾康复服务的机构74个，提供肢体残疾康复服务的机构151个，提供智力残疾康复服务的机构120个，提供精神残疾康复服务的机构79个，提供孤独症儿童康复服务的机构104个，提供辅助器具服务的机构71个。康复机构在岗人员达11377人，其中，管理人员1309人、专业技术人员7788人、其他人员2280人。

二、教育

2017年，基本实现残疾学生从学前到大学全过程免费教育，继续对高中及高等教育阶段残疾学生发放教育专项补贴，残疾人受教育权进一步得到保障。

实施残疾人事业专项彩票公益金助学项目，为779人次家庭经济困难的残疾儿童享受普惠性学前教育提供资助。各地多渠道争取资金支持，对357名残疾儿童给予学前教育资助。

全省共有特殊教育普通高中班（部）4个，在校生762人，其中聋生670人、盲生92人。残疾人中等职业学校（班）12个，在校生1164人，毕业生336人，其中294人获得职业资格证书。全省有375名残疾人被普通高等院校录取，183名残疾人进入特殊教育学院学习。

继续实施《“十三五”残疾青壮年文盲扫盲行动方案》。2576名残疾青壮年文盲接受了扫盲教育。

三、就业

2017年各地采取多种形式促进残疾人就业，努力扩大残疾人就业规模。对残疾人就业能力进行科学评估，制定就业计划。省和南京市共同举办3场残疾人就业专场招聘会。在全省确定了10家人力资源公司开展购买残疾人就业服务试点，帮助680名残疾人上岗就业。参加2017年全国残疾人岗位精英职业技能竞赛，3名选手获得个人名次，并获得团体总分第三名。

2017年全省城乡持证残疾人就业人数为46.4万人，全省城乡持证残疾人新增就业13236人，其中，城镇新增就业9834人，农村新增就业3402人；培训城乡残疾人11973人。

盲人按摩事业稳步发展，按摩机构持续增长。2017年度，全省共培训盲人保健按摩人员819名、盲人医疗按摩人员224名；保健按摩机构达到1018个，医疗按摩机构达到27个；在专业技术职务资格评审中，有28人通过医疗按摩人员初级职称评审。

四、社会保障

全省残疾人保障水平持续提高。全面落实《省政府关于完善困难残疾人生活补贴和重度残疾人护理补贴制度的意见》（苏政发〔2016〕15号），加强政策宣传，努力做到符合“两项补贴”政策条件的残疾人应补尽补。加强与省人社厅、省卫生计生委沟通协调，加快推进残疾人参加社会保险工作。截至2017年底，城乡残疾居民参加城乡社会养老保险人数达到140.4万，参保率92.5%；60岁以下的参保残疾人中有24.2万重度残疾人，其中23.7万人得到了政府的参保扶助，代缴养老保险费比例达到98.0%。有19.7万非重度残疾人也享受了全额或部分代缴养老保险费的优惠政策。62.3万残疾人领取养老金。

残疾人托养服务工作稳步推进，残疾人托养服务机构达到1425个，其中寄宿制托养服务机构112个、日间照料机构536个、综合性托养服务机构777个，全年共为2.9万残疾人提供了托养服务，其中寄宿制机构中托养残疾人0.3万人，日间照料机构中托养残疾人0.9万人，综合托养服务机构中托养残疾人1.7万人。机构之外接受居家服务的残疾人达到20488人。全年共有1030名托养服务管理和服务人员接受了各级各类专业培训。

五、扶贫开发

全省各级残联认真落实中国残联《贫困残疾人脱贫攻坚行动计划（2016—2020）》、省委省政府《关于实施脱贫致富奔小康工程的意见》和《关于聚焦富民持续提高城乡居民收入水平的若干意见》，以建档立卡低收入残疾人为重点，推动分类施策、精准帮扶，扎实推进低收入残疾人脱贫攻坚行动。

2017年，贫困残疾人得到有效扶持，残疾人生产生活状况得到进一步改善，全省脱贫人数为59157人；接受实用技术培训的残疾人达到10233人次。

康复扶贫贴息贷款扶持678名农村残疾人。324个残疾人扶贫基地安置8305名残疾人就业，扶持带动11594户残疾人家庭。

全省共完成847户农村贫困残疾人危房改造，各地投入危房资金905.8万元。

六、宣传文化

残疾人宣传文化服务更加活跃。开展“三采三深入”活动，协调主流新闻媒体集中采访报道，做好残疾人专题专栏宣传工作；编印《江苏省残疾人事业好新闻集萃》；“江苏残联”微信公众号正式上线运营。成立省残疾人文联及6个文学艺术专业协会；扶持9个残疾人文化创业和特殊艺术人才培养基地建设；成功举办中荷文化艺术交流活动；举办首期残疾人文学创作培训班；推进文化进残疾人家庭“五个一工程”。残疾人受到社会广泛关注并更加全面地参与到社会生活当中。截至2017年底，省市县三级公共图书馆共设立盲文及盲文有声读物阅览室51个，共开展残疾人文化周活动493场次；省市两级残联共举办残疾人文化艺术类的比赛及展览44次，共有各类残疾人艺术团18个。

截至2017年底，共有省级残疾人专题广播节目1个、电视手语栏目2个；地市级残疾人专题广播节目14个、电视手语栏目15个。

七、体育

2017年，全省进一步规范15支省残疾人运动队集训和管理工作。与江苏开放大学合作开设残疾人运动员中等职业教育学历班。省残疾人体育训练中心更名为文化体育指导中心。

全省共完成残疾人康复体育关爱家庭服务7128户，建设残疾人体育健身示范点164个，培养健身指导员926名。组织省级残疾人体育比赛2次，参与的残疾人运动员299人次，省级残疾人体育训练基地2个，聘任教练员达38人。

省与苏州、镇江、海门、仪征等地成功承办全国残疾人民间足球（东部赛区）争霸赛、全国残疾人田径锦标赛、全国自行车（场地）锦标赛、全国残疾人排舞指导员训练营、第二届特殊教育学校排舞公开赛；在射阳县举办了省第七届特奥会暨2017年田径锦标赛；组队参加13项国内和17项国际比赛，取得106金46银52铜的优异成绩。

八、维权

残疾人维权服务不断拓展。部署全省残联系统“七五”普法宣传教育工作。配合省人大开展《残疾人保障法》和《江苏省残疾人保障条例》执法检查。组织全省维护残疾人合法权益十大典型案例评选活动。建立法律手语翻译登记备案制度。召开部分市县残疾人人大代表和政协委员座谈会，推动残疾人参政议政。

2017年，全省有2个市级、7个县级制定或修改保障残疾人权益的规范性文件；县级以上人大开展《中华人民共和国残疾人保障法》执法检查和专题调研 14 次；政协开展视察和专题调研 12 次。开展省级普法宣传教育活动 1 次，90 人参加。

截至 2017 年底，成立残疾人法律救助工作协调机构 96 个，建立残疾人法律救助工作站 89 个，办理案件 140 件，有力地促进了法律救助和法律援助工作。

残疾人参政议政工作稳步开展，各地残联协助人大代表、政协委员提出议案、建议、提案 28 件，办理议案、建议、提案 73 件。

无障碍建设法规、标准进一步完善。全省共有 11 个地市出台了无障碍建设与管理法规、规章和规范性文件；省本级、11 个市、55 个县（市、区）成立了无障碍建设领导协调组织；系统开展无障碍建设市、县、区 54 个；全省开展无障碍建设检查 142 次，无障碍培训 2412 人次。为 41181 户残疾人家庭实施了无障碍改造，其中包括 7243 户贫困重度残疾人(无障碍改造数据来源为 2017 年全国残疾人基本服务状况和需求信息数据动态更新)；为 22356 名残疾人发放了残疾人机动轮椅车燃油补贴。

各级残联共处理残疾人群众来信 698 件，接待残疾人群众来访 3507 人次，其中集体来访 37 批次、345 人次，省、市两级来电 1001 通，省、市、县三级网上投诉 550 件。

九、组织建设

继续实施“强基育人”工程，基层残疾人组织规范化建设进一步深入，残疾人工作者队伍建设力度进一步加大，城乡社区残疾人组织建设不断规范。扎实做好残疾人专职委员选聘、培训以及日常动态管理、考核工作，不断提升专职委员队伍素质。统筹推进全省各级残联换届工作。率先出台《江苏省残疾人证管理实施办法》和《江苏省残疾人残疾类别等级评定工作规程》。举办残疾人证管理人员和智力、精神残疾评定医生培训班，省、市、县三级评残委员会和专家库基本建成。指导苏州开展第三代智能化残疾人证国家级试点工作。

2017 年，市县乡共建立残联 1454 个，其中设区市残联 13 个，县（市、区）残联 102 个，乡镇（街道）残联 1339 个。已建社区（村）残协 20400 个。

全省 13 个设区市残联中，7 个领导班子配备了残疾人领导干部共 17 人；102 个县（市、区）残联中，44 个配备了残疾人干部共 54 人。在残疾人专职委员选聘方面，1341 个乡镇（街道）选聘残疾人专职委员 2215 名；15644 个村(含农村社区)和 4767 个城市社区选聘残疾人专职委员 19778 名。

省市县乡四级残联实有工作人员 4951 人。干部培训工作取得新进展，省市县三级残联共举办培训班 463 期，培训机关干部、协会干部及残疾人专职委员 1.4 万人次，对提高残联系统干部队伍素质起到了重要作用。

全省共建立省级及以下各类残疾人专门协会 550 个，其中盲人协会 112 个、聋人协会 112 个、肢残人协会 112 个、智力残疾人及亲友协会 102 个、精神残疾人及亲友协会 102 个、智力和精神残疾人及亲友协会合一的协会 10 个。省级专门协会已建 5 个，市级专门协会已建 65 个，县级专门协会已建 480 个，各级各类残疾人专门协会活动日益活跃。

全省助残社会组织共建有 306 个。

十、服务设施建设

残疾人服务设施建设得到全面发展。截至 2017 年底，全省已竣工并投入使用的各级残疾人综合服务设施 81 个，总建设规模 52.3 万平方米，总投资 19.4 亿元；已竣工并投入使用的各级残疾人康复设施 60 个，总建设规模 20.8 万平方米，总投资 7.1 亿元；已竣工并投入使用的各级残疾人托养服务设施 58 个，总建设规模 30.4 万平方米，总投资 10.2 亿元。

十一、信息化建设

残疾人事业信息化建设得到加强。2017 年省残联门户网站共录入信息 4223 条，围绕省残联重大活动和重点工作制作“学习宣传贯彻十九大精神”和“助残日活动”等网上专题。地方残联全面推进网站建设，目前省残联、13 个设区市残联和 86 个县级残联开通了公众服务网站，为残联系统网站集群服务奠定了基础，残联系统网上信息服务正在逐步覆盖全省。

截至 2017 年底，全省残疾人人口基础数据库入库持证残疾人 150.7 万人。基于残疾人人口基础数据库，省残联开发了相关业务应用，为工作开展提供了有效数据支撑。向 4 个市级残联提供残疾人数据每日推送服务。残疾人事业统计工作科学规范，残疾人工作业务信息数据库不断完善，为政策制定和执行评估提供了可靠依据，残疾人事业现代化研究取得新的成果。

2017年浙江省残疾人事业发展统计公报

2017年，全省残疾人工作围绕省委省政府决策部署和中国残联提出的新要求，以《浙江省人民政府关于加快推进残疾人全面小康实施意见》和《浙江省残疾人事业发展“十三五”规划》的实施为重点，深入组织实施残疾人全面小康十大提升计划，全省残疾人基本医疗、基本康复服务、基本社会保险、基本权益维护、基本文化健身进家庭和家庭无障碍改造等各项工作稳步推进，成效明显。

一、康复

2017年，56.5万名残疾儿童及持证残疾人得到基本康复服务，其中0-6岁残疾儿童6102人，持证视力残疾人56821名、听力残疾人54587名、言语残疾人3414名、肢体残疾人22.1万名、智力残疾人88211名、精神残疾人11.9万名、多重残疾人20378名。全年共为88788名残疾人提供各类辅助器具适配服务。

截至2017年底，全省已有残疾人康复机构190个，其中，提供视力残疾康复服务的机构25个，提供听力言语残疾康复服务的机构45个，提供肢体残疾康复服务的机构82个，提供智力残疾康复服务的机构92个，提供精神残疾康复服务的机构39个，提供孤独症儿童康复服务的机构79个，提供辅助器具服务的机构58个。康复机构在岗人员5735人，其中，管理人员656人，专业技术人员3970人，其他人员1109人。

二、教育

实施残疾人事业专项彩票公益金助学项目，522名家庭经济困难的残疾儿童得到学前教育资助。各地也积极争取其他资金支持，对348名残疾儿童给予学前教育资助。

全省共有特殊教育普通高中班（部）5个，在校生744人，其中聋生482人，盲生262人。残疾人中等职业学校（班）13个，在校生497人，毕业生152人，其中82人获得职业资格证书。全省有384名残疾人被普通高等院校录取，330名残疾人进入高等特殊教育学院学习。

2017年，有2539名残疾青壮年文盲接受了扫盲教育。

三、就业

2017年，全省新增残疾人就业14255人，其中，新增按比例就业5023人，新增电商就业创业2669人。

全省持证残疾人就业人数为33.1万人，其中按比例就业86484人，集中就业46724人，个体就业48803人，社区就业1649人，公益性岗位就业5314人，辅助性就业7097人，居家就业9166人，灵活就业65998人，从事农业种养殖59770人。

盲人按摩事业稳步发展。2017年，全省共培训盲人保健按摩人员346名、盲人医疗按摩人员240名；保健按摩机构971个，医疗按摩机构89个；有1人和60人分别获得盲人医疗按摩人员中级和初级职务任职资格。

四、扶贫

2017年，残疾人接受实用技术培训13952人次。康复扶贫贴息贷款扶持2375名农村残疾人。1042个残疾人扶贫基地安置7614名残疾人就业，扶持带动18497户残疾人家庭。

全省共完成2346户农村贫困残疾人家庭危房改造，各地投入危房改造资金2275.9万元。

五、社会保障

截至2017年底，全省困难残疾人生活补贴惠及40.7万名残疾人，重度残疾人护理补贴惠及45.3万名残疾人。城乡残疾居民参加城乡社会养老保险人数63.4万名，13.6万名参保的60岁以下重度残疾人中，有13.2万名得到政府的参保扶助，代缴养老保险费比例达97.0%。有15.6万名非重度残疾人享受了全额或部分代缴养老保险费的优惠政策。28.1万人领取养老金。

残疾人托养服务工作稳步推进。残疾人托养服务机构1112个，其中寄宿制托养服务机构461个，日间照料机构378个，综合性托养服务机构273个，为29329名残疾人提供了托养服务。接受居家服务的残疾人达28.6万人。全年有1731名托养服务管理和服务人员接受了各级各类专业培训。

六、宣传文化

截至2017年底，共有省级残疾人专题广播节目1个、电视手语栏目3个；市级残疾人专题广播节目12个、电视手语栏目11个。省市县三级公共图书馆共设立盲文及盲文有声读物阅览室71个，共开展残疾人文化周活动605场次；省市两级残联共举办残疾人文化艺术类的比赛及展览30次，共有各类残疾人艺术团26个。

七、体育

全省残疾人康复体育关爱家庭服务2500户，新建残疾人体育健身示范点109个，新增培养健身指导员1150名。

八、维权

2017年，制定或修改保障残疾人权益的规范性文件市级2个、县级19个。县级以上人大开展《中华人民共和国残疾人保障法》执法检查和专题调研47次；县级以上政协开展视察和专题调研50次。开展省级普法宣传教育活动1次，189人参加；举办省级法律培训班1个，130人参加。

截至2017年底，全省成立残疾人法律救助工作协调机构102个，建立残疾人法律救助工作站102个（含开发区）。

开展残疾人参政议政工作，各地残联协助人大代表、政协委员提出议案、建议、提案148件，办理议案、建议、提案185件。

无障碍建设法规、标准进一步完善。全省2个市出台无障碍环境建设与管理法规，14个县出台无障碍环境建设与管理规范性文件；11个市和65个县（市、区）系统开展无障碍环境建设；开展无障碍建设检查395次，无障碍建设培训2226人次。

九、组织建设

2017年，市县乡三级共建立残联组织1477个，其中，各市已建残联11个，县（市、区）已建残联92个（含开发区），乡镇（街道）已建残联1374个；村（社区）已建残协23717个。

截至2017年12月底，省市县乡残联实有人员4872人，乡镇（街道）、村（社区）选聘残疾人专职委员总计23894名。市级残联配备残疾人领导干部11人，县级残联配备残疾人干部73人。

全省共建立省级及以下各类残疾人专门协会486个，其中省级专门协会已建5个，市级专门协会已建55个，县级专门协会已建426个。助残社会组织共有223个。

十、服务设施

残疾人服务设施建设稳步推进。截至2017年底，全省已竣

工并投入使用的各级残疾人综合服务设施95个，总建设规模56.8万平方米，总投资21.4亿元；已竣工并投入使用的各级残疾人康复设施38个，总建设规模25.2万平方米，总投资9.7亿元；已竣工并投入使用的各级残疾人托养服务设施26个，总建设规模18.3万平方米，总投资7.4亿元。

十一、信息化

截至2017年底，11个设区市、76个县级残联开通网站。

2017年安徽省残疾人事业发展统计公报

2017年，全省残联系统深入学习党的十九大精神，认真贯彻落实党中央、国务院和省委、省政府关于残疾人事业发展的一系列重要部署，加快推进实现残疾人小康进程，推动残疾人事业不断发展。

一、康复

2017年，709632名残疾儿童及持证残疾人得到基本康复服务。得到康复服务的持证残疾人中，有视力残疾人81265名、听力残疾人26410名、言语残疾人5085名、肢体残疾人350723名、智力残疾人72692名、精神残疾人133318名、多重残疾人39667名。

截至2017年底，全省已有残疾儿童康复机构228个，其中，提供视力残疾康复服务的机构13个，提供听力言语残疾康复服务的机构84个，提供肢体残疾康复服务的机构79个，提供智力残疾康复服务的机构127个，提供精神残疾康复服务的机构7个，提供孤独症儿童康复服务的机构102个，提供辅助器具服务的机构42个。康复机构在岗人员达5914人，其中，管理人员704人，专业技术人员4424人，其他人员786人。

二、教育

2017年，全省残联实施残疾人事业专项彩票公益金助学项目，为835人次家庭经济困难的残疾儿童享受普惠性学前教育提供资助。各地也积极多渠道争取资金支持，对278名残疾儿童给予学前教育资助。

共有特殊教育普通高中班（部）2个，在校生386人，其中聋生379人，盲生7人。残疾人中等职业学校（班）3个，在校生934人，毕业生255人，其中57人获得职业资格证书。有496名残疾人被普通高等院校录取。

1161名残疾青壮年文盲接受了扫盲教育。

三、就业

2017年，全省残疾人就业规模总体保持稳定。城乡持证残疾人就业人数为500543人，其中按比例就业12469人，集中就业7217人，个体就业37022人，社区就业3076人，公益性岗位就业2698人，辅助性就业10762人，居家就业91889人，从事农业种养加279050人，灵活就业56360人。

培训盲人保健按摩人员1692名、盲人医疗按摩人员217名；保健按摩机构达到552个，医疗按摩机构达到71个；在专业技术职务资格评审中，分别有5人和68人通过医疗按摩人员中级和初级职称评审。

四、社会保障

截至2017年底，城乡残疾居民参加城乡社会养老保险人数达到1310420名，348670名60岁以下的重度残疾人参保，其中345814名得到了政府的参保扶助，代缴养老保险费比例达到99.2%。有55269名非重度残疾人也享受了全额或部分代缴养老保险费的优惠政策。487339人领取养老金。

残疾人托养服务工作稳步推进，残疾人托养服务机构达到243个，其中寄宿制托养服务机构154个，日间照料机构18个，综合性托养服务机构71个，为6233名残疾人提供了托养服务。接受居家服务的残疾人达到10168人。全年359名托养服务管理和服务人员接受了各级各类专业培训。

五、扶贫开发

2017年，贫困残疾人得到有效扶持，其中68611人通过扶贫开发实际脱贫；接受实用技术培训的残疾人达到24662人次。

康复扶贫贴息贷款扶持1731名农村残疾人。达到166个残疾人扶贫基地，安置2059名残疾人就业，扶持带动3062名残疾人户。

完成11245户农村贫困残疾人危房改造，各地投入危房资金128256755元。

六、宣传文化

截至2017年底，共有省级残疾人专题广播节目1个、电视手语栏目1个；地市级残疾人专题广播节目12个、电视手语栏目16个。

截至2017年底，省地县三级公共图书馆共设立盲文及盲文有声读物阅览室52个，共开展残疾人文化周活动208场次；省地两级残联共举办残疾人文化艺术类的比赛及展览14次，共有各类残疾人艺术团6个。

七、体育

2017年，全省深入开展残疾人体育工作。全国残疾人康复体育关爱家庭服务1000户，建设残疾人体育健身示范点44个，培养健身指导员1600名。

八、维权

2017年，全省各级残联维权组织建设得到加强，残疾人事业法律法规体系进一步完善，残疾人维权工作全面开展。制定或修改保障残疾人权益的规范性文件地市级4个、县级21个。县级以上人大开展《中华人民共和国残疾人保障法》执法检查和专题调研12次；政协开展视察和专题调研14次。开展省级普法宣传教育活动4次，420人参加；举办省级法律培训班1个，126人参加。

截至2017年底，成立残疾人法律救助工作协调机构42个，建立残疾人法律救助工作站36个。

残疾人参政议政工作稳步开展，各地残联协助人大代表、政协委员提出议案、建议、提案24件，办理议案、建议、提案43件。

无障碍建设法规、标准进一步完善。系统开展无障碍建设市、县、区80个；开展无障碍建设检查36次，无障碍培训818人次。

九、组织建设

2017年，市县乡共建立残联1695个，各地市已建残联16个，县（市、区）残联已建117个，乡镇（街道）残联已建1562个；已建社区（村）残协16279个。

省市县乡残联实有人员达3697人，乡镇（街道）、村（社区）选聘残疾人专职委员总计18832名。地市级残联配备了残疾人领导干部8人，县级残联配备了残疾人干部65人。

共建立省级及以下各类残疾人专门协会553个，其中省级专门协会已建5个，市级专门协会已建75个，县级专门协会已建473。助残社会组织共有42个。

十、综合服务设施建设

截至2017年底，已竣工并投入使用的各级残疾人综合服务设施85个，总建设规模191555平方米，总投资42683万元；已竣工并投入使用的各级残疾人康复设施17个，总建设规模63500平方米，总投资28909万元；已竣工并投入使用的各级残疾人托养服务设施8个，总建设规模19469平方米，总投资6078万元。

十一、信息化建设

2017年，省残联门户网站共计发布各级各类信息约6000条，初审并报批中国残联2100多条。截至2017年底，15个地市、65个县级残联开通网站，及时对外提供信息服务。据中国残联第二代残疾人证办证系统数据显示，截至2017年底，全省持证的各类各等级残疾人约有164万人。

2017 年福建省残疾人事业发展统计公报

2017 年，全省残联系统在省委、省政府的正确领导和中国残联的精心指导下，深入学习贯彻党的十九大精神，认真贯彻落实党中央、国务院关于残疾人事业发展的一系列重要部署，主动担当，积极作为，推动残疾人事业持续健康发展。

一、康复

2017 年，16.1 万名残疾儿童及持证残疾人得到基本康复服务。得到康复服务的持证残疾人中，有视力残疾人 4409 名、听力残疾人 4544 名、言语残疾人 25 名、肢体残疾人 8.7 万名、智力残疾人 2.7 万名、精神残疾人 2.8 万名、多重残疾人 7676 名。

截至 2017 年底，全省已有残疾人康复机构 253 个，其中，提供视力残疾康复服务的机构 27 个，提供听力言语残疾康复服务的机构 35 个，提供肢体残疾康复服务的机构 62 个，提供智力残疾康复服务的机构 71 个，提供精神残疾康复服务的机构 46 个，提供孤独症儿童康复服务的机构 81 个，提供辅助器具服务的机构 63 个。康复机构在岗人员达 6212 人，其中，管理人员 824 人，专业技术人员 3848 人，其他人员 1540 人。

二、教育

家庭经济困难残疾学生全部纳入国家（政府）资助政策实施范围，实现就学资助全覆盖。实施残疾人事业专项彩票公益金助学项目，对 411 人次家庭经济困难的残疾儿童接受学前教育提供资助；实施“扶贫助学大学圆梦行动”，对 498 名残疾大学生和低保户残疾人子女大学生给予资助；实施“通向明天——交通银行残疾青少年助学计划”，对 110 残疾大学生新生进行资助。各地也积极多渠道争取资金支持，对 119 名残疾儿童给予学前教育资助。

2017 年，全省共有特殊教育普通高中班（部）3 个，在校生 139 人。残疾人中等职业学校（班）6 个，在校生 148 人，毕业生 62 人。全省有 205 名残疾人被普通高等院校录取，27 名残疾人进入特殊教育学院学习。1175 名残疾青壮年文盲接受了扫盲教育。

三、就业

2017 年，城乡持证残疾人就业人数为 21.6 万人，其中按比例就业 1.5 万人，集中就业 6005 人，个体就业 2.5 万人，社区就业 2937 人，公益性岗位就业 2428 人，辅助性就业 4276 人，居家就业 2.6 万人，从事农业种养加 9.9 万人，灵活就业 3.5 万人。

2017 年度，全省共培训盲人保健按摩人员 361 名、盲人医疗按摩人员 245 名；保健按摩机构达到 322 个，医疗按摩机构达到 33 个；在专业技术职务资格评审中，有 16 人通过医疗按摩人员初级职称评审。

四、扶贫

2017 年，残疾人脱贫攻坚持续推进，精准帮扶、精准脱贫力度不断加大，有 33752 名建档立卡残疾人实现脱贫。全年共完成 2518 户农村贫困残疾人危房改造，投入改造资金 3600 万元；有 3783 户残疾人家庭完成易地搬迁，受益家庭人口 13607 人，补助资金超过 5442 万元。对 8703 名残疾人进行实用技术培训。全省 136 个残疾人扶贫基地安置 2307 名残疾人就业，并扶持带动 3161 个残疾人户。

五、社会保障

截至 2017 年底，城乡残疾居民参加城乡社会养老保险人数达到 68.7 万名。16.1 万名 60 岁以下的重度残疾人参保，其中 159667 名得到了政府的参保扶助，代缴养老保险费比例达到 99.3%。有 16.2 万名非重度残疾人也享受了全额或部分代缴养老保险费的优惠政策。34.7 万人领取养老金。

残疾人托养服务工作稳步推进，残疾人托养服务机构达到 119 个，其中寄宿制托养服务机构 44 个，日间照料机构 46 个，综合性托养服务机构 29 个，为 3502 名残疾人提供了托养服务。接受居家服务的残疾人达到 1.7 万人。全年 127 名托养服务管理和服务人员接受了各级各类专业培训。

六、宣传体育

截至2017年底，全省共有省级电视手语栏目1个；地市级残疾人专题广播节目5个、电视手语栏目8个。

残疾人文化体育工作持续推进。围绕第二十七次全国助残日主题，举办“第七届闽台残疾人文化周”，开展了第五届盲童助学行动、省高校手语表演赛、闽台残疾人文化交流进基层等系列活动，近40名台湾嘉宾参加，受到媒体广泛关注，社会反响良好。

成功举办第六届全省特奥会以及残疾人乒乓球等6个单项赛事，组织116名运动员参加全国11个残疾人体育单项赛事，获得41金、23银、17铜；输送运动员32人次参加国际残疾人体育赛事，共获得22金、7银、9铜。

七、维权

各级残联维权组织建设进一步加强，残疾人事业法律法规体系更加完善，无障碍环境建设取得新成果，残疾人维权工作全面开展。

2017年，制定或修改了关于残疾人的专门法规、规章省级1个、地市级2个；制定或修改保障残疾人权益的规范性文件地市级6个、县级5个。县级以上人大开展《中华人民共和国残疾人保障法》执法检查和专题调研3次；政协开展视察和专题调研3次。开展省级普法宣传教育活动3次，326人参加；举办省级法律培训班1个，43人参加。

截至2017年底，成立残疾人法律救助工作协调机构64个，建立残疾人法律救助工作站56个。

残疾人参政议政工作稳步开展，各地残联协助人大代表、政协委员提出议案、建议、提案16件，办理议案、建议、提案36件。

无障碍建设法规、标准进一步完善。系统开展无障碍建设市、县、区48个；开展无障碍建设检查35次，无障碍培训961人次。

八、组织建设

2017年，全省市县乡共建立残联1201个，各县（市、区）残联已建84个，乡镇（街道）残联已建1108个；已建社区（村）残协16069个。

省市县乡残联实有人员达2645人，乡镇（街道）、村（社区）选聘残疾人联络员总计17415名。地市级残联配备了残疾人领导干部12人，县级残联配备了残疾人干部32人。

全省共建立省级及以下各类残疾人专门协会453个，其中省级专门协会已建5个，市级专门协会已建45个，县级专门协会已建403。助残社会组织共有103个。

九、服务设施

截至2017年底，已竣工并投入使用的各级残疾人综合服务设施85个，总建设规模20.1万平方米；已竣工并投入使用的各级残疾人康复设施217个，总建设规模4.0万平方米，总投资12113万元；已竣工并投入使用的各级残疾人托养服务设施45个，总建设规模6.4万平方米。

十、信息化建设

截至2017年底，省残联门户网站共发稿2904篇，网站页面年浏览量47.2万人次，在残疾人事业新闻宣传、政务公开、信息服务等方面发挥了重要作用。推行电子政务应用，发送政务短信9240条，通过政务邮箱向各级残联发送政务文件通知4707份（次）。继续推广“福建省残疾人综合信息服务平台”应用，为残疾人提供网络无障碍服务。

注重加强与纵向、横向部门(单位)的沟通协作，实现数据交换共享。与省人社厅交换全民参保的数据，获得93.4万条全省残疾人参加各类养老保险、医疗保险情况。与省民政厅交换低保数据，获得17.7万残疾人享受低保的数据。

2017年江西省残疾人事业发展统计公报

2017年，在省委省政府的坚强领导下，在中国残联的精心指导下，江西省残联深入学习贯彻十九大精神，牢牢抓住富裕美丽幸福现代化江西建设发展理念，积极推进残疾人事业健康发展。

一、康复

2017年，23.1万名残疾儿童及持证残疾人得到基本康复服务,其中包括0-6岁残疾儿童3623人。其中，有视力残疾人2.9万名、听力残疾人1万名、言语残疾人53名、肢体残疾人13.5万名、智力残疾人9717名、精神残疾人3.8万名、多重残疾人8942名。

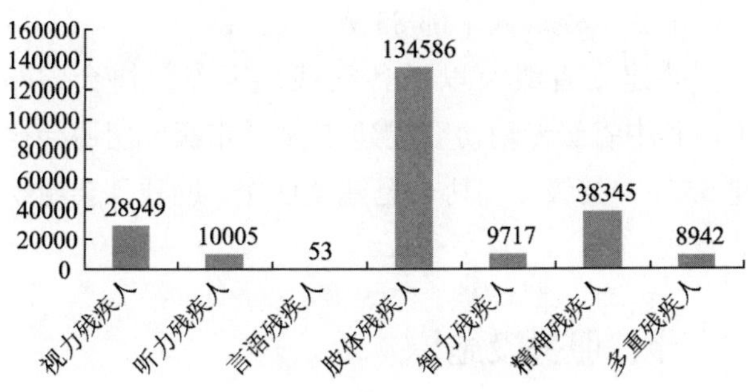

图1　得到康复服务的持证残疾人

截至2017年底，有残疾人康复机构204个，其中，提供视力残疾康复服务的机构8个，提供听力言语残疾康复服务的机构40个，提供肢体残疾康复服务的机构51个，提供智力残疾康复服务的机构62个，提供精神残疾康复服务的机构64个，提供孤独症儿童康复服务的机构30个，提供辅助器具服务的机构28个。康复机构在岗人员达5184人，其中，管理人员800人，专业技术人员3525人，其他人员859人。

二、教育

实施残疾人事业专项彩票公益金助学项目，为500人次家庭经济困难的残疾儿童享受普惠性学前教育提供资助。

共有特殊教育普通高中班（部）2个，在校生287人，其中聋生287人。残疾人中等职业学校（班）5个，在校生517人，毕业生97人，其中41人获得职业资格证书。有327名残疾人被普通高等院校录取。839名残疾青壮年文盲接受了扫盲教育。

三、就业

城乡持证残疾人就业人数为35.2万人，其中按比例就业1.2万人，集中就业2.1万人，个体就业4.8万人，社区就业8576人，公益性岗位就业6949人，辅助性就业7977人，居家就业6万人，从事农业种养加11.8万人，灵活就业6.9万人。

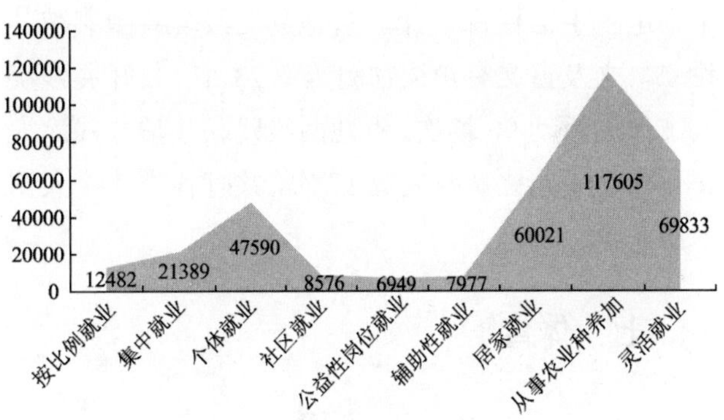

图2　城乡持证残疾人就业人数

培训盲人保健按摩人员134名、盲人医疗按摩人员61名；保健按摩机构达到473个，医疗按摩机构达到75个；在专业技术职务资格评审中，分别有10人和23人通过医疗按摩人员中级和初级职称评审。

四、扶贫

2017年，贫困残疾人得到有效扶持，其中5.1万人通过扶贫开发实际脱贫；接受实用技术培训的残疾人达到1.1万人次。

康复扶贫贴息贷款扶持34名农村残疾人。达到391个残疾人扶贫基地，安置2700名残疾人就业，扶持带动3275名残疾人户。

完成2583户农村贫困残疾人危房改造，各地投入危房资金2791.0万元。

五、社会保障

截至2017年底，城乡残疾居民参加城乡社会养老保险人数达到 84.5 万名，17.3 万名 60 岁以下的重度残疾人参保，其中 16.9 万名得到了政府的参保扶助，代缴养老保险费比例达到 98.2%。有 11.7 万名非重度残疾人也享受了全额或部分代缴养老保险费的优惠政策。32 万人领取养老金。

残疾人托养服务工作稳步推进，残疾人托养服务机构达到 41 个，其中寄宿制托养服务机构 13 个，日间照料机构 19 个，综合性托养服务机构 9 个，为 2463 名残疾人提供了托养服务。接受居家服务的残疾人达到 5065 人。全年 333 名托养服务管理和服务人员接受了各级各类专业培训。

六、宣传文化

截至 2017 年底，地市级残疾人专题广播节目 7 个、电视手语栏目 5 个。省地县三级公共图书馆共设立盲文及盲文有声读物阅览室 23 个，共开展残疾人文化周活动 90 场次；省地两级残联共举办残疾人文化艺术类的比赛及展览 17 次，共有各类残疾人艺术团 7 个。

七、体育

2017 年为全省 8000 户中重度残疾人实施残疾人康复体育进家庭关爱服务，全省、市、县各级创建残疾人体育健身示范点 89 个，培训为残疾人服务的社会体育健身指导员 223 名，各级举办各类体育赛事及体育健身活动 100 余次，参加各类体育赛事及体育健身活动的残疾人达 5400 余名。

八、维权

2017 年，制定或修改了关于残疾人的专门法规、规章省级 1 个、地市级 1 个；制定或修改保障残疾人权益的规范性文件地市级 3 个、县级 3 个。县级以上人大开展《中华人民共和国残疾人保障法》执法检查和专题调研 9 次；政协开展视察和专题调研 7 次。开展省级普法宣传教育活动 7 次，402 人参加；举办省级法律培训班 2 个，160 人参加。

截至 2017 年底，成立残疾人法律救助工作协调机构 54 个，建立残疾人法律救助工作站 41 个。

残疾人参政议政工作稳步开展，各地残联协助人大代表、政协委员提出议案、建议、提案 40 件，办理议案、建议、提案 16 件。

无障碍建设法规、标准进一步完善。系统开展无障碍建设市、县、区 111 个；开展无障碍建设检查 23 次，无障碍培训 117 人次。

九、组织建设

2017 年，市县乡共建立残联 1748 个，其中，各地市已建残联 11 个，县（市、区）残联已建 111 个，乡镇（街道）残联已建 1626 个；已建社区（村）残协 1.8 万个。

省市县乡残联实有人员达 4000 人，乡镇（街道）、村（社区）选聘残疾人专职委员总计 1.7 万名。地市级残联配备了残疾人领导干部 13 人，县级残联配备了残疾人干部 83 人。

共建立省级及以下各类残疾人专门协会 463 个，其中省级专门协会已建 5 个，市级专门协会已建 55 个，县级专门协会已建 403 个。助残社会组织共有 23 个。

十、服务设施

截至 2017 年底，已竣工、投入使用及在建的各级残疾人综合服务设施 73 个，总建设规模 7.4 万平方米，总投资 17651 万元；已竣工并投入使用的各级残疾人康复设施 5 个，总建设规模 4.9 万平方米，总投资 9020 万元；已竣工并投入使用的各级残疾人托养服务设施 14 个，总建设规模 4.5 万平方米，总投资 10344 万元。

十一、信息化

截至 2017 年底，8 个地市、32 个县级残联开通网站。全国残疾人人口数据库江西省持证残疾人 105 万，积极配合全省 OA 办公系统部署。大力推动软件正版化工作。

2017年山东省残疾人事业发展统计公报

2017年，在省委、省政府的坚强领导下，在各级各部门和社会各界的大力支持下，各级残联牢牢把握工作重点，加大工作力度，强化工作措施，狠抓任务落实，推动各项工作取得了新成效。

一、康复

2017年，全省38.3万残疾儿童及持证残疾人得到基本康复服务，其中包括0-6岁残疾儿童11665人、7-17岁残疾儿童14631人。得到康复服务的持证残疾人中,有视力残疾人30490人、听力残疾人13793人、言语残疾人156人、肢体残疾人256730人、智力残疾人17804人、精神残疾人46221人、多重残疾人17070人。全年共为21.0万残疾人提供各类辅助器具适配服务。

截至2017年底，全省共有残疾人康复机构552个，其中：提供视力残疾康复服务的机构65个、提供听力言语残疾康复服务的机构77个、提供肢体残疾康复服务的机构227个、提供智力残疾康复服务的机构156个、提供精神残疾康复服务的机构96个、提供孤独症儿童康复服务的机构127个、提供辅助器具服务的机构82个。康复机构在岗人员达2.6万人，其中：管理人员3190人、专业技术人员18472人、其他人员3843人。

二、教育

实施残疾人事业专项彩票公益金助学项目，944名家庭经济困难的残疾儿童享受普惠性学前教育提供资助。各地多渠道争取资金支持，对157名残疾儿童给予学前教育资助。

全省共有特殊教育普通高中班（部）7个、在校生461人，其中聋生333人、盲生128人。残疾人中等职业学校（班）5个、在校生393人、毕业生12人，其中49人获得职业资格证书。587名残疾学生被普通高等院校录取，161名残疾学生进入高等特殊教育学院学习。

三、就业

城乡持证残疾人就业人数为57.8万人，其中：按比例就业6.6万人、集中就业2.1万人、个体就业3.1万人、公益性岗位就业0.3万人、辅助性就业0.5万人、社区就业0.7万人、居家就业4.2万人、灵活就业5.1万人、从事农业种养殖35.1万人。2017年城乡持证残疾人新增就业2.4万人。

2017年全省共培训盲人保健按摩人员1280名、盲人医疗按摩人员656名；共有保健按摩机构1401个、医疗按摩机构103个；有62人获得盲医疗按摩人员初级职务任职资格。

四、社会保障

截至2017年底，残疾居民参加城乡社会养老保险人数154.0万人。在37.0万60岁以下参保的重度残疾人中，有35.5万得到政府的参保扶助，代缴养老保险费比例95.9%。11.1万非重度残疾人享受全额或部分代缴养老保险费的优惠政策。60.8万残疾人领取养老金。

全省共有残疾人托养服务机构519个，其中寄宿制托养服务机构234个，日间照料机构87个，综合性托养服务机构198个，为2.6万残疾人提供了托养服务。0.9万残疾人接受居家服务。全年2083名托养服务管理和服务人员接受了各级各类专业培训。

五、扶贫

贫困残疾人脱贫攻坚取得阶段性成效，残疾人生产生活状况得到进一步改善，4.6万残疾人退出建档立卡。残疾人接受实用技术培训2.6万人次，扫盲教育1541人，地方投入经费873.3万元。566个残疾人扶贫基地安置9871名残疾人就业，扶持带动1.5万户残疾人家庭。通过开展结对帮扶服务，使9802名残疾人受益。全省各地投入危房改造资金579.0万元，完成645户农村贫困残疾人危房改造。

六、文化体育

截至2017年底，省、市两级开播残疾人专题广播节目15个、电视手语新闻栏目10个。省市县三级公共图书馆共设立盲文及盲文有声读物阅览室53个，共开展残疾人文化周活动284场次。省市两级共举办残疾人文化艺术类的比赛及展览36次，共有各类残疾人艺术团31个。

全年省市县共组织残疾人群众体育健身活动677次，1.7万残疾人参与了活动。全省已建成残疾人体育健身示范点363个，配备1858名残疾人体育社区指导员。完成残疾人康复体育关爱家庭服务850户。

七、政策法规与维权

2017年，省市两级制定或修改了关于残疾人的专门法规、规章3个；市县两级制定或修改保障残疾人权益的规范性文件9个。县级以上人大开展《中华人民共和国残疾人保障法》执法检查和专题调研22次，政协开展视察和专题调研21次。省级开展普法宣传教育活动4次，551人参加。

无障碍建设法规、标准进一步完善，全省共出台了12个省市县级无障碍建设与管理法规、规章和规范性文件，57个市县区系统开展无障碍建设。全省累计开展无障碍建设检查91次，无障碍培训736人次。

截至2017年底，全省已成立残疾人法律救助工作协调机构82个，建立残疾人法律救助工作站83个。

八、组织建设

截至2017年底，省市县乡四级残联机关和事业单位共有编制5879个，实有人员6308人。82.4%市级残联领导班子配备了残疾人，38.6%县级残联配备残疾人干部。选聘乡镇（街道）残疾人专职干事1805人、村（社区）残疾人专职委员6.2万人。

省市两级残联举办综合类培训班36期、培训1726人次，举办残疾人干部培训班18期、培训1345人次。县乡两级残联举办各类培训班1941期、培训4.5万人次。

全省已建立省级及以下各类残疾人专门协会725个，其中市级各专门协会已建率96.5%，县级各专门协会已建率93.1%。全省共有助残社会组织37个。

在县级及以上残疾人及其亲友和残疾人工作者中，共有人大代表22人、政协委员84人。残联系统协助人大代表、政协委员提出议案、建议、提案27件，办理建议、提案58件。

九、服务设施

截至2017年底，全省已竣工并投入使用的各级残疾人综合服务设施126个、总建设规模32.2万平方米、总投资7.7亿元。已竣工并投入使用的各级残疾人康复设施94个、总建设规模56.3万平方米、总投资15.5亿元。已竣工并投入使用的各级残疾人托养服务设施37个、总建设规模11.3万平方米、总投资3.3亿元。

十、信息化与统计

截至2017年底，全省各级共有74个残联开通了门户网站。在《全国残疾人人口基础数据库中》中共有持证残疾人211.6万人，占全省残疾人总人口的37.2%，其中：视力残疾16.9万人、听力残疾13.1万人、言语残疾2.4万人、肢体残疾30.7万人、智力残疾19.2万人、精神残疾19.2万人、多重残疾10.0万人；一级残疾30.6万人、二级残疾64.3万人、三级残疾54.7万人、四级残疾61.9万人。

继续开展残疾人基本服务状况和需求信息数据动态更新工作，全省共完成调查203.5万人，平均入户调查率99.01%。

2017年河南省残疾人事业发展统计公报

2017年，在河南省委、省政府正确领导下，在中国残联有力指导下，在全省各级残联共同努力下，省残联党组理事会坚持以习近平新时代中国特色社会主义思想为指导，深入学习宣传贯彻党的十九大精神，认真落实“发展残疾人事业，加强残疾康复服务”总体要求和省委、省政府关于残疾人工作的决策部署，将以人民为中心的发展思想落实到为残疾人提供精准服务之中，紧紧围绕年初确定的工作目标，团结奋进、攻坚克难，推动全省残疾人事业和残联工作取得了新发展。

一、康复

聚焦残疾人康复需求，实施精准康复服务，在各级残联的共同努力下，2017年全省残疾人康复各项业务深入开展。

2017年，全省54.1万名残疾儿童及持证残疾人得到基本康复服务。其中包括0-6岁残疾儿童1.4万人，得到辅助器具适配服务的残疾人20.6万人，康复服务覆盖率达到70.8%。在得到康复服务的持证残疾人中，有视力残疾人5.3万人、听力残疾人2.3万人、言语残疾人0.2万人、肢体残疾人36.8万人、智力残疾人3.9万名、精神残疾人3.6万人、多重残疾人1.3万名。

截至2017年底，全省已有残疾人康复机构364个，其中，提供视力残疾康复服务的机构40个，提供听力言语残疾康复服务的机构109个，提供肢体残疾康复服务的机构154个，提供智力残疾康复服务的机构141个，提供精神残疾康复服务的机构88个，提供孤独症儿童康复服务的机构86个，提供辅助器具服务的机构65个。康复机构在岗人员达1.6万人，其中，管理人员0.2万人，专业技术人员1.1万人，其他人员0.3万人。

二、教育

2017年全省实施残疾人事业专项彩票公益金助学项目，为1607人次家庭经济困难的残疾儿童享受普惠性学前教育提供资助。

全省共有特殊教育普通高中班（部）4个，在校生234人，其中聋生215人，盲生19人。残疾人中等职业学校（班）7个，在校生487人，毕业生182人，其中118人获得职业资格证书。有626名残疾人被普通高等院校录取，332名残疾人进入特殊教育学院学习。

全省各地有1373名残疾青壮年文盲接受了扫盲教育。

三、就业

2017年，全省城乡持证残疾人就业人数为56.6万人，其中按比例就业2.7万人，集中就业1.4万人，个体就业11.3万人，社区就业0.4万人，公益性岗位就业0.4万人，辅助性就业1.7万人，居家就业3.8万人，从事农业种养加33.4万人，灵活就业1.5万人。

全省培训盲人保健按摩人员0.3万名、盲人医疗按摩人员0.1万名；保健按摩机构达到928个，医疗按摩机构达到111个；在专业技术职务资格评审中，10人通过医疗按摩人员初级职称评审。

四、扶贫

2017年，贫困残疾人得到有效扶持，其中5.4万人通过扶贫开发实际脱贫；接受实用技术培训的残疾人达到5万人次。

全省残疾人扶贫基地达到289个，安置0.9万名残疾人就业，扶持带动1.7万户残疾人家庭。

完成0.3万户农村贫困残疾人危房改造，各地投入危房资金1790万元。

五、社会保障

截至2017年底，全省城乡残疾居民参加城乡社会养老保险人数达到330.9万名，65.3万名60岁以下的重度残疾人参保，其中62.5万名得到了政府的参保扶助，代缴养老保险费比例达到95.7%。有3.8

万名非重度残疾人也享受了全额或部分代缴养老保险费的优惠政策。137.5 万人领取养老金。

全省残疾人托养服务工作稳步推进，残疾人托养服务机构达到 195 个，其中寄宿制托养服务机构 88 个，日间照料机构 22 个，综合性托养服务机构 85 个，为 0.9 万名残疾人提供了托养服务。接受居家服务的残疾人达到 1.1 万人。全年共有 68 名托养服务管理和服务人员接受了各级各类专业培训。

六、宣传文化

截至 2017 年底，全省有省级残疾人专题广播节目 1 个、电视手语栏目 1 个，省级残疾人电视台专题节目 1 个，录制播放 49 期；地市级残疾人专题广播节目 13 个、电视手语栏目 8 个。

截至 2017 年底，省地县三级公共图书馆共设立盲文及盲文有声读物阅览室 60 个，共开展残疾人文化周活动 170 场次；省地两级残联共举办残疾人文化艺术类的比赛及展览 18 次，共有各类残疾人艺术团 5 个。

七、体育

2017 年，全省实施残疾人康复体育关爱家庭服务 2000 户，建设残疾人体育健身示范点 224 个，培养健身指导员 1859 名。

八、维权

2017 年，全省制定或修改保障残疾人权益的规范性文件地市级 5 个、县级 2 个。县级以上人大开展《中华人民共和国残疾人保障法》执法检查和专题调研 13 次；政协开展视察和专题调研 7 次。

截至 2017 年底，全省成立残疾人法律救助工作协调机构 137 个，建立残疾人法律救助工作站 110 个。

残疾人参政议政工作稳步开展，各地残联协助人大代表、政协委员提出议案、建议、提案 13 件，办理议案、建议、提案 22 件。

无障碍建设法规、标准进一步完善。全省系统开展无障碍建设市、县、区 58 个；开展无障碍建设检查 126 次，无障碍培训 442 人次。

九、组织建设

2017 年，全省市县乡共建立残联 0.3 万个，各地市已建残联 18 个，县（市、区）残联已建 168 个，乡镇（街道）残联已建 0.2 万个；已建社区（村）残协 4.7 万个。

省市县乡残联实有人员达 0.8 万人，乡镇（街道）、村（社区）选聘残疾人专职委员总计 5 万名。地市级残联配备了残疾人领导干部 14 人，县级残联配备了残疾人干部 121 人。

全省建立省级及以下各类残疾人专门协会 887 个，其中省级专门协会已建 5 个，市级专门协会已建 90 个，县级专门协会已建 792。助残社会组织共有 50 个。

十、服务设施

截至 2017 年底，全省已竣工并投入使用的各级残疾人综合服务设施 144 个，总建设规模 22.6 万平方米，总投资 39273 万元；已竣工并投入使用的各级残疾人康复设施 15 个，总建设规模 9.5 万平方米，总投资 19962 万元；已竣工并投入使用的各级残疾人托养服务设施 17 个，总建设规模 5 万平方米，总投资 9678 万元。

十一、信息化

截至 2017 年底，15 个地市、43 个县级残联开通网站。2017 年省级残联网站发布信息 3175 条，向中国残联网站推荐发布信息 2059 条。

2017年湖北省残疾人事业发展统计公报

2017年，在省委、省政府坚强领导和中国残联的正确指导下，全省残联系统深入贯彻落实党的十九大精神，紧紧围绕“加快推进残疾人小康进程”这条主线,牢牢把握残疾人“两不愁、三保障、两扩面”这个重点，聚力“打赢贫困残疾人脱贫攻坚战”这个难点，各项工作取得了明显成效。

一、康复

推动出台《湖北省残疾预防行动计划（2017-2020年）》。2017年，全省483612名残疾儿童及持证残疾人得到基本康复服务,其中包括0-6岁残疾儿童5868人。得到康复服务的持证残疾人中，有视力残疾人75613名、听力残疾人38211名、言语残疾人15816名、肢体残疾人191204名、智力残疾人39494名、精神残疾人83177名、多重残疾人38368名。

截至2017年底，全省已有残疾人康复机构220个，其中，提供视力残疾康复服务的机构16个，提供听力言语残疾康复服务的机构37个，提供肢体残疾康复服务的机构64个，提供智力残疾康复服务的机构69个，提供精神残疾康复服务的机构64个，提供孤独症儿童康复服务的机构32个，提供辅助器具服务的机构52个。康复机构在岗人员达9123人，其中，管理人员1178人，专业技术人员6493人，其他人员1452人。

二、教育

实施残疾人事业专项彩票公益金助学项目，为750人次家庭经济困难的残疾儿童提供普惠性学前教育资助。全省共有特殊教育普通高中班（部）7个，在校生697人，其中聋生604人，盲生93人。残疾人中等职业学校（班）5个，在校生578人，毕业生141人，其中60人获得职业资格证书。有369名残疾人被普通高等院校录取。1021名残疾青壮年文盲接受了扫盲教育。

三、就业

对接省财政厅等部门出台《湖北省残疾人就业保障金征收使用管理实施办法》。实施“十百千万”残疾人创业就业扶持计划，对20个残疾人创业就业品牌基地、600名农家小店主和集镇小老板给予扶持。截至2017年底，城乡持证残疾人就业人数为421105人，其中按比例就业33624人，集中就业23989人，个体就业27015人，社区就业4801人，公益性岗位就业3912人，辅助性就业7889人，居家就业61417人，从事农业种养加194204人，灵活就业64254人。

2017年，全省培训盲人保健按摩人员426名、盲人医疗按摩人员49名;保健按摩机构达到912个，医疗按摩机构达到43个;在专业技术职务资格评审中，有25人通过医疗按摩人员初级职称评审。

四、扶贫

2017年，全省各地认真贯彻落实《湖北省残疾人脱贫攻坚行动实施方案（2016-2019年）》，通过精准识别帮扶对象、精准纳入帮扶项目、精准实施帮扶措施、严格考核脱贫成效等措施，全力推进残疾人脱贫攻坚工作，93895人通过扶贫开发实际脱贫。接受实用技术培训的残疾人达到23904人次。

康复扶贫贴息贷款扶持633名农村残疾人。全省80个残疾人扶贫基地，安置2888名残疾人就业，扶持带动6376名残疾人户。

五、社会保障

截至2017年底，城乡残疾居民参加城乡社会养老保险人数达到1262882名，292651名60岁以下的重度残疾人参保，其中277517名得到了政府的参保扶助，代缴养老保险费比例达到94.8%。有193760名非重度残疾人也享受了全额或部分代缴养老保险费的优惠政策。493016人领取养老金。

残疾人托养服务工作稳步推进，残疾人托养服务机构达到236个,其中寄宿制托养服务机构78个,日间照料机构102个,综合性托养服务机构56个,为8404名残疾人提供了托养服务。接受居家服务的残疾人达到7634人。

六、宣传文化

荆风楚韵"——湖北省残疾人艺术团走进台湾,被国台办列为2017年对台宣传品项目,在台湾苗栗、台北、花莲举办了3场高水平的公益演出。人民日报海外版以头版头条全面详实地报道省残疾人艺术团走进台湾演出盛况。新华社在《参考清样》发表了《用高水平的交流活动打动台湾民心——湖北省残疾人艺术团赴台演出观察》。

截至2017年底,全省共有省级残疾人专题广播节目1个,地市级残疾人专题广播节目6个、电视手语栏目8个。省市县三级公共图书馆共设立盲文及盲文有声读物阅览室24个,共开展残疾人文化周活动113场次;省、市两级残联共举办残疾人文化艺术类的比赛及展览27次,共有各类残疾人艺术团8个。

七、体育

全国残疾人康复体育关爱家庭服务1500户,建设残疾人体育健身示范点41个,培养健身指导员1218名。成功承办2017年全国残疾人游泳锦标赛,组队参加全国残疾人乒乓球、举重、田径、游泳锦标赛等10项全国残疾人体育赛事,斩获16金22银15铜。

八、维权

2017年,县级以上人大开展《中华人民共和国残疾人保障法》执法检查和专题调研10次;政协开展视察和专题调研10次。开展省级普法宣传教育活动2次,200人参加;举办省级法律培训班1个,200人参加。 截至2017年底,全省成立残疾人法律救助工作协调机构112个,建立残疾人法律救助工作站59个。

残疾人参政议政工作稳步开展,各地残联协助人大代表、政协委员提出议案、建议、提案34件,办理议案、建议、提案67件。

无障碍建设法规、标准进一步完善。系统开展无障碍建设市、县、区84个;开展无障碍建设检查36次,无障碍培训264人次。

九、组织建设

2017年,全省已建立市县乡残联1340个,各地市已建残联13个,县(市、区)残联已建106个,乡镇(街道)残联已建1221个;已建社区(村)残协24222个。

省市县乡残联实有人员达3446人,乡镇(街道)、村(社区)选聘残疾人专职委员总计21021名。地市级残联配备了残疾人领导干部11人,县级残联配备了残疾人干部52人。

共建立省级及以下各类残疾人专门协会520个,其中省级专门协会已建5个,市级专门协会已建65个,县级专门协会已建450。助残社会组织共有682个。

十、服务设施

截至2017年底,全省已竣工并投入使用的各级残疾人综合服务设施88个,总建设规模182795平方米,总投资34661万元;已竣工并投入使用的各级残疾人康复设施16个,总建设规模59758平方米,总投资18774万元;已竣工并投入使用的各级残疾人托养服务设施21个,总建设规模41006平方米,总投资7698万元。

十一、信息化建设

截至2017年底,省残联网站全年发布信息2252条,12个地市、32个县级(含直管市)残联开通网站。积极与省民政厅对接,实现残疾人社会保障相关数据共享。

2017 年湖南省残疾人事业发展统计公报

2017 年，湖南省残疾人工作在省委省政府正确领导和中国残联指导下，各项任务圆满完成，残疾人事业持续发展，残疾人得到服务和保障水平进一步提高。现将 2017 年度湖南残疾人事业发展统计情况公报如下：

一、康复

2017 年，375581 名持证残疾人及残疾儿童得到基本康复服务,其中包括 0-6 岁残疾儿童 7932 人。得到康复服务的持证残疾人中，有视力残疾人 50525 名、听力残疾人 12995 名、言语残疾人 970 名、肢体残疾人 209753 名、智力残疾人 20649 名、精神残疾人 64773 名、多重残疾人 12839 名。

截至 2017 年底,全省有残疾人康复机构 374 个，其中，提供视力残疾康复服务的机构 52 个，提供听力言语残疾康复服务的机构 70 个，提供肢体残疾康复服务的机构 88 个，提供智力残疾康复服务的机构 112 个，提供精神残疾康复服务的机构 70 个，提供孤独症儿童康复服务的机构 71 个，提供辅助器具服务的机构 107 个。康复机构在岗人员达 11682 人，其中，管理人员 1230 人，专业技术人员 8106 人，其他人员 2346 人。

共完成复明手术定向行走康复 8103 人次，为 37328 名视力残疾人配发盲杖助视器等进行了服务，为其他 7036 名有视力障碍残疾人进行了康复服务。共为 17064 名听力言语残疾人进行了人工耳蜗手术及助听器适配服务，为 478 名听力言语残疾人进行了功能训练，为其他 2099 名听力言语残疾人进行了康复服务。2017 年共为 37152 名肢体残疾人进行了矫治手术和运动功能训练，为 150767 名肢体残疾人进行了假肢、矫形器等辅具适配服务，为其他 30289 名肢体残疾人做了不同程度的康复服务。全年共为 25651 名智力残疾人进行了康复服务。为 1455 名孤独症儿童沟通及适应训练，为 68558 名不同程度精神残疾人进行药物治疗及作业疗法训练和其他方式康复服务。

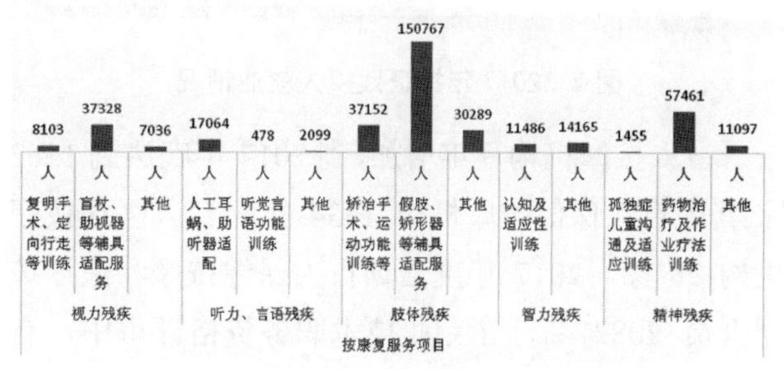

图 1　2017 年康复服务项目情况

在 37 个市辖区和 88 个县（市）开展社区康复，配备 25327 名社区康复协调员。

二、教育

2017 年，残疾人受教育权利进一步得到了更好保障，实施残疾人事业专项彩票公益金助学项目，为 910 人次家庭经济困难的残疾儿童享受普惠性学前教育提供资助。各地也积极多渠道争取资金支持，对 776 名残疾儿童给予学前教育资助。

共有特殊教育普通高中班（部）4 个，在校生 349 人，其中聋生 349 人。残疾人中等职业学校（班）7 个，在校生）833 人，毕业生 284 人，其中 139 人获得职业资格证书。有 369 名残疾人被普通高等院校录取，104 名残疾人进入特殊教育学院学习。1353 名残疾青壮年文盲接受了扫盲教育。

2017 年统计台帐有 910 名学前残疾儿童接受专项彩票公益金助学项目资助，其中视力残疾儿童 8 名，听力残疾儿童 186 名，言语残疾儿童 55 名，肢体残疾儿童 100 名，智力残疾儿童 380 名，精神残疾儿童 76 名，多重残疾儿童 105 名。

三、就业

2017 年，残疾人就业稳步增长。城乡持证残疾人就业人数为 413075 人，其中按比例就业 25631 人，集中就业 15038 人，个体就业 36618 人，社区就业 2954 人，公益性岗位就业 2332 人，辅助性就业 5797 人，居家就业 72766 人，从事农业种养加 196494 人，灵活就业 55445 人。

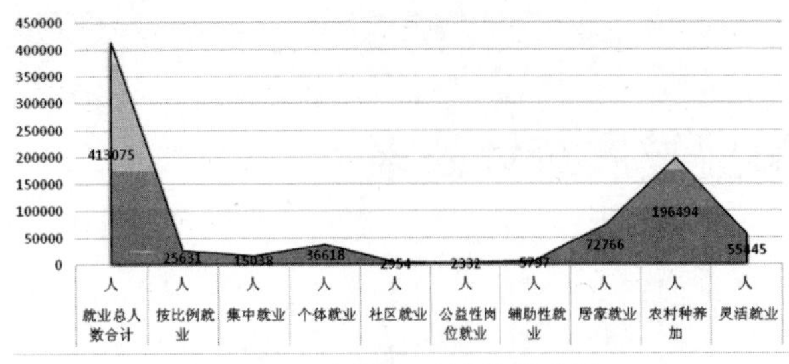

图 2　2017 年持证残疾人就业情况

盲人按摩机构逐年增加，到 2017 年底达到 1362 家,其中盲人保健按摩机构 1334 家，盲人医疗按摩机构 28 家。2017 年度培训盲人保健按摩和医疗按摩人员 2082 名，在专业技术职务资格评审中，有 41 人通过医疗按摩人员初级职称评审。

四、扶贫开发

残疾人扶贫工作持续加力，贫困残疾人生产生活状况得到进一步改善，2017 年，贫困残疾人得到有效扶持，其中 76142 人通过扶贫开发实际脱贫；接受实用技术培训的残疾人达到 20894 人次。

325 个残疾人扶贫基地，安置 6237 名残疾人就业，扶持带动 11192 名残疾人户。完成 13695 户农村贫困残疾人危房改造，各地投入危房资金 130275374 元。

五、社会保障

截至 2017 年底，城乡残疾居民参加城乡社会养老保险人数达到 1727881 名，330550 名 60 岁以下的重度残疾人参保，其中 328097 名得到了政府的参保扶助，代缴养老保险费比例达到 99.3%。有 94186 名非重度残疾人也享受了全额或部分代缴养老保险费的优惠政策。666565 人领取养老金。

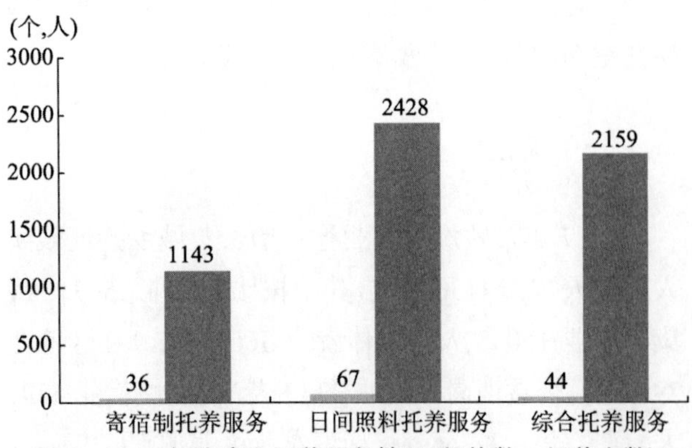

图 3　2017 年残疾人托养服务情况（机构数、托养人数）

残疾人托养服务工作稳步推进，残疾人托养服务机构达到 147 个，其中寄宿制托养服务机构 36 个，日间照料机构 67 个，综合性托养服务机构 44 个，为 5730 名残疾人提供了托养服务。接受居家服务的残疾人达到 16025 人。全年 795 名托养服务管理和服务人员接受了各级各类专业培训。

六、宣传文体

截至 2017 年底，省市县三级公共图书馆共设立盲文及盲文有声读物图书室 10 个，共开展残疾人文化周活动 230 场次；省市两级残联共举办残疾人文化艺术类的比赛及展览 73 次，共有各类残疾人艺术团 26 个。残疾人事业宣传紧密围绕事业大局，大力弘扬人道主义，营造了良好的舆论氛围。组织省级新闻发布会 2 次，电视手语栏目 1 个，省级残疾人专题广播节目 1 个；地市级残疾人专题广播节目 9 个、电视手语栏目 3 个。

七、维权

2017 年，制定或修改了关于残疾人的专门法规、规章省级 1 个、地市级 0 个；制定或修改保障残疾人权益的规范性文件省级 0 个、地市级 1 个、县级 8 个。县级以上人大开展《中华人民共和国残疾人保障法》执法检查和专题调研 20 次；政协开展视察和专题调研 22 次。开展省级普法宣传教育活动 3 次，200 余人参加；举办省级法律培训班 6 个，600 人参加。

截至 2017 年底，成立残疾人法律救助工作协调机构 106 个，建立残疾人法律救助工作站 105 个。

残疾人参政议政工作稳步开展，各地残联协助人大代表、政协委员提出议案、建议、提案 32 件，办理议案、建议、提案 31 件。无障碍建设法规、标准进一步完善。系统开展无障碍建设市、县、区 6 个；开展无障碍建设检查 83 次，无障碍培训 760 人次。2017 年全省各级残联处理残疾人群众来信 4531 件，接待来访 12401 人次，其中集体上访 39 批次，个体上访 11933 人次，从数据上看，上访人数和上访批次比上年大幅度下降。

八、组织建设

2017 年，市县乡共建立残联 2149 个，各地市已建残联 14 个，县（市、区）残联已建 125 个，乡镇（街道）残联已建 2010 个；已建社区（村）残协 30994 个。省市县乡残联实有人员达 4906 人，乡镇（街道）、村（社区）选聘残疾人专职委员总计 26639 名。地市级残联配备了残疾人领导干部 14 人，县级残联配备了残疾人干部 97 人。

共建立省级及以下各类残疾人专门协会 674 个，其中省级专门协会已建 5 个，市级专门协会已建 70 个，县级专门协会已建 599。助残社会组织共有 53 个。

九、服务设施建设

残疾人服务设施建设得到全面发展。截至 2017 年底，已竣工并投入使用的各级残疾人综合服务设施 101 个，总建设规模 127243 平方米，总投资 24258 万元；已竣工并投入使用的各级残疾人康复设施 40 个，总建设规模 86207 平方米，总投资 18942 万元；已竣工并投入使用的各级残疾人托养服务设施 51 个，总建设规模 51934 平方米，总投资 6856 万元。

十、信息化建设

全省各级残联共有 152 名统计员，信息化专业人才 198 人，截至 2017 年底，14 个地市、42 个县级残联开通网站。2017 年度省残联门户网站共发布信息类稿件 3800 篇。

2017 年广东省残疾人事业发展统计公报

2017 年，在省委、省政府的领导和中国残联的指导下，全省各级残联共同努力，积极推动残疾人康复、教育、就业、社会保障、权益保障、信息助残等专项服务工作，残疾人事业发展取得了新的成绩。

一、康复

2017 年，180249 名残疾儿童及持证残疾人得到基本康复服务,其中包括 0-6 岁残疾儿童 9906 人。得到康复服务的持证残疾人中，有视力残疾人 13144 名、听力残疾人 6837 名、言语残疾人 288 名、肢体残疾人 76381 名、智力残疾人 10699 名、精神残疾人 62985 名、多重残疾人 7662 名。

截至 2017 年底，我省已有残疾人康复机构 570 个，其中，提供视力残疾康复服务的机构 72 个，提供听力言语残疾康复服务的机构 76 个，提供肢体残疾康复服务的机构 181 个，提供智力残疾康复服务的机构 201 个，提供精神残疾康复服务的机构 96 个，提供孤独症儿童康复服务的机构 195 个，提供辅助器具服务的机构 86 个。康复机构在岗人员达 18037 人，其中，管理人员 2038 人，专业技术人员 12195 人，其他人员 3804 人。

二、教育

实施残疾人事业专项彩票公益金助学项目，为 1403 人次家庭经济困难的残疾儿童享受普惠性学前教育提供资助。各地也积极多渠道争取资金支持，对 119 名残疾儿童给予学前教育资助。

截至 2017 年底，共有特殊教育普通高中班（部）6 个，在校生 462 人，其中聋生 409 人，盲生 53 人。残疾人中等职业学校（班）10 个，在校生 1547 人，毕业生 399 人，其中 53 人获得职业资格证书。有 550 名残疾人被普通高等院校录取，76 名残疾人进入特殊教育学院学习。

2345 名残疾青壮年文盲接受了扫盲教育。

三、就业

截至 2017 年底，我省城乡持证残疾人就业人数为 278333 人，其中按比例就业 58746 人，集中就业 7321 人，个体就业 12911 人，社区就业 3958 人，公益性岗位就业 4981 人，辅助性就业 4606 人，居家就业 35193 人，从事农业种养加 129367 人，灵活就业 21250 人。

2017 年度培训盲人保健按摩人员 469 名、盲人医疗按摩人员 397 名；共有保健按摩机构 734 个，医疗按摩机构 10 个。

四、扶贫

2017 年，贫困残疾人得到有效扶持，其中 18326 人通过扶贫开发实际脱贫；接受实用技术培训的残疾人达到 15654 人次。康复扶贫贴息贷款扶持 344 名农村残疾人。残疾人扶贫基地 103 个，安置 3291 名残疾人就业，扶持带动 5682 名残疾人户。完成 3656 户农村贫困残疾人危房改造。

五、社会保障

截至 2017 年底，城乡残疾居民参加城乡社会养老保险人数达到 964864 人；316250 名 60 岁以下的重度残疾人参保，其中 302988 名得到了政府的参保扶助，代缴养老保险费比例达到 95.8%。有 79239 名非重度残疾人也享受了全额或部分代缴养老保险费的优惠政策。383286 人领取养老金。

残疾人托养服务工作稳步推进，残疾人托养服务机构达到 1017 个，其中寄宿制托养服务机构 39 个，日间照料机构 875 个，综合性托养服务机构 103 个，为 26859 名残疾人提供了托养服务。接受居家服务的残疾人达到 14273 人。全年 1794 名托养服务管理和服务人员接受了各级各类专业培训。

六、宣传文化与体育

截至2017年底，共有省级残疾人专题广播节目1个、电视手语栏目1个；地市级残疾人专题广播节目14个、电视手语栏目11个。

截至2017年底，省地县三级公共图书馆共设立盲文及盲文有声读物阅览室44个，共开展残疾人文化周活动250场次；省地两级残联共举办残疾人文化艺术类的比赛及展览44次，共有各类残疾人艺术团35个。

全省残疾人康复体育关爱家庭服务2650户，建设残疾人体育健身示范点372个，培养健身指导员2986名。

七、法制建设与维权

2017年，制定或修改保障残疾人权益的规范性文件省级1个、地市级5个、县级2个。县级以上人大开展《中华人民共和国残疾人保障法》执法检查和专题调研11次；政协开展视察和专题调研13次。开展省级普法宣传教育活动1次，315人参加。截至2017年底，成立残疾人法律救助工作协调机构57个，建立残疾人法律救助工作站47个。残疾人参政议政工作稳步开展，各地残联协助人大代表、政协委员提出议案、建议、提案28件，办理议案、建议、提案120件。无障碍建设法规、标准进一步完善。系统开展无障碍建设市、县、区145个；开展无障碍建设检查283次，无障碍培训1054人次。

八、组织建设

2017年，市县乡共建立残联1798个，各地市已建残联21个，县（市、区）残联已建137个，乡镇（街道）残联已建1640个；已建社区（村）残协23929个。

省市县乡残联实有人员达7714人，乡镇（街道）、村（社区）选聘残疾人专职委员总计24657名。地市级残联配备了残疾人领导干部16人，县级残联配备了残疾人干部55人。

共建立省级及以下各类残疾人专门协会698个，其中省级专门协会已建5个，市级专门协会已建105个，县级专门协会已建588。助残社会组织共有119个。

九、服务设施建设

截至2017年底，已竣工并投入使用的各级残疾人综合服务设施104个，总建设规模544206平方米，总投资158774万元；已竣工并投入使用的各级残疾人康复设施55个，总建设规模167478平方米，总投资44903万元；已竣工并投入使用的各级残疾人托养服务设施47个，总建设规模69919平方米，总投资13057万元。

2017年广西壮族自治区残疾人事业发展统计公报

2017年，广西残疾人事业在中国残联和自治区党委、政府的正确领导下，全区各级残联深入贯彻自治区党委、政府关于全区残疾人事业的新部署新要求，加快推进残疾人小康进程，积极完成“十三五”规划年度目标任务，残疾人事业发展取得更好的成绩，广大残疾人得到更多福祉。现根据我区2017年度残疾人事业统计年报数据和实际情况进行分析，并公报如下：

一、康复

截至2017年底，共有残疾人康复机构220个，其中，残联办康复机构110个。康复机构在岗人员达6868人。其中，管理人员713人，业务人员4620人，其他人员1535人。

在39个市辖区和75个县（市）开展社区康复工作，配备14079名社区康复协调员，为156709人次提供社区康复服务。

二、教育

本年度实施残疾人事业专项彩票公益金助学项目，为1220人次家庭经济困难的残疾儿童享受普惠性学前教育提供资助。各地也积极多渠道争取资金支持，对8名残疾儿童给予学前教育资助。

共有特殊教育普通高中学校（班）2个，在校生44人，都属聋生，毕业生12人。残疾人中等职业学校（班）1个，在校生219人，其中盲生54人，聋生165人，毕业生62人。有315名残疾人被普通高等院校录取。

三、就业

就业实名制人数为322419人，其中按比例就业9034人，集中就业1995人，个体就业14600人，社区就业1270人，公益性岗位就业2018人，辅助性就业2487人，居家就业39700人，226523人从事农业种养加，灵活就业24792人。

培训盲人保健按摩人员540名、盲人医疗按摩人员56名；保健按摩机构达到324个，医疗按摩机构达到5个。

四、扶贫

2017年，残疾人扶贫开发成效显著，贫困残疾人生产生活状况得到进一步改善。贫困残疾人得到有效扶持，其中81099人通过扶贫开发实际脱贫；接受实用技术培训的残疾人达到29944人次。

残疾人扶贫基地达到132个，安置3347名残疾人就业，扶持带动15755名残疾人。

完成2207户农村贫困残疾人危房改造，各地投入危房资金2431.4万元。

五、社会保障

截至2017年底，城乡残疾居民参加城乡社会养老保险人数达到112.3万名，参保率达79.5%，60岁以下的参保残疾人中有17.6万名重度残疾人，其中16.6万名得到了政府的参保扶助，代缴养老保险费比例达到94.5%。有35.4万名非重度残疾人也享受了全额或部分代缴养老保险费的优惠政策。领取养老金待遇的人数达到59.2万人。

残疾人托养服务工作稳步推进，残疾人托养服务机构达到55个，共为28792名残疾人提供了托养服务。其中寄宿制托养服务机构23个；日间照料机构26个；综合性托养服务机构6个。接受居家服务的残疾人达到25432人。全年共有779名托养服务管理和服务人员接受了各级各类专业培训。

六、宣传文化

2017年，共有省级残疾人专题广播节目1个、电视手语栏目1个；地市级残疾人专题广播节目3个、电视手语栏目6个。

截至2017年底，省地县三级公共图书馆共设立盲文及盲文有声读物阅览室共19个，共开展残疾人文化周活动80场次；省地两级残联共举办残疾人文化艺术类的比赛及展览12次，共有各类残疾人艺术团 6 个。

七、体育

省级建设社区健身示范点 3 个，培养健身指导员 130 名。

八、维权

2017 年，县级以上人大进行《残疾人保障法》执法检查和专题调研 3 次；政协进行视察和专题调研 2 次。

截至 2017 年底，成立残疾人法律救助工作协调机构 45 个，建立残疾人法律救助工作站 43 个，办理案件 67 件。

残疾人参政议政工作稳步开展，各地残联协助人大代表、政协委员提出议案、建议、提案 12 件，办理议案、建议、提案 6 件。

无障碍建设法规、标准进一步完善。125 个市、县、区系统开展无障碍建设；开展无障碍建设检查 43 次，无障碍培训 169 人次。

各级残联共处理残疾人群众来信 643 件，接待残疾人群众来访 9147 人次，其中集体访 17 批次、205 人次，来电 579 通，网上投诉 2 件。

九、组织建设

2017 年，市县乡共建立残联 1378 个，其中各地市残联已建 15 个，县（市、区）残联已建 114 个，乡镇（街道）残联已建 1249 个；已建社区（村）残协 14658 个。

省市县乡残联实有人员达 3352 人，乡镇（街道）、村（社区）选聘残疾人专职委员总计 17453 名。地市级残联配备了残疾人领导干部 11 人，县级残联配备了残疾人干部 62 人。

共建立省级及以下各类残疾人专门协会 630 个，其中省级专门协会已建 5 个，市级专门协会已建 70 个，县级专门协会已建 555 个。助残社会组织共有 17 个。

十、服务设施

残疾人服务设施建设得到全面发展。截至 2017 年底，已竣工并投入使用的各级残疾人综合服务设施 101 个，总建设规模 145134.3 平方米，总投资 25680.1 万元；已竣工并投入使用的各级残疾人康复设施 5 个，总建设规模 22300.5 平方米，总投资 6324 万元；已竣工并投入使用的各级残疾人托养服务设施 7 个，总建设规模 11315.3 平方米，总投资 1780.3 万元。

2017 年海南省残疾人事业发展统计公报

2017 年,在海南省委、省政府的领导和中国残联的指导下，省残联系统深入学习贯彻党的十九大精神，围绕海南国际旅游岛建设，积极推进残疾人康复、教育、就业、社会保障、信息助残等专项服务工作，团结进取、务实创新，加快推进残疾人小康进程，残疾人事业发展取得了新的成绩，使广大残疾人得到了更多的福祉。

一、康复

2017 年，6.9 万名残疾儿童及持证残疾人得到基本康复服务,其中包括 0-6 岁残疾儿童 1380 人。得到康复服务的持证残疾人中，有视力残疾人 7804 名、听力残疾人 2063 名、言语残疾人 268 名、肢体残疾人 3.1 万名、智力残疾人 7159 名、精神残疾人 1.7 万名、多重残疾人 3607 名。

截至 2017 年底，全省已有残疾人康复机构 34 个，其中，提供视力残疾康复服务的机构 4 个，提供听力言语残疾康复服务的机构 5 个，提供肢体残疾康复服务的机构 18 个，提供智力残疾康复服务的机构 11 个，提供精神残疾康复服务的机构 6 个，提供孤独症儿童康复服务的机构 10 个，提供辅助器具服务的机构 4 个。康复机构在岗人员达 1258 人，其中，管理人员 129 人，专业技术人员 919 人，其他人员 210 人。

二、教育

实施残疾人事业专项彩票公益金助学项目，为 345 人次家庭经济困难的残疾儿童享受普惠性学前教育提供资助。各地也积极多渠道自筹资金支持，对 6 名残疾儿童给予学前教育资助。

共有特殊教育普通高中班（部）1 个，在校生 90 人，其中聋生 90 人。残疾人中等职业学校（班）1 个，在校生 120 人，毕业生 40 人，其中 40 人获得职业资格证书。有 83 名残疾人被普通高等院校录取。1024 名残疾青壮年文盲接受了扫盲教育。

三、就业

采取优惠和扶持保护措施，多渠道、多层次、多种形式促进残疾人实现就业。城乡持证残疾人就业人数为 3.4 万人，其中按比例就业 4825 人，集中就业 406 人，个体就业 1186 人，社区就业 823 人，公益性岗位就业 419 人，辅助性就业 206 人，居家就业 3355 人，从事农业种养加 2.1 万人，灵活就业 2467 人。培训盲人保健按摩人员 145 名、盲人医疗按摩人员 17 名；保健按摩机构达到 227 个，医疗按摩机构达到 4 个；在专业技术职务资格评审中，分别有 1 人和 7 人通过医疗按摩人员中级和初级职称评审。

四、扶贫开发

2017 年，贫困残疾人得到有效扶持，其中 5495 人通过扶贫开发实际脱贫；接受实用技术培训的残疾人达到 6168 人次。达到 41 个残疾人扶贫基地，安置 220 名残疾人就业，扶持带动 300 名残疾人户。完成 297 户农村贫困残疾人危房改造，各地投入危房资金 901 万元。

五、社会保障

截至 2017 年底，城乡残疾居民参加城乡社会养老保险人数达到 16.1 万名，50121 名 60 岁以下的重度残疾人参保，其中 49995 名得到了政府的参保扶助，代缴养老保险费比例达到 99.7%。有 6311 名非重度残疾人也享受了全额或部分代缴养老保险费的优惠政策。5.7 万人领取养老金。

残疾人托养服务工作稳步推进，残疾人托养服务机构达到 14 个，其中寄宿制托养服务机构 11 个，综合性托养服务机构 3 个，为 1343 名残疾人提供了托养服务。接受居家服务的残疾人达到 2 万人。全年 5 名托养服务管理和服务人员接受了各级各类专业培训。

六、宣传文化和体育

截至 2017 年底，共有省级残疾人专题广播节目 1 个、电视手语栏目 1 个；地市级电视手语栏目 1 个。

截至 2017 年底，省地县三级公共图书馆共设立盲文及盲文有声读物阅览室 2 个，共开展残疾人文化周活动 13 场次；省地两级残联共举办残疾人文化艺术类的比赛及展览 1 次，共有各类残疾人艺术团 2 个。

全国残疾人康复体育关爱家庭服务 50 户，建设残疾人体育健身示范点 6 个，培养健身指导员 412 名。

七、维权

2017 年，制定或修改了关于残疾人的专门法规、地市级 1 个；制定或修改保障残疾人权益的规范性文件地市级 1 个、县级 2 个。县级以上人大开展《中华人民共和国残疾人保障法》执法检查和专题调研 3 次；开展省级普法宣传教育活动 4 次，506 人参加；举办省级法律培训班 4 个，374 人参加。

截至 2017 年底，成立残疾人法律救助工作协调机构 17 个，建立残疾人法律救助工作站 21 个。

残疾人参政议政工作稳步开展，各地残联协助人大代表、政协委员提出议案、建议、提案 7 件，办理议案、建议、提案 1 件。

无障碍建设法规、标准进一步完善。系统开展无障碍建设市、县、区 2 个；开展无障碍建设检查 4 次，无障碍培训 304 人次。

八、组织建设

2017 年，市县乡共建立残联 246 个，各地市已建残联 3 个，县（市、区）残联已建 20 个，乡镇（街道）残联已建 223 个；已建社区（村）残协 2583 个。

省市县乡残联实有人员达 734 人，乡镇（街道）、村（社区）选聘残疾人专职委员总计 3041 名。地市级残联配备了残疾人领导干部 3 人，县级残联配备了残疾人干部 8 人。

共建立省级及以下各类残疾人专门协会 109 个，其中省级专门协会已建 5 个，市级专门协会已建 15 个，县级专门协会已建 89。助残社会组织共有 7 个。

九、服务设施和信息化建设

截至 2017 年底，已竣工并投入使用的各级残疾人综合服务设施 10 个，总建设规模 1.3 万平方米，总投资 3919 万元；已竣工并投入使用的各级残疾人康复设施 2 个，总建设规模 2205 平方米，总投资 525 万元。

截至 2017 年底，3 个地市、12 个县级残联开通网站。

2017年重庆市残疾人事业发展统计公报

2017年，在重庆市委、市政府的坚强领导下，在中国残联的关怀指导下，在社会各界的关心支持下，全市各级残联以习近平新时代中国特色社会主义思想为指导，深入贯彻落实市委五届三次全会精神，扎实落实《重庆市人民政府关于印发重庆市“十三五”加快残疾人小康进程规划的通知》（渝府发〔2017〕11号），着力加快推进残疾人小康进程，各项工作取得显著成绩。

一、残疾人康复工作

推进康复机构规范化管理，完善基层服务网络。全市共有残疾人康复机构262个，其中，提供视力残疾康复服务的机构44个，提供听力言语残疾康复服务的机构43个，提供肢体残疾康复服务的机构87个，提供智力残疾康复服务的机构67个，提供精神残疾康复服务的机构48个，提供孤独症儿童康复服务的机构31个，提供辅助器具服务的机构39个。康复机构在岗人员达7952人，其中，管理人员952人，专业技术人员4835人，其他人员2165人。

通过实施精准康复服务，全市167725名残疾儿童及持证残疾人得到基本康复服务，其中包括0-6岁残疾儿童2580人。得到康复服务的持证残疾人中，有视力残疾人21781名、听力残疾人7345名、言语残疾人137名、肢体残疾人74988名、智力残疾人14803名、精神残疾人42496名、多重残疾人5709名。

二、残疾人教育工作

实施残疾人事业专项彩票公益金助学项目，为374人次家庭经济困难的残疾儿童享受普惠性学前教育提供资助。

全市共有特殊教育普通高中班（部）3个，在校生131人，其中聋生34人，盲生97人。残疾人中等职业学校（班）1个，在校生）77人，毕业生25人。有317名残疾人被普通高等院校录取。

2134名残疾青壮年文盲接受了扫盲教育。

三、残疾人就业工作

大力推进残疾人按比例就业，采取集中就业、个体就业、公益岗位就业、灵活就业、居家就业、辅助性就业等多种形式就业，大力促进残疾人就业增收。截至2017年，城乡持证残疾人就业248840人，其中按比例就业15001人，集中就业11096人，个体就业20296人，社区就业3055人，公益性岗位就业2081人，辅助性就业3147人，居家就业28525人，从事农业种养加125286人，灵活就业40353人。

进一步推动盲人保健按摩行业规范化管理。培训盲人保健按摩人员139名、盲人医疗按摩人员255名；保健按摩机构达到874个，医疗按摩机构达到18个。

四、残疾人扶贫开发工作

推进精准脱贫工作，贫困残疾人得到有效扶持。通过扶贫开发实际脱贫13923人，接受实用技术培训的残疾人19849人次。

康复扶贫贴息贷款扶持587名农村残疾人,残疾人扶贫基地达到115个，安置1145名残疾人就业，扶持带动1513名残疾人户。

全力实施农村贫困残疾人危房改造。2017年，共投入危房资金5882.2万元，对3550户农村贫困残疾人危房进行改造

五、社会保障工作

截至2017年底，城乡残疾居民参加城乡社会养老保险人数达到527352名，128310名60岁以下的重度残疾人参保，其中126728名得到了政府的参保扶助，代缴养老保险费比例达到98.8%。有33136名非重度残疾人也享受了全额或部分代缴养老保险费的优惠政策。领取养老金待遇的人数达到201023人。

残疾人托养服务工作稳步推进，残疾人托养服务机构达到80个。其中寄宿制托养服务机构24个；日间照料机构37个；综合性托养服务机构19个，

为2051名残疾人提供了机构托养服务。接受居家服务的残疾人达到28102人。全年共有1634名托养服务管理和服务人员接受了各级各类专业培训。

六、残疾人宣传文体工作

加大宣传工作力度。截止2017年底，共有市级残疾人专题广播节目1个、电视手语栏目1个；区级残疾人专题广播节目6个、电视手语栏目25个。

残疾人群众性文化活动更加丰富。全市公共图书馆共设立盲文及盲文有声读物阅览室42个，开展残疾人文化周活动197场次；举办残疾人文化艺术类的比赛及展览6次，成立残疾人艺术团1个。

深入开展残疾人体育工作。完成残疾人康复体育关爱家庭服务10000户，建设残疾人体育健身示范点204个，培养健身指导员425名。

七、残疾人维权工作

抓好“大维权、大接访、大稳定”机制的贯彻落实。2017年，全市制定或修改保障残疾人权益的规范性文件6个。县级以上人大开展《中华人民共和国残疾人保障法》执法检查和专题调研9次；政协开展视察和专题调研13次。开展市级普法宣传教育活动3次，640人参加了活动；举办市级法律培训班1期，92人参加了培训。

截至2017年底，成立残疾人法律救助工作协调机构29个，建立残疾人法律救助工作站29个。

残疾人参政议政工作稳步开展，各级残联协助人大代表、政协委员提出议案、建议、提案41件，办理议案、建议、提案36件。

无障碍建设法规、标准进一步完善。38个区县均系统开展无障碍建设；开展无障碍建设检查55次，无障碍培训1642人次。

八、残疾人组织建设工作

残疾人基层组织体系建设更加完善，推进基层残疾人组织能力建设，全面落实和提高了全市乡镇（街道）残联理事长、残疾人专职委员的待遇，巩固稳定了基层残疾人队伍。2017年，全市共建立各级残联1063个，其中区县残联40个，乡镇（街道）残联1023个；已建村（社区）残协10986个。

全市残联系统实有人员1975人，乡镇（街道）、村（社区）选聘残疾人专职委员11390名。区县残联配备残疾人干部38人。

建立各类残疾人专门协会199个，助残社会组织46个。

九、残疾人综合服务设施建设

残疾人服务设施建设得到全面发展。截至2017年底，已竣工并投入使用的各级残疾人综合服务设施27个，总建设规模79819平方米，总投资23289万元；已竣工并投入使用的各级残疾人康复设施9个，总建设规模52814平方米，总投资22363万元；已竣工并投入使用的各级残疾人托养服务设施2个，总建设规模5968平方米，总投资1708万元。

十、残疾人信息化建设

全市共有27个区县残联开通了网站，其中：独立建立网站17个，搭载上级残联或同级政府网站或集约到同级群团网站11个。

截至2017年底，全国残疾人人口基础数据库入库重庆籍持证残疾人84.3万人。扎实开展残疾人基本服务状况和需求信息动态更新工作，全面掌握残疾人基本服务和需求信息，为业务工作的开展、残疾人精准服务提供了有效数据支撑。与政府相关涉残部门开展数据共享与交换，为整合残疾人服务和管理资源提供了信息保障。

2017年四川省残疾人事业发展统计公报

2017年，在省委、省政府的正确领导下，在中国残联的大力指导和支持下，在社会各界的关爱和帮助下，四川省残疾人工作继续保持良好的发展势头，“量体裁衣”式残疾人服务持续深化，在残疾人康复、教育、就业、扶贫、组织建设、维权、宣传文化、体育、服务设施建设等业务领域均取得了新进步、新成效，为广大残疾人带来更多的福祉。现根据我省2017年度残疾人事业统计数据进行分析，并公报如下：

一、康复

2017年，通过实施精准康复服务，共为126.8万名残疾儿童及持证残疾人提供基本康复服务。其中：视力残疾人7.8万名，听力言语残疾人1.3万名，肢体残疾人89万名，智力残疾人10.1万名，精神残疾人15.3万名,多重残疾人3.3万名。共有9813名0-6岁残疾儿童得到基本康复服务。

截止2017年底，全省共建有残疾人康复机构263个，其中，提供视力残疾康复服务的机构50个，提供听力言语残疾康复服务的机构58个，提供肢体残疾康复服务的机构111个，提供智力残疾康复服务的机构117个，提供精神残疾康复服务的机构81个，提供孤独症儿童康复服务的机构58个，提供辅助器具服务的机构68个。康复机构在岗人员达1.1万人。

二、教育

2017年，通过实施残疾人事业专项彩票公益金助学项目，为家庭经济困难的残疾儿童享受普惠性学前教育提供资助共计1004人次；各地也积极多渠道争取资金支持，对182名残疾儿童给予了学前教育资助。

截止2017年底，全省共有特殊教育普通高中班（部）4个，残疾人中等职业学校（班）3个；全年共有682名残疾人被普通高等院校录取。

三、就业

城乡持证残疾人就业人数为89.3万人。其中：按比例就业2.1万人，集中就业1.3万人，个体就业5.6万人，社区就业9390人，公益性岗位就业7295人，辅助性就业1.7万人，居家就业32.7万人，从事农业种养加34.6万人，灵活就业9.6万人。

共培训盲人保健按摩人员994名、盲人医疗按摩人员63名；全省盲人保健按摩机构达到1727个，盲人医疗按摩机构达到57个。

四、扶贫

全省残疾人扶贫开发成效显著，贫困残疾人生产生活状况得到进一步改善。有效扶持贫困残疾人，其中5.2万人通过扶贫开发实际脱贫；为残疾人提供实用技术培训15.4万人次。

全省残疾人扶贫基地达到385个，共安置6564名残疾人就业，扶持带动1.2万户残疾人。

全年共完成2985户农村贫困残疾人危房改造，各地投入危房改造资金共计3034.2万元。

五、社会保障

截至2017年底，城乡残疾居民参加城乡社会养老保险人数达到223万名。60岁以下的参保残疾人中有41.7万名重度残疾人，其中40.4万名得到了政府的参保扶助，代缴养老保险费比例达到97.1%。有26.3万名非重度残疾人也享受了全额或部分代缴养老保险费的优惠政策。

残疾人托养服务工作继续规范推进。残疾人托养服务机构达到167个，共为6104名残疾人提供托养服务；共有524名托养服务管理和服务人员接受了专业培训。

六、宣传文化体育

截止2017年底，全省共有残疾人专题广播节目

7 个，电视手语新闻栏目 8 个。

共设立盲文及盲文有声读物阅览室 40 个；共有各类残疾人艺术团 9 个；全年开展残疾人文化周活动 225 场次；省、市两级举办残疾人文化艺术类比赛及展览 18 次。

全年共开展全国残疾人康复体育关爱家庭服务 4.6 万户；建设残疾人体育健身示范点 129 个，培养健身指导员 807 名。

七、维权

截至 2017 年底，全省已成立残疾人法律救助工作协调机构 115 个，建立残疾人法律救助工作站 93 个。

残疾人参政议政工作稳步开展，各级残联协助人大代表、政协委员提出议案、建议、提案 38 件，办理议案、建议、提案 59 件。

在无障碍建设领域，全省已有 37 个市、县、区系统开展无障碍建设；全年共开展无障碍建设检查 279 次，无障碍培训 5073 人次。

八、组织建设

截止 2017 年底，市县乡共建立残联 4724 个，其中市级残联 21 个，县级残联 189 个，乡镇（街道）残联已建 4514 个；社区（村）残协已建 46438 个。

省、市、县、乡残联实有人员达到 9180 人，乡镇（街道）、村（社区）选聘残疾人专职委员共计 45396 名。

共建立省级以下各类残疾人专门协会 978 个，建立助残社会组织 154 个。

九、服务设施

深入推进残疾人服务设施建设工作。截至 2017 年底，已竣工并投入使用的各级残疾人综合服务设施达 141 个，总建设规模 33.8 万平方米；已竣工并投入使用的各级残疾人康复设施达 38 个，总建设规模 16.3 万平方米；已竣工并投入使用的各级残疾人托养服务设施达 21 个，总建设规模 4 万平方米。

十、信息化

2017 年，依托四川省“量体裁衣”式残疾人服务平台，持续深化“量体裁衣”式残疾人服务工作。根据“量体裁衣”式残疾人服务平台的统计结果显示，2017 年，全省各级残疾人工作者共为 331.1 万名残疾人提供 3025.2 万项次的服务。

2017年贵州省残疾人事业发展统计公报

2017年，在省委、省政府的领导、中国残联的指导及相关部门的支持下，贵州省残疾人联合会深入学习贯彻党的十九大精神，认真贯彻落实党中央、国务院关于残疾人事业发展的一系列重要部署，主动担当，积极作为，着力加强促进残疾人事业发展的制度建设、民生建设、环境建设和机关建设，大力推进着残疾人事业的各项工作任务，推动残疾人事业持续健康发展。

一、康复

2017年，15.2万名残疾儿童及持证残疾人得到基本康复服务,其中包括0-6岁残疾儿童2684人。得到康复服务的持证残疾人中，有视力残疾人2.1万名、听力残疾人7892名、言语残疾人654名、肢体残疾人9.2万名、智力残疾人8817名、精神残疾人1.1万名、多重残疾人9719名。

截至2017年底，有残疾人康复机构185个，其中，提供视力残疾康复服务的机构46个，提供听力言语残疾康复服务的机构50个，提供肢体残疾康复服务的机构63个，提供智力残疾康复服务的机构60个，提供精神残疾康复服务的机构56个，提供孤独症儿童康复服务的机构37个，提供辅助器具服务的机构44个。康复机构在岗人员达8273人，其中，管理人员989人，专业技术人员5502人，其他人员1782人。

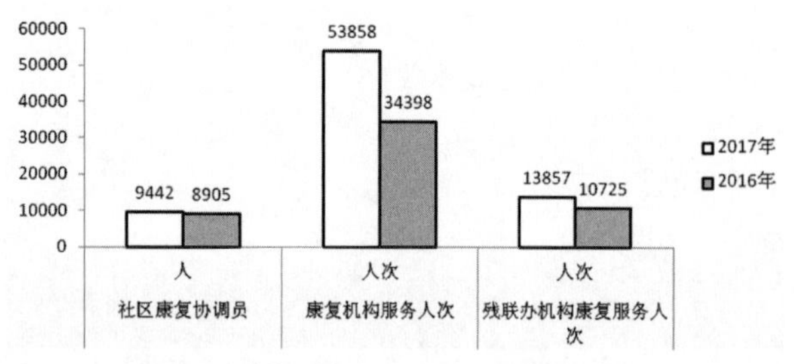

图1 2017年与2016年康复情况对比

二、教育

实施残疾人事业专项彩票公益金助学项目，为582人次家庭经济困难的残疾儿童享受普惠性学前教育提供资助。

全省共有特殊教育学校75所，在校三残学生1.6万人；残疾人中等职业学校1所；有612名残疾人学生被普通高等院校录取；全年对1419名残疾青壮年文盲接受了扫盲教育。

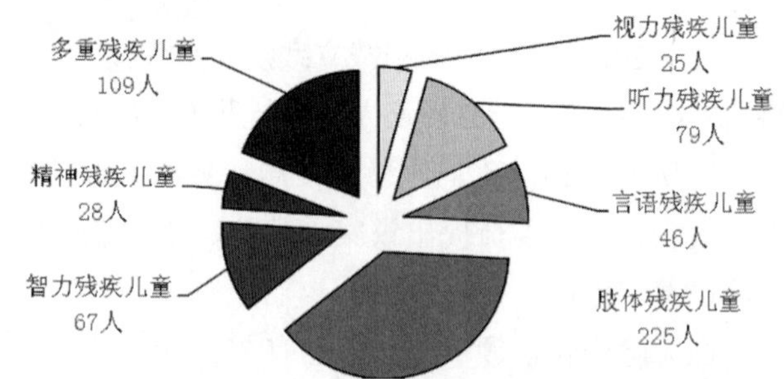

图2 2017年度接受残疾人事业专项彩票公益金助学项目资情况分析

三、就业

城乡持证残疾人就业人数为33.5万人，其中按比例就业7758人，集中就业5745人，个体就业1.9万人，社区就业2070人，公益性岗位就业1398人，辅助性就业3055人，居家就业4.9万人，从事农业种养加20.3万人，灵活就业4.5万人。

全年共培训盲人保健按摩人员710名、盲人医疗按摩人员171名；保健按摩机构达717个，医疗按摩机构达26个；专业技术职务资格评审中，有82人通过医疗按摩人员初级职称评审。

四、扶贫

2017年，贫困残疾人得到有效扶持，其中4.2万人通过扶贫开发实际脱贫；接受实用技术培训的残疾人达到1.2万人次。康复扶贫贴息贷款扶持824名农村残疾人。残疾人扶贫基地安置1840名残疾人就业，扶持带动3583名残疾人户。

完成353户农村贫困残疾人危房改造，各地投入危房资金232.0万元。

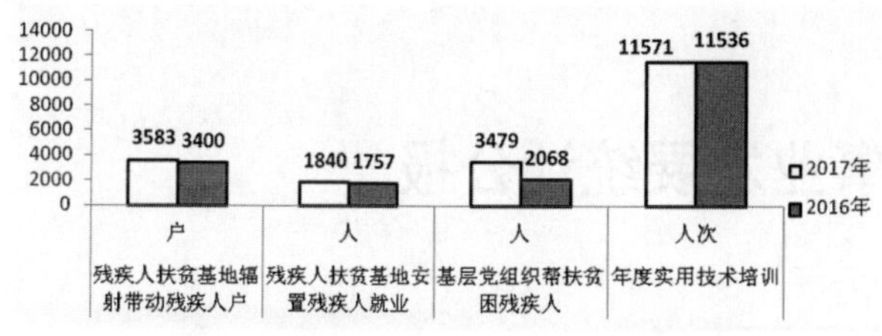

图 3　2017 年与 2016 年扶贫情况比较

五、社会保障

截至 2017 年底，城乡残疾居民参加城乡社会养老保险人数达到 76.6 万名，9.9 万名 60 岁以下的重度残疾人参保，其中 8.8 万名得到了政府的参保扶助，代缴养老保险费比例达到 88.4%。有 6.1 万名非重度残疾人也享受了全额或部分代缴养老保险费的优惠政策。38.2 万人领取养老金。

残疾人托养服务工作稳步推进，残疾人托养服务机构达到 26 个，其中寄宿制托养服务机构 8 个，日间照料机构 3 个，综合性托养服务机构 15 个，为 2048 名残疾人提供了托养服务。接受居家服务的残疾人达到 6398 人。全年 68 名托养服务管理和服务人员接受了各级各类专业培训。

六、宣传文化

截至 2017 年底，共有省级残疾人专题广播节目 3 个、电视手语栏目 1 个；地市级残疾人专题广播节目 4 个、电视手语栏目 6 个。

截至 2017 年底，省地县三级公共图书馆共设立盲文及盲文有声读物阅览室 23 个，共开展残疾人文化周活动 199 场次；省地两级残联共举办残疾人文化艺术类的比赛及展览 4 次，共有各类残疾人艺术团 2 个。

七、体育

全省建设残疾人体育健身示范点 46 个，培养健身指导员 241 名。

八、维权

2017 年，制定或修改保障残疾人权益的规范性文件省级 2 个、地市级 1 个、县级 11 个。县级以上人大开展《中华人民共和国残疾人保障法》执法检查和专题调研 7 次；政协开展视察和专题调研 7 次。开展省级普法宣传教育活动 2 次，400 人参加；举办省级法律培训班 2 个，400 人参加。

截至 2017 年底，成立残疾人法律救助工作协调机构 74 个，建立残疾人法律救助工作站 64 个。

残疾人参政议政工作稳步开展，各地残联协助人大代表、政协委员提出议案、建议、提案 5 件，办理议案、建议、提案 9 件。

无障碍建设法规、标准进一步完善。系统开展无障碍建设市、县、区 26 个；开展无障碍建设检查 25 次，无障碍培训 76 人次。

九、组织建设

2017 年，市县乡共建立残联 1523 个，各地市已建残联 10 个，县（市、区）残联已建 88 个，乡镇（街道）残联已建 1425 个；已建社区（村）残协 1.6 万个。

省市县乡残联实有人员达 3221 人，乡镇（街道）、村（社区）选聘残疾人专职委员总计 1.6 万名。地市级残联配备了残疾人领导干部 11 人，县级残联配备了残疾人干部 96 人。

共建立省级及以下各类残疾人专门协会 404 个，其中省级专门协会已建 5 个，市级专门协会已建 31 个，县级专门协会已建 368。助残社会组织共有 13 个。

十、服务设施建设

截至 2017 年底，已竣工并投入使用的各级残疾人综合服务设施 58 个，总建设规模 6.2 万平方米，总投资 1.2 亿元；已竣工并投入使用的各级残疾人康复设施 6 个，总建设规模 4.2 万平方米，总投资 1.0 亿元；已竣工并投入使用的各级残疾人托养服务设施 9 个，总建设规模 3.5 万平方米，总投资 9122 万元。

十一、信息化建设

截至 2017 年底，3 个地市、21 个县级残联开通网站。

2017 年云南省残疾人事业发展统计公报

2017 年全省各级残联深入学习党的十九大及省委九届、十届全会精神，认真贯彻落实党中央、国务院关于残疾人事业发展的一系列决策部署，全省残疾人工作者凝聚精、气、神，以人道、廉洁、服务、奉献为宗旨，充分发挥服务弱势、强势推进的工作理念，圆满完成各项工作任务，云南省残疾人事业取得了良好的发展，广大残疾人得到了更多的实惠和帮助，各级人民政府、各级政府残工委单位、社会各界、社会公众对于残疾人群体的关注进一步提高。

一、康复

2017 年，云南省残疾人康复工作坚持以“保基本、强基础、建机制”的原则，紧紧围绕构建与经济社会发展相协调、与残疾人康复需求相适应的多元化康复服务体系、多层次康复保障制度，为实现 2020 年，残疾儿童及有需求的持证残疾人接受基本康复服务的比例达 80%以上，采取更有针对性的措施，以实施残疾人精准康复服务行动为重点，全面部署“十三五”残疾人康复工作，制定并印发《云南省残疾人康复服务“十三五”实施方案》《云南省辅助器具推广和服务“十三五”实施方案》《云南省残疾预防综合试验区创建试点工作实施方案》；认真贯彻落实《残疾预防和残疾人康复条例》，已形成《云南省残疾预防和残疾人康复规定》（申报稿），为下一步的立法申请做好了准备；全面落实残疾预防工作，认真贯彻落实《云南省人民政府办公厅关于印发云南省残疾预防行动计划（2016—2020 年）的通知》精神；全面落实残疾人康复工作，制定《云南省 0—6 岁残疾儿童康复救助管理办法》，认真做好 2017 年云南省残联系统康复专业人才实名制培训工作，认真组织实施国际合作项目。

2017 年，全省共有 273241 名残疾儿童及持证残疾人得到基本康复服务,其中包括 0-6 岁残疾儿童 2977 人，7-17 岁残疾儿童 14474 人。得到康复服务的持证残疾人中，有视力残疾人 35484 名、听力残疾人 21101 名、言语残疾人 2238 名、肢体残疾人 140731 名、智力残疾人 18846 名、精神残疾人 40851 名、多重残疾人 13832 名，其中共有 70773 人得到辅助器具适配服务。

截至 2017 年底，全省共有残疾人康复机构 240 个，其中，提供视力残疾康复服务的机构 47 个，提供听力言语残疾康复服务的机构 45 个，提供肢体残疾康复服务的机构 70 个，提供智力残疾康复服务的机构 70 个，提供精神残疾康复服务的机构 63 个，提供孤独症儿童康复服务的机构 29 个，提供辅助器具服务的机构 92 个。康复机构在岗人员达 7173 人，其中，管理人员 815 人，专业技术人员 4018 人，其他人员 2340 人。全省 2017 年度共培训康复机构管理人员 1670 人次，培训康复机构业务人员 10084 人次。

二、教育

2017 年云南特殊教育职业学院获批成立，有力地促进了我省以职业教育为主的残疾人高中阶段教育发展。云南省教育厅、云南省残联等七部门联合印发了《云南省特殊教育提升计划实施方案（2017-2020 年）》，以期到 2020 年，全省各级各类特殊教育普及水平全面提高，保障能力全面增强，教育质量全面提升。

2017 年继续实施残疾人事业专项彩票公益金助学项目，为全省 465 人次家庭经济困难的残疾儿童享受普惠性学前教育提供资助。各地也积极获得其他资金支持，对 11 名残疾儿童给予学前教育资助。

全省共有特殊教育普通高中班 1 个，在校生 272 人，其中聋生 232 人，盲生 40 人。残疾人中等职业学校 4 个，2017 年招生 286 人，在校生 819 人，2017 年度毕业生 229 人，毕业生中 215 人获得职业资格证书。

全省 2017 年共有 1298 名残疾人考生达到高等教育录取分数线，其中有 917 名残疾人被普通高等院校录取，其中研究生 1 人、本科生 357 人，专科（高职）生 559 人。

全省全年通过培训对 3560 名残疾青壮年文盲

进行了扫盲教育。

三、就业

2017 年全省城乡持证残疾人就业人数为 450019 人，其中按比例就业 18370 人，全年新增 335 人；集中就业 7703 人，全年新增 154 人；个体就业 17132 人，全年新增 643 人；社区就业 989 人，全年新增 41 人；公益性岗位就业 973 人，全年新增 40 人；辅助性就业 5064 人，全年新增 51 人；居家就业 44788 人，全年新增 952 人；从事农业种养加 306197 人，全年新增 4225 人；灵活就业 48803 人，全年新增 2209 人。

全省盲人按摩事业发展迅速，2017 年全省培训盲人保健按摩人员 1437 名、盲人医疗按摩人员 399 名；全省保健按摩机构达到 855 个，其中通过积极稳妥推动“助盲脱贫”实现盲人保健按摩机构规范化建设暨量化分级 350 家。

2017 年全省新注册医疗按摩机构 4 个。机构建设有力促进盲人就业，全年促进盲人保健按摩人员就业 538 人，盲人医疗按摩人员在医疗机构中就业 9 人，在专业技术职务资格评审中，有 23 人通过医疗按摩人员初级职称的评审。

四、扶贫

2017 年，贫困残疾人脱贫攻坚取得阶段性成效，贫困残疾人得到有效扶持，贫困残疾人户退出建档立卡共 34746 户，涉及残疾人共 43376 人实际脱贫；全省接受实用技术培训的残疾人达到 35208 人次。

2017 年全省实际落实康复扶贫贴息贷款 159 万元，本年度财政贴息金额 5.8 万元，共扶持 20 名农村残疾人生产创业。全省残疾人扶贫基地建设稳步推进，共建设 385 个残疾人扶贫基地，安置 3263 名残疾人就业，扶持带动 25410 名残疾人户。

2017 年全省共完成 3317 户农村贫困残疾人危房改造，各地投入危房资金 2242.2 万元，其中省级资金 17.5 万元，州（市）残联资金 1028 万元，县级资金 1196.7 万元。

五、社会保障与托养

截至 2017 年底，全省符合参保条件的残疾居民为 99.2 万人，其中符合参保条件的重度残疾人 33.3 万人，城乡残疾居民参加城乡社会养老保险人数达到 86.3 万名，其中 60 岁以下的重度残疾人参保 18.1 万名，其中 17.4 万名得到了政府的参保优惠政策扶助，获得全额或部分代缴养老保险，代缴养老保险费比例达到重度残疾人数的 96.1%。全省有 19.0 万名非重度残疾人也享受了全额或部分代缴养老保险费的优惠政策。31.0 万人领取养老金。

全省残疾人托养服务工作稳步推进，截止 2017 年全省共建设残疾人托养服务机构 74 个，其中寄宿制托养服务机构 33 个，托养残疾人 965 人，日间照料托养服务机构 8 个，托养残疾人 742 人，综合性托养服务机构 33 个，托养残疾人 473 人，机构共为 2180 名残疾人提供了托养服务。全省全年共有 942 名托养服务管理和服务人员接受了各级各类专业培训，其中机构内人员 135 人接受培训，807 名居家人员接受了居家托养服务人员培训，全省获得居家托养服务的残疾人达到 13453 人，

六、宣传文化

2017 年全省残联紧紧围绕残疾人事业大局，统筹做好重大政策、重点工作、重要活动的宣传报道，传播社会主义核心价值观，弘扬人道主义思想和“平等、参与、共享”的现代文明社会残疾人观。

2017 年由省残联会与云南广播电视台国际频道《Hi 云南》栏目携手创办的宣传残疾人事业的节目《追梦》，组织记者采访 50 多次，每周 1 期从未间断，对我省残疾人事业相关活动、各项工作开展情况和所取得的成就、残疾人重要节日及相关活动、残疾人自强不息的先进典型和残疾人工作优秀代表进行宣传，将《追梦》栏目办成了我省大力宣传残疾人事业的主要阵地和重要平台。全年云南日报刊登宣传残疾人事业的新闻、专题等文章 20 余篇。

截至 2017 年底，全省共有省级残疾人专题电视手语栏目 1 个，组织省级新闻发布会 1 次，开通 1 个省级残疾人联合会官方微信；州（市）残联残疾人专题广播节目 6 个、电视手语栏目 10 个，组织州（市）残联新闻发布会 2 次，累计成立新促会 9 个。

2017 年我省着力推进公共图书馆盲人阅览室、文化进社区、文化进家庭、残疾人特殊艺术人才培养基地、残疾人文化创意产业基地等项目建设，努力保障残疾人平等享有文化公共服务的权益，进一步建立公共文化服务网络。在第八届全国残疾人艺

术汇演西部赛区比赛中，获一等奖 1 个、二等奖 2 个、三等奖 3 个，并获组织奖，获一等奖的声乐类节目《赶马哥》被指定参加在北京举行的第九届全国残疾人艺术汇演进行汇报演出。

截至 2017 年底，省、州（市）、县（市、区）三级公共图书馆共设立盲文及盲文有声读物阅览室 28 个，共开展残疾人文化周活动 267 场次，其中省级举办 1 次，参与人次 280 人；州（市）残联举办 40 次，参与人次 2298 人；县（市、区）残联举办 226 次，参与人次 15976 人。省、州（市）两级残联共举办残疾人文化艺术类的比赛及展览 13 次，共有各类残疾人艺术团 8 个。

七、体育

2017 年云南省残疾人体育事业蓬勃发展，运动员、教练员和工作人员狠抓各时期集训队伍的管理和参赛工作，全年参加国内国际各种比赛共获得金牌 40 枚、银牌 32 枚、铜牌 22 枚，实现了竞技体育和群众体育和谐持续发展的良好局面。

2017 年全年全省共 1000 户家庭接受了全国残疾人康复体育关爱家庭服务。全省截止 2017 年底建设残疾人体育健身示范点 20 个。其中省级残疾人群众体育健身示范点 5 个，参与人次 180 人次；州（市）级残疾人体育健身示范点 4 个，参与人次 25 人次；残疾人体育健身示范点 11 个，参与人次 7618 人次。省、州（市）、县（市、区）三级累计共培养残疾人体育健身指导员 765 名。

八、维权与信访

2017 年，全省共有 2 个县（市、区）制定或修改了保障残疾人权益的规范性文件。县（市、区）以上人大开展《中华人民共和国残疾人保障法》执法检查或专题调研 6 次；政协开展视察或专题调研 4 次。

截至 2017 年底，全省共成立残疾人法律救助工作协调机构 35 个，其中省级 1 个，州（市）残联 8 个，县（市、区）残联 26 个；建立残疾人法律救助工作站 32 个，其中省级 1 个并办理案件 12 起，州（市）残联 8 个并办理案件 5 起，县（市、区）残联 23 个并办理案件 62 起。

全省残疾人参政议政工作稳步开展，各地残联协助人大代表、政协委员提出议案、建议、提案 34 件，办理人大建议、政协提案 19 件。各级共有 72 名残疾人担任人大代表，其中省级 1 人，州（市）残联 12 人，县（市、区）残联 59 人；各级共有 126 名残疾人担任政协委员，其中省级 2 人，州（市）残联 18 人，县（市、区）残联 106 人。

2017 年无障碍建设法规、标准进一步完善。全省各级共建立无障碍建设领导协调组织 49 个，其中州（市）残联 14 个，县（市、区）残联 35 个，2017 年共有 5 个州（市）和 69 个县（市、区）系统开展无障碍环境建设。全省 2017 年共开展无障碍建设检查 52 次，其中州（市）残联开展 11 次，县（市、区）残联开展 41 次；全省全年共开展无障碍培训 414 人次，其中州（市）残联 1 人次，县（市、区）残联 413 人次。

2017 年省级共接到残疾人来信 41 件；全年共接待残疾人来访 404 人次，其中个人访 404 人次，无集体来访事件；全年共受理 22 件网上投诉，无电话投诉。

2017 年州（市）残联共接到残疾人来信 69 件；全年共接待残疾人来访 753 人次，其中个人访 753 人次，无集体来访事件；共受理来电 1266 通，受理网上投诉件 4 件。

2017 年县（市、区）残联共接到残疾人来信 2300 件；全年共接待残疾人来访 12609 人次，其中个人访 12514 人次，集体来访 9 批次共 95 人次；共受理网上投诉件 24 件。

九、组织建设

2017 年，全省州（市）、县（市、区）、乡镇（街道）共建立残联 1555 个。其中省级残联机关 1 个，实有人员 59 人，省级残联事业单位 8 个，实有人员 253 人。

全省各州（市）已建残联机关 16 个，其中 12 个州（市）残联配备了残疾人领导干部，州（市）残联机关共有 196 人，州（市）残联事业单位共 27 个，实有人员 121 人；各州市 2017 年共举办综合培训班 24 期，参加培训人次达 2036 人次；共举办残疾人干部培训班 14 期，参加培训人次 1314 人次；共有 156 名助残志愿者为 442 名残疾人提供了志愿助残服务。

全省共有 134 个县（市、区）建立了残联，其中 89 个残联机关配备了残疾人领导干部，县（市、区）残联机关实有人员 1287 人，县（市、区）残联残联事业单位 109 个，实有人员 347 人。各县（市、区）共举办 218 期培训班，参加培训人次 10374 人次；共有 1832 名助残志愿者为 36400 名残疾人提供了志愿助残服务。

全省共有 1405 个乡镇（街道）建立了残联；其中专职理事长有 460 名，兼职理事长 470 名，残疾人专职委员 1429 名。乡镇（街道）残联共举办培训班 594 期，参加培训人次 8892 人次；共有 4403 名助残志愿者为 73201 名残疾人提供了志愿助残服务。

全省已建社区（村）残协 14164 个，其中城市社区建立残协 1513 个，农村社区建立残协 12651 个；配备残疾人专职委员 13589 名，其中城市社区配备 1485 名，农村社区配备 12104 名 ；共有 5622 名助残志愿者为 39429 名残疾人提供了志愿助残服务。

截止到 2017 年全省共建立省级及以下各类残疾人专门协会 707 个，其中盲人协会省级 1 个、州（市）残联 16 个、县（市、区）残联 126 个，聋人协会省级 1 个、州（市）残联 16 个、县（市、区）残联 126 个，肢残人协会省级 1 个、州（市）残联 16 个、县（市、区）残联 126 个，智力残疾人及亲友协会省级 1 个、州（市）残联 16 个、县（市、区）残联 119 个，精神残疾人及亲友协会省级 1 个、州（市）残联 15 个、县（市、区）残联 119 个，

全省各级 2017 年累计有助残社会组织共有 14 个，其中有 10 个社会团体、1 个基金会、3 个社会服务组织。

十、服务设施

截至 2017 年底，全省已竣工并投入使用的各级残疾人综合服务设施 127 个，总建设规模 164455 平方米，总投资 31714 万元；在建项目 5 个，总建设规模 17315 平方米，总投资 3530 万元。已竣工并投入使用的各级残疾人康复设施 3 个，总建设规模 6450 平方米，总投资 1009 万元；在建项目 10 个，总规模 100118 平方米，总投资 27701 万元。已竣工并投入使用的各级残疾人托养服务设施 5 个，总建设规模 11714 平方米，总投资 3522 万元；在建项目 23 个，总规模 55580 平方米，总投资 14286 万元。

十一、信息化建设与统计

2017 年全省各级残联按照《云南省人民政府关于加快推进残疾人小康进程的实施意见》要求，认真做好我省残疾人事业信息化和统计工作，对加快推进我省残疾人小康进程，服务于残疾人社会保障和基本公共服务水平的提高，取得了明显的成效。

2017 年省残联对门户网站进行再次改版，加大政府信息公开力度，突出宣传重点，提升网站整体视觉效果，对现有信息无障碍功能进行升级，进一步方便盲人朋友访问网站。完成了省残联“互联网+政务服务”事项梳理，共梳理政务服务事项 18 项，下一步将按照省政府办公厅要求做好残疾人证网上办理的前期准备工作。2017 年省残联还完成了云南省残联协同办公平台（OA）建设，转变工作方式、提高工作效率。

截至 2017 年底，省残联网站全年共发布稿件 1700 多篇，省残联官方微信通过公众号发布稿件 420 多篇；全省共有 11 个州（市）残联、21 个县（市、区）残联开通门户网站，其中独立建立网站 9 个，搭载上级残联或同级政府部门网站 24 个；全省残疾人事业统计数据连续 2 年纳入省统计局统计年鉴。

2017年西藏自治区残疾人事业发展统计公报

2017年，在中国残联的精心指导和大力支持下，在自治区党委、政府的高度重视和亲切关怀下，我区残联系统认真学习领会党的十九大和自治区第九次党代会精神，贯彻落实党中央国务院和区党委政府发展残疾人事业的决策部署，紧紧围绕工作大局，认真总结残疾人事业发展成就和经验，主动作为、务求创新、攻坚克难、扎实肯干，努力推进残疾人小康进程取得新进展。

一、康复

2017年，全区共有725名残疾儿童及持证残疾人得到基本康复服务，其中包括0-6岁残疾儿童27人，接受辅助器具适配服务328人。得到康复服务的持证残疾人中，有视力残疾人71名、听力残疾人42名、肢体残疾人501名、智力残疾人18名、精神残疾人14名、多重残疾人79名。

截至2017年底，20个县及3个市辖区开展了社区康复服务，全区共有社区康复协调员87人，其中15人接受过培训。

截至2017年底，全区已有残疾人康复机构5个，其中，提供视力残疾康复服务的机构1个，提供听力言语残疾康复服务的机构1个，提供肢体残疾康复服务的机构4个，提供智力残疾康复服务的机构2个，提供辅助器具服务的机构5个。康复机构在岗人员78人，其中，管理人员12人，专业技术人员38人，其他人员28人。

二、教育、就业、扶贫

继续实施残疾人事业专项彩票公益金助学项目，为107人次家庭经济困难的残疾儿童享受普惠性学前教育提供资助。 2017年，全区共有36名残疾人被普通高等院校录取。

城乡持证残疾人就业人数为18228人，其中按比例就业368人，集中就业294人，个体就业616人，社区就业57人，公益性岗位就业111人，辅助性就业62人，居家就业7657人，从事农业种养加工6731人，灵活就业2332人。

培训盲人保健按摩人员13名、盲人医疗按摩人员4名；保健按摩机构4个，在专业技术职务资格评审中2人通过医疗按摩人员初级职称评审。

2017年，贫困残疾人得到有效扶持，其中771人通过扶贫开发实际脱贫；接受实用技术培训的残疾人达到1417人次。

三、社会保障

截至2017年底，城乡残疾居民参加城乡社会养老保险人数达到20093名，2866名60岁以下的重度残疾人参保，其中2842名得到了政府的参保扶助，代缴养老保险费比例达到99.2%。有6487名非重度残疾人也享受了全额或部分代缴养老保险费的优惠政策，9259人领取养老金。

残疾人托养服务工作稳步推进，拉萨市建立了寄宿制残疾人托养服务机构，13名残疾人享受了托养服务，接受居家服务的残疾人达到708人。全年有4名托养服务管理和服务人员接受了各级各类专业培训。

四、组织建设

2017年，市县乡共建立残联81个，其中地市已建残联7个，县（市、区）残联已建74个，省市县乡残联实有人员达293人。地市级残联配备了残疾人领导干部5人，县级残联配备了残疾人干部9人。共建立省级各类残疾人专门协会3个。

五、服务设施

截至2017年底，已竣工并投入使用的各级残疾人综合服务设施28个，总建设规模32637平方米，总投资10542万元；已竣工并投入使用的各级残疾人康复设施13个，总建设规模22369平方米，总投资8358万元；已竣工并投入使用的各级残疾人托养服务设施3个，总建设规模11109平方米，总投资3415万元。

六、信息化建设

全年，在西藏残联官方网站、官方微博、微信公众号累计发稿 180 篇，举办各类信息化培训 3 期，累计参加人数达 200 人。

2017 年陕西省残疾人事业发展统计公报

2017 年，在省委、省政府的坚强领导下和中国残联的正确指导下，我省残联系统深入学习贯彻党的十九大精神，认真贯彻落实党中央、国务院关于残疾人事业发展的一系列重要部署，主动担当，积极作为，推动残疾人事业持续健康发展。

一、康复

2017 年，249468 名残疾儿童及持证残疾人得到基本康复服务,其中包括 0-6 岁残疾儿童 3189 人。得到康复服务的持证残疾人中，有视力残疾人 27764 名、听力残疾人 18320 名、言语残疾人 1224 名、肢体残疾人 139130 名、智力残疾人 9514 名、精神残疾人 39750 名、多重残疾人 12375 名。

截至 2017 年底，全省已有残疾人康复机构 316 个，其中，提供视力残疾康复服务的机构 64 个，提供听力言语残疾康复服务的机构 47 个，提供肢体残疾康复服务的机构 190 个，提供智力残疾康复服务的机构 67 个，提供精神残疾康复服务的机构 57 个，提供孤独症儿童康复服务的机构 32 个，提供辅助器具服务的机构 62 个。康复机构在岗人员达 9468 人，其中，管理人员 1240 人，专业技术人员 5908 人，其他人员 2320 人。

二、教育

实施残疾人事业专项彩票公益金助学项目，为 223 人次家庭经济困难的残疾儿童享受普惠性学前教育提供资助。各地也积极多渠道争取资金支持，对 10 名残疾儿童给予学前教育资助。

共有特殊教育普通高中班（部）3 个，在校生 102 人，其中聋生 89 人，盲生 13 人。残疾人中等职业学校（班）3 个，在校生）1104 人，毕业生 282 人，其中 170 人获得职业资格证书。有 224 名残疾人被普通高等院校录取。

966 名残疾青壮年文盲接受了扫盲教育。

三、就业

城乡持证残疾人就业人数为 262540 人，其中按比例就业 12530 人，集中就业 4678 人，个体就业 13989 人，社区就业 2171 人，公益性岗位就业 3837 人，辅助性就业 5669 人，居家就业 37503 人，从事农业种养加 150294 人，灵活就业 31869 人。

培训盲人保健按摩人员 484 名、盲人医疗按摩人员 30 名；保健按摩机构达到 450 个，医疗按摩机构达到 72 个；在专业技术职务资格评审中， 53 人通过医疗按摩初级职称评审。

四、扶贫

2017 年，贫困残疾人得到有效扶持，其中 37093 人通过扶贫开发实际脱贫；接受实用技术培训的残疾人达到 41264 人次。

具有 168 个残疾人扶贫基地，安置 3067 名残疾人就业，扶持带动 7115 名残疾人户。

完成 418 户农村贫困残疾人危房改造，各地投入危房资金 2329000 元。

五、社会保障

截至 2017 年底，城乡残疾居民参加城乡社会养老保险人数达到 773153 名，133908 名 60 岁以下的重度残疾人参保，其中 133572 名得到了政府的参保扶助，代缴养老保险费比例达到 99.7%。有 182411 名非重度残疾人也享受了全额或部分代缴养老保险费的优惠政策。270399 人领取养老金。

残疾人托养服务工作稳步推进，残疾人托养服务机构达到 143 个，其中寄宿制托养服务机构 80 个，日间照料机构 13 个，综合性托养服务机构 50 个，为 8371 名残疾人提供了托养服务。接受居家服务的残疾人达到 7767 人。全年 153 名托养服务管理和服务人员接受了各级各类专业培训。

六、宣传文化

截至 2017 年底，共有省级残疾人专题广播节目 1 个、电视手语栏目 1 个；地市级电视手语栏目 8 个。

截至 2017 年底，省地县三级公共图书馆共设立盲文及盲文有声读物阅览室 41 个，共开展残疾人文化周活动 213 场次；省地两级残联共举办残疾人文化艺术类的比赛及展览 12 次，共有各类残疾人艺术团 7 个。

七、体育

全省残疾人康复体育关爱家庭服务 1435 户，建设残疾人体育健身示范点 20 个，培养健身指导员 2492 名。

八、维权

2017 年，制定或修改保障残疾人权益的规范性文件县级 1 个。县级以上人大开展《中华人民共和国残疾人保障法》执法检查和专题调研 1 次。

截至 2017 年底，成立残疾人法律救助工作协调机构 99 个，建立残疾人法律救助工作站 91 个。

残疾人参政议政工作稳步开展，各地残联协助人大代表、政协委员提出议案、建议、提案 8 件，办理议案、建议、提案 14 件。

无障碍建设法规、标准进一步完善。系统开展无障碍建设市、县、区 43 个；开展无障碍建设检查 18 次，无障碍培训 320 人次。

九、组织建设

2017 年，市县乡共建立残联 1524 个，各地市已建残联 10 个，县（市、区）残联已建 113 个，乡镇（街道）残联已建 1401 个；已建社区（村）残协 26437 个。

省市县乡残联实有人员达 4211 人，乡镇（街道）、村（社区）选聘残疾人专职委员总计 27859 名。地市级残联配备了残疾人领导干部 17 人，县级残联配备了残疾人干部 96 人。

共建立省级及以下各类残疾人专门协会 592 个，其中省级专门协会已建 5 个，市级专门协会已建 50 个，县级专门协会已建 537。助残社会组织共有 11 个。

十、服务设施

截至 2017 年底，已竣工并投入使用的各级残疾人综合服务设施 77 个，总建设规模 161881 平方米，总投资 35470 万元；已竣工并投入使用的各级残疾人康复设施 39 个，总建设规模 80231 平方米，总投资 19540 万元；已竣工并投入使用的各级残疾人托养服务设施 50 个，总建设规模 114889 平方米，总投资 15176 万元。

十一、信息化

截至 2017 年底，10 个地市、47 个县级残联开通网站。

2017 年甘肃省残疾人事业发展统计公报

2017 年，全省残疾人工作在习近平新时代中国特色社会主义思想指引下，各级各部门各单位攻坚克难、狠抓落实，基础管理持续提升、项目建设成效卓著。我省残疾人事业快速发展、残疾人项目投入持续增加、残疾人群体受益覆盖面持续扩大。

一、康复

2017 年，通过实施一批残疾人康复项目，有效改善残疾人的生活状况和参与水平。特别是争取投入和利用外资，为全省 5.5 万名听力障碍患者开展精准听力障碍筛查工作，集中培训 1000 名残疾人服务机构专业人才、为 1000 名听障残疾儿童提供人工耳蜗术后康复强化训练；与美国斯达克公司联合实施“世界从此欢声笑语”中国（甘肃）项目为兰州、天水两市 5717 名贫困听障人士免费适配助听器。

全省 18 个市辖区、69 个县（市）的 13568 个社区（村）开展了社区康复工作。全省配备社区康复协调员 1.18 万人。累计接受康复服务 57.65 万人次。

图 1 2013-2017 年累计接受社区康复残疾人

实施精准康复服务，为 242864 名残疾儿童及持证残疾人提供了基本康复服务，其中 0-17 岁未持证残疾儿童 113 人。得到康复服务的残疾人中，有视力残疾 2.71 万名、听力残疾 1.59 万名、言语残疾 789 名、肢体残疾 13.63 万名、智力残疾 2.37 万名、精神残疾 1.9 万名、多重残疾 20 万名。

6752 名视力残疾人得到白内障复明手术、定向行走等训练。10567 名低视力残疾人得到适配盲杖、助视器等辅助器具服务。开展视力残疾康复机构总数达到 38 个。

16654 名听力残疾人、言语残疾人接受人工耳蜗、助听器适配的康复服务。听力言语功能训练 71 名。已建设省级听力语言康复机构 1 个，市县级听力语言康复机构 32 个。

2.53 万名肢体残疾人接受矫治手术、运动功能训练等康复服务。为 4.93 万名肢体残疾人进行假肢、矫形器辅具适配。开展肢体残疾康复训练服务机构数达 54 个（省级康复机构 1 个、市县级康复机构 53 个）。

对 7154 名智力残疾人进行认知及适应性训练。开展智力残疾康复训练服务机构数达 45 个（省级康复机构 1 个、市县级康复机构 44 个）。

为 191 名孤独症儿童进行沟通及适应训练，7384 名精神残疾人进行药物治疗及作业疗法训练。建立 1 个省级孤独症儿童康复训练机构。

深入开展辅助器具适配服务，为 7.69 万残疾人进行了辅助器具适配。

康复机构在岗人员达 2474 人，其中，管理人员 394 人、专业技术人员 1564 人、其他人员 516 人。

表 1 2017 年康复训练服务机构（个）

级 别	类 别					
	视力	听力语言	肢体	智力	精神	辅助器具
省 级	1	1	1	1	1	1
市州级	8	9	15	15	2	8
县 级	29	23	38	29	21	58
合 计	38	33	54	45	24	67

二、教育

省残联与省教育厅等七部门联合印发《甘肃省第二期特殊教育提升计划（2017—2020 年）》，出台《全面推进残疾青壮年扫盲工作方案》推动提高残疾人受教育水平。

通过实施残疾人事业专项彩票公益金助学项

目，为 162 所学前教育机构提供资助，资助贫困残疾幼儿 1178 人。

全省共有特殊教育普通高中班（部）3 个，在校生 168 人（聋生 158 人、盲生 10 人）。残疾人中等职业学校（班）2 个，在校生 155 人，毕业 41 人，41 人获得职业资格证书。有 523 名残疾学生被普通高等院校录取。

三、就业

2017 年城乡持证残疾人新增就业 7707 人，其中，城镇新增就业 1887 人，农村新增就业 5820 人。

城乡持证残疾人就业 26.73 万人。其中按比例残疾人就业 7638 人，集中就业 2083 人，个体就业 1.83 万人，社区就业 1909 人，公益性岗位就业 2677 人，辅助性就业 4145 人，居家就业 3.5 万人，从事农业种养加 16.76 万人,灵活就业 2.8 万人。

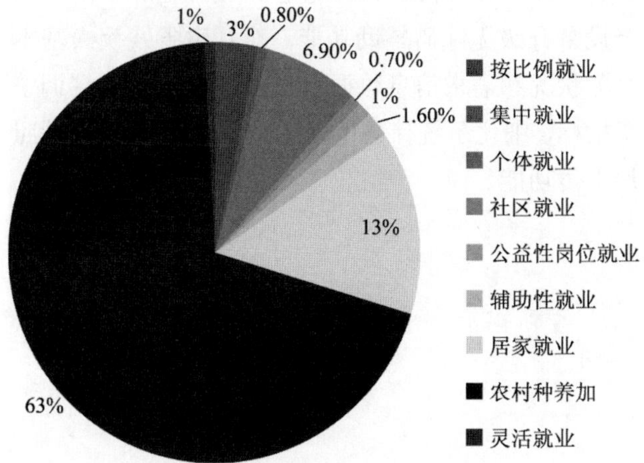

图 2　全省城乡持证残疾人就业情况

盲人按摩事业稳步发展，全年度培训盲人保健按摩人员 774 名,盲人医疗按摩人员 137 名。保健按摩机构数量达到 341 个，医疗按摩机构数量达到 29 个。在专业技术职务资格评审中 11 人通过医疗按摩人员初级职称评审。

四、扶贫

2017 年，积极争取将符合条件的贫困残疾人纳入精准扶贫建档立卡范围。全省精准脱贫 2.2 万人，接受实用技术培训的残疾人达到 3.2 万人次。

扶持新建残疾人扶贫基地 167 个，安置 2419 名残疾人就业。带动 5563 户残疾人家庭增产增收。完成 9115 户农村贫困残疾人危房改造。

五、社会保障

积极推行重度残疾人参保优惠政策。全省已有 103.9 万城乡残疾居民参加养老参保，60 岁以下的参保残疾人中有 23.5 万重度残疾人享受了由政府代缴全额或部分保费。有 8.07 万非重度残疾人也享受了全额或部分代缴养老保险费的优惠政策。

残疾人托养服务工作规范推进，残疾人托养服务机构达到 85 个(寄宿制托养服务机构 28 个、日间照料机构 19 个、综合性托养服务机构 38 个)。托养残疾人总数达 1.14 万。

六、宣传文化

2017 年，甘肃省第二十七次全国助残日活动暨省委省政府为民办实事贫困残疾人精准脱贫“百千万”行动启动仪式在兰州举行。组织参加全国“第九届残疾人艺术汇演”并取得优异成绩。

全年省市组织新闻发布会和新闻媒体采访 75 次。省市级专题广播节目 23 个，电视手语新闻栏目 14 个。全省开展残疾人文化周活动 207 场次。举办残疾人文化艺术比赛及展览 31 场次。推动建立省、市、县公共图书馆及盲人有声读物图书室 51 个。

七、体育活动

建立省级群众体育活动示范点 69 个。建立地市级、县级群众活动示范点 69 个。全省已培养残疾人社会体育指导员 630 人。开展残疾人康复体育进家庭 5000 户。

八、维权

全省制定或修改关于残疾人的专门法规、规章 8 个,制定或修改保障残疾人权益的规范性文件 39 份。全省各级人大执法检查 22 次，政协专题调研 18 次。举办普法活动 4 次，共计 3000 人参加。

残疾人参政议政工作得到加强，各级残联协助人大代表、政协委员提出议案、建议及提案 27 件。办理人大建议、政协提案 21 件。

全省出台 9 个无障碍环境建设法规政府令。开展无障碍建设检查 48 次，无障碍培训 114 人次。

全省建立残疾人法律救助工作协调机构 102 个。建立残疾人法律救助工作站 102 个，办理案件

180件。

各级残联接收残疾人来信 1016 件，接待来访 3256人次，接听来电444通。

表2　2016年全省各级残疾人法律救助情况

级 别	法律救助协调机构（个）	法律救助	
		工作站（个）	办理案件（件）
省　级	1	1	0
市州级	15	15	7
县　级	86	86	179
合　计	102	102	180

九、组织建设

省市残联领导班子配备残疾人理事长或副理事长16人。省市县残联机关配备残疾人干部152人。省市县乡残联实有人员4148人。

已建乡镇（街道）残联1379个，已建社区（村）残协17243个。选聘残疾人专职委员17660人(乡镇专职委员1638人、村社区专职委员16022人)。

全省建立省级及以下各类残疾人专门协会 510个，其中省级专门协会5个，市级专门协会75个，县级专门协会430。助残社会组织29个。

十、服务设施

截至 2017 年底，已竣工并投入使用的各级残疾人综合服务设施90个，总建设规模9.4万平方米，总投资3亿元；已竣工并投入使用的各级残疾人康复设施7个，总建设规模3.0万平方米，总投资7975万元；已竣工并投入使用的各级残疾人托养服务设施 9 个，总建设规模 1.9 万平方米，总投资 4500万元。

十一、信息化建设

省残联门户网站全年刊发残联系统政务信息3580条。中国残联网站采用2839条。采用率达80%。对省残联门户无障碍网站进行改版，增加了网络安全设备升级无障碍辅助功能。对甘肃省残疾人基本服务状况和需求信息数据动态更新系统 PC 端调整了指标，细化了统计分析功能和APP移动客户端照片上传功能。

2017年青海省残疾人事业发展统计公报

2017年，在省委、省政府的坚强领导和中国残联的有力指导下，青海省残联以残疾人社会保障和服务体系建设为核心任务，全面完成了各项业务指标，残疾人生活状况进一步改善，残疾人事业实现新发展。

一、康复

2017年，63104名残疾儿童及持证残疾人得到基本康复服务,其中包括0-6岁残疾儿童1246人。得到康复服务的持证残疾人中，有视力残疾人9065名、听力残疾人8754名、言语残疾人1439名、肢体残疾人31052名、智力残疾人5063名、精神残疾人1967名、多重残疾人5721名。

截至2017年底，有残疾人康复机构35个，其中，提供视力残疾康复服务的机构12个，提供听力言语残疾康复服务的机构12个，提供肢体残疾康复服务的机构20个，提供智力残疾康复服务的机构21个，提供精神残疾康复服务的机构6个，提供孤独症儿童康复服务的机构15个，提供辅助器具服务的机构16个。康复机构在岗人员达489人，其中，管理人员91人，专业技术人员258人，其他人员140人。

二、教育

实施残疾人事业专项彩票公益金助学项目，为201人次家庭经济困难的残疾儿童享受普惠性学前教育提供资助。各地也积极多渠道争取资金支持，对16名残疾儿童给予学前教育资助。共有特殊教育普通高中班（部）1个，有135名残疾人被普通高等院校录取，890名残疾青壮年文盲接受了扫盲教育。

三、就业

城乡持证残疾人就业人数为44893人，其中按比例就业1660人，集中就业2005人，个体就业2773人，社区就业245人，公益性岗位就业848人，辅助性就业573人，居家就业4667人，从事农业种养加23426人，灵活就业8696人。

培训盲人保健按摩人员145名、盲人医疗按摩人员24名；保健按摩机构达到234个，医疗按摩机构达到5个；在专业技术职务资格评审中，分别有2人和9人通过医疗按摩人员中级和初级职称评审。

四、扶贫

2017年，贫困残疾人得到有效扶持，其中5348人通过扶贫开发实际脱贫；接受实用技术培训的残疾人达到7237人次。达到64个残疾人扶贫基地，安置892名残疾人就业，扶持带动1311名残疾人户。完成557户农村贫困残疾人危房改造，各地投入危房资金17598500元。

五、社保保障

截至2017年底，城乡残疾居民参加城乡社会养老保险人数达到124705名，39373名60岁以下的重度残疾人参保，其中39331名得到了政府的参保扶助，代缴养老保险费比例达到99.9%。有29758名非重度残疾人也享受了全额或部分代缴养老保险费的优惠政策。49079人领取养老金。

残疾人托养服务工作稳步推进，残疾人托养服务机构达到46个，其中寄宿制托养服务机构15个，综合性托养服务机构21个，为1414名残疾人提供了托养服务。接受居家服务的残疾人达到1195人。全年25名托养服务管理和服务人员接受了各级各类专业培训。

六、宣传文化

截至2017年底，共有省级残疾人专题广播节目1个、电视手语栏目2个；电视手语栏目4个。

截至2017年底，省地县三级公共图书馆共设立盲文及盲文有声读物阅览室11个，共开展残疾人文化周活动79场次；省地两级残联共举办残疾人文化艺术类的比赛及展览13次，共有各类残疾人艺术团2个。

七、体育

全国残疾人康复体育关爱家庭服务1500户，建设残疾人体育健身示范点6个，培养健身指导员80名。

八、维权

2017年，制定或修改保障残疾人权益的规范性文件县级4个。县级以上人大开展《中华人民共和国残疾人保障法》执法检查和专题调研3次；政协开展视察和专题调研3次。开展省级普法宣传教育活动7次，1800人参加；举办省级法律培训班1个，96人参加。

截至2017年底，成立残疾人法律救助工作协调机构39个，建立残疾人法律救助工作站36个。

残疾人参政议政工作稳步开展，各地残联协助人大代表、政协委员提出议案、建议、提案9件，办理议案、建议、提案6件。无障碍建设法规、标准进一步完善。系统开展无障碍建设市、县、区11个；开展无障碍建设检查28次，无障碍培训51人次。

九、组织建设

2017年，市县乡共建立残联464个，各地市已建残联8个，县（市、区）残联已建46个，乡镇（街道）残联已建410个；已建社区（村）残协4542个。

省市县乡残联实有人员达1234人，乡镇（街道）、村（社区）选聘残疾人专职委员总计2245名。地市级残联配备了残疾人领导干部11人，县级残联配备了残疾人干部26人。

共建立省级及以下各类残疾人专门协会275个，其中省级专门协会已建5个，市级专门协会已建40个，县级专门协会已建230。助残社会组织共有4个。

十、服务设施

截至2017年底，已竣工并投入使用的各级残疾人综合服务设施22个，总建设规模41105平方米，总投资13648万元；已竣工并投入使用的各级残疾人康复设施3个，总建设规模14625平方米，总投资3680万元；已竣工并投入使用的各级残疾人托养服务设施28个，总建设规模53545平方米，总投资15131万元。

十一、信息化

截至2017年底，3个地市、7个县级残联开通网站。

2017 年宁夏回族自治区残疾人事业发展统计公报

2017 年，在自治区党委、政府的正确领导下，在中国残联业务部门的精心指导下，在社会各界的关爱支持和广大残疾人工作者的共同努力下，全区残疾人事业发展取得新的重大进展。

一、康复

2017 年，115132 名残疾儿童及持证残疾人得到基本康复服务,其中包括 0-6 岁残疾儿童 1445 人。得到康复服务的持证残疾人中，有视力残疾人 15157 名、听力残疾人 11720 名、言语残疾人 1356 名、肢体残疾人 54444 名、智力残疾人 13218 名、精神残疾人 11976 名、多重残疾人 7032 名。

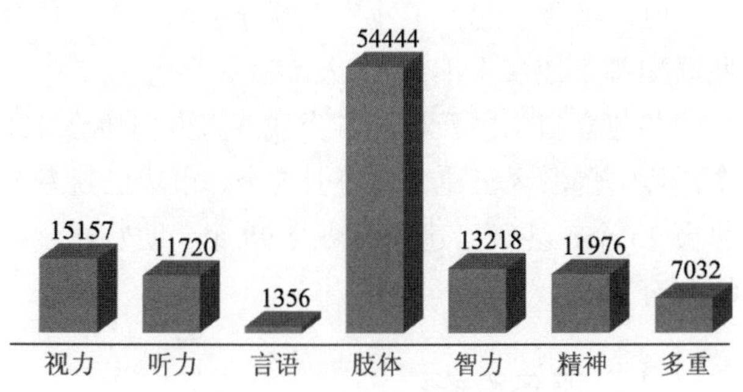

图 1　残疾人得到基本服务状况

截至 2017 年底，全区有残疾人康复机构 29 个，其中，提供视力残疾康复服务的机构 7 个，提供听力言语残疾康复服务的机构 6 个，提供肢体残疾康复服务的机构 21 个，提供智力残疾康复服务的机构 22 个，提供精神残疾康复服务的机构 5 个，提供孤独症儿童康复服务的机构 17 个，提供辅助器具服务的机构 7 个。康复机构在岗人员达 585 人，其中，管理人员 87 人，专业技术人员 424 人，其他人员 74 人。

二、教育

实施残疾人事业专项彩票公益金助学项目，为 177 人次家庭经济困难的残疾儿童享受普惠性学前教育提供资助。各地也积极多渠道争取资金支持，对 11 名残疾儿童给予学前教育资助。

2017 年，全区共有特殊教育普通高中班 1 个，在校生 37 人，其中聋生 36 人，盲生 1 人。有 151 名残疾人被普通高等院校录取。1822 名残疾青壮年文盲接受了扫盲教育。

三、就业

城乡持证残疾人就业人数为 58342 人，其中按比例就业 7041

人，集中就业 1805 人，个体就业 4912 人，社区就业 345 人，公益性岗位就业 607 人，辅助性就业 1223 人，居家就业 12238 人，从事农业种养加 23169 人，灵活就业 7002 人。

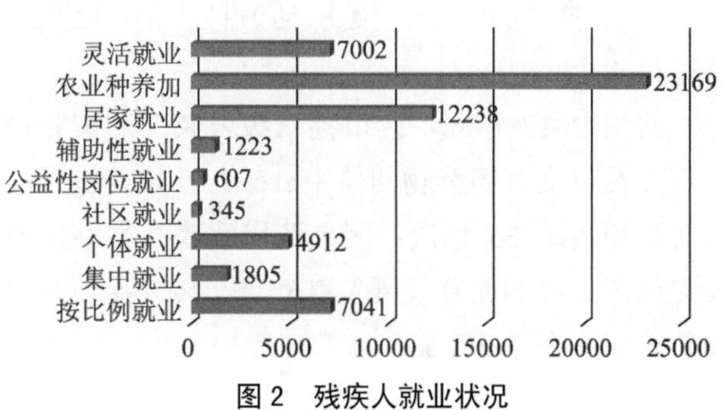

图 2　残疾人就业状况

盲人按摩事业稳步发展，按摩机构持续增长。2017 年度，全区共培训盲人保健按摩人员 328 名、盲人医疗按摩人员 65 名；保健按摩机构达到 309 个，医疗按摩机构达到 11 个；在专业技术职务资格评审中，分别有 6 人和 2 人通过医疗按摩人员中级和初级职称评审。

四、扶贫开发

2017 年，贫困残疾人得到有效扶持，其中 8115 人通过扶贫开发实际脱贫；接受实用技术培训的残疾人达到 6881 人次。康复扶贫贴息贷款扶持 1500 名农村残疾人。建立 55 个残疾人扶贫基地，安置 1106 名残疾人就业，扶持带动 2704 名残疾人户。完成 178 户农村贫困残疾人危房改造，各地投入危房资金 489 万元。

五、社会保障

截至 2017 年底，城乡残疾居民参加城乡社会养老保险人数达到 210726 名，50049 名 60 岁以下的重度残疾人参保，其中 49759 名得到了政府的参保扶助，代缴养老保险费比例达到 99.4%。有 33227 名非重度残疾人也享受了全额或部分代缴养老保险费的优惠政策。102108 人领取养老金。

残疾人托养服务工作稳步推进，残疾人托养服务机构达到 69 个，其中寄宿制托养服务机构 15 个，日间照料机构 46 个，综合性托养服务机构 8 个，为 2402 名残疾人提供了托养服务。接受居家服务的残疾人达到 3473 人。全年 86 名托养服务管理和服务人员接受了各级各类专业培训。

六、宣传文化

截至 2017 年底，自治区级残疾人专题广播节目 1 个；地市级残疾人专题广播节目 2 个、电视手语栏目 4 个。

截至 2017 年底，区市县三级公共图书馆共设立盲文及盲文有声读物阅览室 16 个，共开展残疾人文化周活动 35 场次；区市两级残联共举办残疾人文化艺术类的比赛及展览 16 次，共有各类残疾人艺术团 2 个。

七、体育

全国残疾人康复体育关爱家庭服务 1000 户，建设残疾人体育健身示范点 8 个，培养健身指导员 15 名。全年组织残疾人参加国际国内体育赛事 12 次，获得 46 枚金牌、42 枚银牌、35 枚铜牌的好成绩，再次刷新历史记录。

八、维权

2017 年，制定或修改保障残疾人权益的规范性文件县级 1 个。县级以上人大开展《中华人民共和国残疾人保障法》执法检查和专题调研 2 次；政协开展视察和专题调研 1 次。自治区开展普法宣传教育活动 5 次，430 人参加；自治区举办法律培训班 1 个，75 人参加。

截至 2017 年底，成立残疾人法律救助工作协调机构 13 个，建立残疾人法律救助工作站 9 个。

残疾人参政议政工作稳步开展，各地残联协助人大代表、政协委员提出议案、建议、提案 14 件，办理议案、建议、提案 10 件。

无障碍建设法规、标准进一步完善。系统开展无障碍建设市、县（区）23 个；开展无障碍建设检查 27 次，无障碍培训 119 人次。

九、组织建设

2017 年，市县乡共建立残联 268 个，各地市已建残联 5 个，县（市、区）残联已建 21 个，乡镇（街道）残联已建 242 个；已建社区（村）残协 2037 个。 区市县乡残联实有人员达 822 人，乡镇（街道）、村（社区）选聘残疾人专职委员总计 1579 名。地市级残联配备了残疾人领导干部 5 人，县级残联配备了残疾人干部 13 人。

共建立自治区及以下各类残疾人专门协会 128 个，其中自治区已建专门协会 5 个，市级已建专门协会 25 个，县级已建专门协会 98 个。助残社会组织共有 44 个。

十、服务设施

截至 2017 年底，已竣工并投入使用的各级残疾人综合服务设施 17 个，总建设规模 31252 平方米，总投资 7757 万元；已竣工并投入使用的各级残疾人康复设施 3 个，总建设规模 15141 平方米，总投资 5060 万元；已竣工并投入使用的各级残疾人托养服务设施 1 个，总建设规模 2000 平方米，总投资 440 万元。

十一、信息化

截至 2017 年底，3 个地市、11 个县级残联开通网站。

2017 年新疆维吾尔自治区残疾人事业发展统计公报

2017 年，在自治区党委、人民政府的坚强领导下，全区各级残联深入学习贯彻党的十九大精神，以维护自治区社会稳定和长治久安为根本，认真贯彻落实自治区党委、人民政府关于残疾人事业发展的一系列重要部署，主动担当，积极作为，努力推进残疾人康复、教育、就业、扶贫、维权、宣传文体等工作。

一、康复

2017 年，63450 名残疾儿童及持证残疾人得到基本康复服务,其中包括 0-6 岁残疾儿童 1693 人。享受康复服务的持证残疾人中，有视力残疾人 7616 名、听力残疾人 5518 名、言语残疾人 191 名、肢体残疾人 32793 名、智力残疾人 5699 名、精神残疾人 7753 名、多重残疾人 3740 名。

截至 2017 年底，有残疾人康复机构 134 个，其中，提供视力残疾康复服务的机构 36 个，提供听力言语残疾康复服务的机构 24 个，提供肢体残疾康复服务的机构 73 个，提供智力残疾康复服务的机构 32 个，提供精神残疾康复服务的机构 19 个，提供孤独症儿童康复服务的机构 8 个，提供辅助器具服务的机构 26 个。康复机构在岗人员达 1955 人，其中，管理人员 470 人，专业技术人员 1156 人，其他人员 329 人。

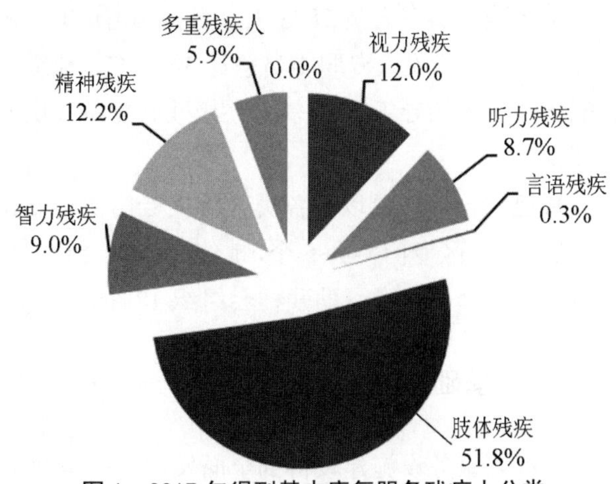

图 1　2017 年得到基本康复服务残疾人分类

二、教育

实施残疾人事业专项彩票公益金助学项目，为 195 人次家庭经济困难的残疾儿童在享受普惠性学前教育优惠的基础上提供资助。各地也积极多渠道争取资金支持，对 33 名残疾儿童给予学前教育资助。

全区共有特殊教育普通高中班（部）1 个，在校生 235 人。残疾人中等职业学校（班）2 个，在校生）351 人，毕业生 151 人。316 名残疾人被普通高等院校录取。

2436 名残疾青壮年文盲接受扫盲教育。

三、就业

城乡持证残疾人就业人数为 179791 人，其中按比例就业 21327 人，集中就业 4442 人，个体就业 13673 人，社区就业 2166 人，公益性岗位就业 2678 人，辅助性就业 1297 人，居家就业 12606 人，从事农业种养加 93902 人，灵活就业 27700 人。

培训盲人保健按摩人员 94 名、盲人医疗按摩人员 27 名；保健按摩机构达到 161 个，医疗按摩机构达到 22 个；在专业技术职务资格评审中，分别有 6 人和 15 人通过医疗按摩人员中级和初级职称评审。

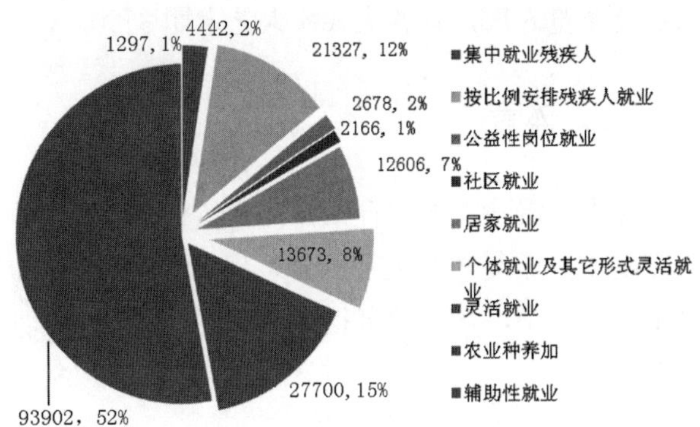

图 2　城乡残疾人就业情况

四、社会保障

截至 2017 年底，城乡残疾居民参加城乡社会养老保险人数达到 358254 名，71315 名 60 岁以下的重度残疾人参保，其中67338名得到了政府的参保扶助，代缴养老保险费比例达到94.4%。有113433名非重度残疾人享受全额或部分代缴养老保险费的优惠政策。117376人领取养老金。

残疾人托养服务工作稳步推进，残疾人托养服务机构达到191个，其中寄宿制托养服务机构36个，日间照料机构86个，综合性托养服务机构69个，为4826名残疾人提供托养服务。接受居家服务的残疾人达到3890人。全年126名托养服务管理和服务人员接受各级各类专业培训。

五、扶贫

2017年，残疾人扶贫开发成效显著，贫困残疾人生产生活状况进一步改善。贫困残疾人得到有效扶持，其中8064人通过扶贫开发实现脱贫；接受实用技术培训的残疾人达到21738人次。

康复扶贫贴息贷款扶持307名农村残疾人。全区共有218个残疾人扶贫基地，安置残疾人就业3564名，扶持带动残疾人户5747名。

完成1182户农村贫困残疾人危房改造，各地共投入危房资金12217800元。

六、宣传文化

截至2017年底，地市级残疾人专题广播节目3个、电视手语栏目4个。

自治区地县三级公共图书馆共设立盲文及盲文有声读物阅览室10个，共开展残疾人文化活动212场次；自治区地两级残联共举办残疾人文化艺术类比赛及展览6次，有各类残疾人艺术团3个。

七、体育

深入开展残疾人体育工作，全区有550户残疾人家庭享受康复体育关爱服务，建设残疾人体育健身示范点8个，培养健身指导员21名。

八、维权

自治区残联深入开展依法保护残疾人权益工作，做好自治区实施《残疾人保障法》办法、《残疾人就业条例》、《无障碍环境建设条例》等有关残疾人权益保障的法律法规的宣传贯彻工作。

2017年，开展自治区级普法宣传教育活动2次，120人参加普法教育。

截至2017年底，成立残疾人法律救助工作协调机构82个，建立残疾人法律救助工作站66个。残疾人参政议政工作稳步开展，各地残联协助人大代表、政协委员提出议案、建议、提案9件，办结议案、建议、提案9件。

无障碍建设法规、标准进一步完善。全区共有无障碍市、县、区3个；开展无障碍建设检查23次，无障碍培训222人次。

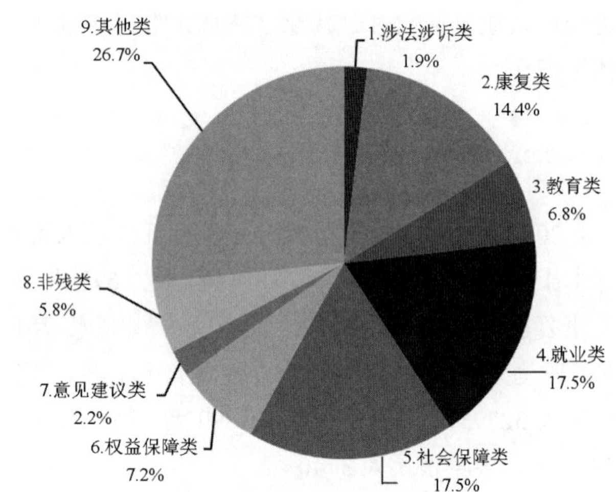

图3 残疾人群众来访分类占比情况图

全区各级残联共处理残疾人群众来信1762件，接待残疾人群众来访5406人次，来电568次。

九、组织建设

2017年，全区共建立残联1172个，其中地州市已建残联14个，县（市、区）残联97个，乡（镇、街道）残联已建1061个；已建社区（村）残协9299个。

全区残联实有人员2873人，乡镇（街道）、村（社区）选聘残疾人专职委员总计3430名。地级残联配备残疾人领导干部26人，县级残联配备残疾人干部92人。

共建立自治区及以下各类残疾人专门协会516个，其中自治区专门协会5个，地级专门协会67个，县级专门协会444个。助残社会组织18个。

十、基础设施

残疾人服务设施建设得到全面发展。截至2017年底，已竣工并投入使用的各级残疾人综合服务设施78个，总建设规模195464平方米，总投资54703

万元；已竣工并投入使用的各级残疾人康复设施 19 个，总建设规模 35600 平方米，总投资 8458 万元；已竣工并投入使用的各级残疾人托养服务设施 28 个，总建设规模 27878 平方米，总投资 6707 万元。

十一、信息化

统计队伍建设进一步加强，各级残联共有 98 名兼职统计人员从事残疾人事业统计工作，统计人员业务素质培养普遍得到重视，自治区残联举办培训班 1 期，参加培训的人员达到 57 人次；地级举办培训班 12 期，参加培训的人员达到 242 人次。

全面推进网站建设，目前自治区残联开通门户网站，自治区网站发稿量 1950 篇；有 7 个地级残联网站和 20 个县级残联开通网站。

2017 年新疆生产建设兵团残疾人事业发展统计公报

2017 年,在中国残联的关心指导和兵团党委的正确领导下，兵团残联系统以习近平新时代中国特色社会主义思想为指导，认真学习宣传贯彻党的十九大精神，深入贯彻落实中央党的群团工作会议精神和兵团第七次党代会、兵团党委七届二次全委会议精神，贯彻落实党中央、国务院关于新时代中国特色残疾人事业新部署新要求，围绕新疆工作总目标，紧紧抓住“全面建成小康社会，残疾人一个不能少”这条主线，聚焦“残疾人脱贫攻坚”、“基本公共服务托底补短”，主动担当、积极作为，扎实有效地开展残疾人扶贫攻坚工作，聚焦精准服务，坚持创新发展、顺势发力，较好地完成了国家和兵团安排部署的各项工作任务，有力推进了残疾人事业的健康发展和残疾人民生的持续改善。现根据 2017 年度残疾人事业统计数据公报如下：

一、康复

2017 年，20575 名残疾儿童及持证残疾人得到基本康复服务,其中包括 0-6 岁残疾儿童 136 人。得到康复服务的持证残疾人中，有视力残疾人 1962 名、听力残疾人 998 名、言语残疾人 0 名、肢体残疾人 9564 名、智力残疾人 2081 名、精神残疾人 5247 名、多重残疾人 723 名。

截至 2017 年底，有残疾人康复机构 50 个，其中，提供视力残疾康复服务的机构 13 个，提供听力言语残疾康复服务的机构 12 个，提供肢体残疾康复服务的机构 42 个，提供智力残疾康复服务的机构 14 个，提供精神残疾康复服务的机构 16 个，提供孤独症儿童康复服务的机构 2 个，提供辅助器具服务的机构 16 个。康复机构在岗人员 1037 人，其中，管理人员 145 人，专业技术人员 679 人，其他人员 213 人。

二、教育

实施残疾人事业专项彩票公益金助学项目，为 33 人次家庭经济困难的残疾儿童享受普惠性学前教育提供资助。各级积极多渠道争取资金支持，对 21 名残疾儿童给予学前教育资助。有 52 名残疾人被普通高等院校录取，1105 名残疾青壮年文盲接受了扫盲教育。

三、就业

城乡持证残疾人就业人数为 22833 人，其中按比例就业 10772 人，集中就业 1214 人，个体就业 2850 人，社区就业 186 人，公益性岗位就业 232 人，辅助性就业 306 人，居家就业 634 人，从事农业种养加 3139 人，灵活就业 3400 人。

培训盲人保健按摩人员 9 名、盲人医疗按摩人员 2 名；保健按摩机构达到 27 个，医疗按摩机构达到 7 个；在专业技术职务资格评审中，有 8 人通过医疗按摩人员初级职称评审。

四、扶贫

2017 年，贫困残疾人得到有效扶持，其中 2512 人通过扶贫开发实际脱贫；接受实用技术培训的残疾人达到 13414 人次。康复扶贫贴息贷款扶持 1284 名农村残疾人。已有 58 个残疾人扶贫基地，安置 1078 名残疾人就业，扶持带动 1626 户残疾人家庭。完成 127 户农村贫困残疾人危房改造，各地投入危房资金 542.9 万元。

五、社会保障

截至 2017 年底，城乡残疾居民参加城乡社会养老保险人数达到 24460 名，8790 名 60 岁以下的重度残疾人参保，其中 8508 名得到了政府的参保扶助，代缴养老保险费比例达到 96.8%。有 2525 名非重度残疾人也享受了全额或部分代缴养老保险费的优惠政策。3057 人领取养老金。

残疾人托养服务工作稳步推进，残疾人托养服务机构达到 60 个，其中寄宿制托养服务机构 22 个，日间照料机构 9 个，综合性托养服务机构 29 个，为 2553 名残疾人提供了托养服务。接受居家服务的残疾人4580人。全年5名托养服务管理和服务人员接受了各级各类专业培训。

六、宣传文化

截至2017年底，共有兵团级电视手语栏目1个，兵师团三级公共图书馆共设立盲文及盲文有声读物阅览室1个，共开展残疾人文化周活动217场次；兵师两级残联共举办残疾人文化艺术类的比赛及展览4次。

七、体育

兵团级建设残疾人体育健身示范点3个，培养健身指导员30名。

八、维权

截至2017年底，成立残疾人法律救助工作协调机构6个，建立残疾人法律救助工作站5个。残疾人参政议政工作稳步开展，各地残联协助人大代表、政协委员提出议案、建议、提案1件，办理议案、建议、提案1件。开展无障碍建设检查2次，无障碍培训15人次。

九、组织建设

2017年，师团已达标残联25个，其中师市级已达标残联14个，团（镇、街道）残联达标11个；达标连（社区、村）残协6个。

兵团各级残联实有人员达110人，团（镇、街道）、（社区、村）选聘残疾人专职委员总计118名。师市级残联配备了残疾人领导干部3人。

共建立兵团级及以下各类残疾人专门协会54个，其中兵团级专门协会已建5个，师市级专门协会已建49个，助残社会组织共有1个。

十、设施

截至2017年底，已竣工并投入使用的各级残疾人综合服务设施10个，总建设规模7183平方米，总投资999万元；已竣工并投入使用的各级残疾人康复设施10个，总建设规模40394平方米，总投资12560万元；已竣工并投入使用的各级残疾人托养服务设施51个，总建设规模80005平方米，总投资15221万元。

十一、信息化

截至2017年底，1个师市残联开通网站。

2017年黑龙江垦区残疾人事业发展统计公报

2017年，黑龙江垦区各级残疾残在中残联的领导下，认真落实党的十八届三中、四中、五中、六中、七中全会精神，认真学习贯彻党的十九大精神，以习近平新时代中国特色社会主义思想为指导，团结进取，务实创新，以全力完成“十三五”规划任务为目标，努力使垦区残疾人事业发展取得新的成绩，令广大残疾人得到更多福祉。

一、康复

2017年，2501名残疾儿童及持证残疾人得到基本康复服务,其中包括0-6岁残疾儿童15人。得到康复服务的持证残疾人中，有视力残疾人1173名、听力残疾人251名、言语残疾人1名、肢体残疾人450名、智力残疾人31名、精神残疾人521名、多重残疾人74名。

截至2017年底，垦区已建成并投入使用的残疾人康复机构共有70个，其中，提供肢体残疾康复服务的机构60个，提供精神残疾康复服务的机构3个，提供辅助器具服务的机构14个。康复机构在岗人员达397人，其中，管理人员111人，专业技术人员224人，其他人员62人。

二、教育

实施残疾人事业专项彩票公益金助学项目，为17人次家庭经济困难的残疾儿童享受普惠性学前教育提供资助，有9名残疾人被普通高等院校录取，14名残疾青壮年文盲接受了扫盲教育。

三、就业

2017年，垦区城乡持证残疾人就业人数为23558人，其中按比例就业11267人，集中就业1221人，个体就业3041人，社区就业186人，公益性岗位就业337人，辅助性就业324人，居家就业651人，从事农业种养加3192人，灵活就业3339人。

培训盲人医疗按摩人员4名；保健按摩机构达到2个，医疗按摩机构达到1个；在专业技术职务资格评审中，分别有4人和5人通过医疗按摩人员中级和初级职称评审。

四、扶贫

2017年，贫困残疾人得到有效扶持，接受实用技术培训的残疾人达到1403人次。

截止到2017年底，垦区残疾人扶贫基地达到4个，安置17名残疾人就业，扶持带动4名残疾人户。

各地积极争取资金，完成8户农村贫困残疾人危房改造，各地投入危房资金17500元。

五、社会保障

截止到2017年底，城乡残疾居民参加城乡社会养老保险人数达到14名，5名60岁以下的重度残疾人参保，4人领取养老金。

残疾人托养服务工作稳步推进，残疾人托养服务机构达到11个，其中寄宿制托养服务机构8个，日间照料机构1个，综合性托养服务机构2个，为473名残疾人提供了托养服务。接受居家服务的残疾人达到121人。

六、维权

2017年，开展省级普法宣传教育活动1次，120人参加；截止到2017年底，垦区成立残疾人法律救助工作协调机构6个。

无障碍建设法规、标准进一步完善。系统开展无障碍建设市、县、区2个；开展无障碍建设检查1次，无障碍培训125人次。

七、组织建设

2017年，市县乡共建立残联112个，各地市已建残联9个，县（市、区）残联已建103个；已建社区（村）残协68个。

省市县乡残联实有人员达221人，乡镇(街道)、村（社区）选聘残疾人专职委员总计88名，县级残联配备了残疾人干部6人。

共建立省级及以下各类残疾人专门协会 565 个，其中省级专门协会已建 5 个，市级专门协会已建45个，县级专门协会已建515。助残社会组织共有5个。

八、服务设施建设

截至 2017 年底，已竣工并投入使用的各级残疾人综合服务设施6个，总建设规模4949平方米，总投资609万元；已竣工并投入使用的各级残疾人康复设施4个，总建设规模24500平方米，总投资4900万元；已竣工并投入使用的各级残疾人托养服务设施4个，总建设规模12521平方米，总投资6777万元。

附 录

Appendix

关于使用 2010 年末全国残疾人总数及各类、不同残疾等级人数的通知

残联〔2012〕25 号

各省、自治区、直辖市及计划单列市残联，新疆生产建设兵团残联，黑龙江农垦总局残联:

根据第六次全国人口普查我国总人口数，及第二次全国残疾人抽样调查我国残疾人占全国总人口的比例和各类残疾人占残疾人总人数的比例，推算了 2010 年末我国残疾人总人数及各类、不同等级的残疾人数，现通知如下:

全国残疾人总数为 8502 万人。

各类残疾人的人数分别为: 视力残疾 1263 万人; 听力残疾 2054 万人; 言语残疾 130 万人; 肢体残疾 2472 万人; 智力残疾 568 万人; 精神残疾 629 万人; 多重残疾 1386 万人。

各残疾等级人数分别为: 重度残疾 2518 万人; 中度和轻度残疾人 5984 万人。

以上数据可在工作中使用并对外公开。

中国残疾人联合会

二〇一二年三月五日

中国残联统计调查项目目录

审批项目一览表

统计调查项目名称	批准文号	有效期截止时间
中国残疾人事业统计调查制度	国统制[2018] 82 号	2021 年 6 月
全国残疾人基本服务状况和需求信息数据动态更新	国统制[2017] 38 号	2019 年 4 月
全国残疾人家庭收入状况调查制度	国统制[2018] 60 号	2021 年 5 月

中国残疾人联合会文件

残联发[2006]1 号

关于印发《中国残联系统统计工作管理办法》的通知

各省、自治区、直辖市及计划单列市残联，新疆生产建设兵团残联、黑龙江农垦总局残联:

为了加强统计工作的管理,规范统计调查行为，提高统计调查的整体效益，充分发挥统计工作的服务和监督作用，中国残联依据《中华人民共和国统计法》、《中华人民共和国统计法实施细则》、《部门统计调查管理暂行办法》，结合工作实际，对原有的《中国残联系统统计工作暂行规定》、《中国残联系统专项业务统计调查项目管理暂行办法》、《中国残联机关统计资料管理暂行办法》等进行了修订和整合，制定了《全国残联系统统计工作管理办法》，现予以印发，请遵照执行。

中国残疾人联合会
二〇〇六年一月三日

中国残联系统统计工作管理办法

一、总　则

第一条　为了科学、有效地组织全国残联系统统计工作，规范统计调查行为，提高统计调查的整体效益，充分发挥统计工作的服务和监督作用，依据《中华人民共和国统计法》(以下简称《统计法》)、《中华人民共和国统计法实施细则》(以下简称《实施细则》)、《部门统计调查管理暂行办法》，结合工作实际，制定本办法。

第二条　全国残联系统统计工作的基本任务是：对全国残疾人事业的发展状况和残联系统的业务工作进行统计调查、统计分析、统计预测和统计监督，为国家和各级人民政府制定与残疾人事业相关的政策、法规提供依据，为领导运筹决策和残联系统工作的发展提供有效的服务。

第三条　全国残联系统统计工作由：中国残疾人事业统计年报制度、中国残疾人事业统计快报制度、中国残疾人事业基础统计台账制度、专项业务统计调查工作组成。

第四条　各级残联应加强统计现代化建设，积极利用信息技术手段，使残疾人事业统计数据更加科学、准确、及时，逐步实现残疾人事业统计数据的电子化和统计数据的社会共享与服务。

二、统计机构、职责和统计人员

第五条　全国残联系统统计工作实行统一领导、分级负责。中国残联负责全国残疾人事业统计工作的组织、协调与管理，并对地方残联统计工作进行指导，具体由中国残联设置的统计机构负责组织实施。地方各级残联的统计工作由地方各级残联设置的统计机构或统计主管部门负责管理和组织实施，并接受上级残联统计机构和同级人民政府统计部门的指导、监督与管理。

第六条　中国残联的统计机构设在中国残联信息中心，负责组织、协调和管理全国残联系统的统计工作。其主要职责是：制定残疾人事业统计调查计划和项目，制定统计标准；组织协调各级残联搜集、整理、提供统计资料，管理统计资料的发布，开展统计分析、统计预测和统计监督工作；指导、检查全国残联系统统计工作，组织统计业务经验交流，开展全国残联系统统计科学研究；做好统计人员培训工作；制订全国残联系统统计工作现代化规划。

各省级残联应设置统计机构或明确统计主管部门并设专职统计人员，负责指导本行政区域内各级残联统计工作，组织管理本级残联的统计工作。其主要职责是：在完成好中国残联和上级残联下达的各项统计调查工作的同时，为本级残疾人事业提供各项统计数据，并开展统计调查活动。

各地级市残联应明确统计主管部门并设专（兼）职统计人员，其主要职责是：在完成好中国残联和上级残联下达的各项统计调查工作的同时，为本级残疾人事业提供各项统计数据，并开展统计调查活动。

各县级残联应明确统计工作主管部门或主管负责人，确定兼职统计人员。其主要职责是：做好基础数据工作，建立统计台账，完成好中国残联和上级残联下达的统计调查任务，为本级残疾人事业提供各项统计数据，并开展统计调查活动。

第七条　各级残联统计人员应保持相对稳定。统计人员的调动，应当征得本级统计主管部门或统计工作负责人的同意；省级专职统计人员的调动，应当征得中国残联统计机构的同意。统计人员调动工作或离职，应当由经过统计业务培训、能够胜任统计业务工作的人员接替，并办理交接手续。各级残联的统计人员应取得同级人民政府统计机构颁发的统计上岗证，具有残联系统业务知识和计算机操作能力。

三、统计报表制度的编制、修改与审批

第八条　中国残疾人事业统计年报、快报制度和统计台账制度中的指标、指标涵义、调查范围、

分类目录、计算方法和统计报表表式、统计编码以及报送时间，由中国残联统一规定，按照国家统计局的要求报送国家统计局进行审批备案。按规定程序经国家统计局批准或备案的统计报表，在报表的右上角标明制表机关名称、表号、批准或备案机关名称及其批准文号。被调查的部门、人员应当准确、及时地按报表规定填报。

不符合前款规定的统计报表（包括以搜集数字为主的调查提纲）是非法报表，被调查的部门可以拒绝填报。

第九条 中国残疾人事业统计年报、快报和统计台账应根据中国残疾人事业发展的需要及时进行调整和补充。中国残联各业务部门因工作需要，调整和补充有关指标时，应进行充分论证并与中国残联统计管理部门联系与协商，经中国残联理事会批准后，报国家统计局批准或备案。

四、统计台账管理

第十条 为了规范中国残联系统统计工作，做到依法统计，发挥统计服务和监督作用，根据《中华人民共和国统计法》和国家相关统计工作的规定，中国残联将制定中国残疾人事业统计台账制度，加强统计台账的管理与数据的报送。

第十一条 中国残疾人事业统计台账（卡）充分利用电子网络化的方式、将科学合理、准确实用的动态管理，与中国残疾人事业统计报表制度相衔接。台账填写内容要符合法律法规政策的要求，填写对象真实、准确；先填卡，后建帐，做到由台账中提取统计数字。

第十二条 各级残联必须依据中国残疾人事业统计台账（卡）中的数据，报送中国残疾人事业统计快报、年报和各项专项业务统计调查的统计报表，做到填报统计报表的数据全面、准确、及时、数出一门。

第十三条 中国残疾人事业统计台账在统一格式、统一软件下实施，由各级地方残联统计人员协调业务部门和人员用计算机或纸质台账、台卡方式进行专门管理。统计人员发生变动时，要严格履行交接手续。

第十四条 省级、地（市）级残联都应建立电子化台账。有条件的县级残联也要实行电子化台账，各级残联应积极推动电子化台账建设，加强统计台账的管理工作。在没有实行全面电子化台账之前，将实行电子化台账和纸质台账、台卡的同时保存。

第十五条 中国残疾人事业统计台账、台卡按中国残疾人事业统计报表逐级汇总上报。

五、专项业务统计调查管理

第十六条 中国残联和地方各级残联开展的专项业务统计调查，以及残联各业务部门与其他部门或单位联合组织实施的统计调查，其调查的统计指标与中国残联年报、快报指标交叉重复或需要对外公布统计数据的统计调查，均属于专项业务统计调查管理范畴。

第十七条 中国残联系统各级统计机构统一管理和协调本级业务部门专项业务统计调查。

第十八条 专项业务统计调查项目必须符合国家统计局《部门统计调查项目管理暂行办法》的基本原则与要求。专项业务统计调查项目的立项必须有充分的理由。调查要有明确的目的和资料使用范围。调查项目应当与中国残联职能范围和各项业务工作相对应。

第十九条 中国残联系统各级统计机构通过建立审批备案制度、调查项目公布制度、跟踪检查制度、举报制度，对会内专项业务统计调查进行管理。

第二十条 专项业务统计调查项目中的统计标准和分类必须与政府综合统计机构规定使用的标准和分类相一致。涉及政府综合统计机构规定以外的专业标准和分类，要与国家有关标准或行业标准相一致。尚无国家标准和行业标准的，必须严格按照标准化及分类科学的原则进行归纳和设计，并在使用前征求政府综合统计机构的意见。

第二十一条 中国残联新增设的统计调查项目在制定好统计调查方案后，须提交中国残联统计机构审核，报国家统计局批准后统一组织实施。

地方残联新增设的统计调查项目，由本级残联统计机构统一管理，报上级残联统计机构和同级人民政府统计局批准后组织实施。地方残联制发的统计调查表内容、指标涵义、计算方法、完成期限等，均不得与中国残联制发的有关统计调查表相抵触。

六、统计资料的管理与发布

第二十二条 残联系统统计资料实行归口管理。全国性残联系统 统计资料，由中国残联统计机构统一管理；地方性残联系统统计资料，由地方残联统计机构或统计人员统一管理。统计机构和统计人员必须建立统计工作责任制和统计资料整理、审查、管理制度，不断提高工作质量和工作效率，保证残联系统统计资料的准确、及时。

各级残联的文件、报告、简报、情况反映、信息等引用综合性的统计数字，必须经本级统计机构或统计人员复核。对外提供和公布的统计资料，必须经本级统计机构或统计人员统一复核和办理并由主管理事长批准。任何部门和个人不得擅自公开和使用未经正式公布的残联系统统计资料。

第二十三条 各级残联统计机构、统计人员必须建立健全统计资料档案，对原始记录、统计台账和综合分析等统计资料，按有关规定保管，不得损坏。对于属于国家秘密的残联系统统计资料，要按照《中华人民共和国保守国家秘密法》、国家统计局《统计资料保密管理办法》等有关规定，妥善保管。

七、奖励和惩罚

第二十四条 各级残联对有下列表现之一的残联统计机构或者人员，给予表扬或奖励:

一、在改革和完善残联系统统计制度、统计方法等方面，有重要贡献的;

二、在完成规定的残联系统统计调查任务，保障残联系统统计资料的准确性、及时性方面，做出显著成绩的;

三、在进行残联系统统计分析、统计预测和统计监督方面取得重要成绩的;

四、在运用和推广现代化信息技术方面，有显著效果的;

五、在残联系统统计科学研究方面有所创新的;

六、坚持实事求是，依法办事，同违反统计法规和本办法的行为作斗争，表现突出的。

第二十五条 各级残联对有下列行为之一的机构或者人员，给予批评或处分:

一、虚报、瞒报、拒报残联系统统计资料的;

二、伪造、篡改残联系统统计资料的;

三、无故迟报残联系统统计资料的;

四、侵犯统计机构、统计人员行使统计法规及本办法所规定的职权或打击报复统计人员的;

五、违反统计法规及本办法，未经批准，自行编制发布残联系统统计报表的;

六、违反统计法规及本办法，未经核定批准，擅自对外提供或公布残联系统统计资料的。

八、附　则

第二十六条 本办法由中国残联负责解释。

第二十七条 本办法自发布之日起试行。

中华人民共和国统计法

（1983 年 12 月 8 日第六届全国人民代表大会常务委员会第三次会议通过。根据 1996 年 5 月 15 日第八届全国人民代表大会常务委员会第十九次会议《关于修改〈中华人民共和国统计法〉的决定》修正。2009 年 6 月 27 日第十一届全国人民代表大会常务委员会第九次会议修订。）

第一章 总 则

第一条 为了科学、有效地组织统计工作，保障统计资料的真实性、准确性、完整性和及时性，发挥统计在了解国情国力、服务经济社会发展中的重要作用，促进社会主义现代化建设事业发展，制定本法。

第二条 本法适用于各级人民政府、县级以上人民政府统计机构和有关部门组织实施的统计活动。

统计的基本任务是对经济社会发展情况进行统计调查、统计分析，提供统计资料和统计咨询意见，实行统计监督。

第三条 国家建立集中统一的统计系统，实行统一领导、分级负责的统计管理体制。

第四条 国务院和地方各级人民政府、各有关部门应当加强对统计工作的组织领导，为统计工作提供必要的保障。

第五条 国家加强统计科学研究，健全科学的统计指标体系，不断改进统计调查方法，提高统计的科学性。

国家有计划地加强统计信息化建设，推进统计信息搜集、处理、传输、共享、存储技术和统计数据库体系的现代化。

第六条 统计机构和统计人员依照本法规定独立行使统计调查、统计报告、统计监督的职权，不受侵犯。

地方各级人民政府、政府统计机构和有关部门以及各单位的负责人，不得自行修改统计机构和统计人员依法搜集、整理的统计资料，不得以任何方式要求统计机构、统计人员及其他机构、人员伪造、篡改统计资料，不得对依法履行职责或者拒绝、抵制统计违法行为的统计人员打击报复。

第七条 国家机关、企业事业单位和其他组织以及个体工商户和个人等统计调查对象，必须依照本法和国家有关规定，真实、准确、完整、及时地提供统计调查所需的资料，不得提供不真实或者不完整的统计资料，不得迟报、拒报统计资料。

第八条 统计工作应当接受社会公众的监督。任何单位和个人有权检举统计中弄虚作假等违法行为。对检举有功的单位和个人应当给予表彰和奖励。

第九条 统计机构和统计人员对在统计工作中知悉的国家秘密、商业秘密和个人信息，应当予以保密。

第十条 任何单位和个人不得利用虚假统计资料骗取荣誉称号、物质利益或者职务晋升。

第二章 统计调查管理

第十一条 统计调查项目包括国家统计调查项目、部门统计调查项目和地方统计调查项目。

国家统计调查项目是指全国性基本情况的统计调查项目。部门统计调查项目是指国务院有关部门的专业性统计调查项目。地方统计调查项目是指县级以上地方人民政府及其部门的地方性统计调查项目。

国家统计调查项目、部门统计调查项目、地方统计调查项目应当明确分工，互相衔接，不得重复。

第十二条 国家统计调查项目由国家统计局制定，或者由国家统计局和国务院有关部门共同制定，报国务院备案；重大的国家统计调查项目报国务院审批。

部门统计调查项目由国务院有关部门制定。统计调查对象属于本部门管辖系统的，报国家统计局备案；统计调查对象超出本部门管辖系统的，报国家统计局审批。

地方统计调查项目由县级以上地方人民政府统计机构和有关部门分别制定或者共同制定。其中，由省级人民政府统计机构单独制定或者和有关部门共同制定的，报国家统计局审批；由省级以下人民政府统计机构单独制定或者和有关部门共同制定的，报省级人民政府统计机构审批；由县级以上地方人民政府有关部门制定的，报本级人民政府统计机构审批。

第十三条 统计调查项目的审批机关应当对调查项目的必要性、可行性、科学性进行审查，对符合法定条件的，作出予以批准的书面决定，并公布；对不符合法定条件的，作出不予批准的书面决定，并说明理由。

第十四条 制定统计调查项目，应当同时制定该项目的统计调查制度，并依照本法第十二条的规定一并报经审批或者备案。

统计调查制度应当对调查目的、调查内容、调查方法、调查对象、调查组织方式、调查表式、统计资料的报送和公布等作出规定。

统计调查应当按照统计调查制度组织实施。变更统计调查制度的内容，应当报经原审批机关批准或者原备案机关备案。

第十五条 统计调查表应当标明表号、制定机关、批准或者备案文号、有效期限等标志。

对未标明前款规定的标志或者超过有效期限的统计调查表，统计调查对象有权拒绝填报；县级以上人民政府统计机构应当依法责令停止有关统计调查活动。

第十六条 搜集、整理统计资料，应当以周期性普查为基础，以经常性抽样调查为主体，综合运用全面调查、重点调查等方法，并充分利用行政记录等资料。

重大国情国力普查由国务院统一领导，国务院和地方人民政府组织统计机构和有关部门共同实施。

第十七条 国家制定统一的统计标准，保障统计调查采用的指标涵义、计算方法、分类目录、调查表式和统计编码等的标准化。

国家统计标准由国家统计局制定，或者由国家统计局和国务院标准化主管部门共同制定。

国务院有关部门可以制定补充性的部门统计标准，报国家统计局审批。部门统计标准不得与国家统计标准相抵触。

第十八条 县级以上人民政府统计机构根据统计任务的需要，可以在统计调查对象中推广使用计算机网络报送统计资料。

第十九条 县级以上人民政府应当将统计工作所需经费列入财政预算。

重大国情国力普查所需经费，由国务院和地方人民政府共同负担，列入相应年度的财政预算，按时拨付，确保到位。

第三章 统计资料的管理和公布

第二十条 县级以上人民政府统计机构和有关部门以及乡、镇人民政府，应当按照国家有关规定建立统计资料的保存、管理制度，建立健全统计信息共享机制。

第二十一条 国家机关、企业事业单位和其他组织等统计调查对象，应当按照国家有关规定设置原始记录、统计台账，建立健全统计资料的审核、签署、交接、归档等管理制度。

统计资料的审核、签署人员应当对其审核、签署的统计资料的真实性、准确性和完整性负责。

第二十二条 县级以上人民政府有关部门应当及时向本级人民政府统计机构提供统计所需的行政记录资料和国民经济核算所需的财务资料、财政资料及其他资料，并按照统计调查制度的规定及时向本级人民政府统计机构报送其组织实施统计调查取得的有关资料。

县级以上人民政府统计机构应当及时向本级人民政府有关部门提供有关统计资料。

第二十三条 县级以上人民政府统计机构按照国家有关规定，定期公布统计资料。

国家统计数据以国家统计局公布的数据为准。

第二十四条 县级以上人民政府有关部门统计调查取得的统计资料，由本部门按照国家有关规定公布。

第二十五条 统计调查中获得的能够识别或者推断单个统计调查对象身份的资料，任何单位和个人不得对外提供、泄露，不得用于统计以外的目的。

第二十六条 县级以上人民政府统计机构和有关部门统计调查取得的统计资料，除依法应当保密的外，应当及时公开，供社会公众查询。

第四章　统计机构和统计人员

第二十七条　国务院设立国家统计局，依法组织领导和协调全国的统计工作。

国家统计局根据工作需要设立的派出调查机构，承担国家统计局布置的统计调查等任务。

县级以上地方人民政府设立独立的统计机构，乡、镇人民政府设置统计工作岗位，配备专职或者兼职统计人员，依法管理、开展统计工作，实施统计调查。

第二十八条　县级以上人民政府有关部门根据统计任务的需要设立统计机构，或者在有关机构中设置统计人员，并指定统计负责人，依法组织、管理本部门职责范围内的统计工作，实施统计调查，在统计业务上受本级人民政府统计机构的指导。

第二十九条　统计机构、统计人员应当依法履行职责，如实搜集、报送统计资料，不得伪造、篡改统计资料，不得以任何方式要求任何单位和个人提供不真实的统计资料，不得有其他违反本法规定的行为。

统计人员应当坚持实事求是，恪守职业道德，对其负责搜集、审核、录入的统计资料与统计调查对象报送的统计资料的一致性负责。

第三十条　统计人员进行统计调查时，有权就与统计有关的问题询问有关人员，要求其如实提供有关情况、资料并改正不真实、不准确的资料。

统计人员进行统计调查时，应当出示县级以上人民政府统计机构或者有关部门颁发的工作证件；未出示的，统计调查对象有权拒绝调查。

第三十一条　国家实行统计专业技术职务资格考试、评聘制度，提高统计人员的专业素质，保障统计队伍的稳定性。

统计人员应当具备与其从事的统计工作相适应的专业知识和业务能力。

县级以上人民政府统计机构和有关部门应当加强对统计人员的专业培训和职业道德教育。

第五章　监督检查

第三十二条　县级以上人民政府及其监察机关对下级人民政府、本级人民政府统计机构和有关部门执行本法的情况，实施监督。

第三十三条　国家统计局组织管理全国统计工作的监督检查，查处重大统计违法行为。

县级以上地方人民政府统计机构依法查处本行政区域内发生的统计违法行为。但是，国家统计局派出的调查机构组织实施的统计调查活动中发生的统计违法行为，由组织实施该项统计调查的调查机构负责查处。

法律、行政法规对有关部门查处统计违法行为另有规定的，从其规定。

第三十四条　县级以上人民政府有关部门应当积极协助本级人民政府统计机构查处统计违法行为，及时向本级人民政府统计机构移送有关统计违法案件材料。

第三十五条　县级以上人民政府统计机构在调查统计违法行为或者核查统计数据时，有权采取下列措施:

（一）发出统计检查查询书，向检查对象查询有关事项;

（二）要求检查对象提供有关原始记录和凭证、统计台账、统计调查表、会计资料及其他相关证明和资料;

（三）就与检查有关的事项询问有关人员;

（四）进入检查对象的业务场所和统计数据处理信息系统进行检查、核对;

（五）经本机构负责人批准，登记保存检查对象的有关原始记录和凭证、统计台账、统计调查表、会计资料及其他相关证明和资料;

（六）对与检查事项有关的情况和资料进行记录、录音、录像、照相和复制。

县级以上人民政府统计机构进行监督检查时，监督检查人员不得少于二人，并应当出示执法证件；未出示的，有关单位和个人有权拒绝检查。

第三十六条　县级以上人民政府统计机构履行监督检查职责时，有关单位和个人应当如实反映情况，提供相关证明和资料，不得拒绝、阻碍检查，不得转移、隐匿、篡改、毁弃原始记录和凭证、统计台账、统计调查表、会计资料及其他相关证明和资料。

第六章　法律责任

第三十七条　地方人民政府、政府统计机构或者有关部门、单位的负责人有下列行为之一的，由任免机关或者监察机关依法给予处分，并由县级以上人民政府统计机构予以通报：

（一）自行修改统计资料、编造虚假统计数据的；

（二）要求统计机构、统计人员或者其他机构、人员伪造、篡改统计资料的；

（三）对依法履行职责或者拒绝、抵制统计违法行为的统计人员打击报复的；

（四）对本地方、本部门、本单位发生的严重统计违法行为失察的。

第三十八条 县级以上人民政府统计机构或者有关部门在组织实施统计调查活动中有下列行为之一的，由本级人民政府、上级人民政府统计机构或者本级人民政府统计机构责令改正，予以通报；对直接负责的主管人员和其他直接责任人员，由任免机关或者监察机关依法给予处分：

（一）未经批准擅自组织实施统计调查的；

（二）未经批准擅自变更统计调查制度的内容的；

（三）伪造、篡改统计资料的；

（四）要求统计调查对象或者其他机构、人员提供不真实的统计资料的；

（五）未按照统计调查制度的规定报送有关资料的。

统计人员有前款第三项至第五项所列行为之一的，责令改正，依法给予处分。

第三十九条 县级以上人民政府统计机构或者有关部门有下列行为之一的，对直接负责的主管人员和其他直接责任人员由任免机关或者监察机关依法给予处分：

（一）违法公布统计资料的；

（二）泄露统计调查对象的商业秘密、个人信息或者提供、泄露在统计调查中获得的能够识别或者推断单个统计调查对象身份的资料的；

（三）违反国家有关规定，造成统计资料毁损、灭失的。

统计人员有前款所列行为之一的，依法给予处分。

第四十条 统计机构、统计人员泄露国家秘密的，依法追究法律责任。

第四十一条 作为统计调查对象的国家机关、企业事业单位或者其他组织有下列行为之一的，由县级以上人民政府统计机构责令改正，给予警告，可以予以通报；其直接负责的主管人员和其他直接责任人员属于国家工作人员的，由任免机关或者监察机关依法给予处分：

（一）拒绝提供统计资料或者经催报后仍未按时提供统计资料的；

（二）提供不真实或者不完整的统计资料的；

（三）拒绝答复或者不如实答复统计检查查询书的；

（四）拒绝、阻碍统计调查、统计检查的；

（五）转移、隐匿、篡改、毁弃或者拒绝提供原始记录和凭证、统计台账、统计调查表及其他相关证明和资料的。

企业事业单位或者其他组织有前款所列行为之一的，可以并处五万元以下的罚款；情节严重的，并处五万元以上二十万元以下的罚款。

个体工商户有本条第一款所列行为之一的，由县级以上人民政府统计机构责令改正，给予警告，可以并处一万元以下的罚款。

第四十二条 作为统计调查对象的国家机关、企业事业单位或者其他组织迟报统计资料，或者未按照国家有关规定设置原始记录、统计台账的，由县级以上人民政府统计机构责令改正，给予警告。

企业事业单位或者其他组织有前款所列行为之一的，可以并处一万元以下的罚款。

个体工商户迟报统计资料的，由县级以上人民政府统计机构责令改正，给予警告，可以并处一千元以下的罚款。

第四十三条 县级以上人民政府统计机构查处统计违法行为时，认为对有关国家工作人员依法应当给予处分的，应当提出给予处分的建议；该国家工作人员的任免机关或者监察机关应当依法及时作出决定，并将结果书面通知县级以上人民政府统计机构。

第四十四条 作为统计调查对象的个人在重大国情国力普查活动中拒绝、阻碍统计调查，或者提供不真实或者不完整的普查资料的，由县级以上人民政府统计机构责令改正，予以批评教育。

第四十五条 违反本法规定，利用虚假统计资料骗取荣誉称号、物质利益或者职务晋升的，除对其编造虚假统计资料或者要求他人编造虚假统计资料的行为依法追究法律责任外，由作出有关决定的单位或者其上级单位、监察机关取消其荣誉称号，追缴获得的物质利益，撤销晋升的职务。

第四十六条　当事人对县级以上人民政府统计机构作出的行政处罚决定不服的，可以依法申请行政复议或者提起行政诉讼。其中，对国家统计局在省、自治区、直辖市派出的调查机构作出的行政处罚决定不服的，向国家统计局申请行政复议；对国家统计局派出的其他调查机构作出的行政处罚决定不服的，向国家统计局在该派出机构所在的省、自治区、直辖市派出的调查机构申请行政复议。

第四十七条　违反本法规定，构成犯罪的，依法追究刑事责任。

第七章　附　则

第四十八条　本法所称县级以上人民政府统计机构，是指国家统计局及其派出的调查机构、县级以上地方人民政府统计机构。

第四十九条　民间统计调查活动的管理办法，由国务院制定。

中华人民共和国境外的组织、个人需要在中华人民共和国境内进行统计调查活动的，应当按照国务院的规定报请审批。

利用统计调查危害国家安全、损害社会公共利益或者进行欺诈活动的，依法追究法律责任。

第五十条　本法自 2010 年 1 月 1 日起施行。

部门统计调查项目管理办法

（中华人民共和国国家统计局令第22号）

第一章　总则

第一条　为加强部门统计调查项目的规范性、统一性管理，提高统计调查的科学性和有效性，减轻统计调查对象负担，推进部门统计信息共享，根据《中华人民共和国统计法》及其实施条例和国务院有关规定，制定本办法。

第二条　本办法适用于国务院各部门制定的统计调查项目。

第三条　本办法所称的统计调查项目，是指国务院有关部门通过调查表格、问卷、行政记录、大数据以及其他方式搜集整理统计资料，用于政府管理和公共服务的各类统计调查项目。

第四条　国家统计局统一组织领导和协调全国统计工作，指导国务院有关部门开展统计调查，统一管理部门统计调查。

第五条　国务院有关部门应当明确统一组织协调统计工作的综合机构，负责归口管理、统一申报本部门统计调查项目。

第二章　部门统计调查项目的制定

第六条　国务院有关部门执行相关法律、行政法规、国务院的决定和履行本部门职责，需要开展统计活动的，应当制定相应的部门统计调查项目。

第七条　制定部门统计调查项目，应当减少调查频率，缩小调查规模，降低调查成本，减轻基层统计人员和统计调查对象的负担。可以通过行政记录和大数据加工整理获得统计资料的，不得开展统计调查；可以通过已经批准实施的各种统计调查整理获得统计资料的，不得重复开展统计调查；抽样调查、重点调查可以满足需要的，不得开展全面统计调查。

第八条　制定部门统计调查项目，应当有组织、人员和经费保障。

第九条　制定部门统计调查项目，应当同时制定该项目的统计调查制度。

统计调查制度内容包括总说明、报表目录、调查表式、分类目录、指标解释、指标间逻辑关系，采用抽样调查方法的还应当包括抽样方案。

统计调查制度总说明应当对调查目的、调查对象、统计范围、调查内容、调查频率、调查时间、调查方法、组织实施方式、质量控制、报送要求、信息共享、资料公布等作出规定。

面向单位的部门统计调查，其统计调查对象应当取自国家基本单位名录库或者部门基本单位名录库。

第十条　部门统计调查应当规范设置统计指标、调查表，指标解释和计算方法应当科学合理。

第十一条　部门统计调查应当使用国家统计标准。无国家统计标准的，可以使用经国家统计局批准的部门统计标准。

第十二条　新制定的部门统计调查项目或者对现行统计调查项目进行较大修订的，应当开展试填试报等工作。其中，重要统计调查项目应当进行试点。

第十三条　部门统计调查项目涉及其他部门职责的，应当事先征求相关部门意见。

第三章　部门统计调查项目审批和备案

第十四条　国务院有关部门制定的统计调查项目，统计调查对象属于本部门管辖系统或者利用行政记录加工获取统计资料的，报国家统计局备案；统计调查对象超出本部门管辖系统的，报国家统计局审批。

部门管辖系统包括本部门直属机构、派出机构和垂直管理的机构，省及省以下与部门对口设立的管理机构。

第十五条　部门统计调查项目审批或者备案包括申报、受理、审查、反馈、决定等程序。

第十六条 部门统计调查项目送审或者备案时，应当通过部门统计调查项目管理平台提交下列材料:

（一）申请审批项目的部门公文或者申请备案项目的部门办公厅（室）公文;

（二）部门统计调查项目审批或者备案申请表;

（三）统计调查制度;

（四）统计调查项目的论证报告、背景材料、经费保障等，修订的统计调查项目还应当提供修订说明;

（五）征求有关地方、部门、统计调查对象和专家意见及其采纳情况;

（六）制定机关按照会议制度集体讨论决定的会议纪要;

（七）重要统计调查项目的试点报告;

（八）由审批机关或者备案机关公布的统计调查制度的主要内容;

（九）防范和惩治统计造假、弄虚作假责任规定。

前款第（一）项的公文应当同时提交纸质文件。

第十七条 申请材料齐全并符合法定形式的，国家统计局予以受理。

申请材料不齐全或者不符合法定形式的，国家统计局应当一次告知需要补正的全部内容，制定机关应当按照国家统计局的要求予以补正。

第十八条 统计调查制度应当列明下列事项:

（一）向国家统计局报送的制定机关组织实施统计调查取得的具体统计资料清单;

（二）主要统计指标公布的时间、渠道;

（三）统计信息共享的内容、方式、时限、渠道、责任单位和责任人;

（四）向统计信息共享数据库提供的统计资料清单;

（五）统计调查对象使用国家基本单位名录库或者部门基本单位名录库的情况。

第十九条 国家统计局对申请审批的部门统计调查项目进行审查，符合下列条件的部门统计调查项目，作出予以批准的书面决定:

（一）具有法定依据或者确为部门公共管理和服务所必需;

（二）与现有的国家统计调查项目和部门统计调查项目的主要内容不重复、不矛盾;

（三）主要统计指标无法通过本部门的行政记录或者已有统计调查资料加工整理取得;

（四）部门统计调查制度科学、合理、可行，并且符合本办法第八条、第九条和第十八条规定;

（五）采用的统计标准符合国家有关规定;

（六）符合统计法律法规和国家有关规定。

不符合前款规定的，国家统计局向制定机关提出修改意见；修改后仍不符合前款规定条件的，国家统计局作出不予批准的书面决定，并说明理由。

第二十条 国家统计局对申请备案的部门统计调查项目进行审查，符合下列条件的部门统计调查项目，作出同意备案的书面决定:

（一）统计调查项目的调查对象属于制定机关管辖系统，或者利用行政记录加工获取统计资料;

（二）与现有的国家统计调查项目和部门统计调查项目的主要内容不重复、不矛盾;

（三）部门统计调查制度科学、合理、可行，并且符合本办法第八条、第九条和第十八条规定。

第二十一条 国家统计局在收到制定机关申请公文及完整的相关资料后，在20个工作日内完成审批，20个工作日内不能作出决定的，经审批机关负责人批准可以延长10日，并应当将延长审批期限的理由告知制定机关；在10个工作日内完成备案。完成时间以复函日期为准。

制定机关修改统计调查项目的时间，不计算在审批期限内。

第二十二条 部门统计调查项目有下列情形之一的，国家统计局简化审批或者备案程序，缩短期限:

（一）发生突发事件，需要迅速实施统计调查;

（二）统计调查内容未做变动，统计调查项目有效期届满需要延长期限。

第二十三条 部门统计调查项目实行有效期管理。审批的统计调查项目有效期为 3 年，备案的统计调查项目有效期为 5 年。统计调查制度对有效期规定少于 3 年的，从其规定。有效期以批准执行或者同意备案的日期为起始时间。

统计调查项目在有效期内需要变更内容的，制定机关应当重新申请审批或者备案。

第二十四条 部门统计调查项目经国家统计局批准或者备案后，应当在统计调查表的右上角标明表号、制定机关、批准机关或者备案机关、批准文号或者备案文号、有效期限等标志。

第二十五条 制定机关收到批准或者备案的书面决定后，在10个工作日内将标注批准文号或者备案文号和有效期限的统计调查制度发送到部门统计调查项目管理平台。

第二十六条 国家统计局及时通过国家统计局网站公布批准或者备案的部门统计调查项目名称、制定机关、批准文号或者备案文号、有效期限和统计调查制度的主要内容。

第四章 部门统计调查的组织实施

第二十七条 国务院有关部门应当健全统计工作流程规范，完善统计数据质量控制办法，夯实统计基础工作，严格按照国家统计局批准或者备案的统计调查制度组织实施统计调查。

第二十八条 国务院有关部门在组织实施统计调查时，应当就统计调查制度的主要内容对组织实施人员进行培训；应当就法定填报义务、主要指标涵义和口径、计算方法、采用的统计标准和其他填报要求，向调查对象作出说明。

第二十九条 国务院有关部门应当按《中华人民共和国统计法实施条例》的要求及时公布主要统计指标涵义、调查范围、调查方法、计算方法、抽样调查样本量等信息，对统计数据进行解释说明。

第三十条 国务院有关部门组织实施统计调查应当遵守国家有关统计资料管理和公布的规定。

第三十一条 部门统计调查取得的统计资料，一般应当在政府部门间共享。

第三十二条 国务院有关部门建立统计调查项目执行情况评估制度，对实施情况、实施效果和存在问题进行评估，认为应当修改的，按规定报请国家统计局审批或者备案。

第五章 国家统计局提供的服务

第三十三条 国家统计局依法开展部门统计调查项目审批和备案工作，为国务院有关部门提供有关统计业务咨询、统计调查制度设计指导、统计业务培训等服务。

第三十四条 国家统计局组织国务院有关部门共同维护、更新国家基本单位名录库，为部门统计调查提供调查单位名录和抽样框。

第三十五条 国家统计局建立统计标准库，为部门统计调查提供国家统计标准和部门统计标准。

第三十六条 国家统计局向国务院有关部门提供部门统计调查项目查询服务。

第三十七条 国家统计局推动建立统计信息共享数据库，为国务院有关部门提供部门统计数据查询服务。

第六章 监督检查

第三十八条 国家统计局依法对部门统计调查制度执行情况进行监督检查，依法查处部门统计调查中的重大违法行为；县级以上地方人民政府统计机构依法查处本级和下级人民政府有关部门和统计调查对象执行部门统计调查制度中发生的统计违法行为。

第三十九条 任何单位和个人有权向国家统计局举报部门统计调查违法行为。

国家统计局公布举报统计违法行为的方式和途径，依法受理、核实、处理举报，并为举报人保密。

第四十条 县级以上人民政府有关部门积极协助本级人民政府统计机构查处统计违法行为，及时向县级以上人民政府统计机构移送有关统计违法案件材料。

第四十一条 县级以上人民政府统计机构在调查部门统计违法行为或者核查部门统计数据时，有权采取《中华人民共和国统计法》第三十五条规定的下列措施：

（一）发出检查查询书，向检查单位和调查对象查询部门统计调查项目有关事项；

（二）要求检查单位和调查对象提供与部门统计调查有关的统计调查制度、调查资料、调查报告及其他相关证明和资料；

（三）就与检查有关的事项询问有关人员；

（四）进入检查单位和调查对象的业务场所和统计数据处理信息系统进行检查、核对；

（五）经本机构负责人批准，登记保存检查单位与统计调查有关的统计调查制度、调查资料、调查报告及其他相关证明和资料；

（六）对与检查事项有关的情况和资料进行记录、录音、录像、照相和复制。

县级以上人民政府统计机构进行监督检查时，监督检查人员不得少于 2 人，并应当出示执法证件；未出示的，有关部门有权拒绝检查。

第四十二条 县级以上人民政府统计机构履行监督检查职责时，有关部门应当如实反映情况，提供相关证明和资料，不得拒绝、阻碍检查，不得转移、隐匿、篡改、毁弃与部门统计调查有关的统计调查制度、调查资料、调查报告及其他相关证明和资料。

第七章 法律责任

第四十三条 县级以上人民政府有关部门在组织实施部门统计调查活动中有下列行为之一的，由上级人民政府统计机构、本级人民政府统计机构责令改正，予以通报：

（一）违法制定、实施部门统计调查项目；

（二）未执行国家统计标准或者经依法批准的部门统计标准；

（三）未执行批准和备案的部门统计调查制度；

（四）在部门统计调查中统计造假、弄虚作假。

第四十四条 县级以上人民政府有关部门及其工作人员有下列行为之一的，由上级人民政府统计机构、本级人民政府统计机构责令改正，予以通报：

（一）拒绝、阻碍对部门统计调查的监督检查和对部门统计违法行为的查处；

（二）包庇、纵容部门统计违法行为；

（三）向存在部门统计违法行为的单位或者个人通风报信，帮助其逃避查处。

第四十五条 县级以上人民政府统计机构在查处部门统计违法行为中，认为对有关国家工作人员依法应当给予处分的，应当提出给予处分的建议，将处分建议和案件材料移送该国家工作人员的任免机关或者监察机关。

第八章 附 则

第四十六条 中央编办管理机构编制的群众团体机关、经授权代主管部门行使统计职能的国家级集团公司和工商领域联合会或者协会等开展的统计调查项目，参照部门统计调查项目管理。

县级以上地方人民政府统计机构对本级人民政府有关部门制定的统计调查项目管理，参照本办法执行。

第四十七条 本办法自 2017 年 10 月 1 日起施行。国家统计局 1999 年公布的《部门统计调查项目管理暂行办法》同时废止。